O N E

I watch movies on streaming services. There are so many interesting ones...
—ONE

Manga creator ONE began *One-Punch Man* as a webcomic, which quickly went viral, garnering over 10 million hits. In addition to *One-Punch Man*, ONE writes and draws the series *Mob Psycho 100* and *Makai no Ossan*.

Y U S U K E
M U R A T A

Never draw a line without purpose.
—Yusuke Murata

A highly decorated and skilled artist best known for his work on *Eyeshield 21*, Yusuke Murata won the 122nd Hop Step Award (1995) for *Partner* and placed second in the 51st Akatsuka Award (1998) for *Samui Hanashi*.

ONE-PUNCH MAN 23

ONE + YUSUKE MURATA

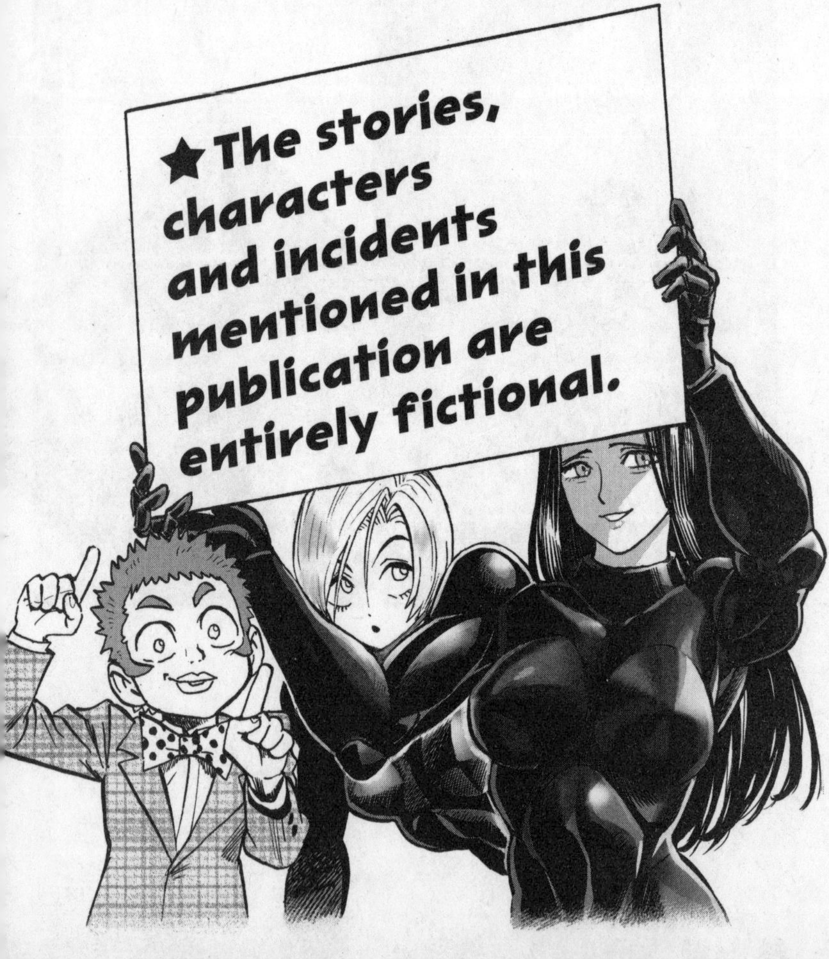
★The stories, characters and incidents mentioned in this publication are entirely fictional.

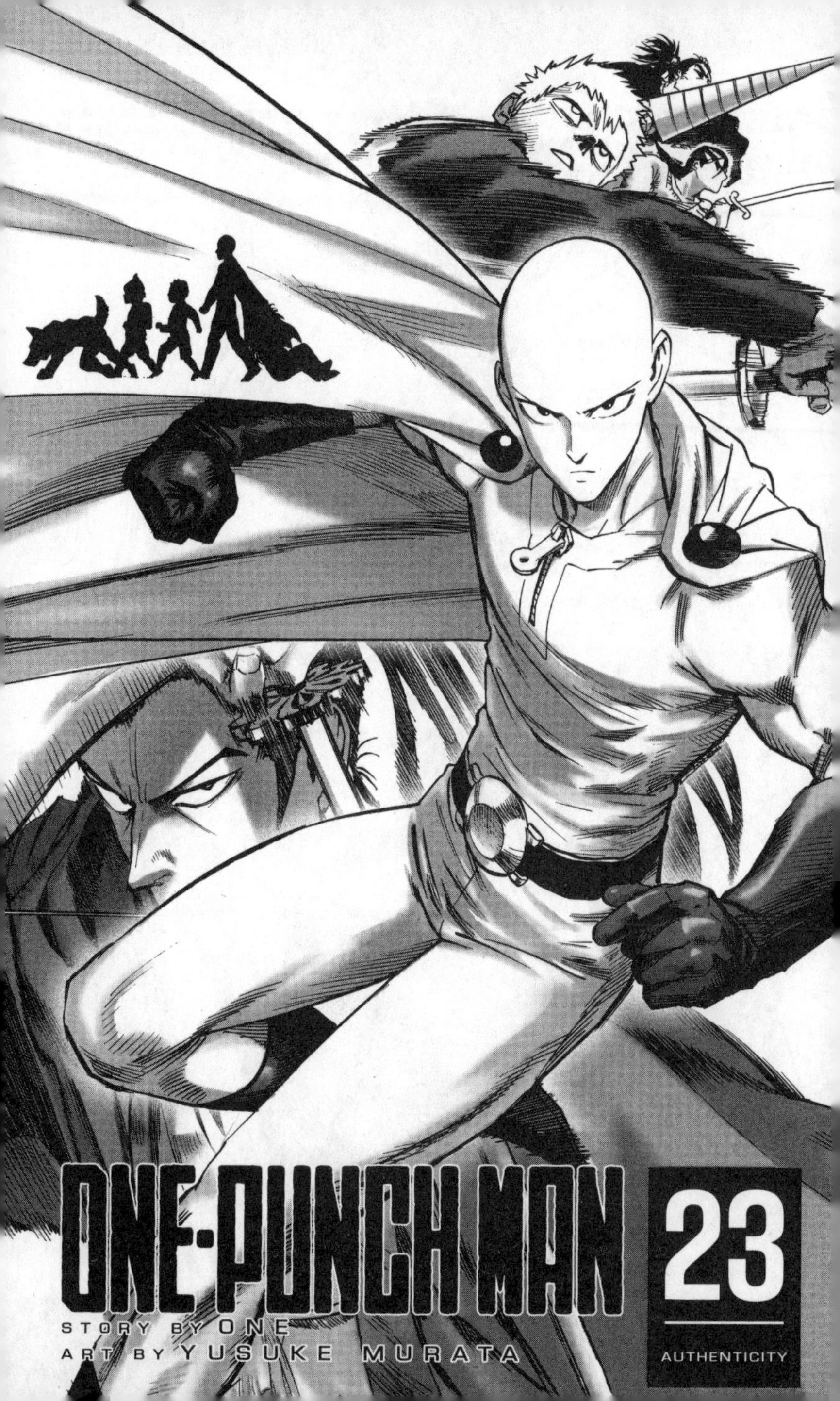

ONE-PUNCH MAN

23

STORY BY ONE

ART BY YUSUKE MURATA

AUTHENTICITY

CHARACTERS

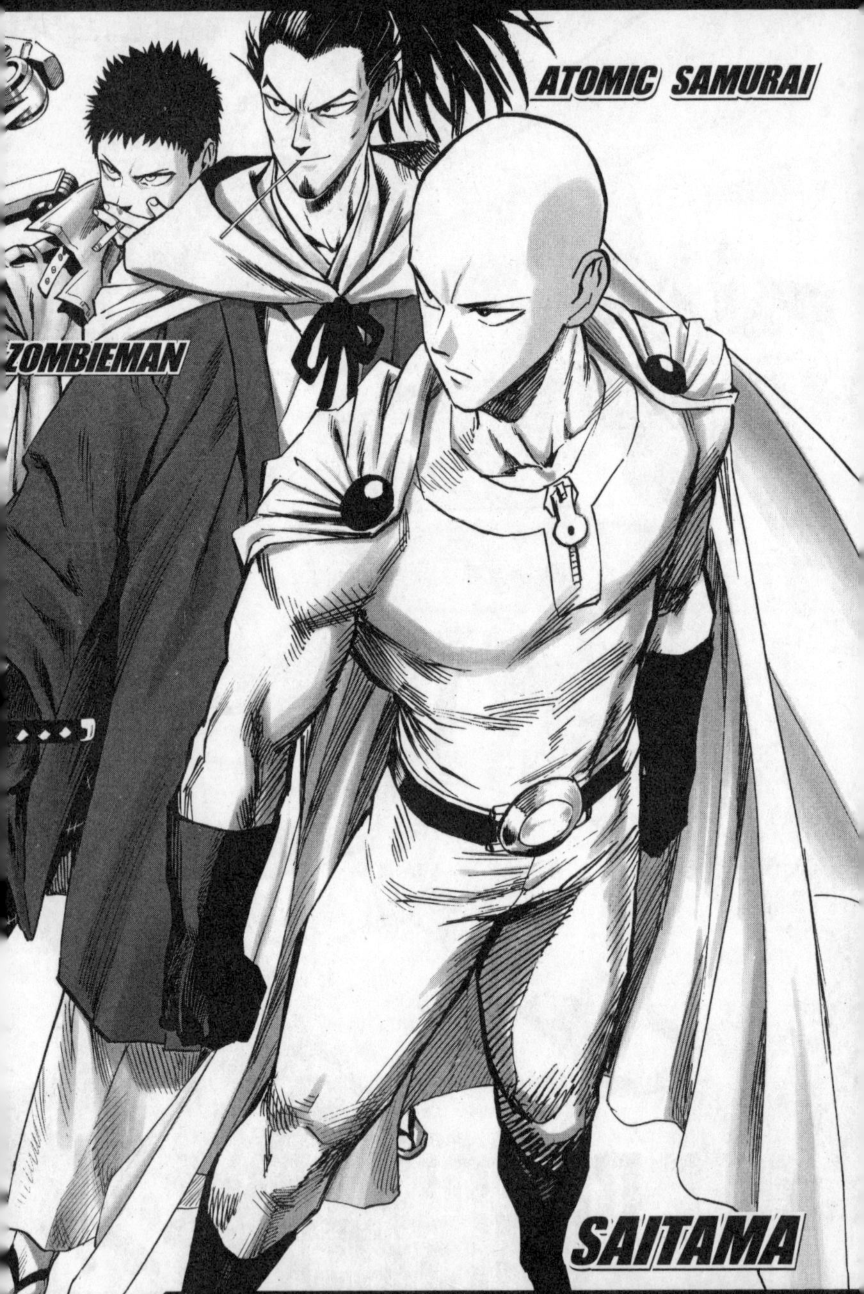
ATOMIC SAMURAI
ZOMBIEMAN
SAITAMA

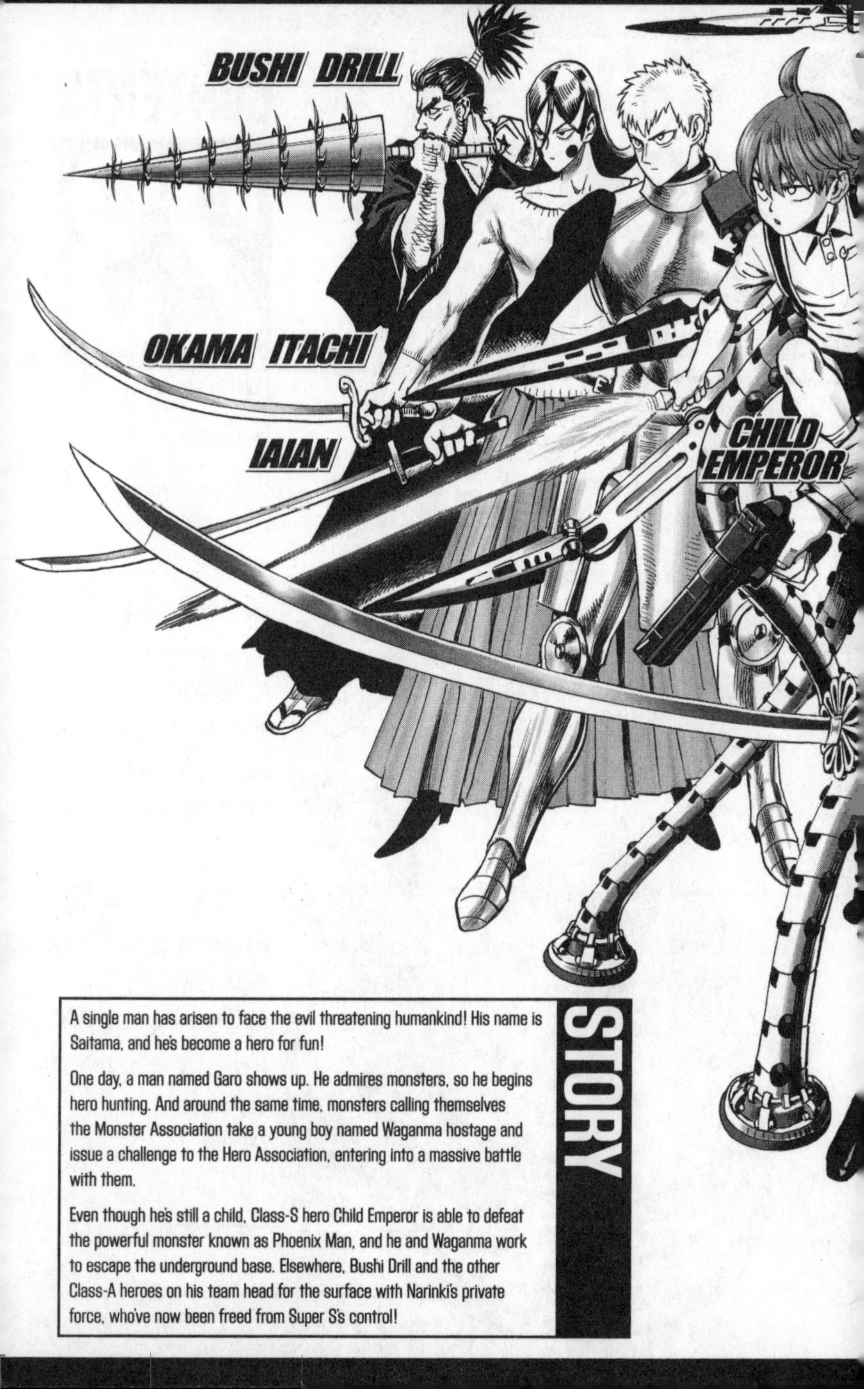
BUSHI DRILL
OKAMA ITACHI
IAIAN
CHILD EMPEROR

STORY

A single man has arisen to face the evil threatening humankind! His name is Saitama, and he's become a hero for fun!

One day, a man named Garo shows up. He admires monsters, so he begins hero hunting. And around the same time, monsters calling themselves the Monster Association take a young boy named Waganma hostage and issue a challenge to the Hero Association, entering into a massive battle with them.

Even though he's still a child, Class-S hero Child Emperor is able to defeat the powerful monster known as Phoenix Man, and he and Waganma work to escape the underground base. Elsewhere, Bushi Drill and the other Class-A heroes on his team head for the surface with Narinki's private force, who've now been freed from Super S's control!

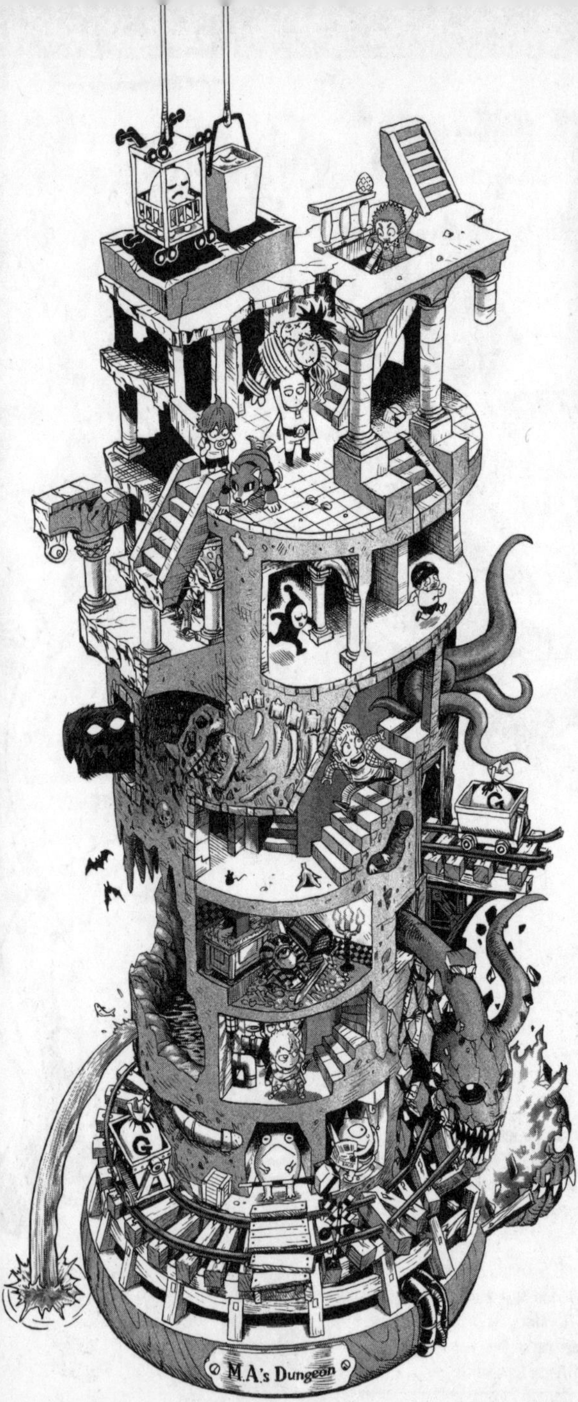
M.A.'s Dungeon

CONTENTS

23

[AUTHENTICITY]

PUNCH 107: BACK

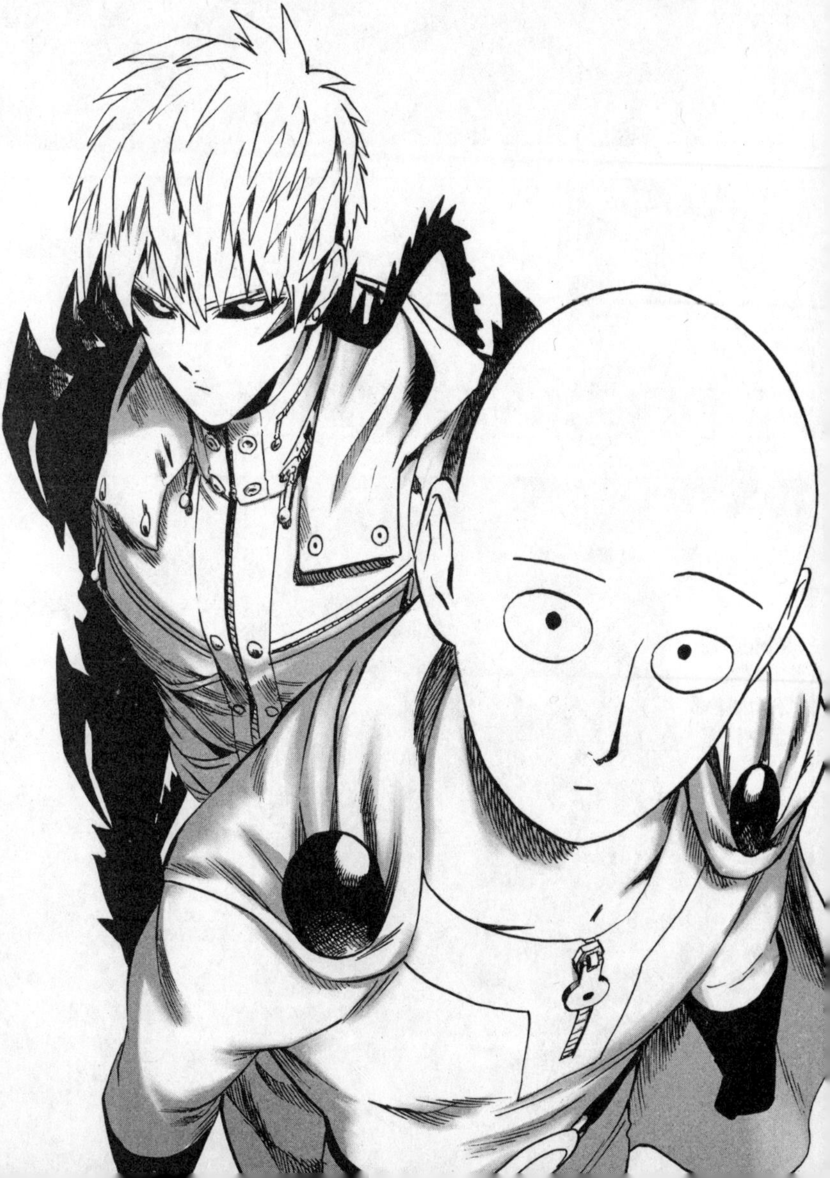

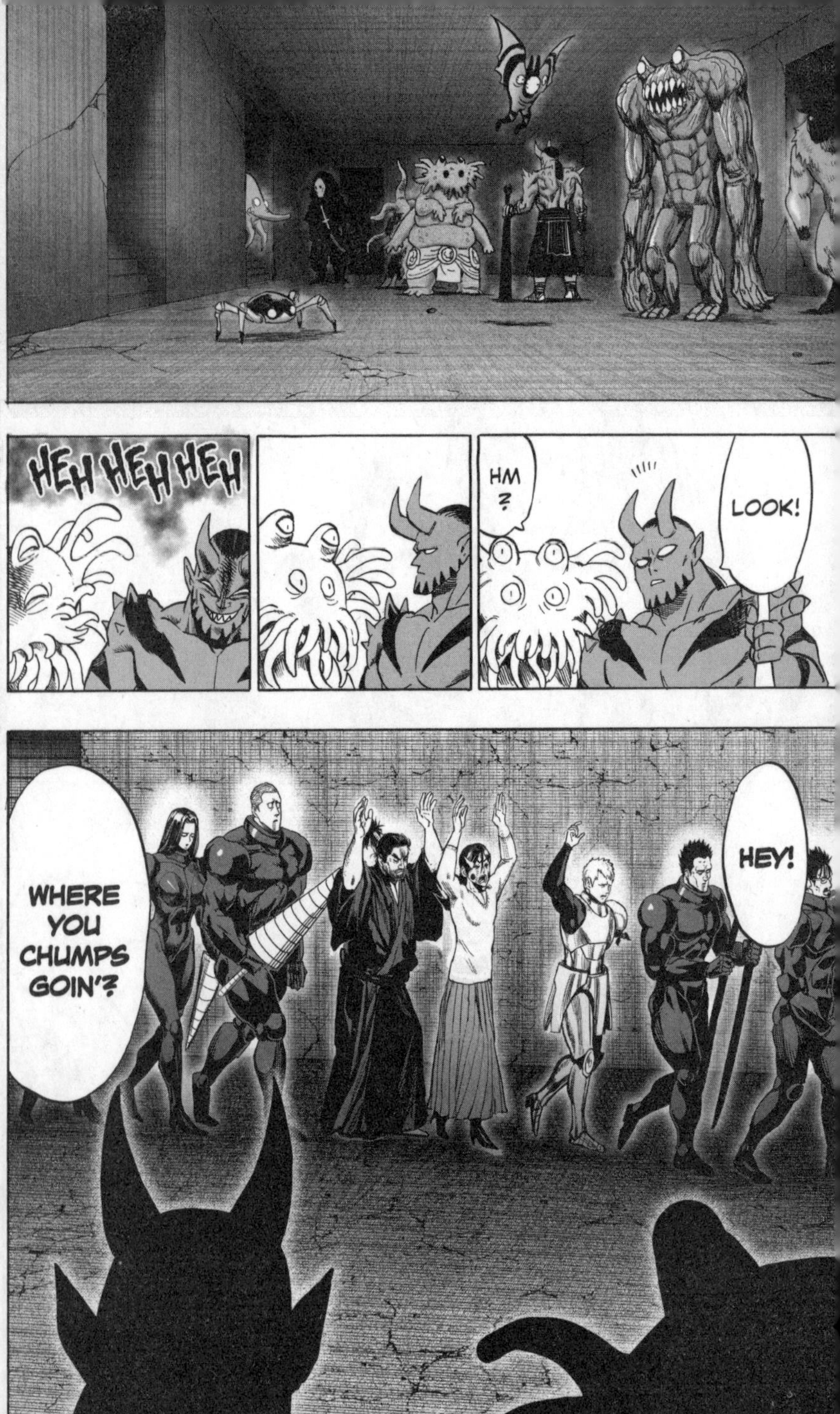
LOOK!
HM ?
HEH HEH HEH
HEY!
WHERE YOU CHUMPS GOIN'?

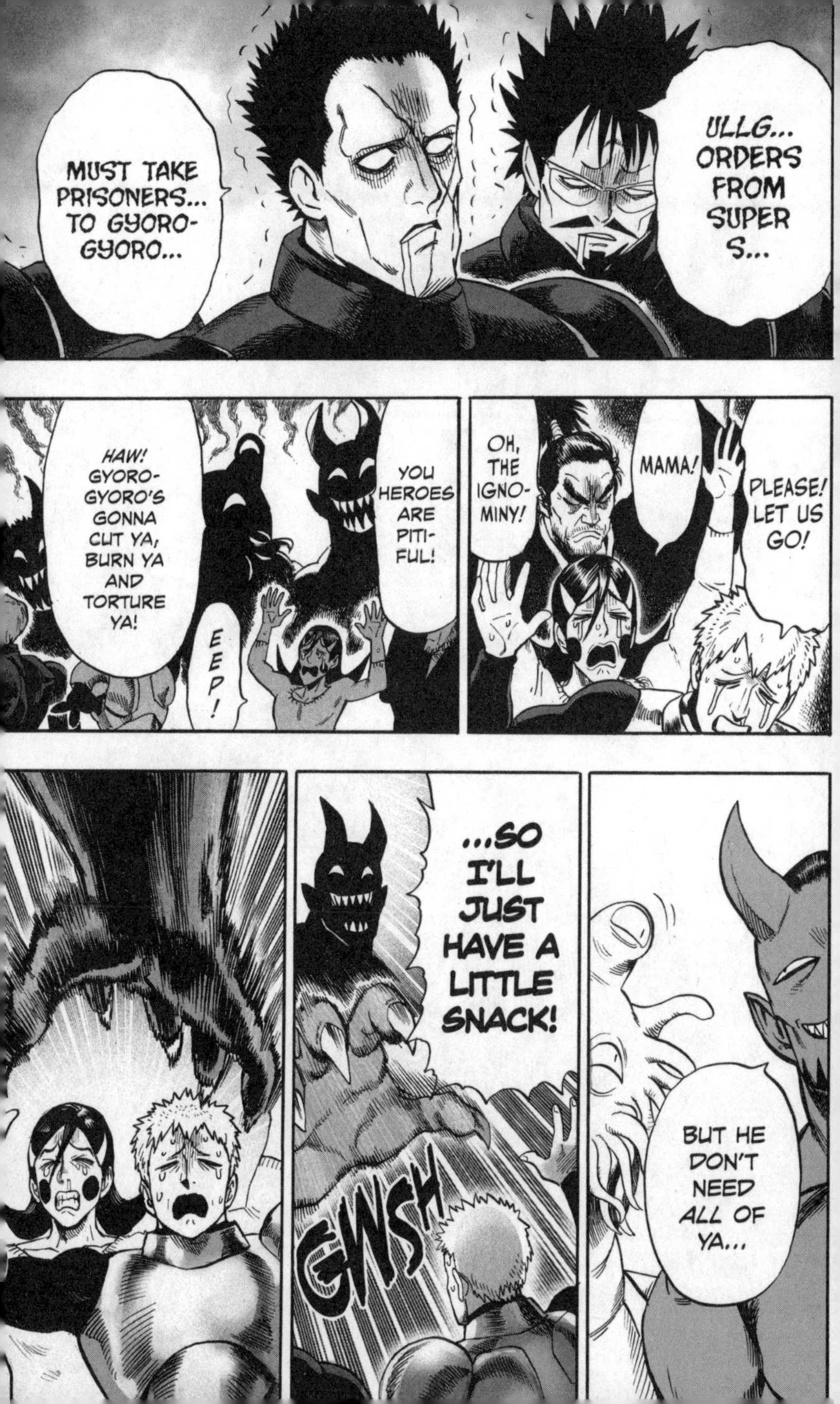
ULLG... ORDERS FROM SUPER S...
MUST TAKE PRISONERS... TO GYORO-GYORO...
PLEASE! LET US GO!
MAMA!
OH, THE IGNOMINY!
YOU HEROES ARE PITIFUL!
HAW! GYORO-GYORO'S GONNA CUT YA, BURN YA AND TORTURE YA!
EEP!
BUT HE DON'T NEED ALL OF YA...
...SO I'LL JUST HAVE A LITTLE SNACK!
GNSH

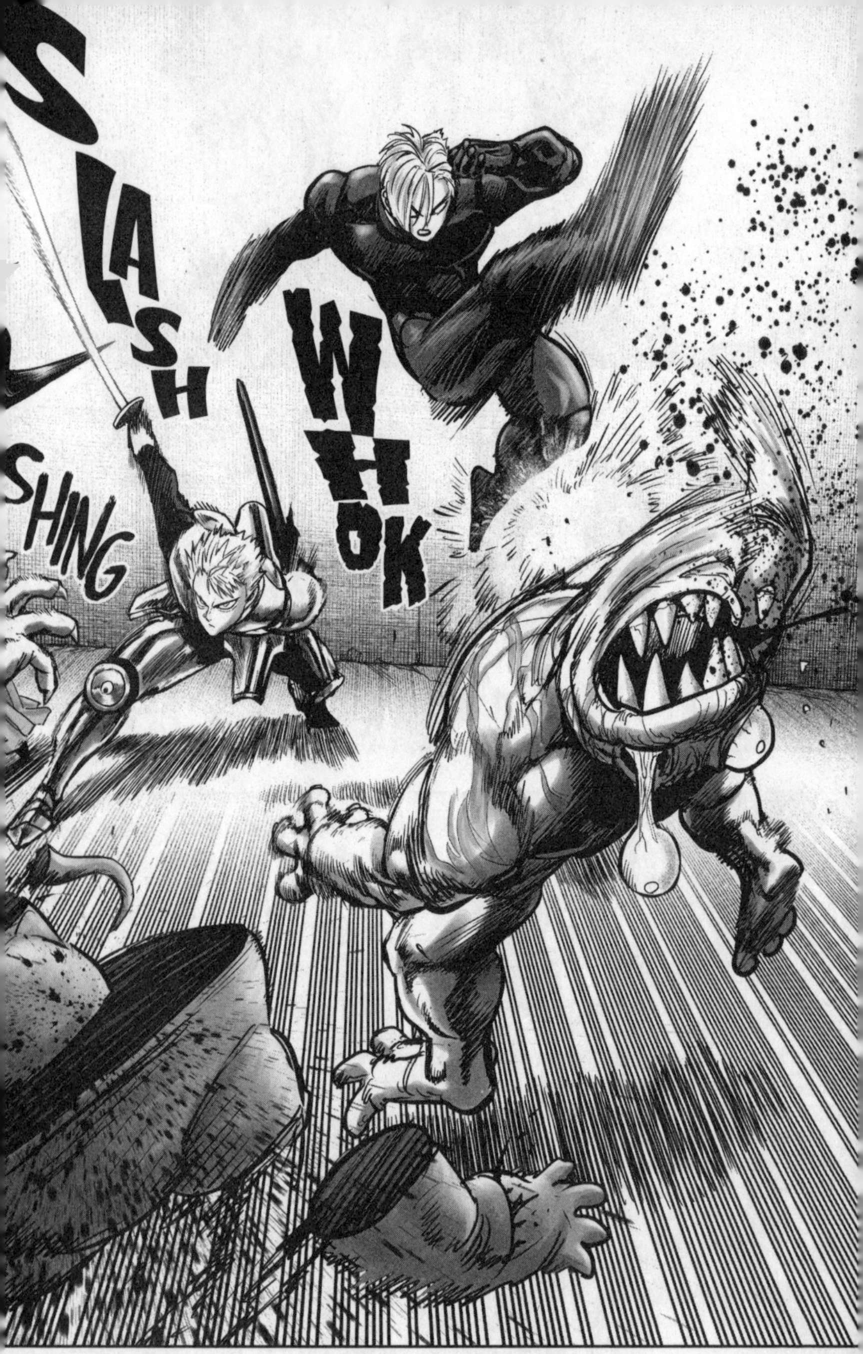
WHOK
SLASH
SHING

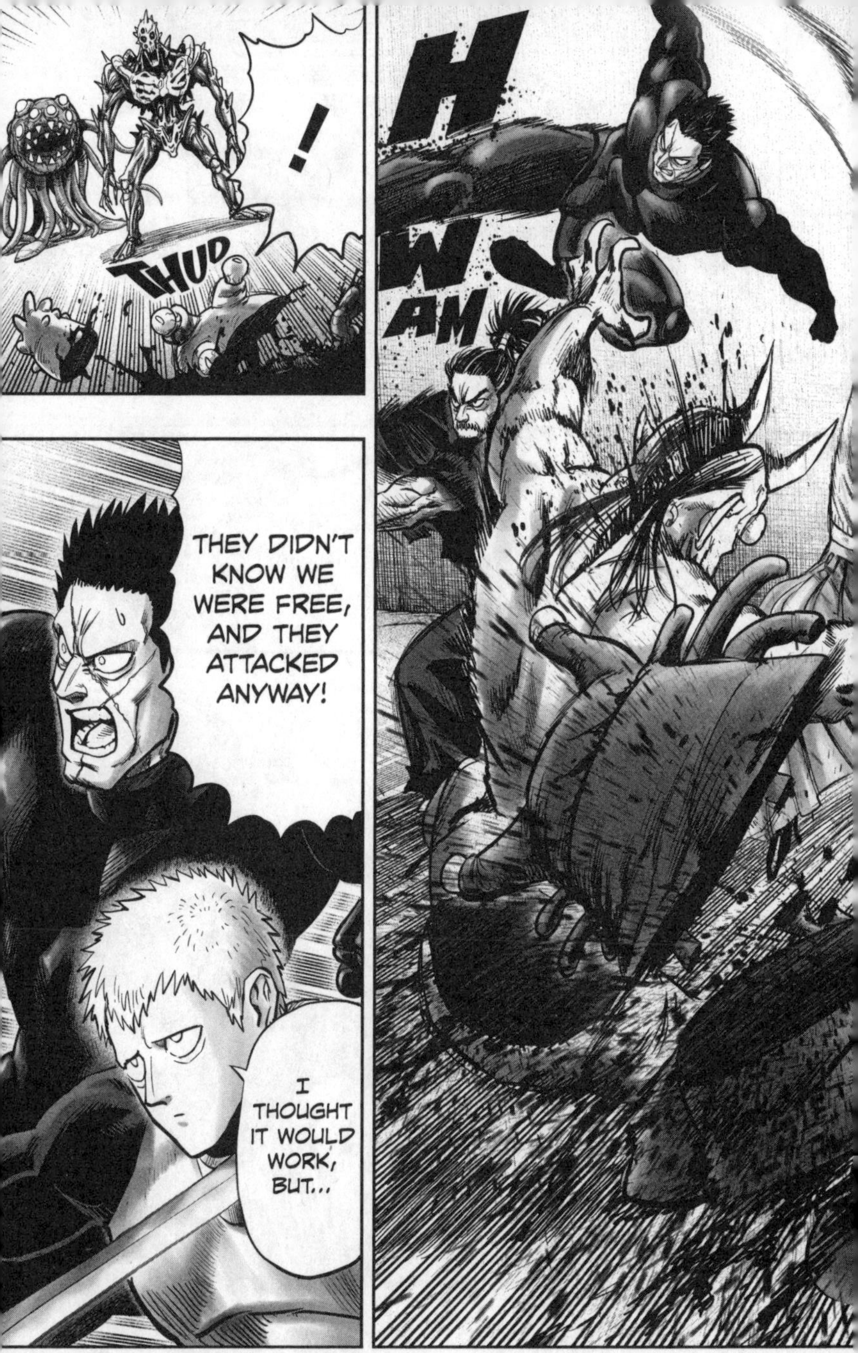
H
W
AM
!
THUD
THEY DIDN'T KNOW WE WERE FREE, AND THEY ATTACKED ANYWAY!
I THOUGHT IT WOULD WORK, BUT...

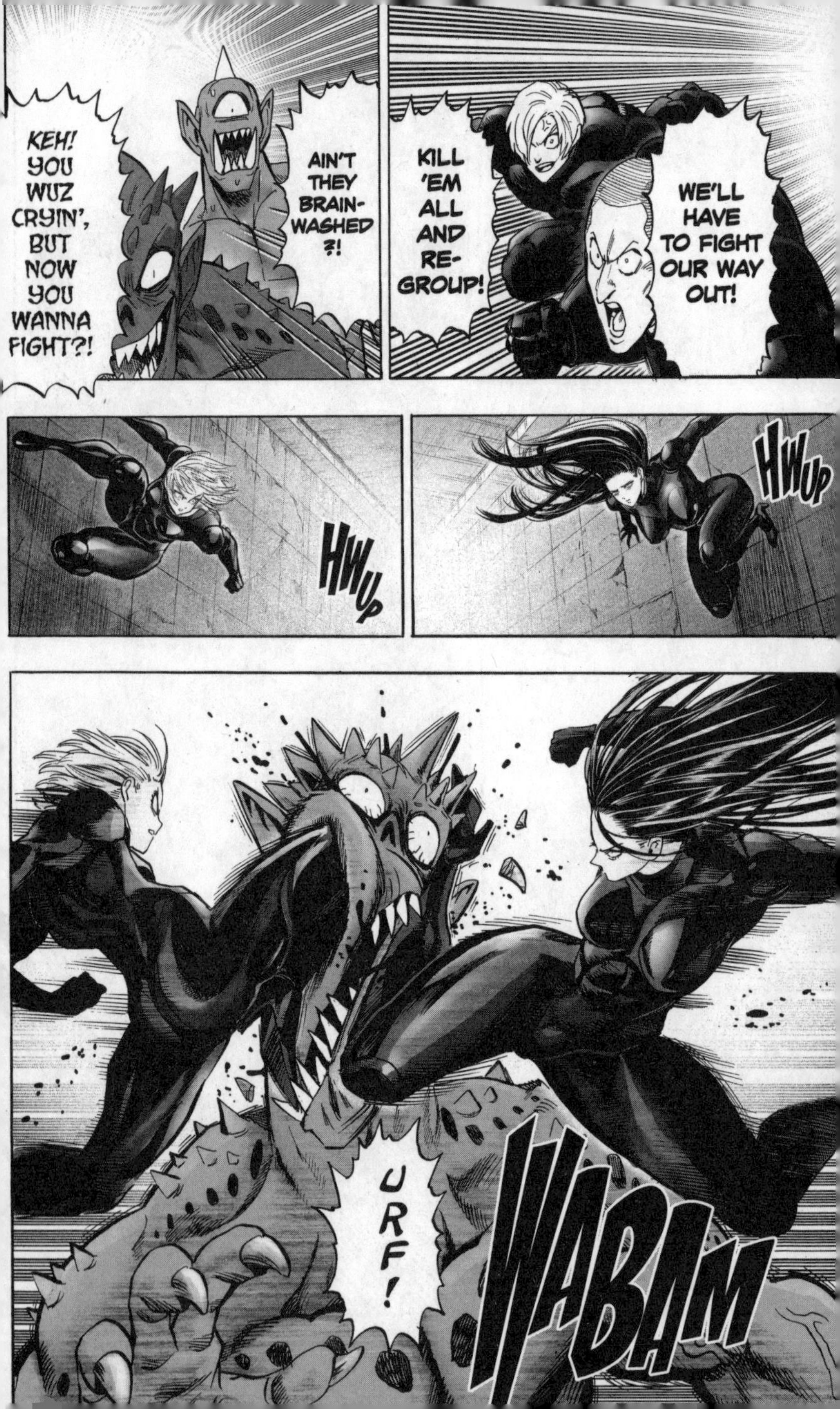
WE'LL HAVE TO FIGHT OUR WAY OUT!
KILL 'EM ALL AND RE-GROUP!
AIN'T THEY BRAIN-WASHED?!
KEH! YOU WUZ CRYIN', BUT NOW YOU WANNA FIGHT?!
HWUP
HWUP
WABAM
URF!

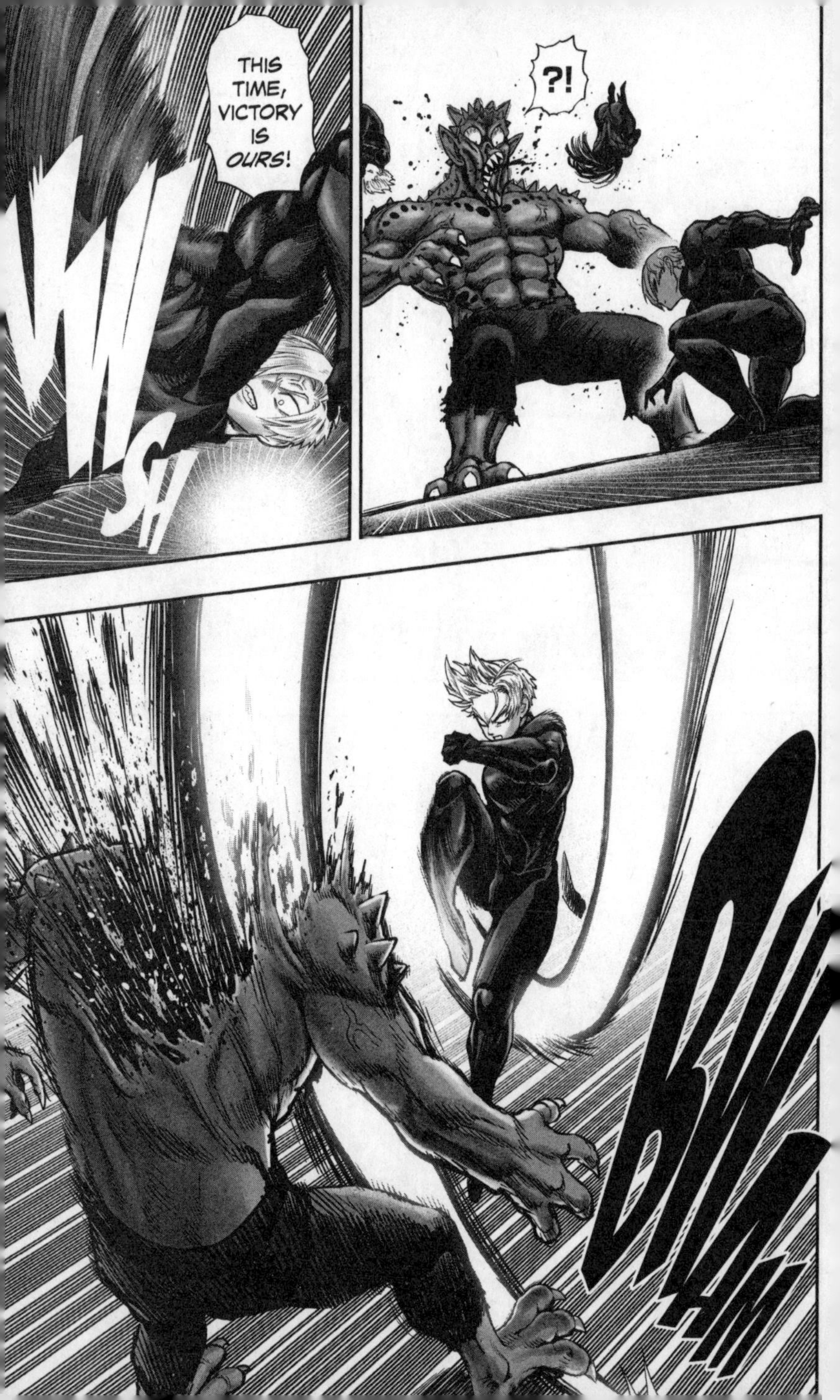
?!
THIS TIME, VICTORY IS OURS!
WHSH

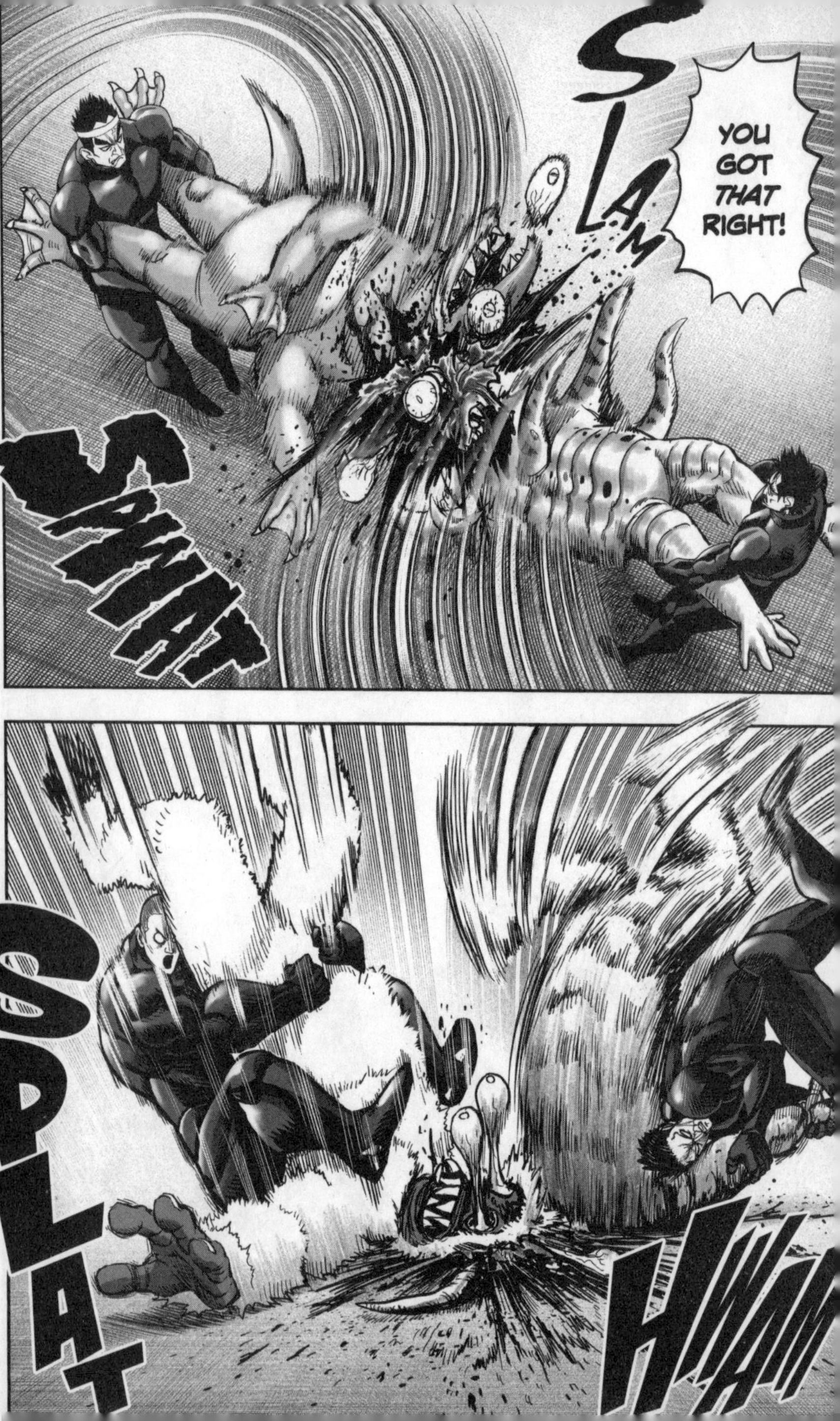
YOU GOT THAT RIGHT!
SLAM
SPLAT

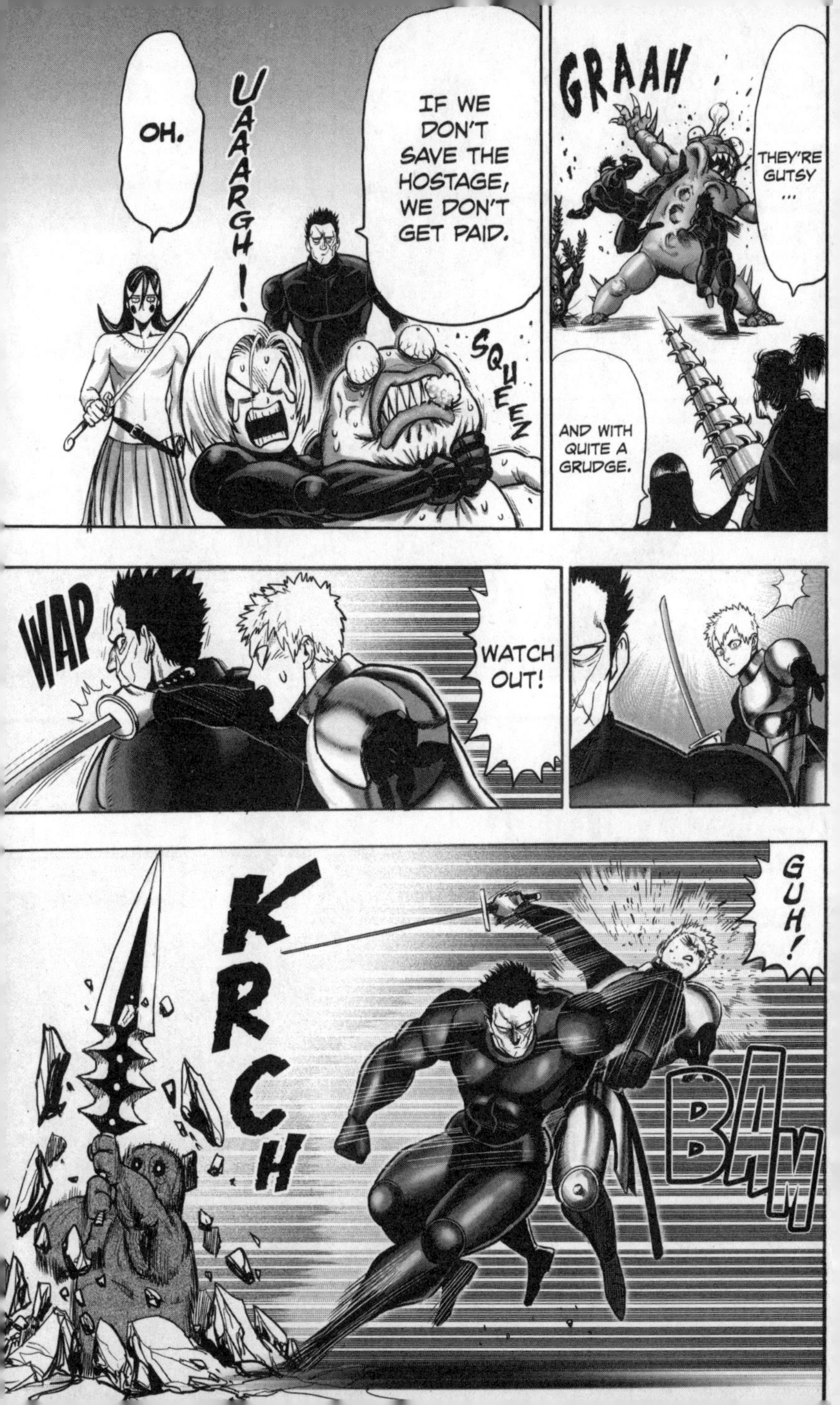
THEY'RE GUTSY ...
GRAAH
AND WITH QUITE A GRUDGE.
IF WE DON'T SAVE THE HOSTAGE, WE DON'T GET PAID.
UAAAARGH!
OH.
SQUEEZ
WATCH OUT!
WAP
GUH!
BAM
KRCH

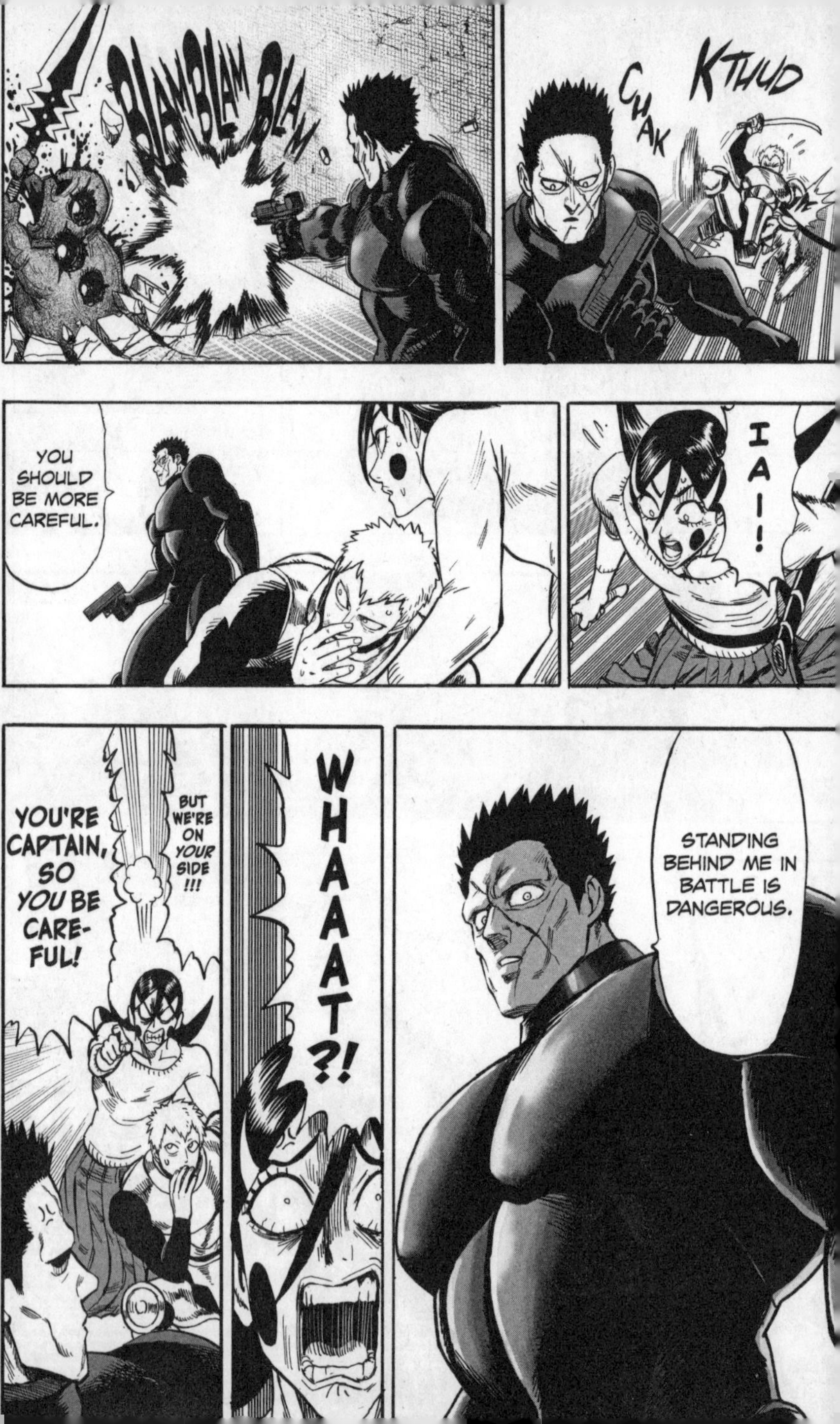
KTHUD
CHAK
BLAM BLAM BLAM
IAI!!
YOU SHOULD BE MORE CAREFUL.
STANDING BEHIND ME IN BATTLE IS DANGEROUS.
WHAAAAT?!
BUT WE'RE ON YOUR SIDE!!!
YOU'RE CAPTAIN, SO YOU BE CARE-FUL!

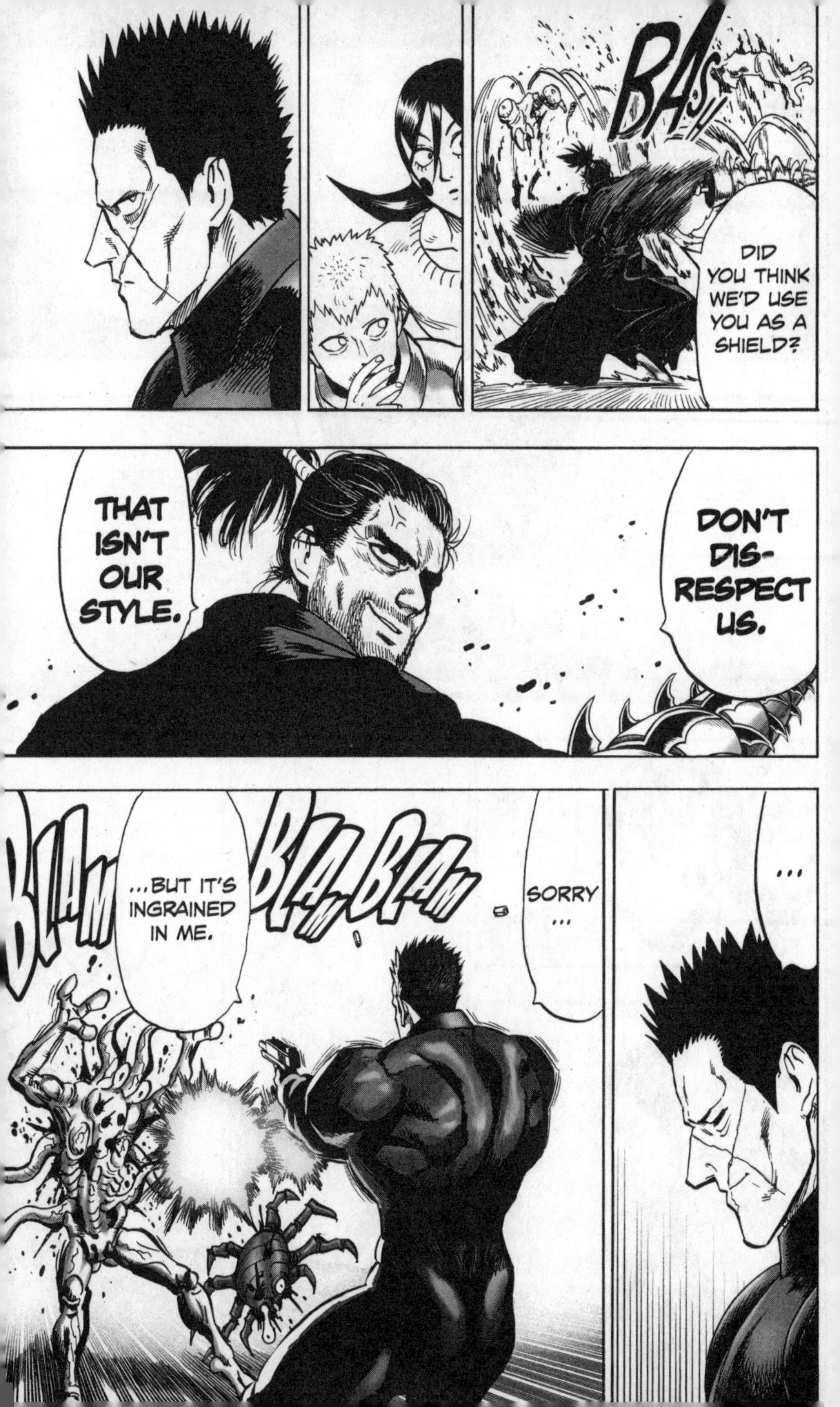
BASH
DID YOU THINK WE'D USE YOU AS A SHIELD?
DON'T DIS-RESPECT US.
THAT ISN'T OUR STYLE.
...
SORRY ...
...BUT IT'S INGRAINED IN ME.
BLAM BLAM
BLAM

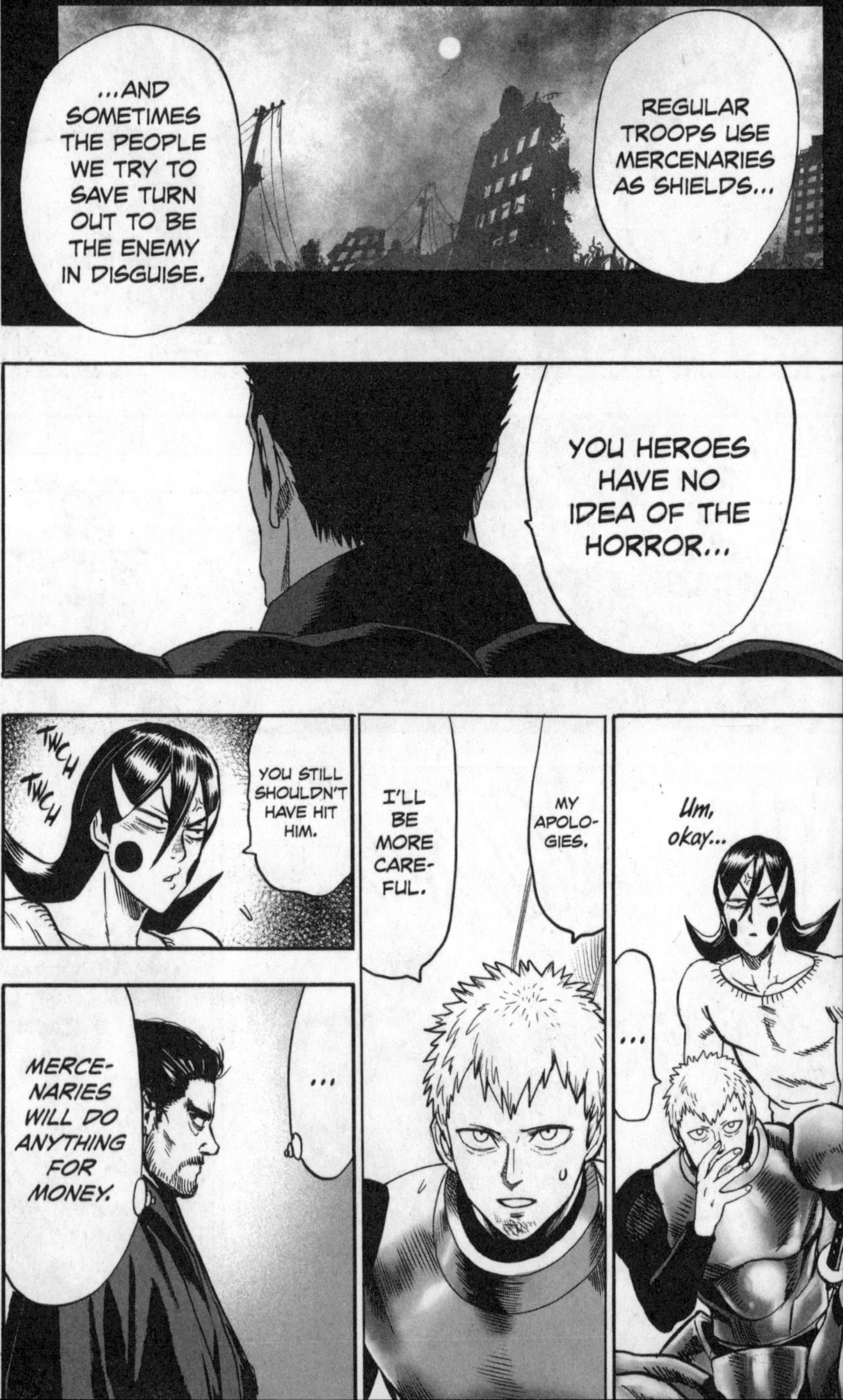
REGULAR TROOPS USE MERCENARIES AS SHIELDS...
...AND SOMETIMES THE PEOPLE WE TRY TO SAVE TURN OUT TO BE THE ENEMY IN DISGUISE.
YOU HEROES HAVE NO IDEA OF THE HORROR...
Um, okay...
...
MY APOLO-GIES.
I'LL BE MORE CARE-FUL.
TWCH TWCH
YOU STILL SHOULDN'T HAVE HIT HIM.
...
MERCE-NARIES WILL DO ANYTHING FOR MONEY.

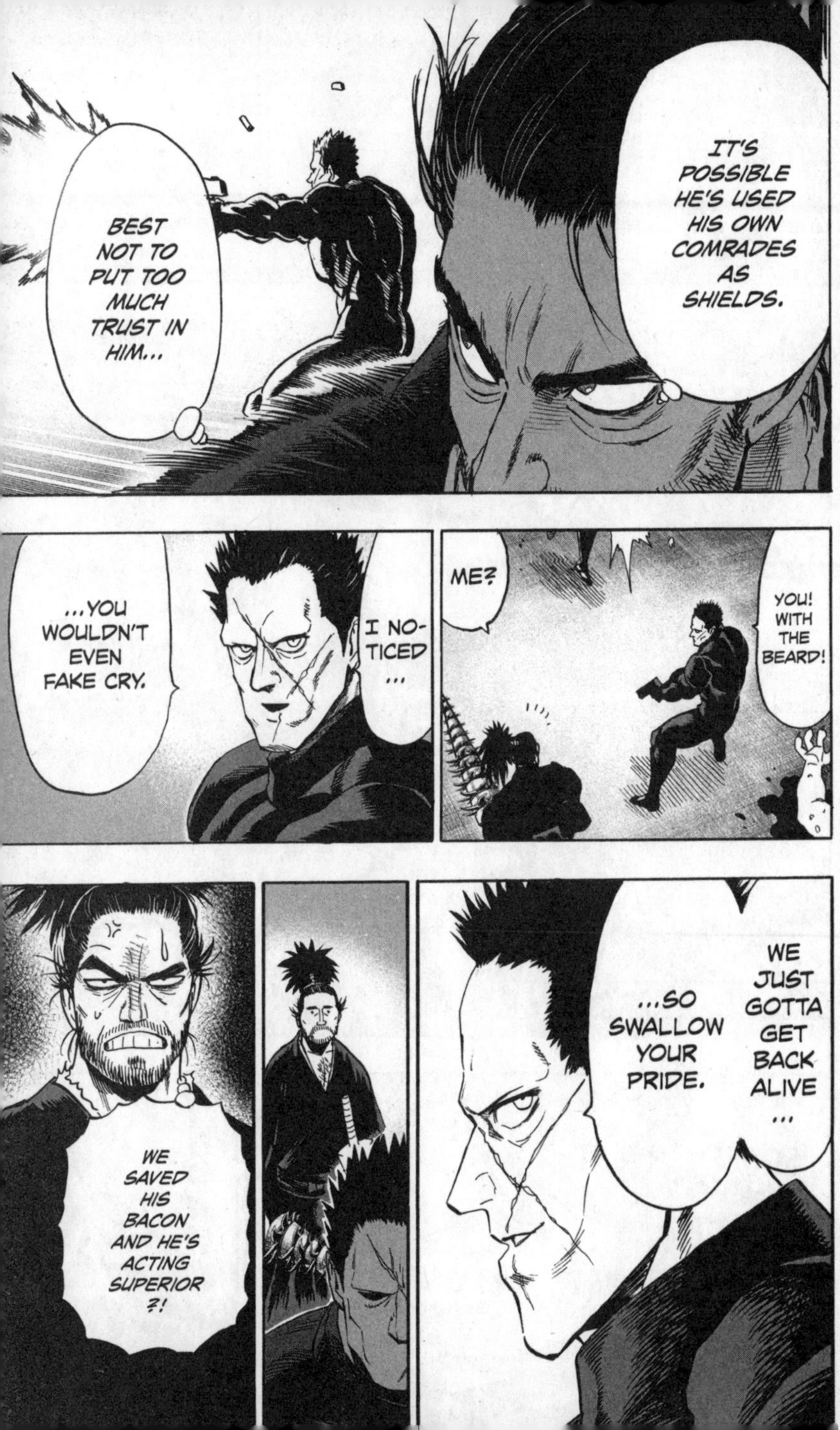
IT'S POSSIBLE HE'S USED HIS OWN COMRADES AS SHIELDS.
BEST NOT TO PUT TOO MUCH TRUST IN HIM...
YOU! WITH THE BEARD!
ME?
I NO-TICED...
...YOU WOULDN'T EVEN FAKE CRY.
WE JUST GOTTA GET BACK ALIVE...
...SO SWALLOW YOUR PRIDE.
WE SAVED HIS BACON AND HE'S ACTING SUPERIOR?!

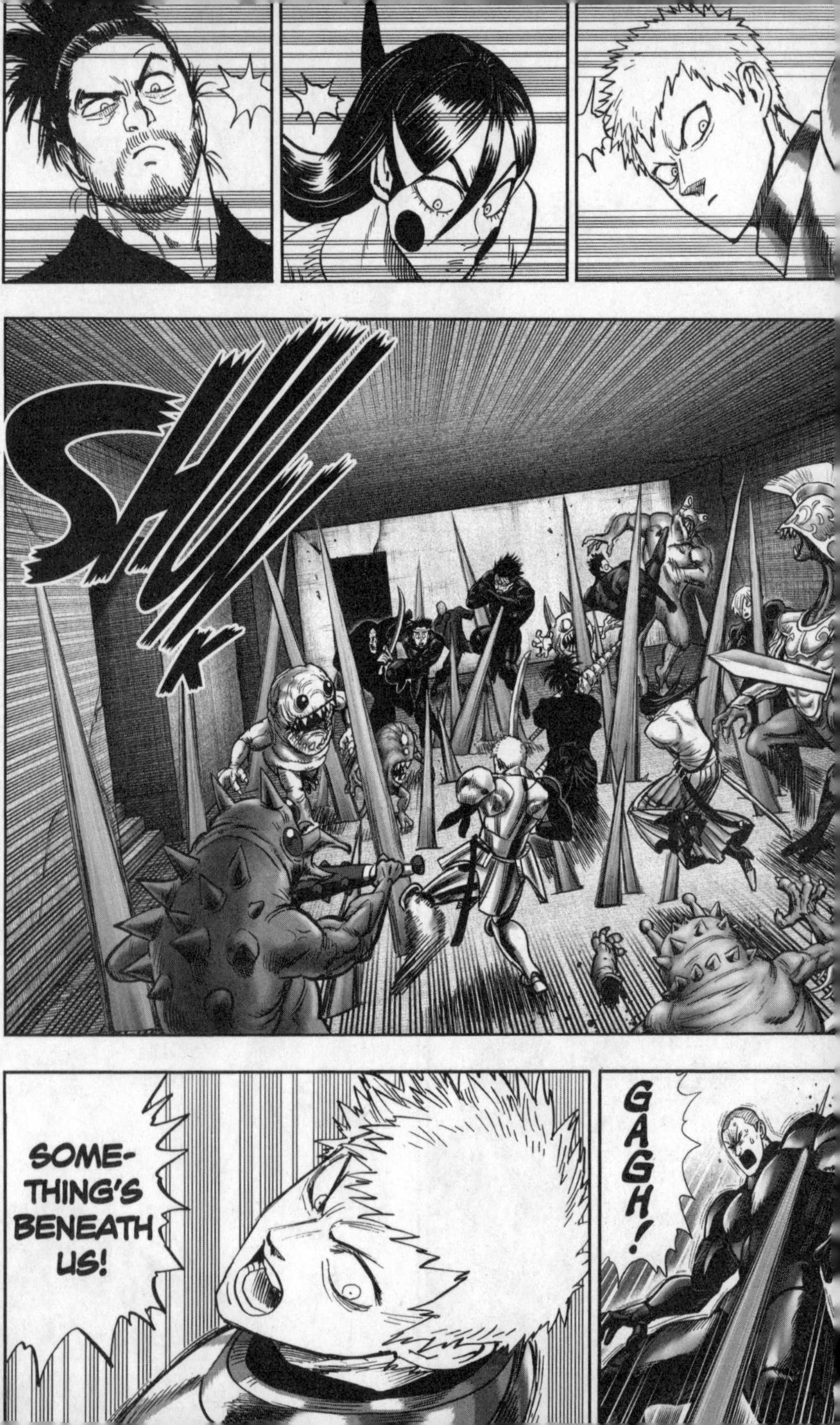
SHUNK
GAGH!
SOME-THING'S BENEATH US!

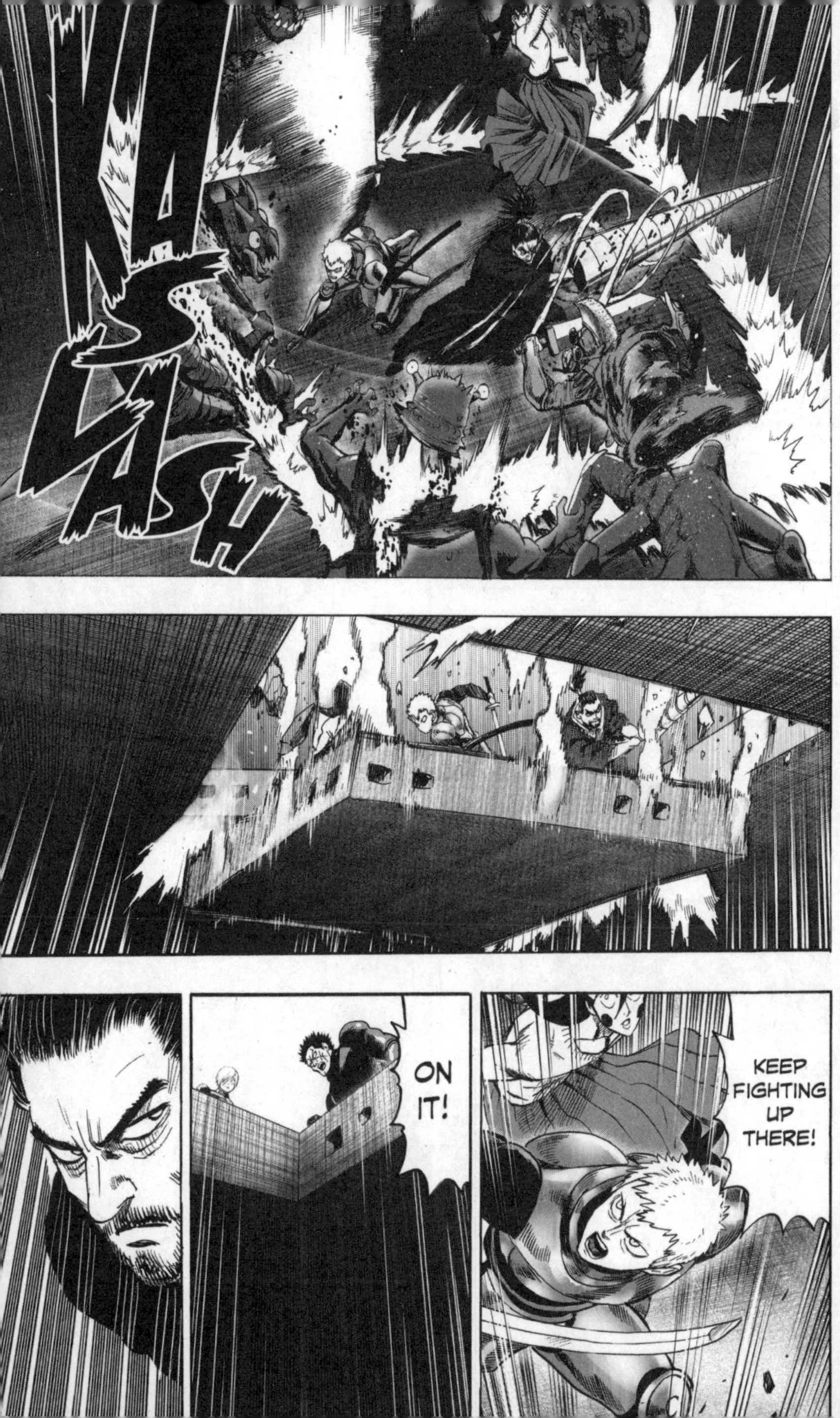
SLASH
KEEP FIGHTING UP THERE!
ON IT!

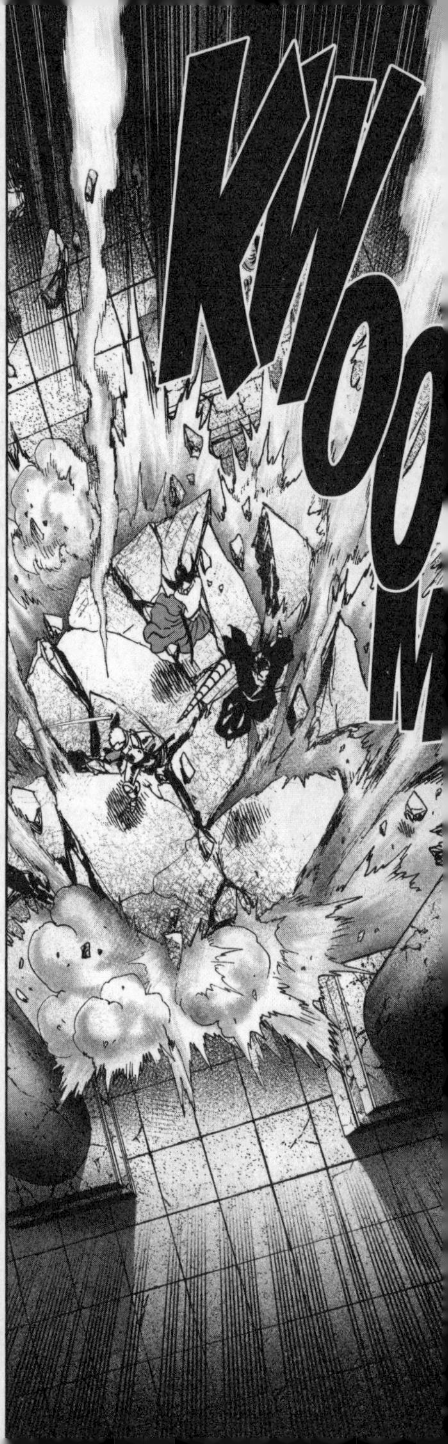
KWOOM
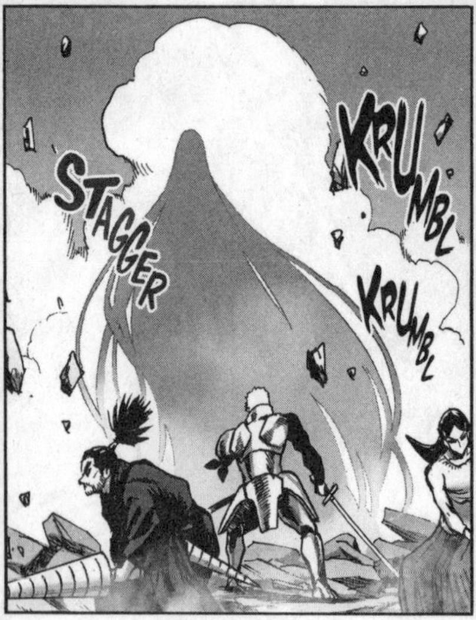
KRUMBL
KRUMBL
STAGGER
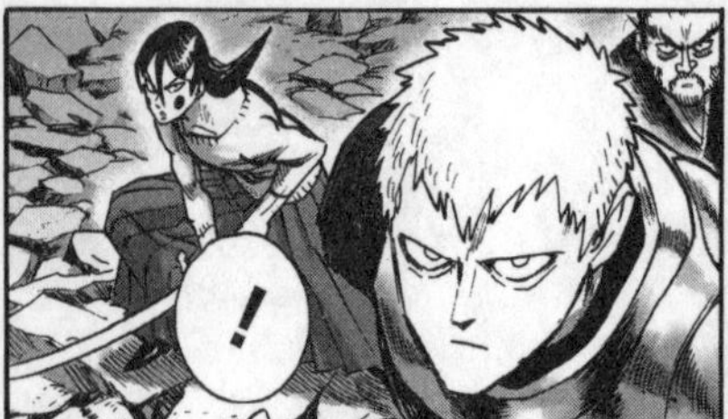
!
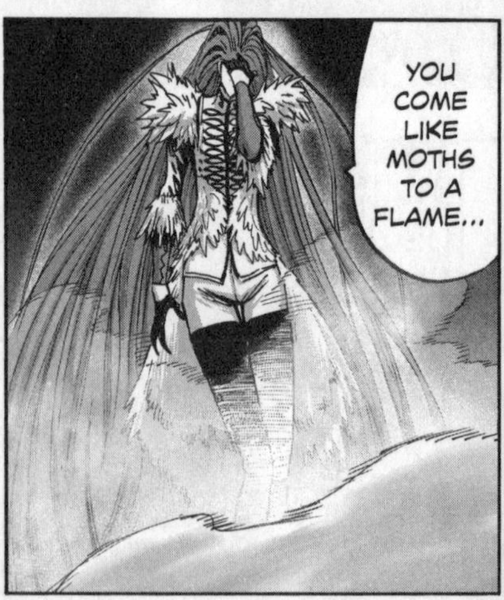
YOU COME LIKE MOTHS TO A FLAME...

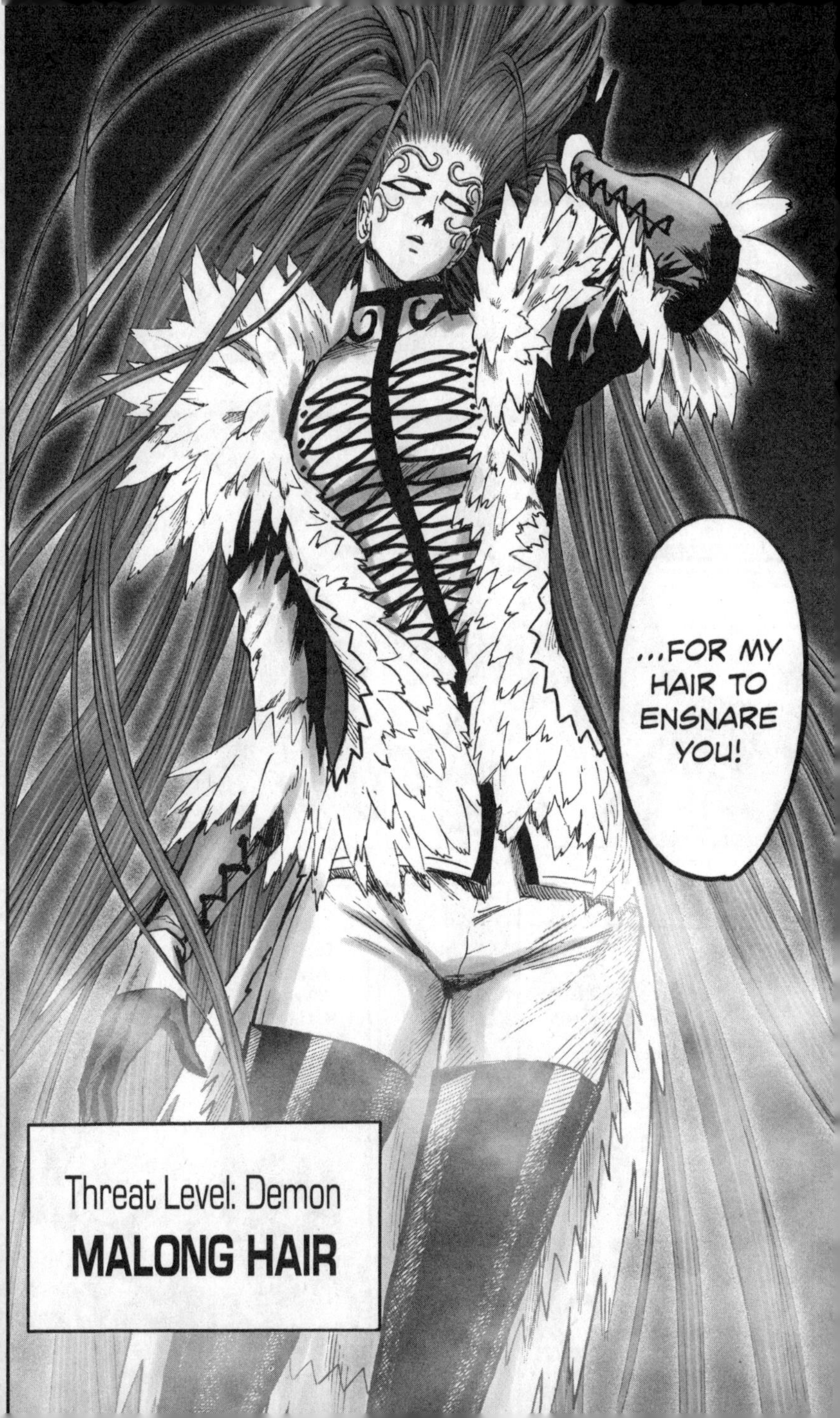
...FOR MY HAIR TO ENSNARE YOU!
Threat Level: Demon
MALONG HAIR

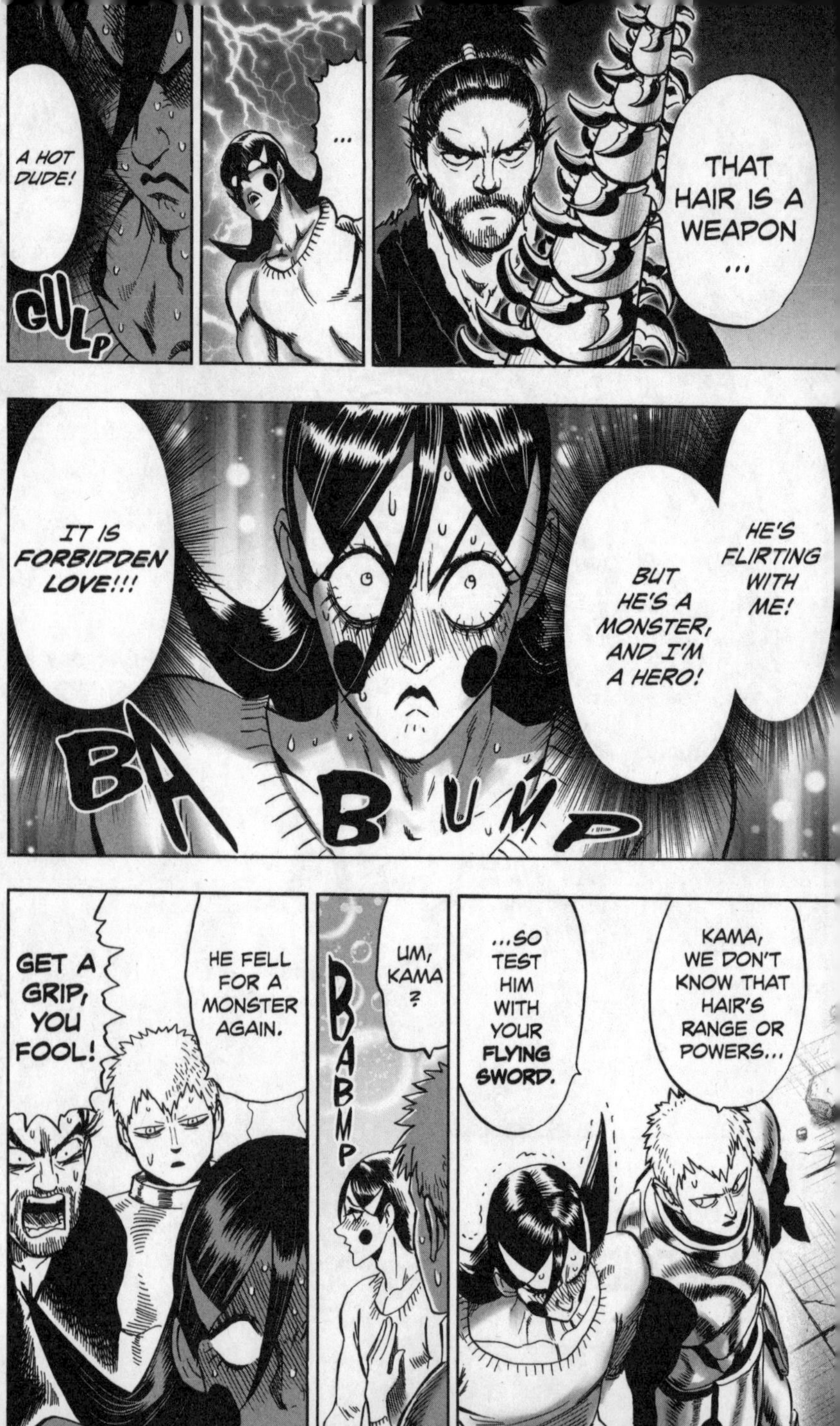
THAT HAIR IS A WEAPON ...
...
A HOT DUDE!
GULP
HE'S FLIRTING WITH ME!
BUT HE'S A MONSTER, AND I'M A HERO!
IT IS FORBIDDEN LOVE!!!
BA BUMP
KAMA, WE DON'T KNOW THAT HAIR'S RANGE OR POWERS...
...SO TEST HIM WITH YOUR FLYING SWORD.
UM, KAMA?
BABUMP
HE FELL FOR A MONSTER AGAIN.
GET A GRIP, YOU FOOL!

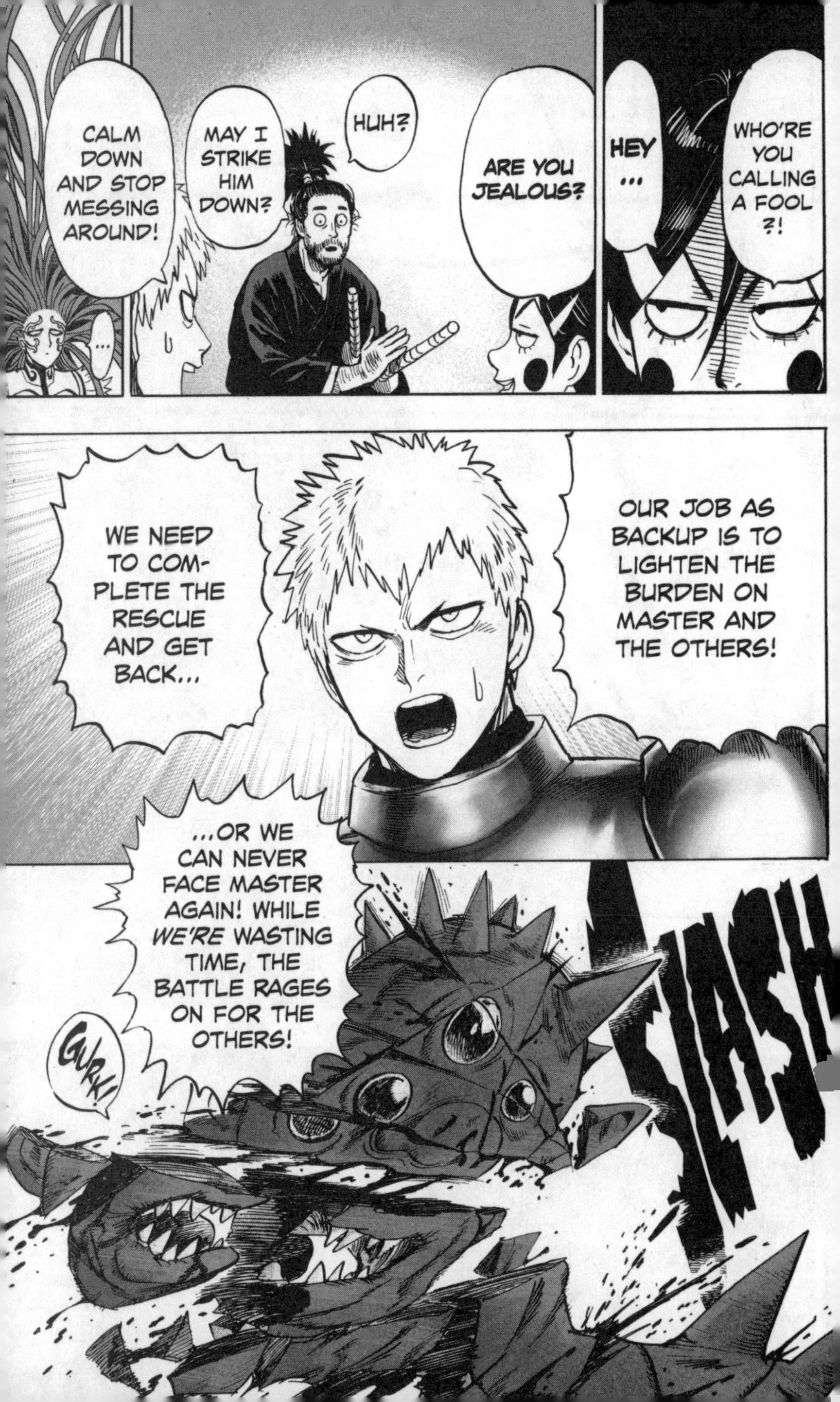
WHO'RE YOU CALLING A FOOL ?!
HEY ...
ARE YOU JEALOUS?
HUH?
MAY I STRIKE HIM DOWN?
CALM DOWN AND STOP MESSING AROUND!
...
OUR JOB AS BACKUP IS TO LIGHTEN THE BURDEN ON MASTER AND THE OTHERS!
WE NEED TO COMPLETE THE RESCUE AND GET BACK...
...OR WE CAN NEVER FACE MASTER AGAIN! WHILE *WE'RE* WASTING TIME, THE BATTLE RAGES ON FOR THE OTHERS!
SLASH
GURK!

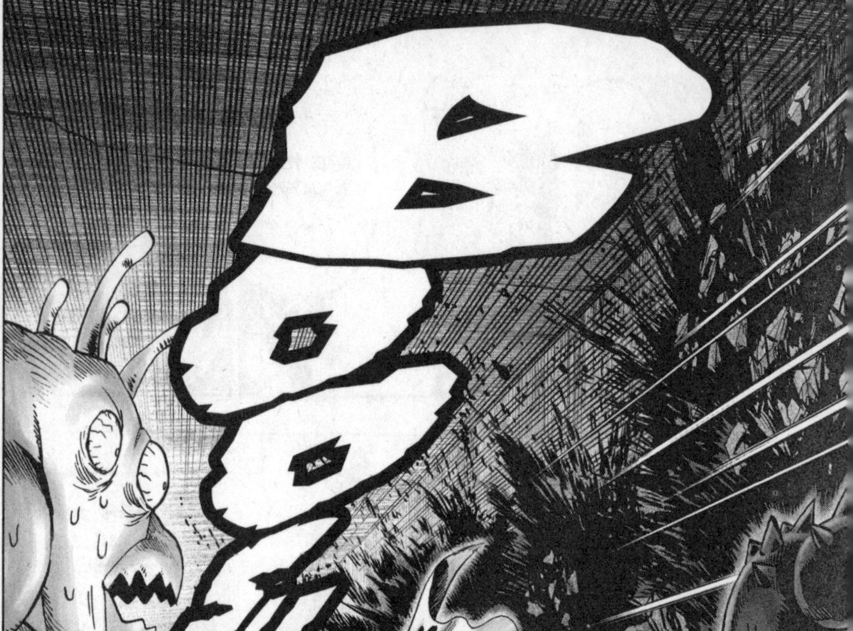
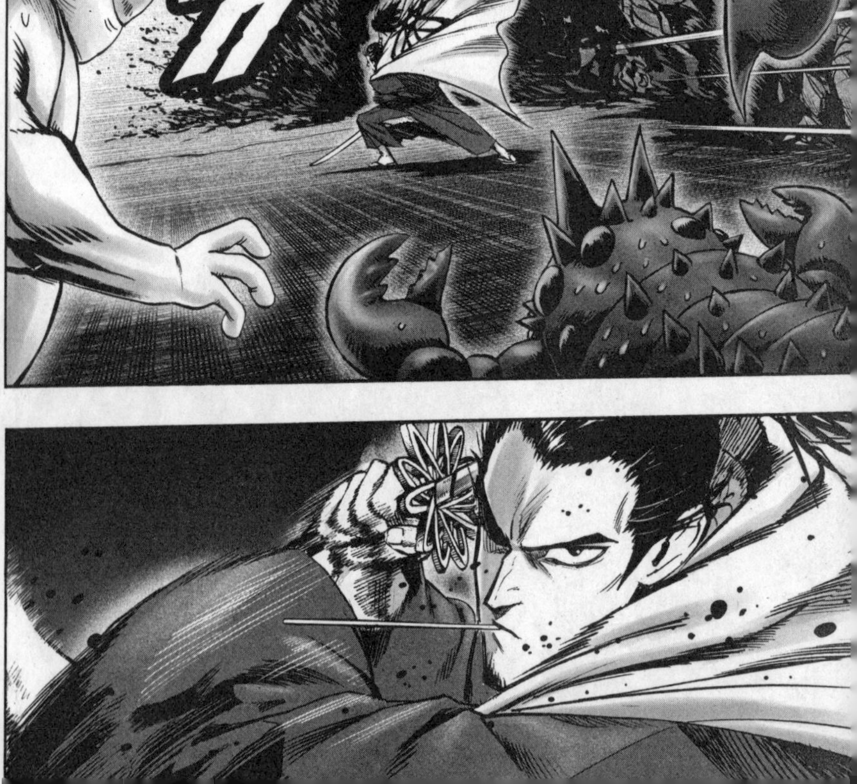

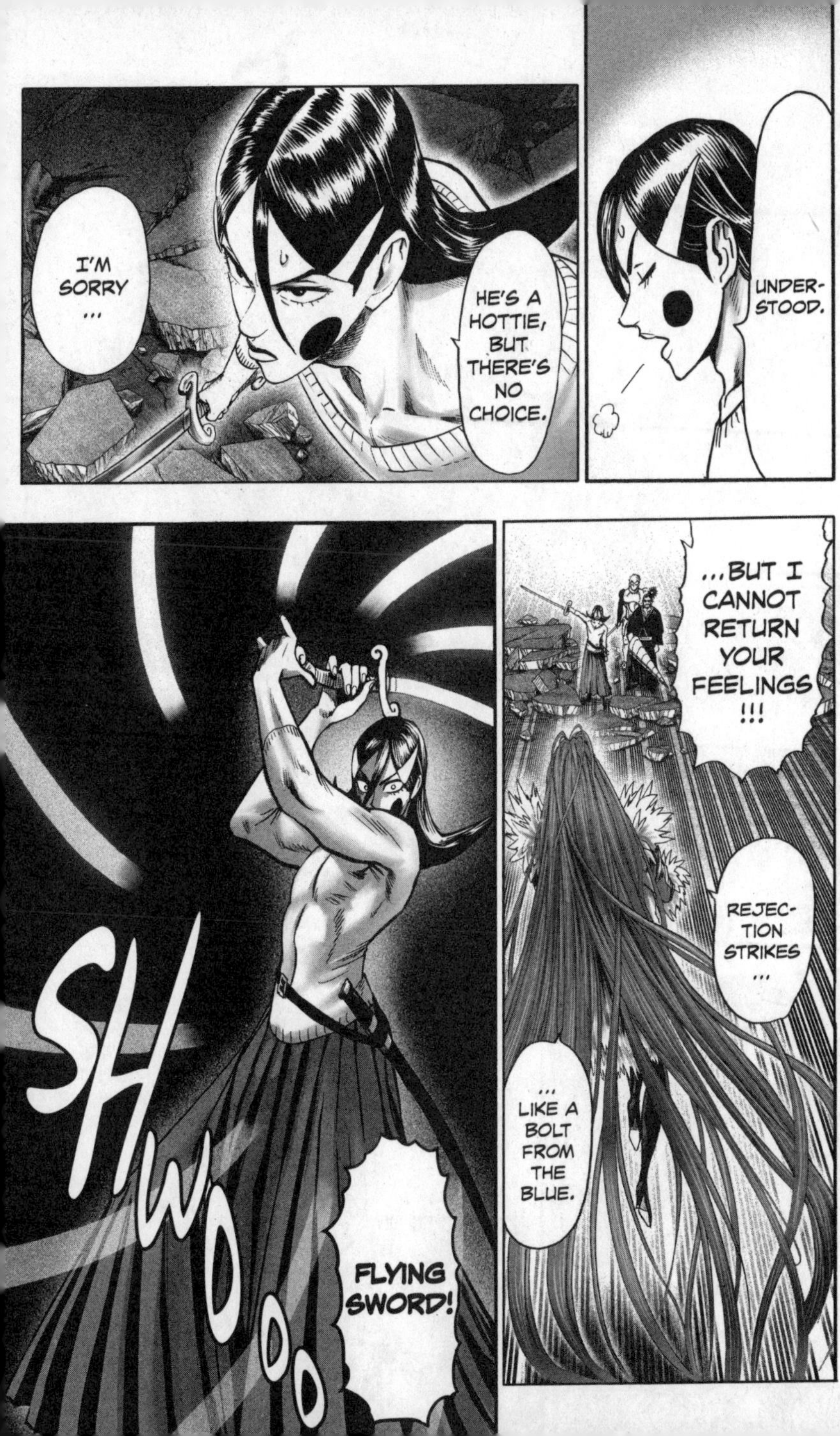
UNDER-STOOD.
HE'S A HOTTIE, BUT THERE'S NO CHOICE.
I'M SORRY ...
...BUT I CANNOT RETURN YOUR FEELINGS !!!
REJEC-TION STRIKES ...
... LIKE A BOLT FROM THE BLUE.
SHWOOOO
FLYING SWORD!

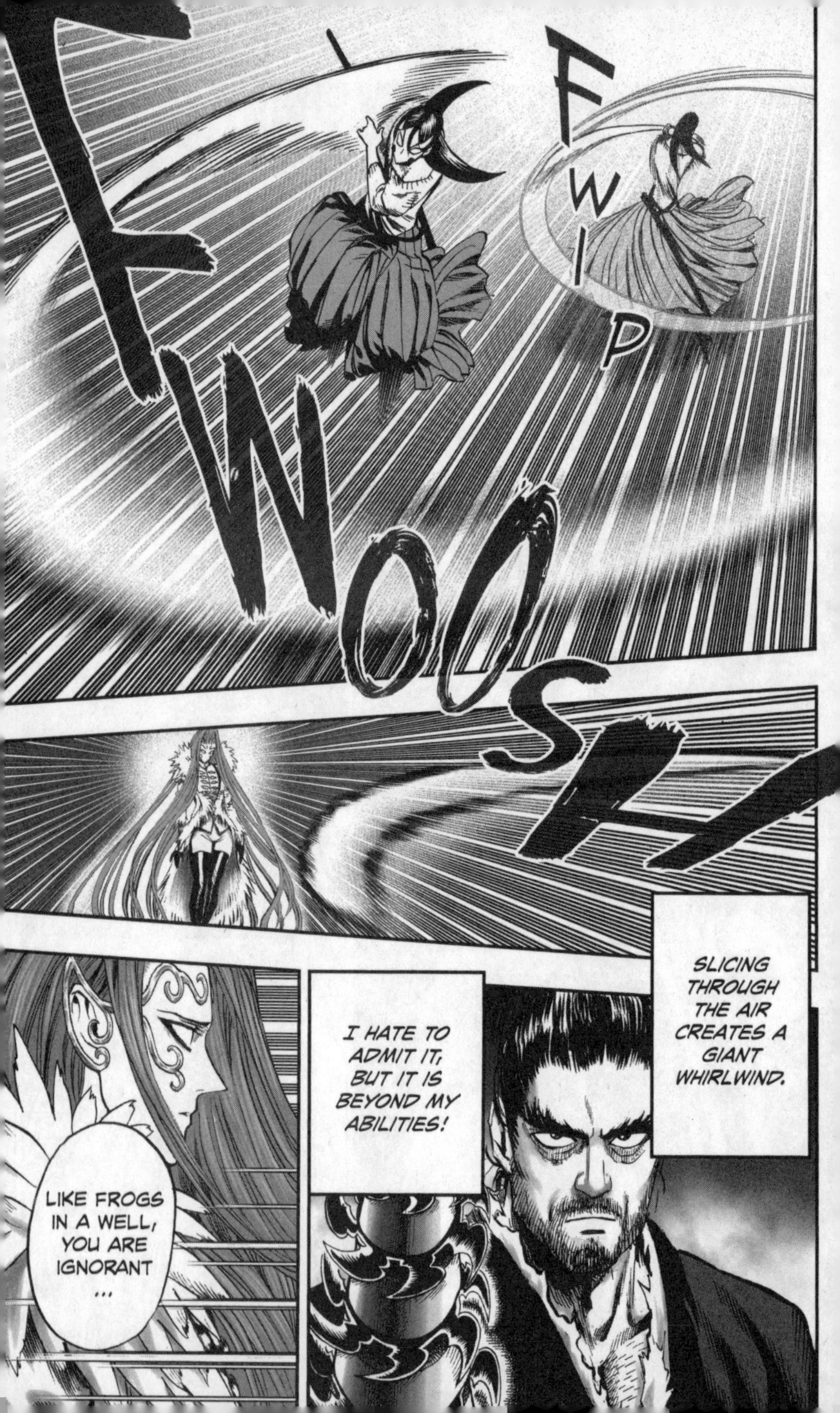
FWIP
FWOOSH
SLICING THROUGH THE AIR CREATES A GIANT WHIRLWIND.
I HATE TO ADMIT IT, BUT IT IS BEYOND MY ABILITIES!
LIKE FROGS IN A WELL, YOU ARE IGNORANT ...

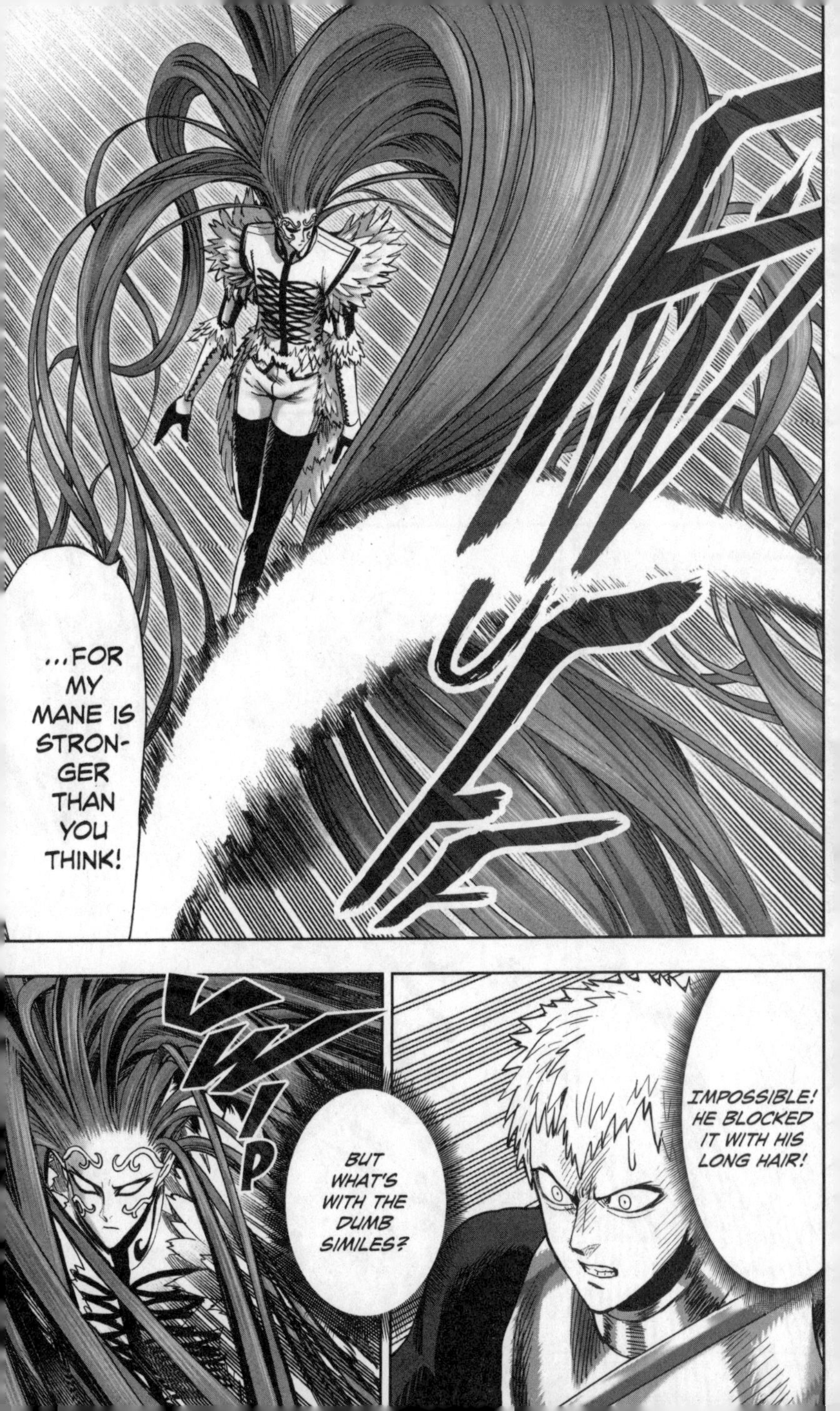
...FOR MY MANE IS STRONGER THAN YOU THINK!
IMPOSSIBLE! HE BLOCKED IT WITH HIS LONG HAIR!
BUT WHAT'S WITH THE DUMB SIMILES?
WHIP

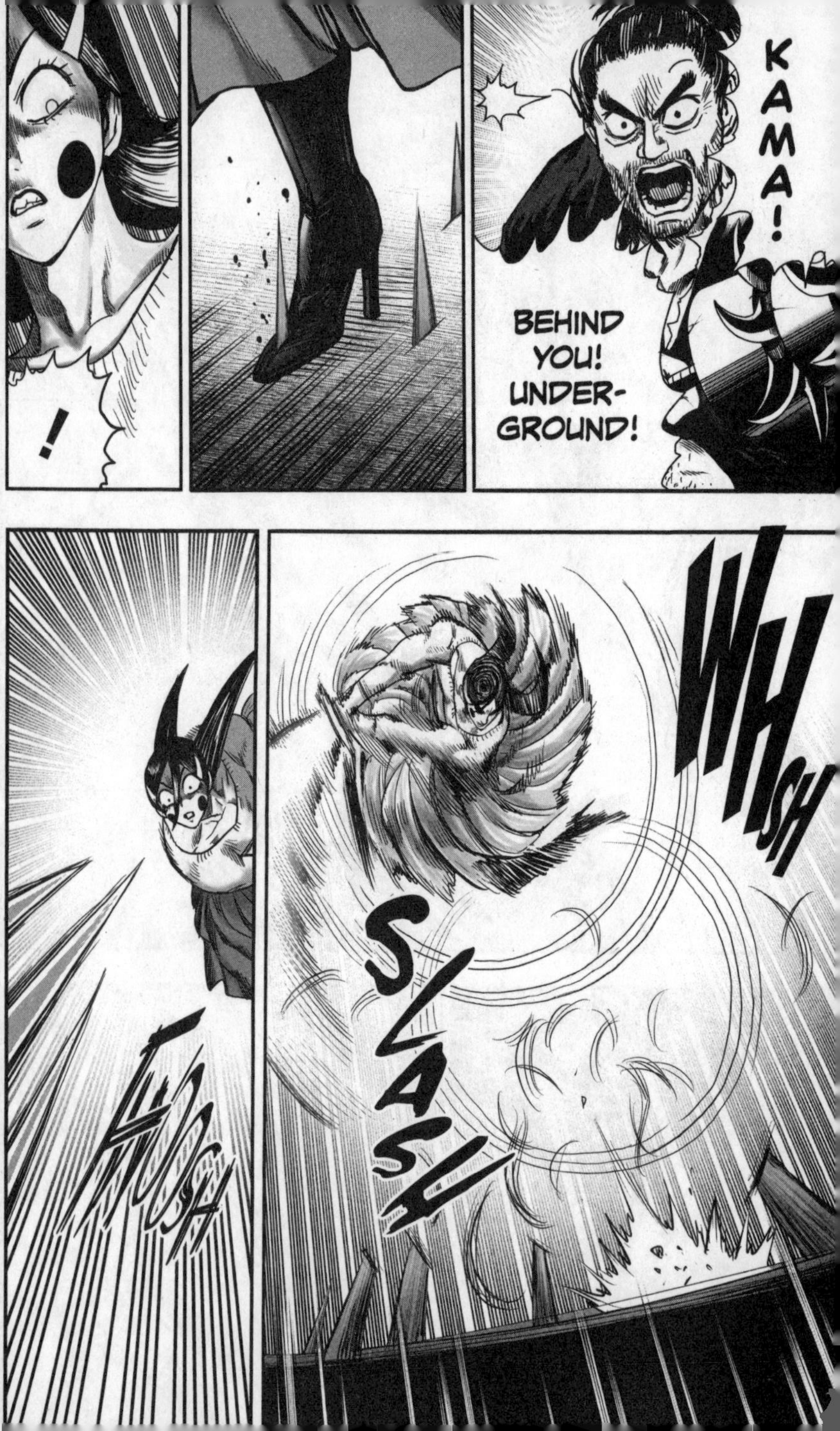
KAMA!
BEHIND YOU! UNDER-GROUND!
!
WHSH
SLASH

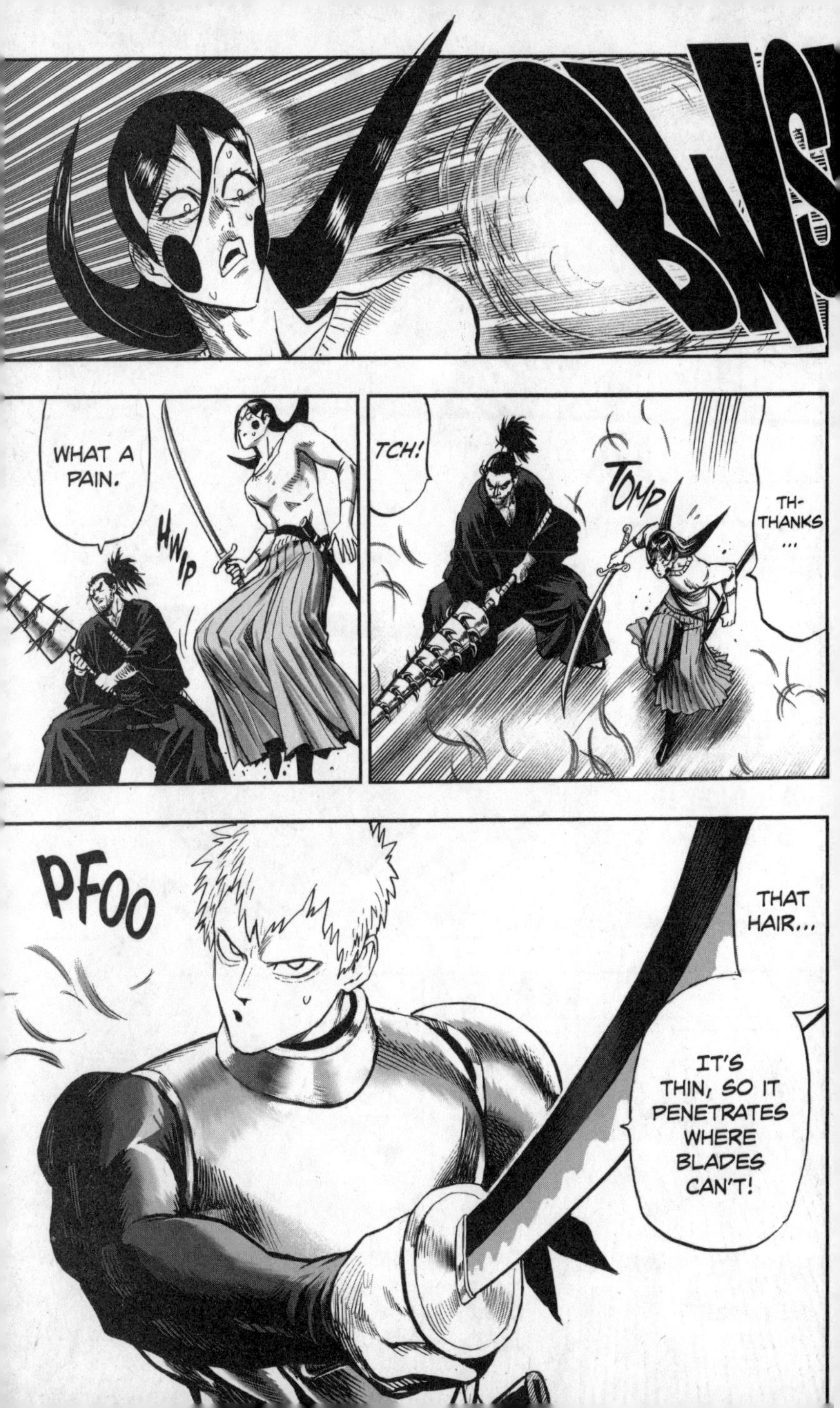
BWS
TCH!
TOMP
TH-THANKS...
WHAT A PAIN.
HWIP
THAT HAIR...
IT'S THIN, SO IT PENETRATES WHERE BLADES CAN'T!
PFOO

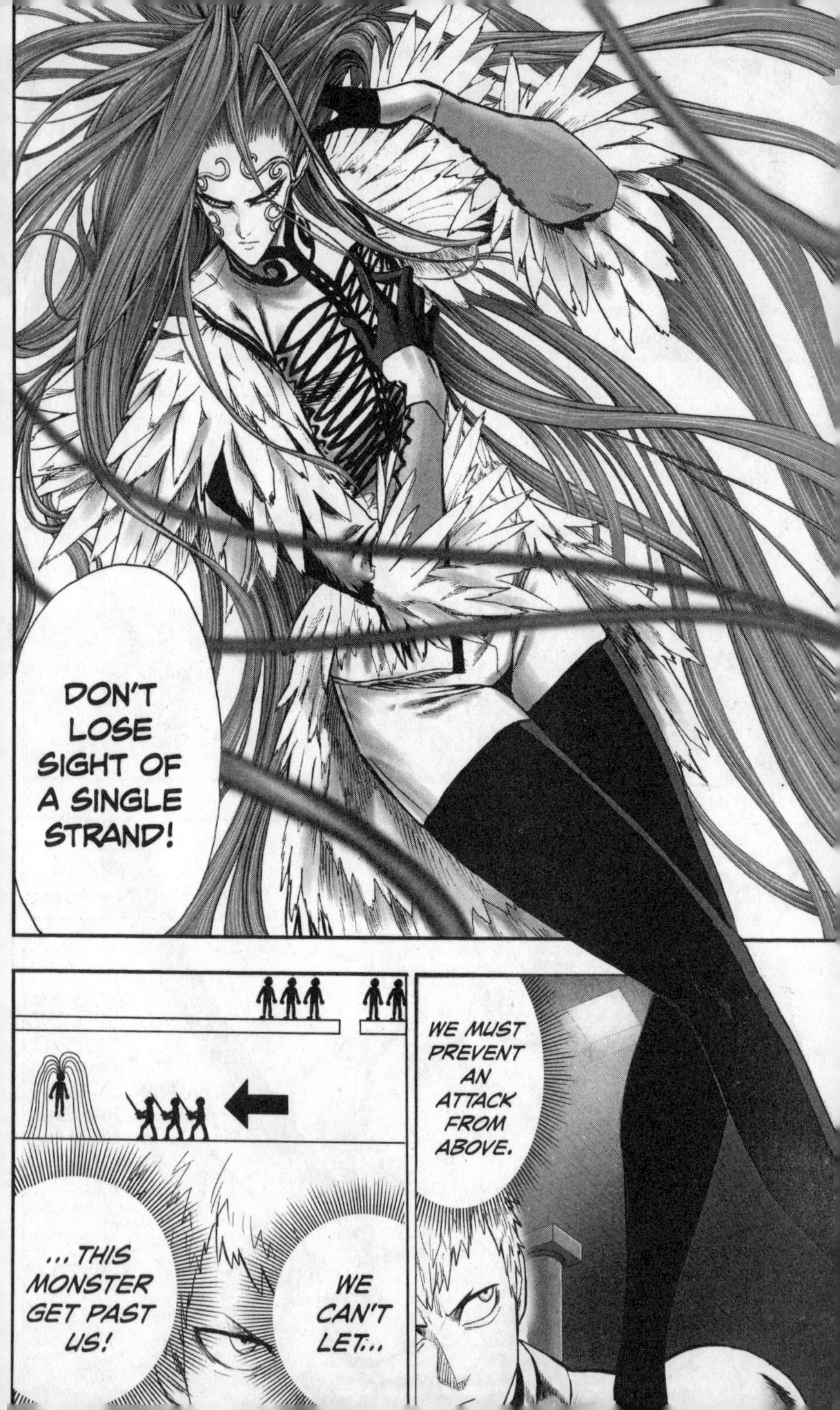
DON'T LOSE SIGHT OF A SINGLE STRAND!
WE MUST PREVENT AN ATTACK FROM ABOVE.
WE CAN'T LET...
...THIS MONSTER GET PAST US!

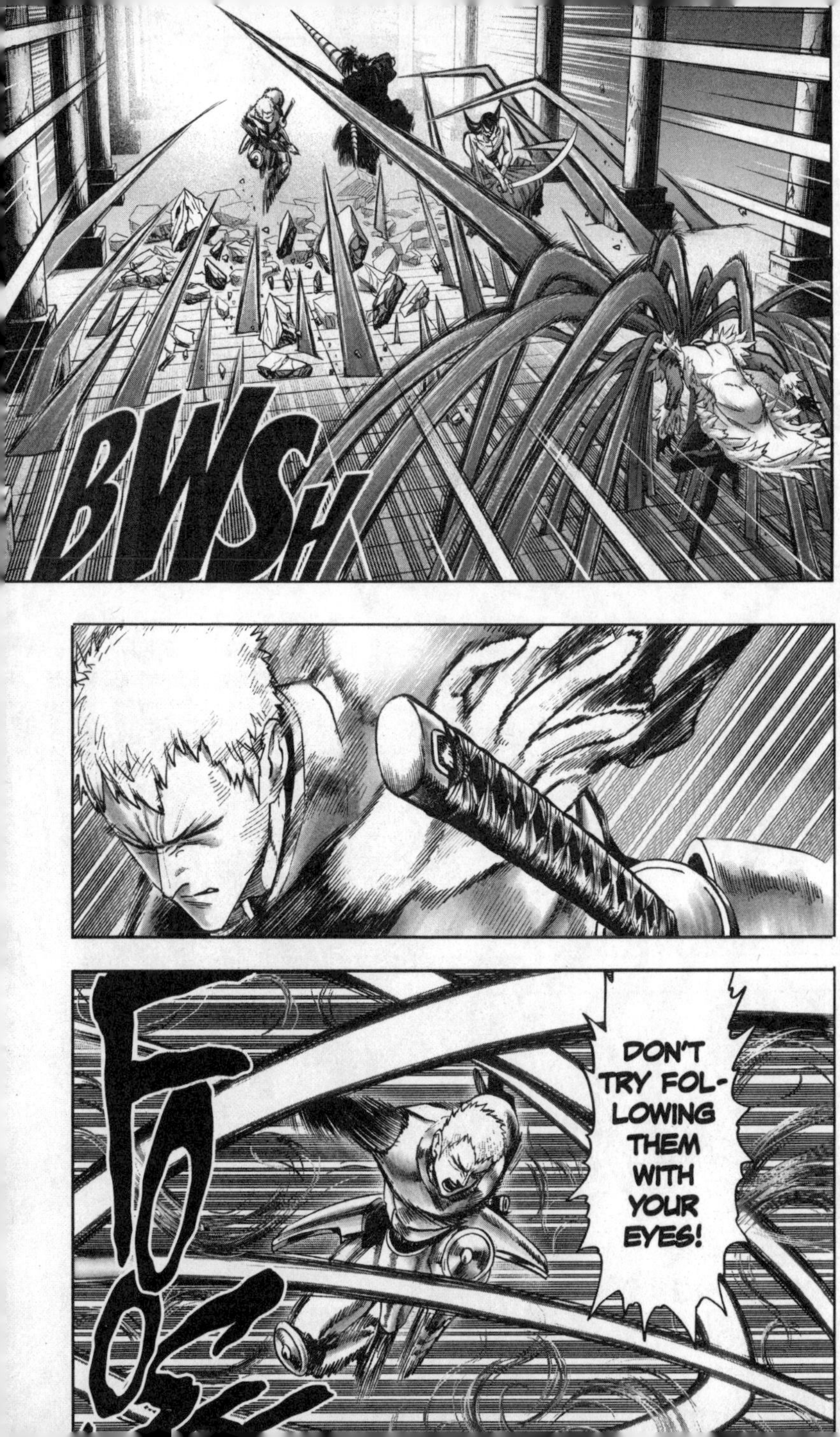
BWSH
DON'T TRY FOL-LOWING THEM WITH YOUR EYES!
FSSH

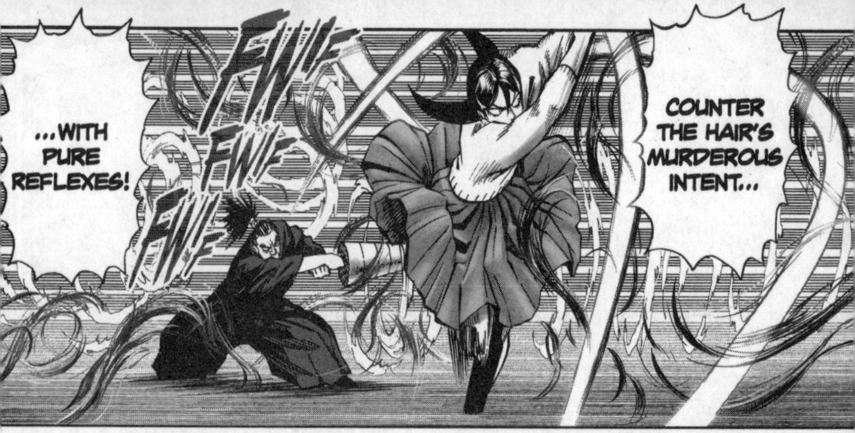
COUNTER THE HAIR'S MURDEROUS INTENT...
...WITH PURE REFLEXES!

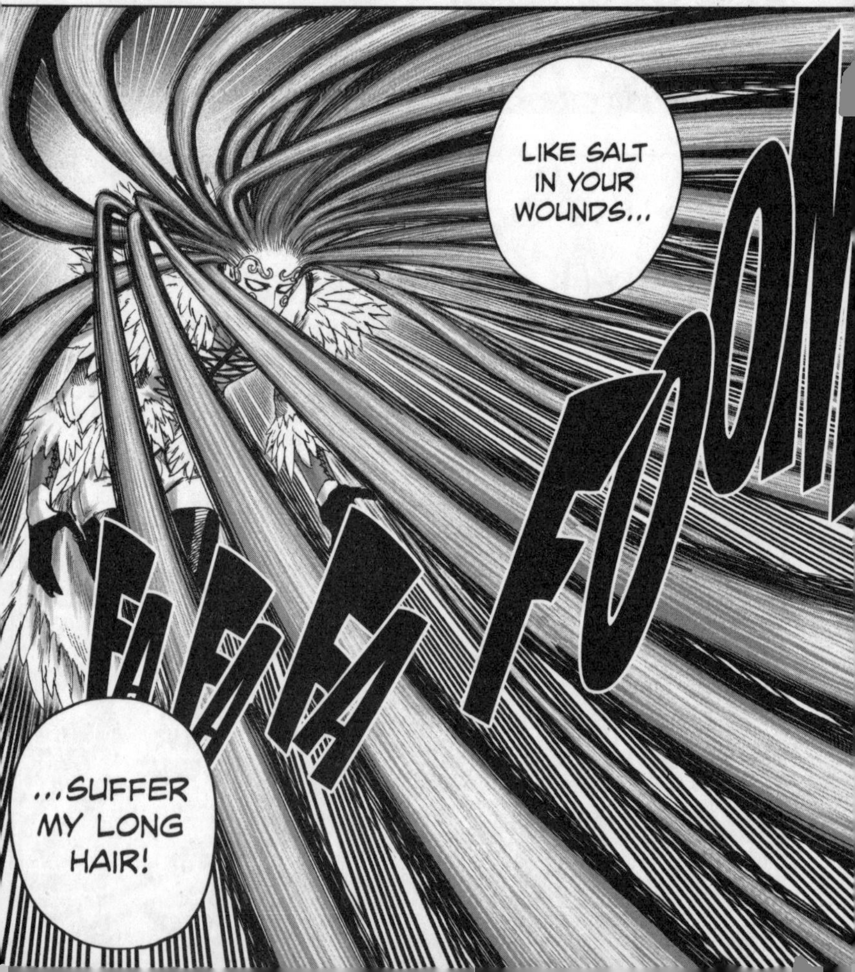
LIKE SALT IN YOUR WOUNDS...
...SUFFER MY LONG HAIR!

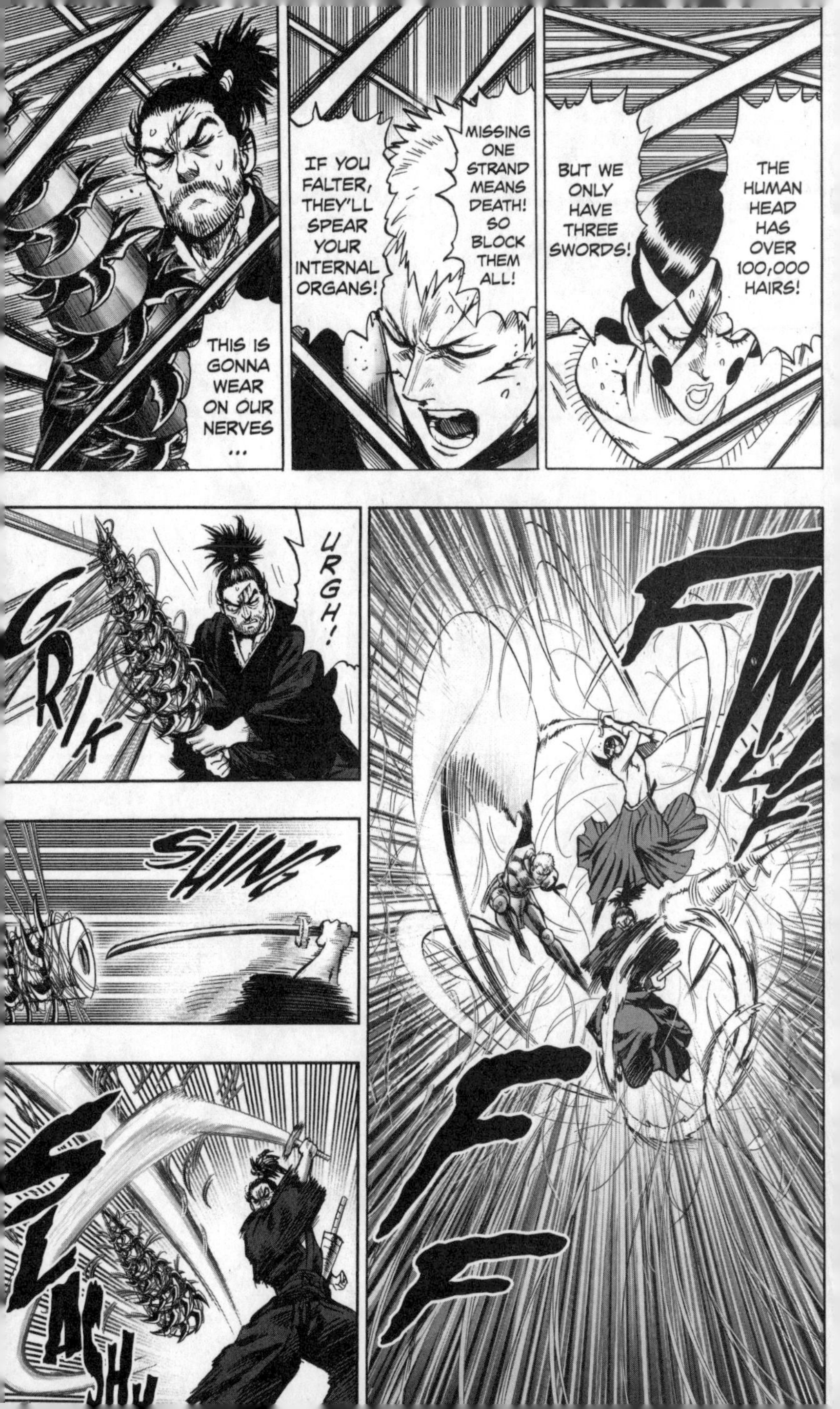
THE HUMAN HEAD HAS OVER 100,000 HAIRS!
BUT WE ONLY HAVE THREE SWORDS!
MISSING ONE STRAND MEANS DEATH! SO BLOCK THEM ALL!
IF YOU FALTER, THEY'LL SPEAR YOUR INTERNAL ORGANS!
THIS IS GONNA WEAR ON OUR NERVES ...
URGH!
GRIK
SHING
SLASH

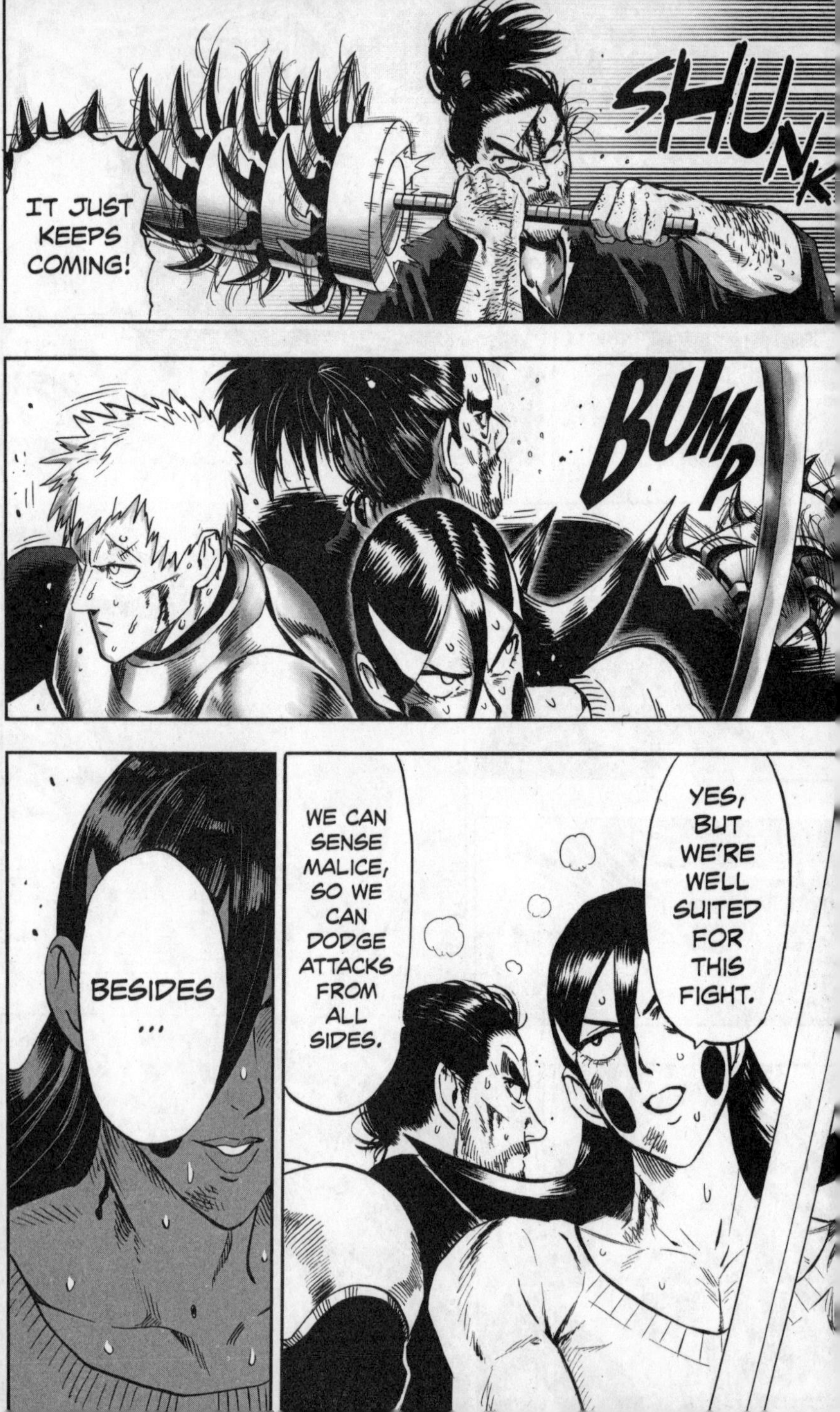
SHUNK
IT JUST KEEPS COMING!
BUMP
YES, BUT WE'RE WELL SUITED FOR THIS FIGHT.
WE CAN SENSE MALICE, SO WE CAN DODGE ATTACKS FROM ALL SIDES.
BESIDES ...

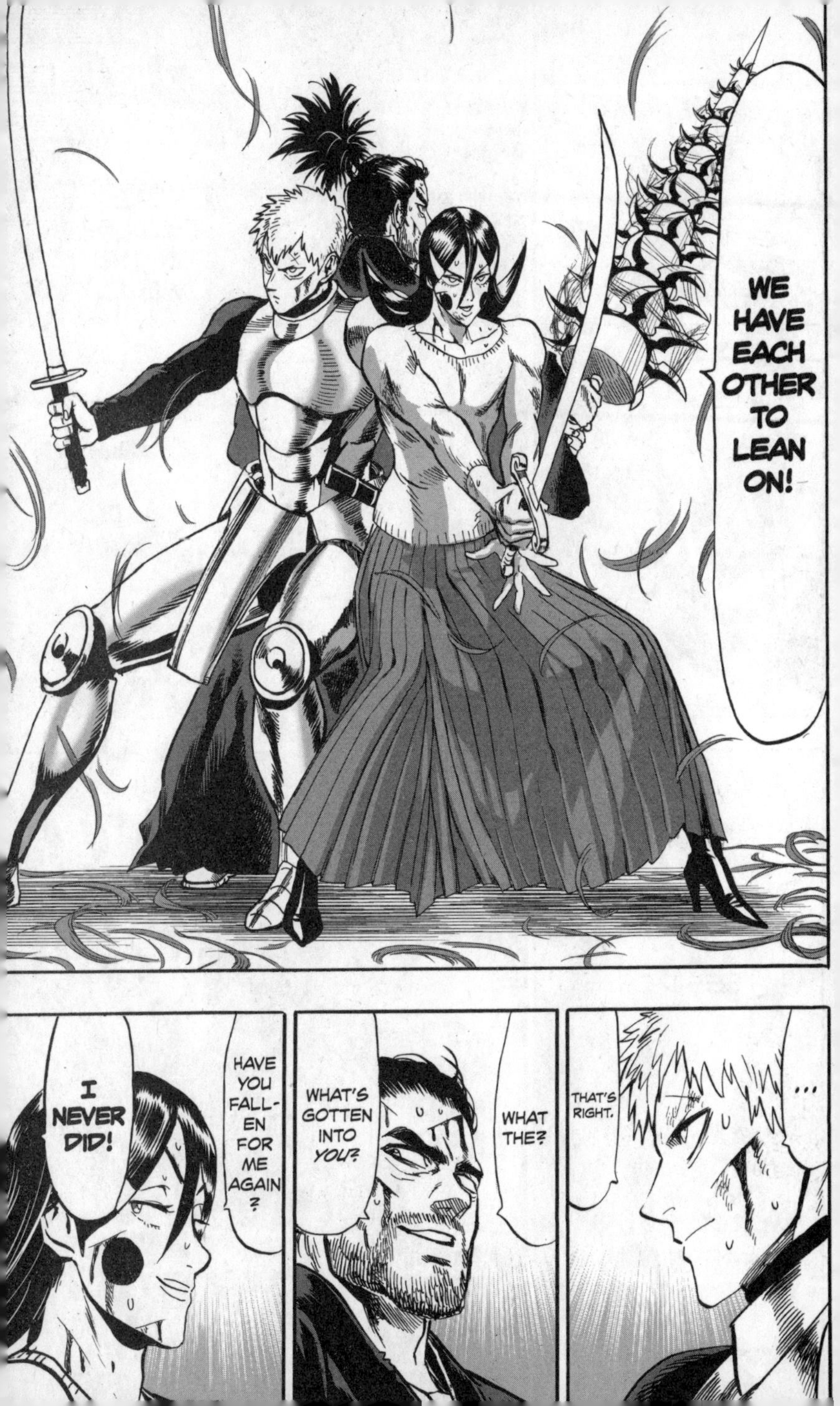

WE HAVE EACH OTHER TO LEAN ON!
...
THAT'S RIGHT.
WHAT THE?
WHAT'S GOTTEN INTO *YOU*?
HAVE YOU FALL-EN FOR ME AGAIN?
I NEVER DID!

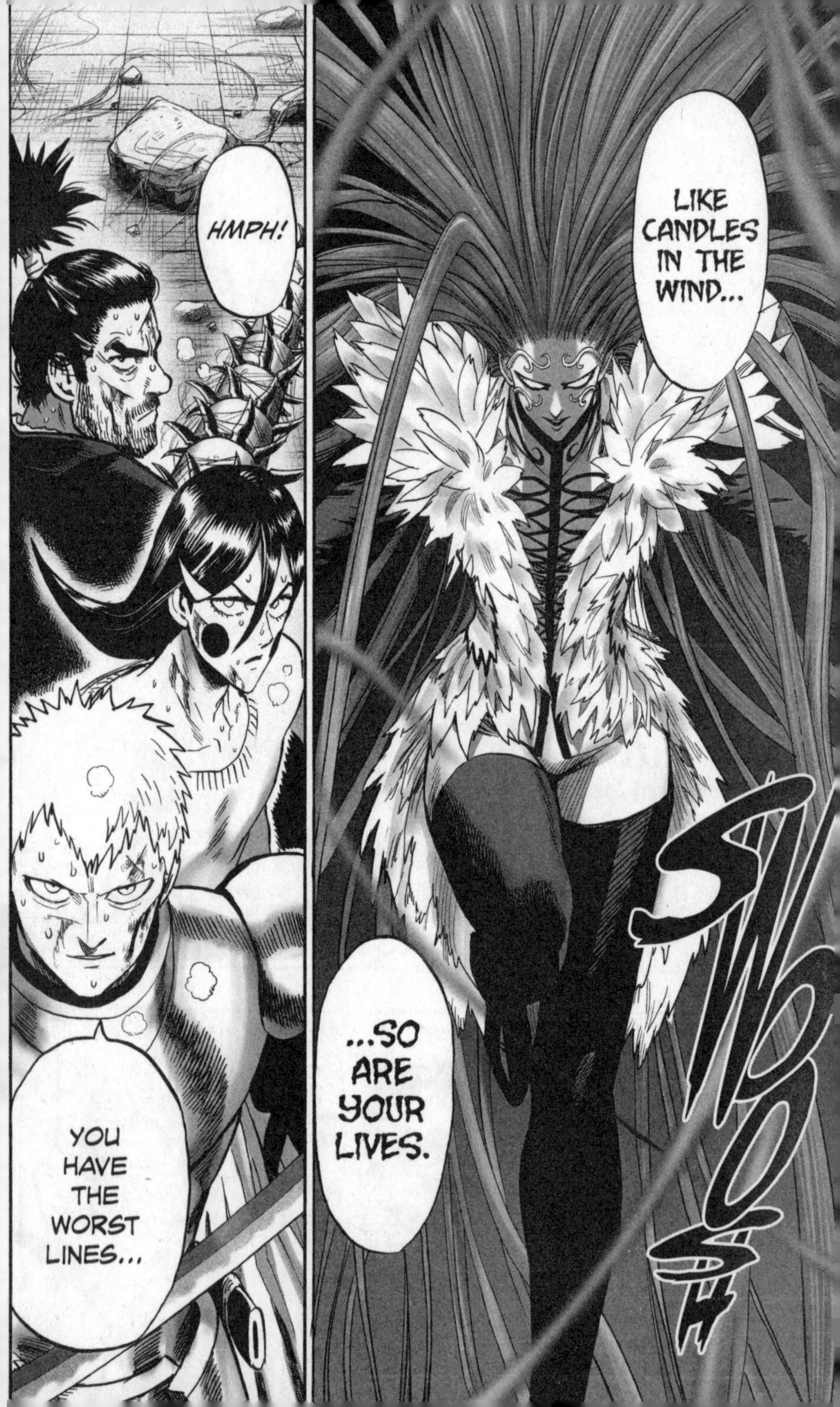
LIKE CANDLES IN THE WIND...
...SO ARE YOUR LIVES.
HMPH!
YOU HAVE THE WORST LINES...

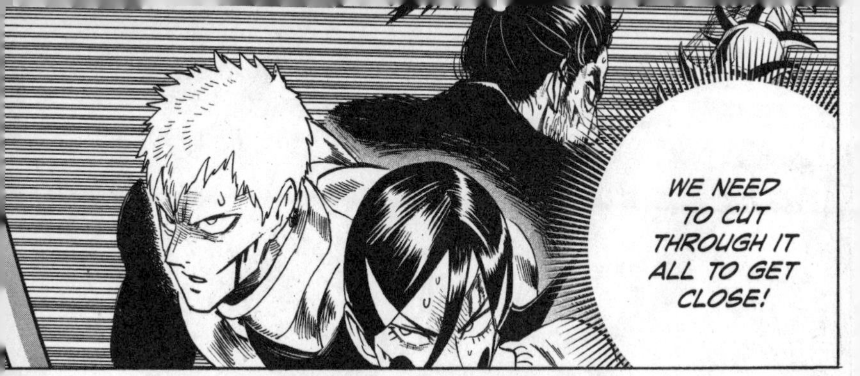
WE NEED TO CUT THROUGH IT ALL TO GET CLOSE!

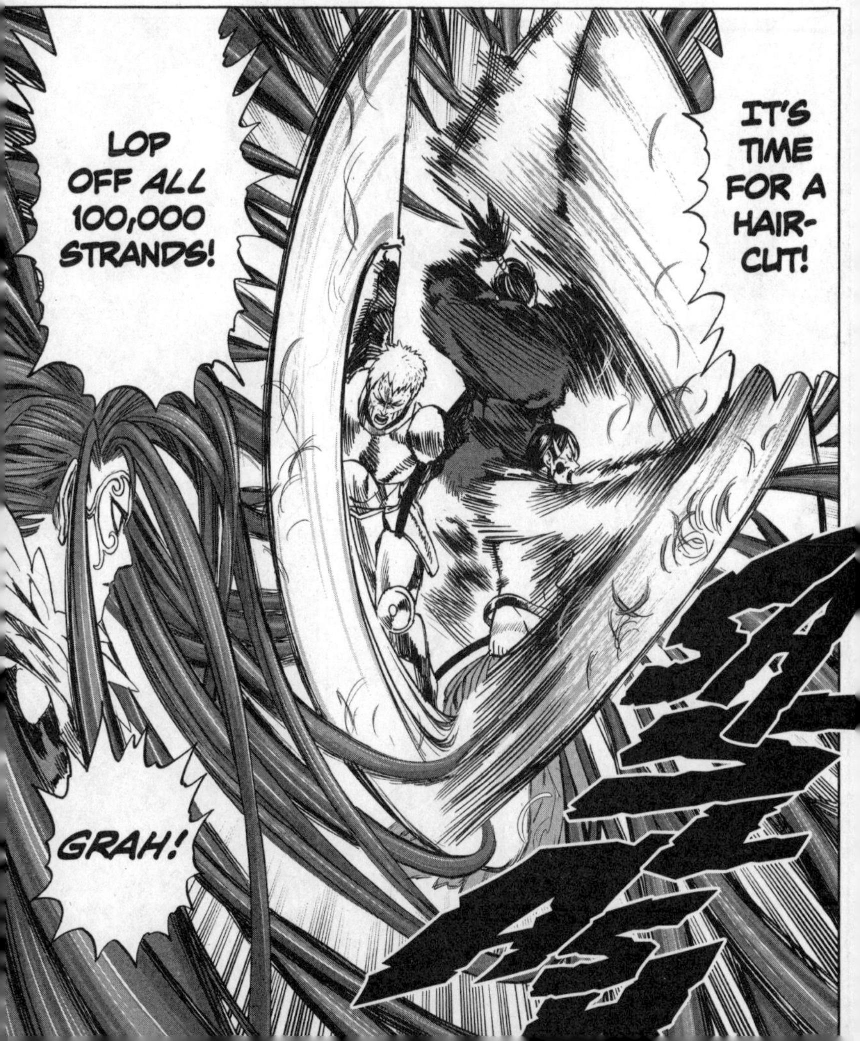
IT'S TIME FOR A HAIR-CUT!
LOP OFF ALL 100,000 STRANDS!
GRAH!

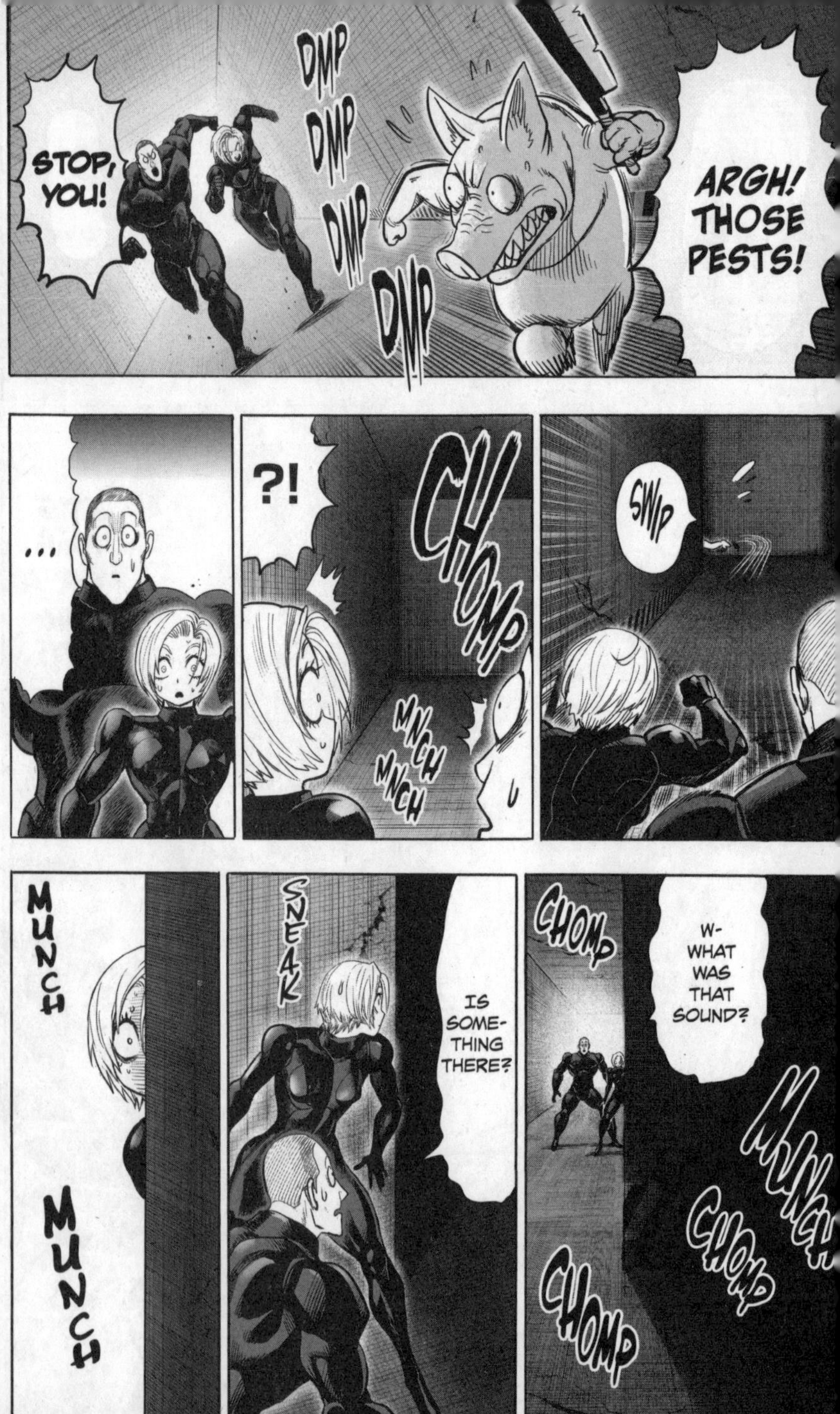
ARGH! THOSE PESTS!
DMP DMP DMP DMP
STOP, YOU!
SWIP
?!
CHOMP
MNCH MNCH
...
W-WHAT WAS THAT SOUND?
CHOMP
MUNCH
CHOMP
CHOMP
SNEAK
IS SOMETHING THERE?
MUNCH
MUNCH

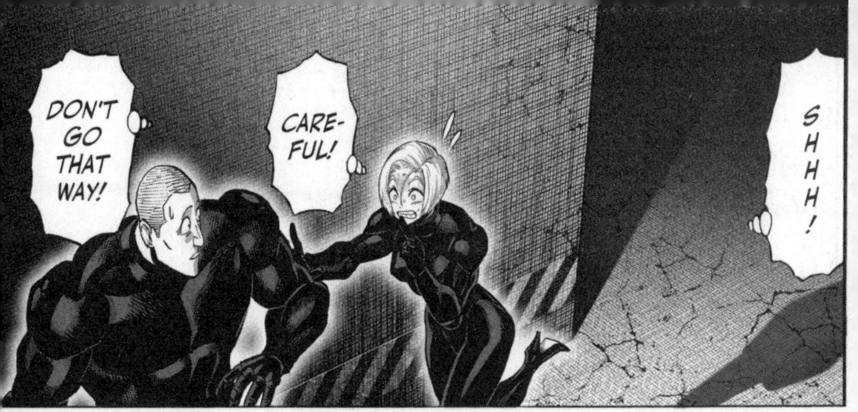
SHHH!
CARE-FUL!
DON'T GO THAT WAY!
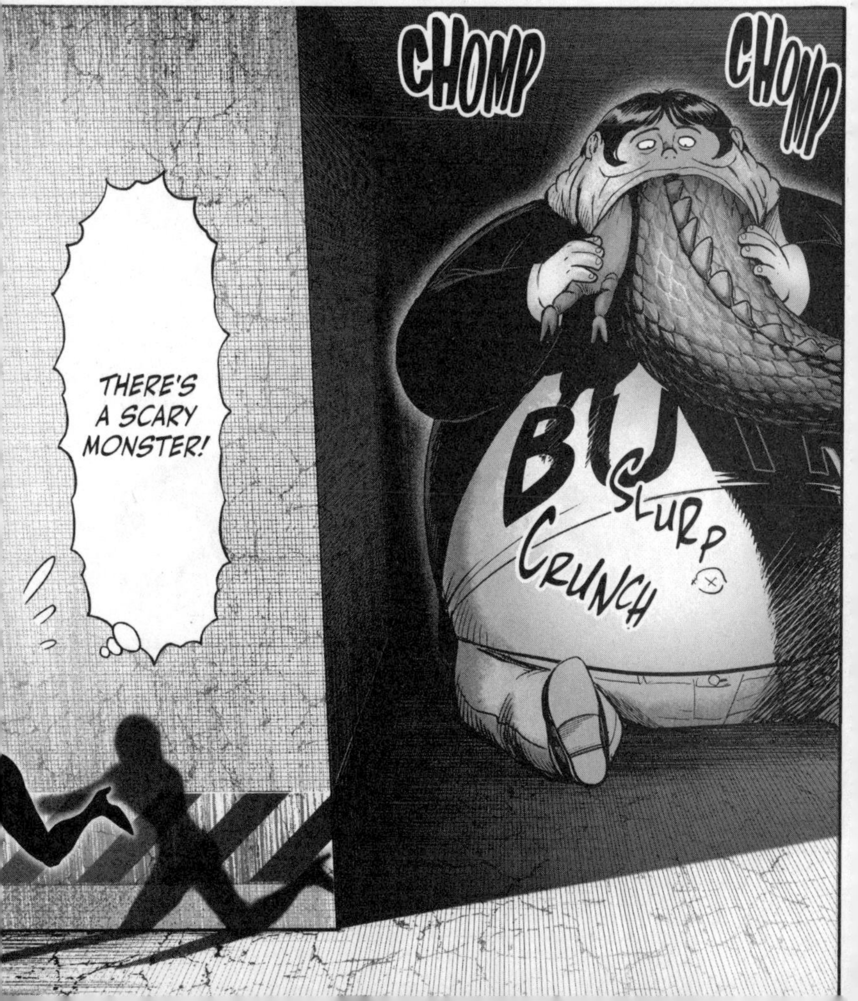
CHOMP
CHOMP
SLURP
CRUNCH
THERE'S A SCARY MONSTER!

26 yrs.

23 yrs.

37 yrs.

PUNCH 108: AUTHENTICITY

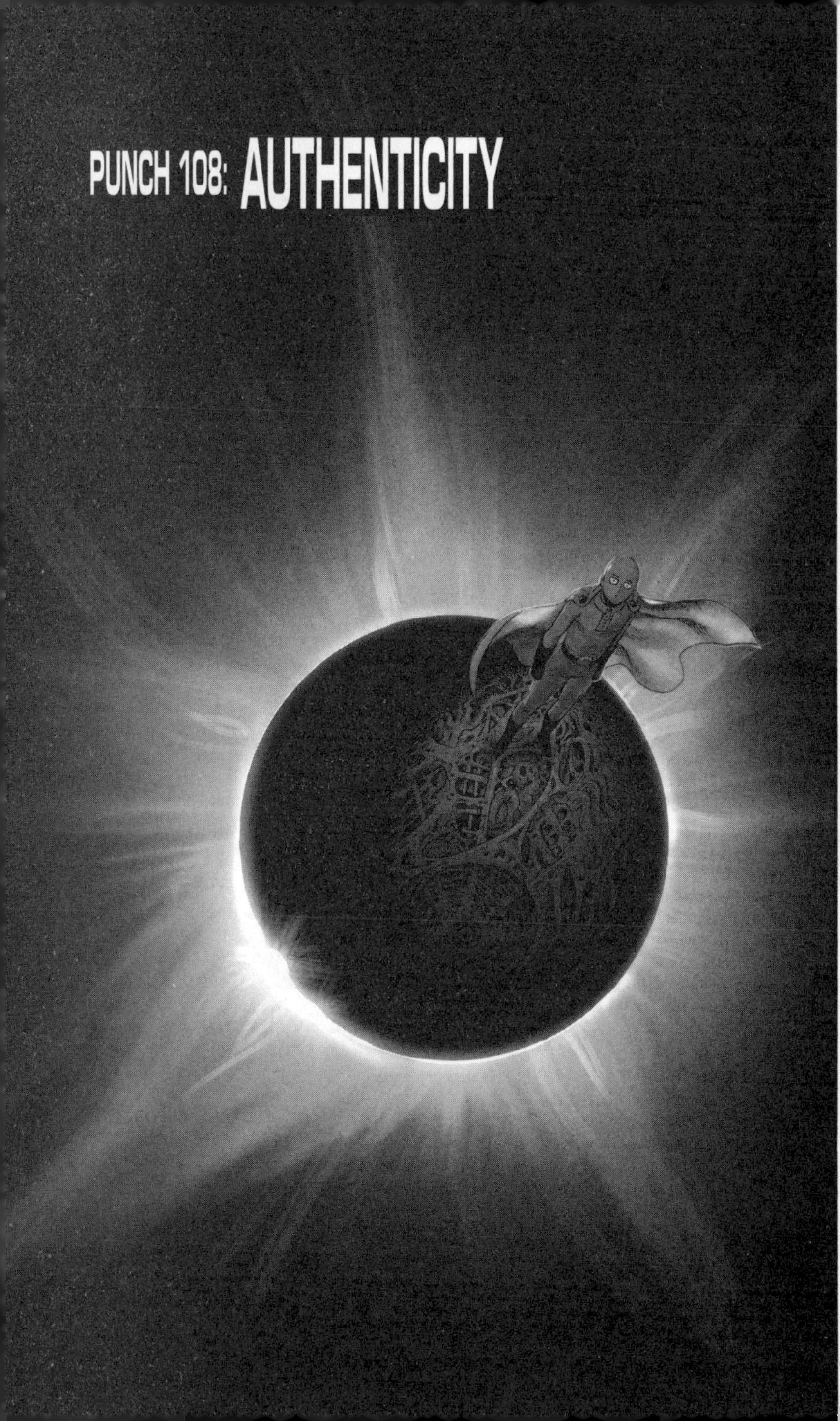

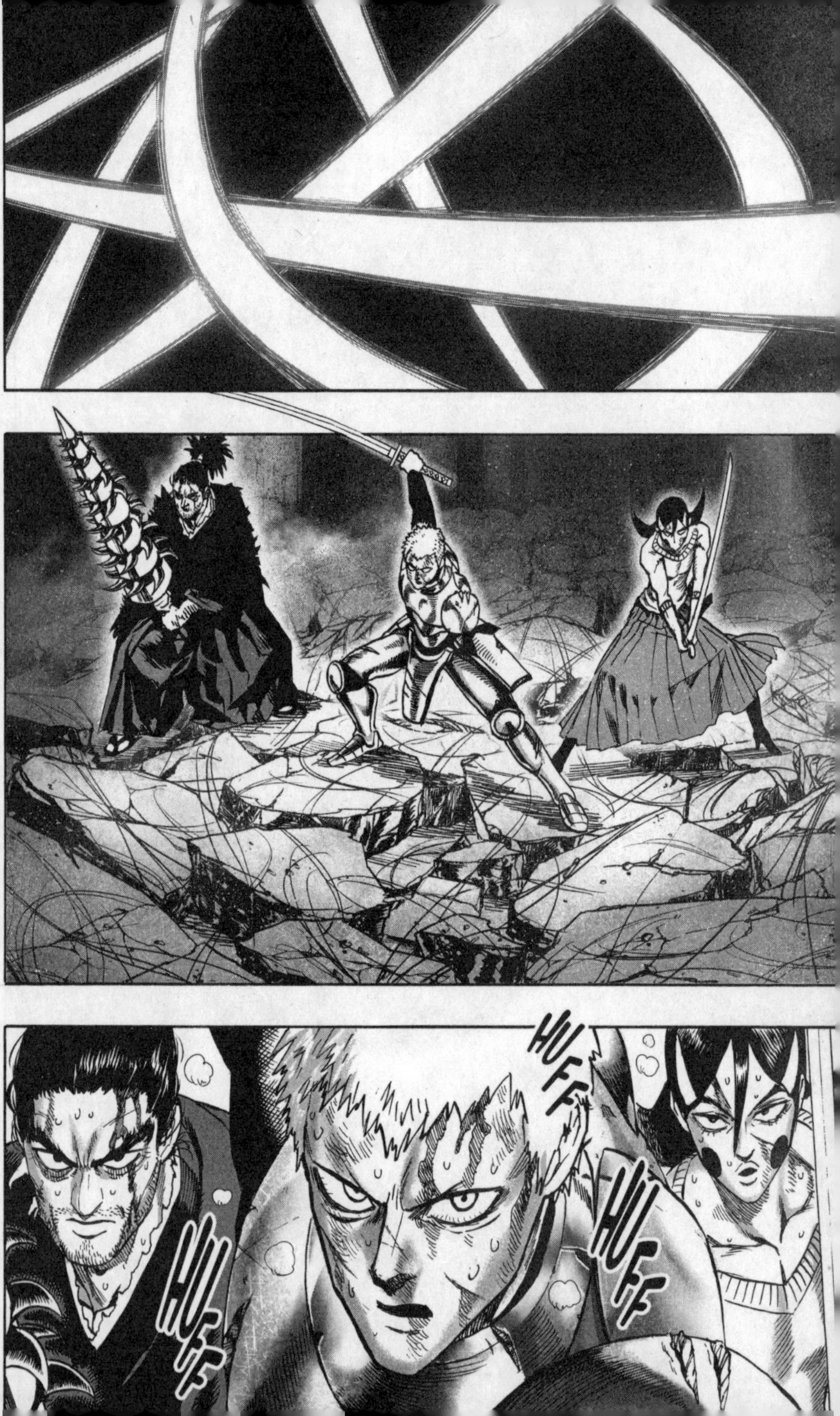
HUFF
HUFF
HUFF
HUFF

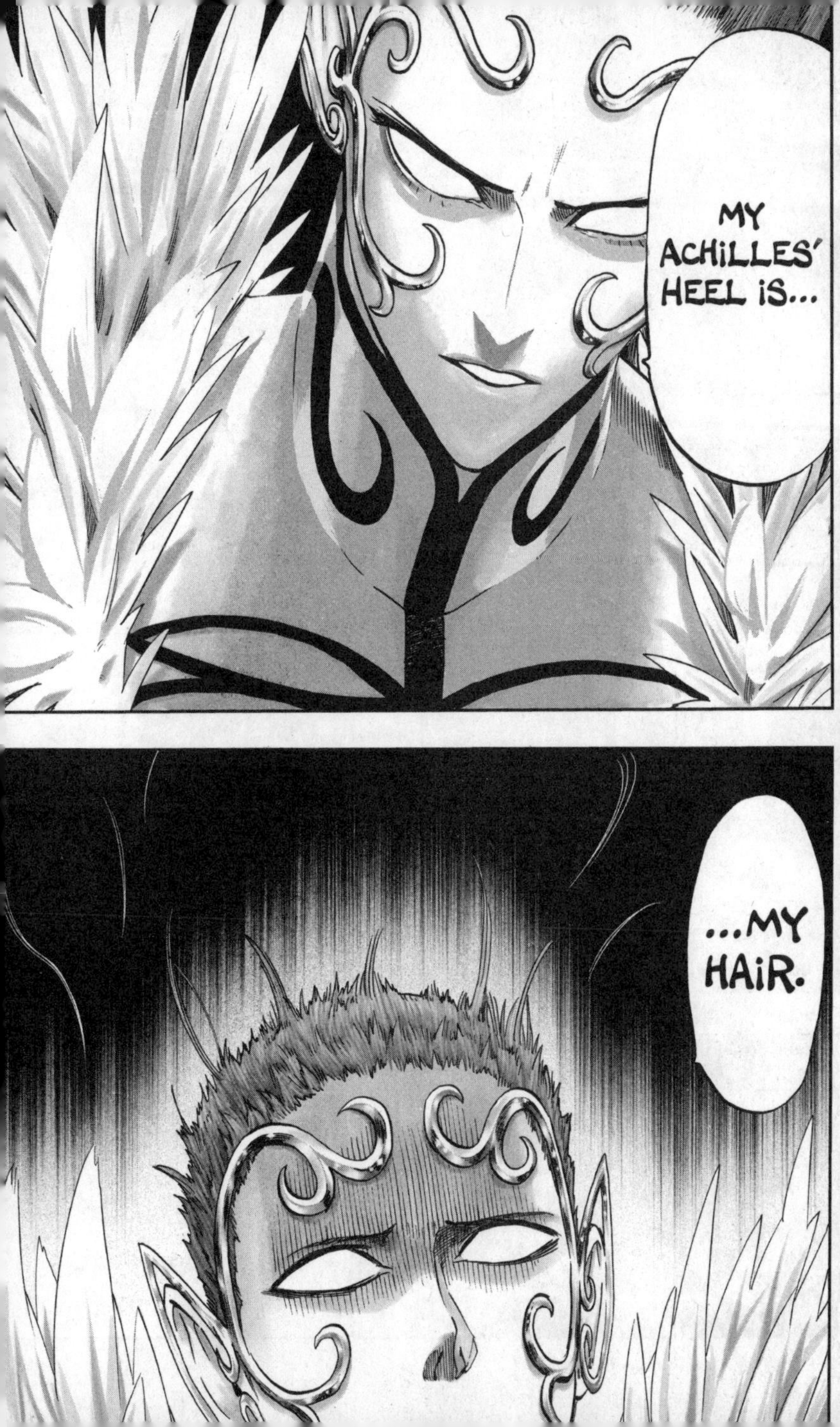
MY ACHILLES' HEEL IS...
...MY HAIR.

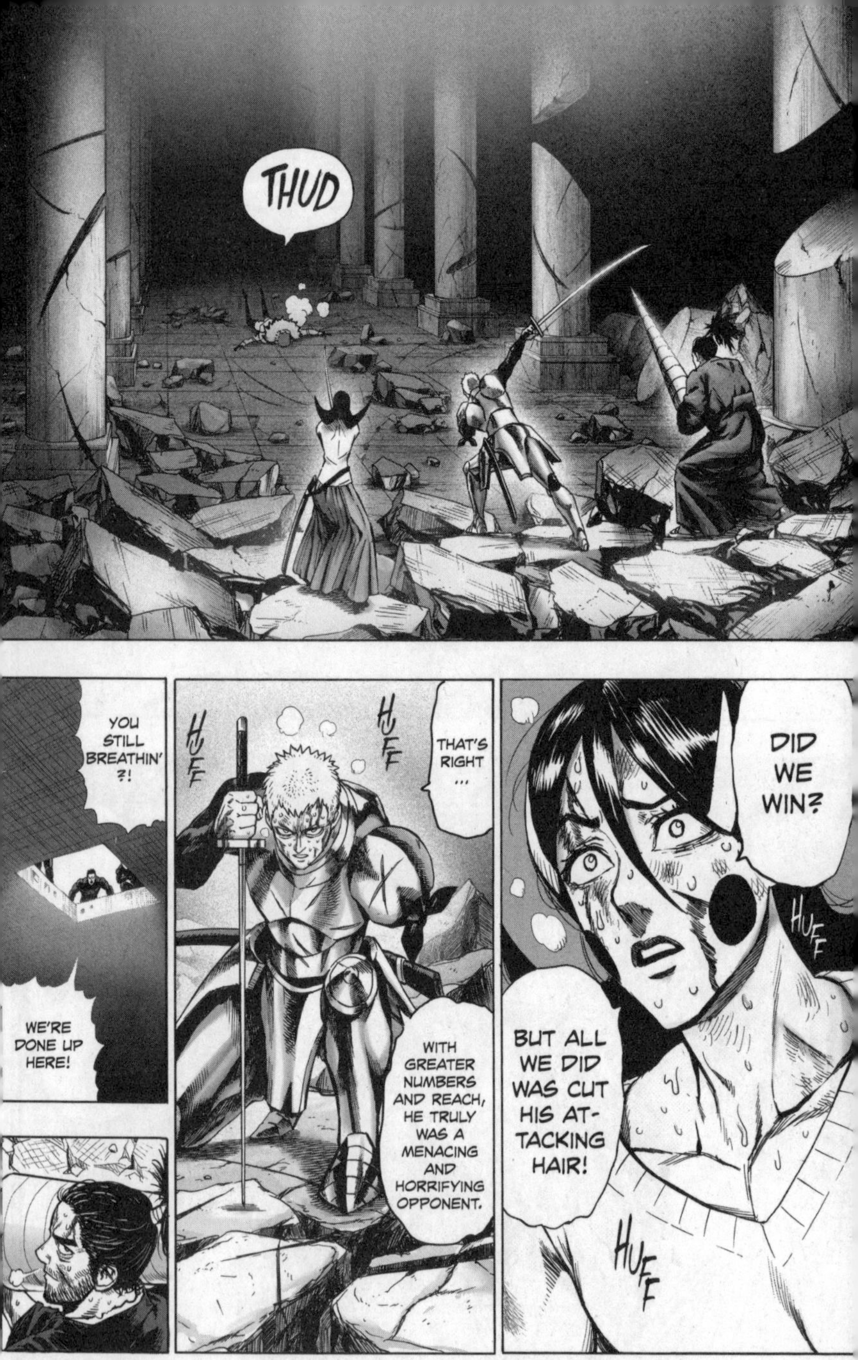
THUD
DID WE WIN?
BUT ALL WE DID WAS CUT HIS AT-TACKING HAIR!
HUFF
HUFF
HUFF
HUFF
THAT'S RIGHT ...
WITH GREATER NUMBERS AND REACH, HE TRULY WAS A MENACING AND HORRIFYING OPPONENT.
YOU STILL BREATHIN' ?!
WE'RE DONE UP HERE!

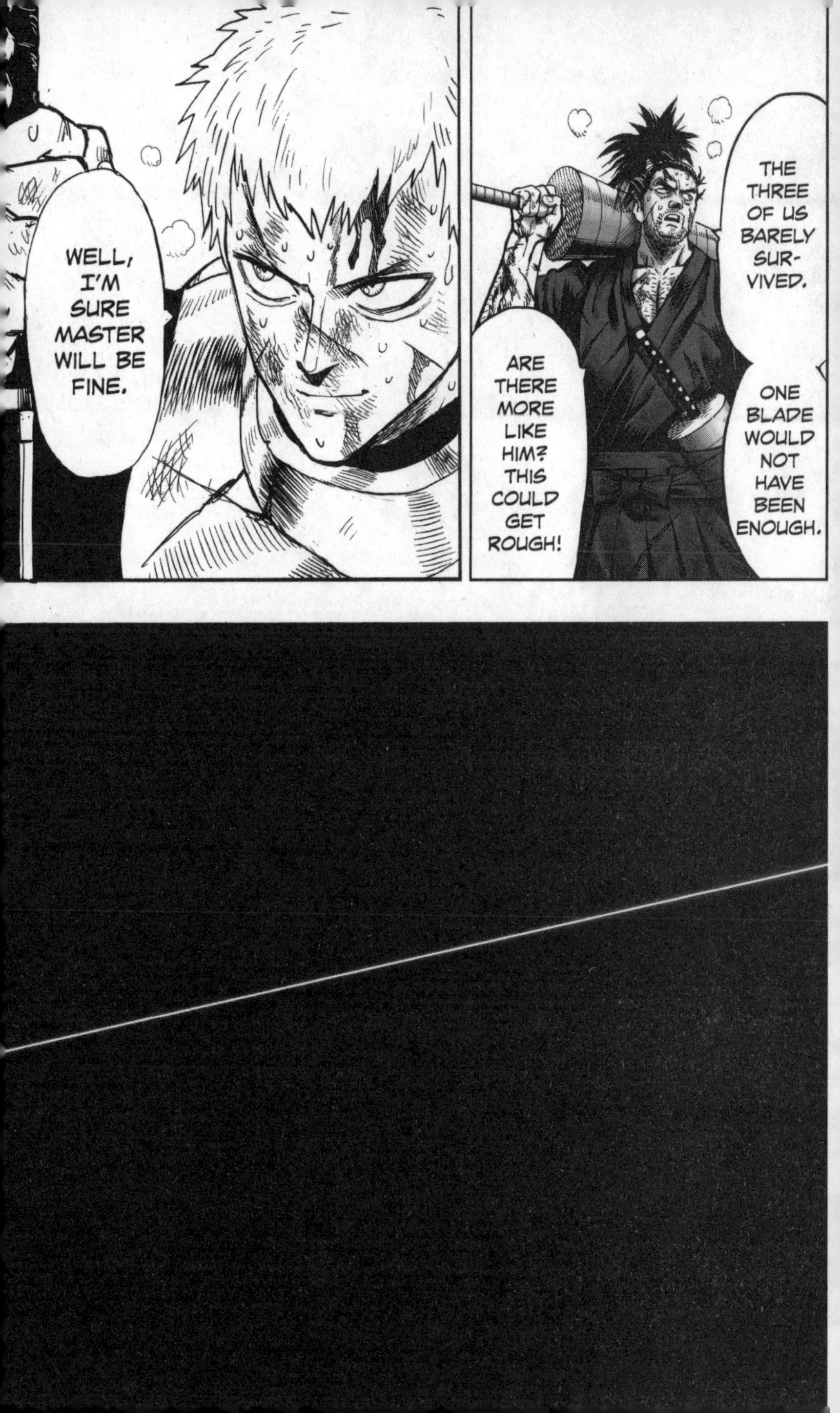
THE THREE OF US BARELY SUR-VIVED.
ONE BLADE WOULD NOT HAVE BEEN ENOUGH.
ARE THERE MORE LIKE HIM? THIS COULD GET ROUGH!
WELL, I'M SURE MASTER WILL BE FINE.

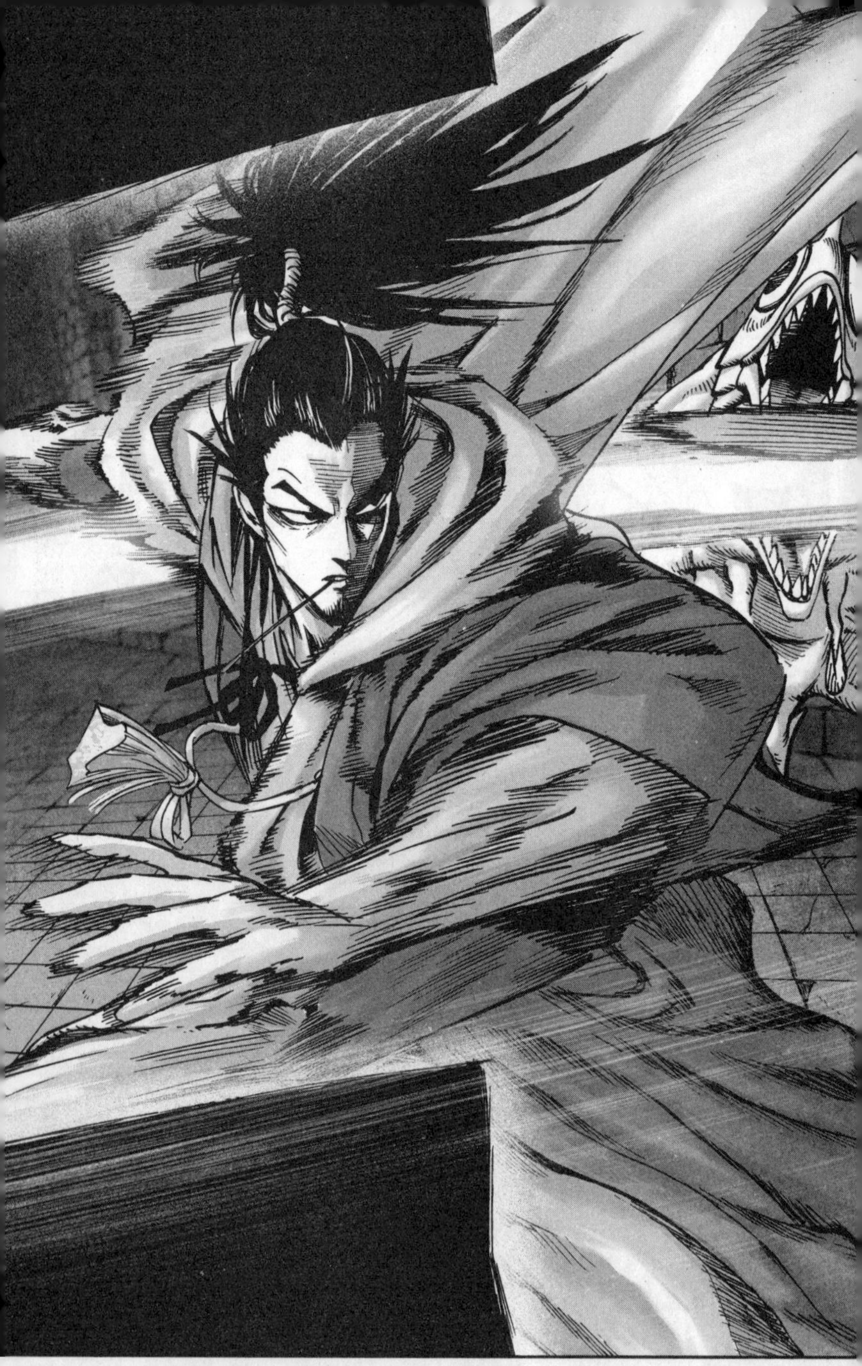

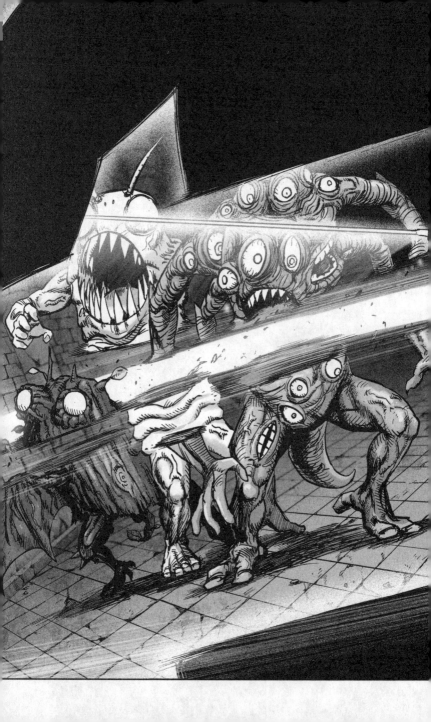

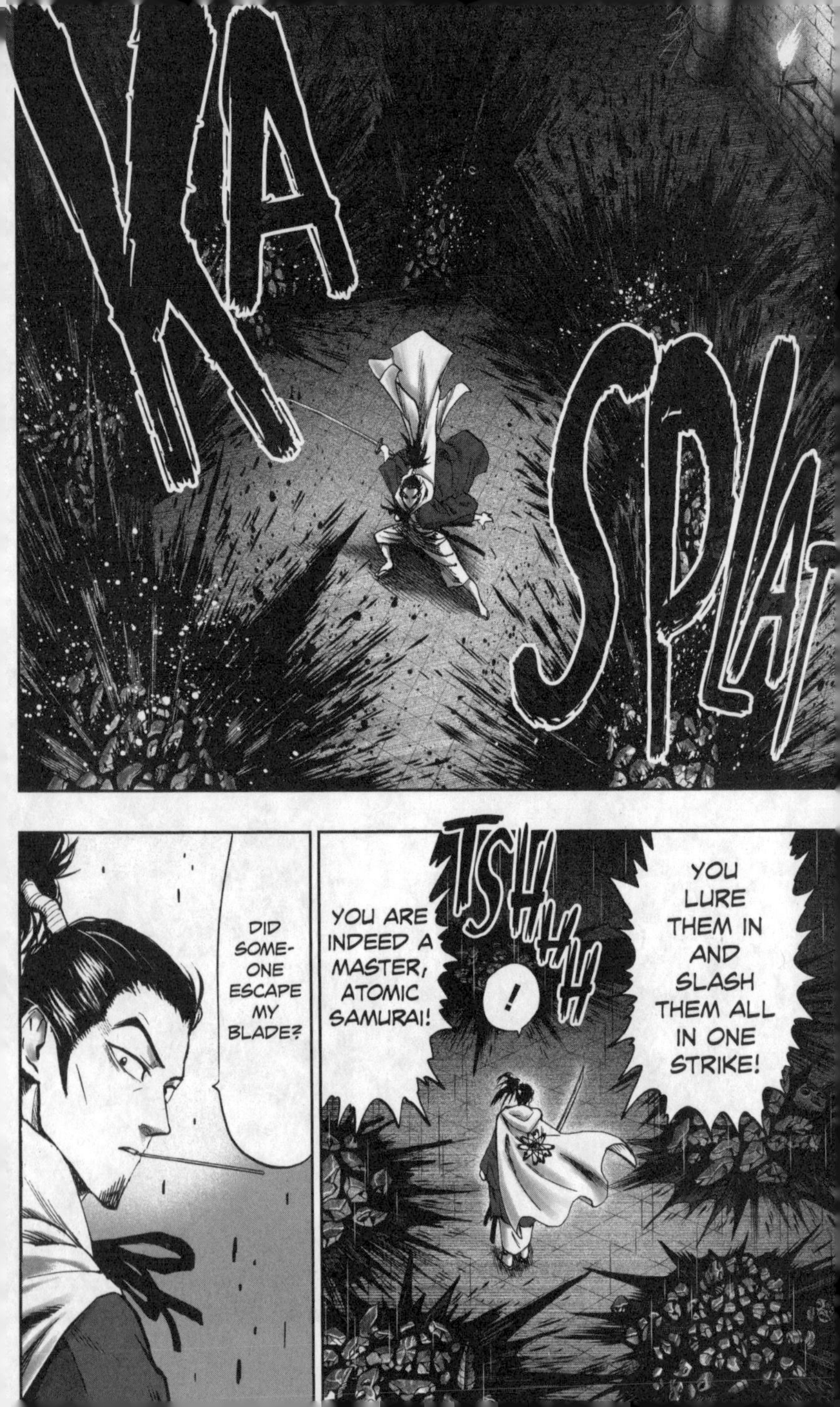
KA
SPLAT
YOU LURE THEM IN AND SLASH THEM ALL IN ONE STRIKE!
TSHHHH
YOU ARE INDEED A MASTER, ATOMIC SAMURAI!
!
DID SOMEONE ESCAPE MY BLADE?

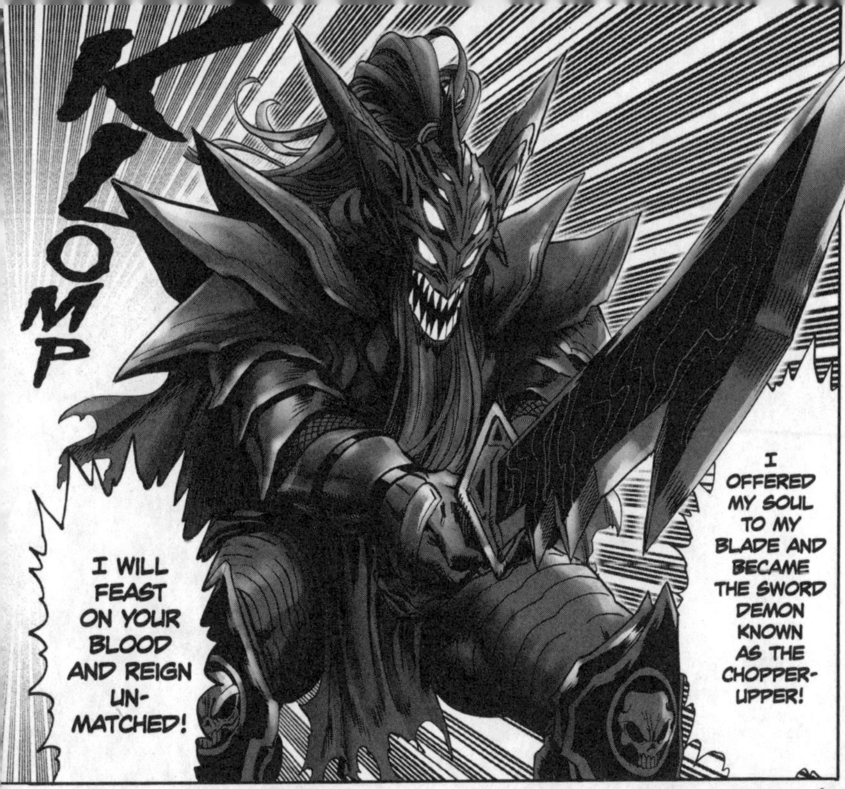
I OFFERED MY SOUL TO MY BLADE AND BECAME THE SWORD DEMON KNOWN AS THE CHOPPER-UPPER!
I WILL FEAST ON YOUR BLOOD AND REIGN UN-MATCHED!
KLOMP

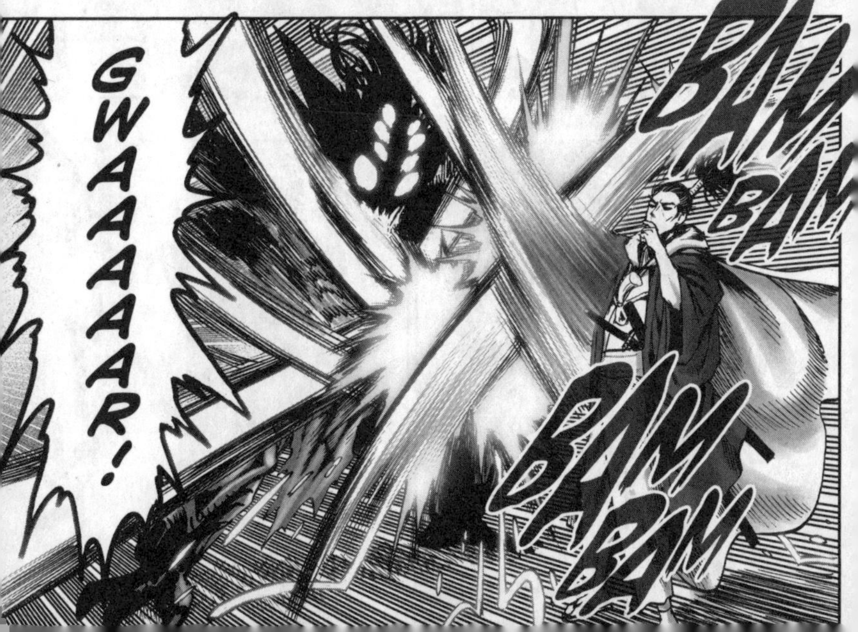
BAM BAM
GWAAAAAAR!
BAM BAM

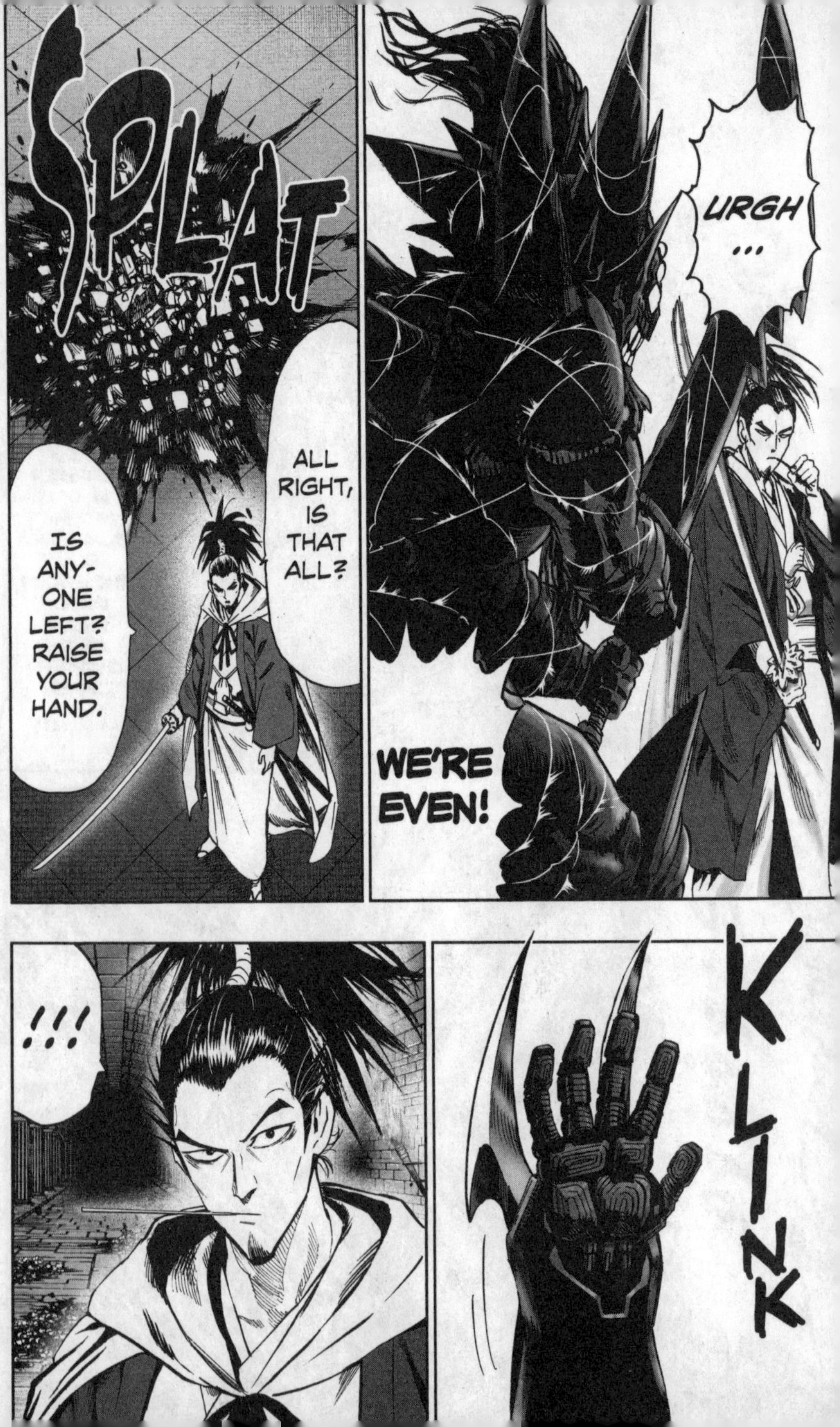
URGH ...
WE'RE EVEN!
SPLAT
ALL RIGHT, IS THAT ALL?
IS ANY-ONE LEFT? RAISE YOUR HAND.
KLLINK
!!!

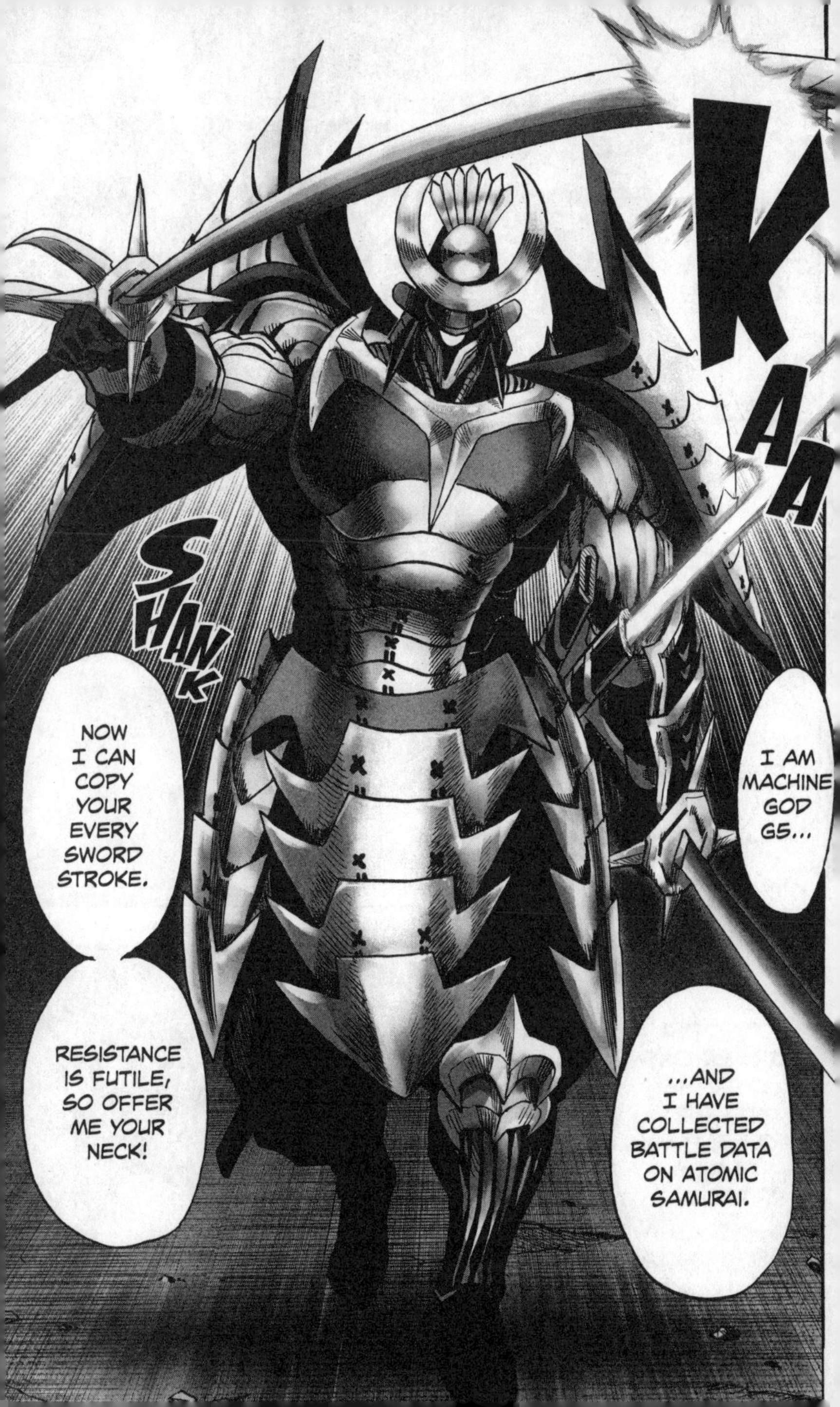
KAA
I AM MACHINE GOD G5...
...AND I HAVE COLLECTED BATTLE DATA ON ATOMIC SAMURAI.
SHANK
NOW I CAN COPY YOUR EVERY SWORD STROKE.
RESISTANCE IS FUTILE, SO OFFER ME YOUR NECK!

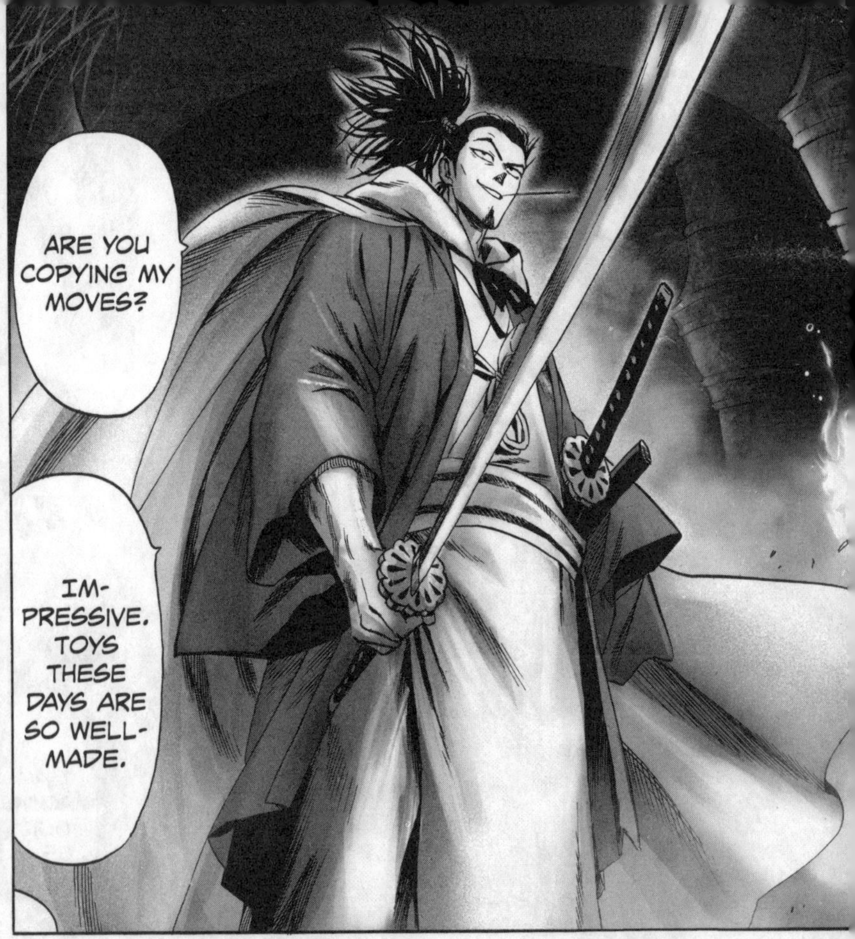
ARE YOU COPYING MY MOVES?
IM-PRESSIVE. TOYS THESE DAYS ARE SO WELL-MADE.
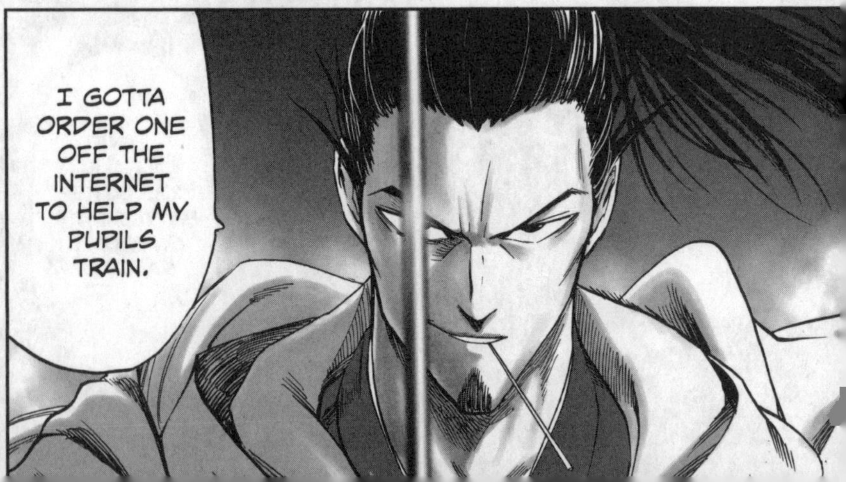
I GOTTA ORDER ONE OFF THE INTERNET TO HELP MY PUPILS TRAIN.

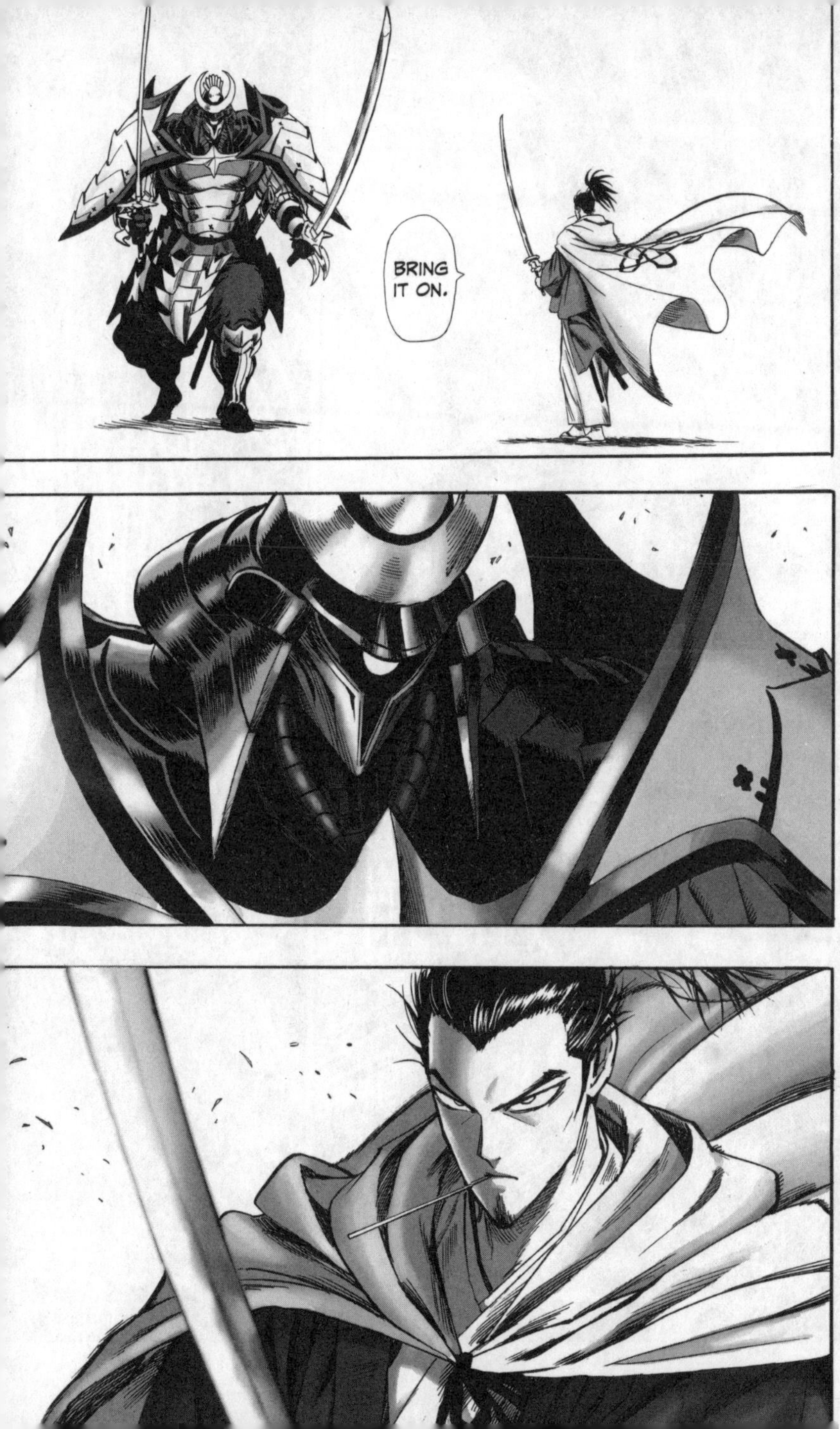
BRING IT ON.

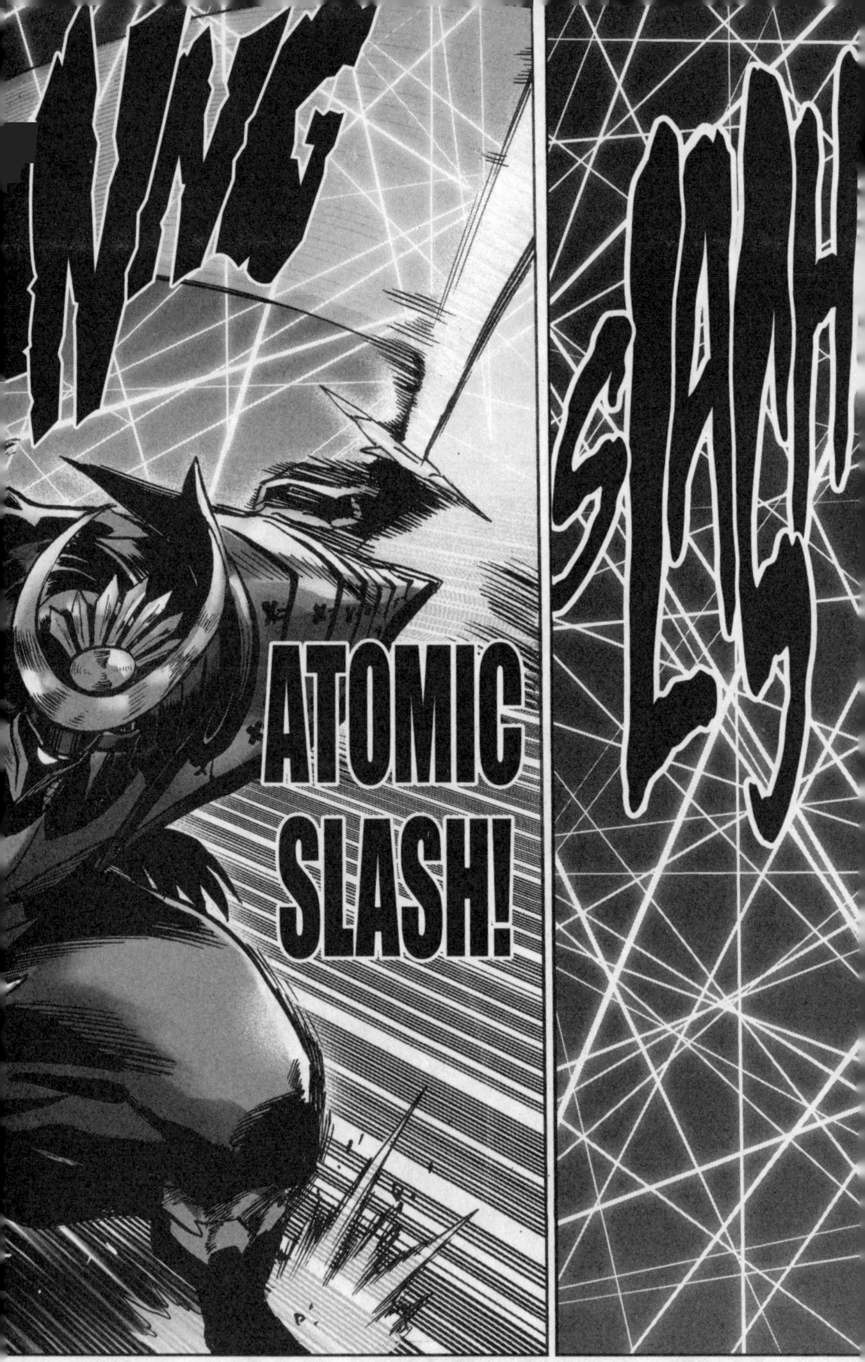
SLASH
WING
ATOMIC SLASH!

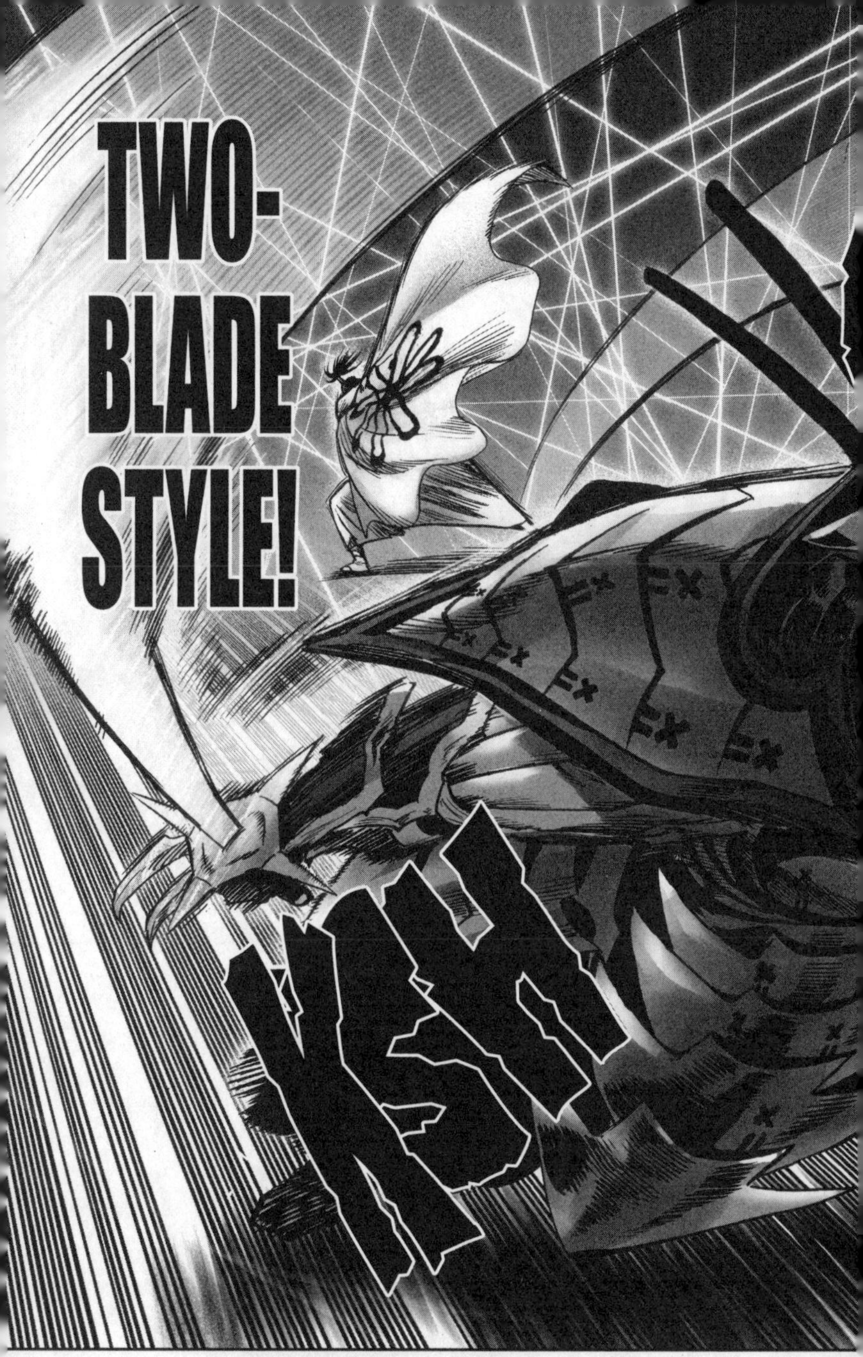
TWO-BLADE STYLE!
KSH!!

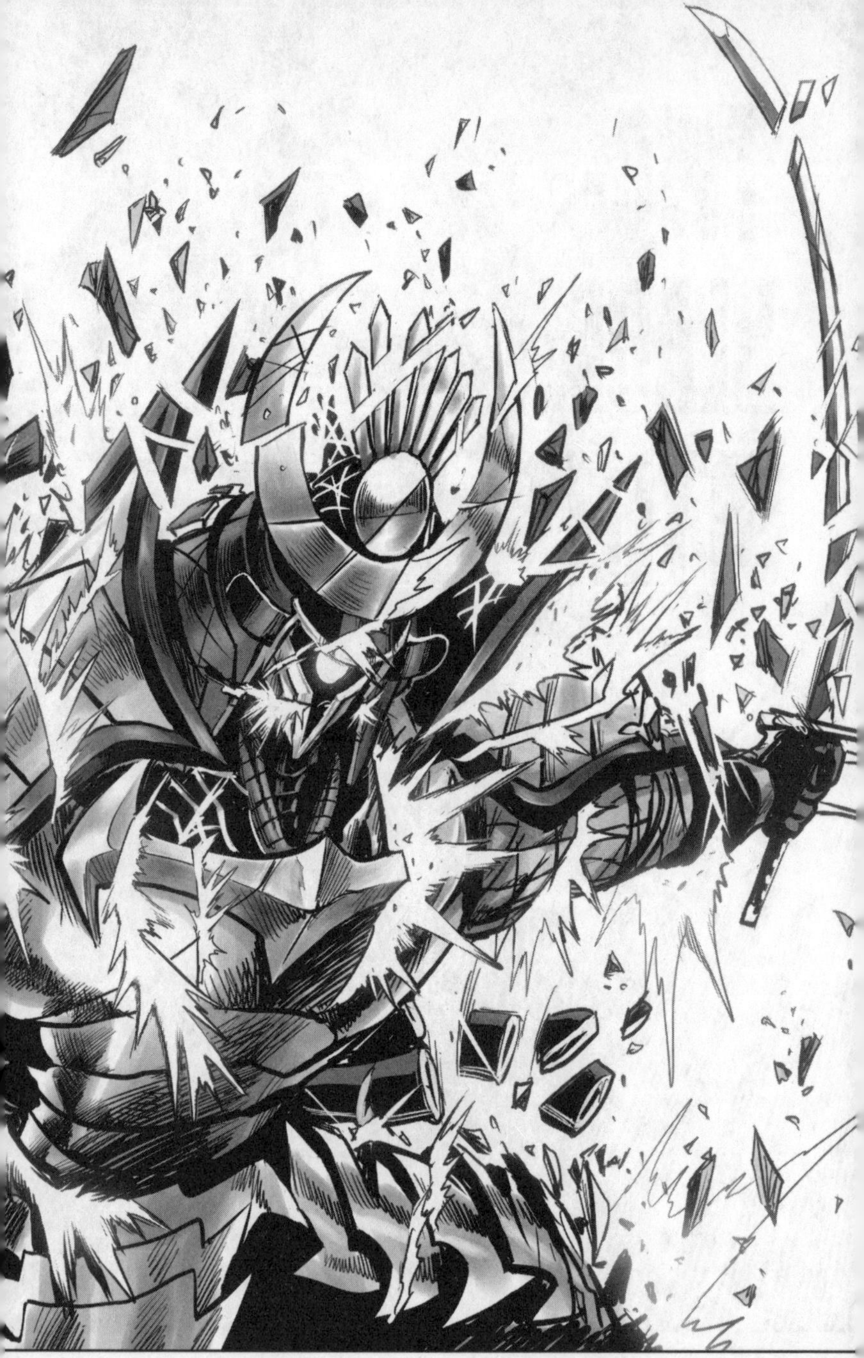

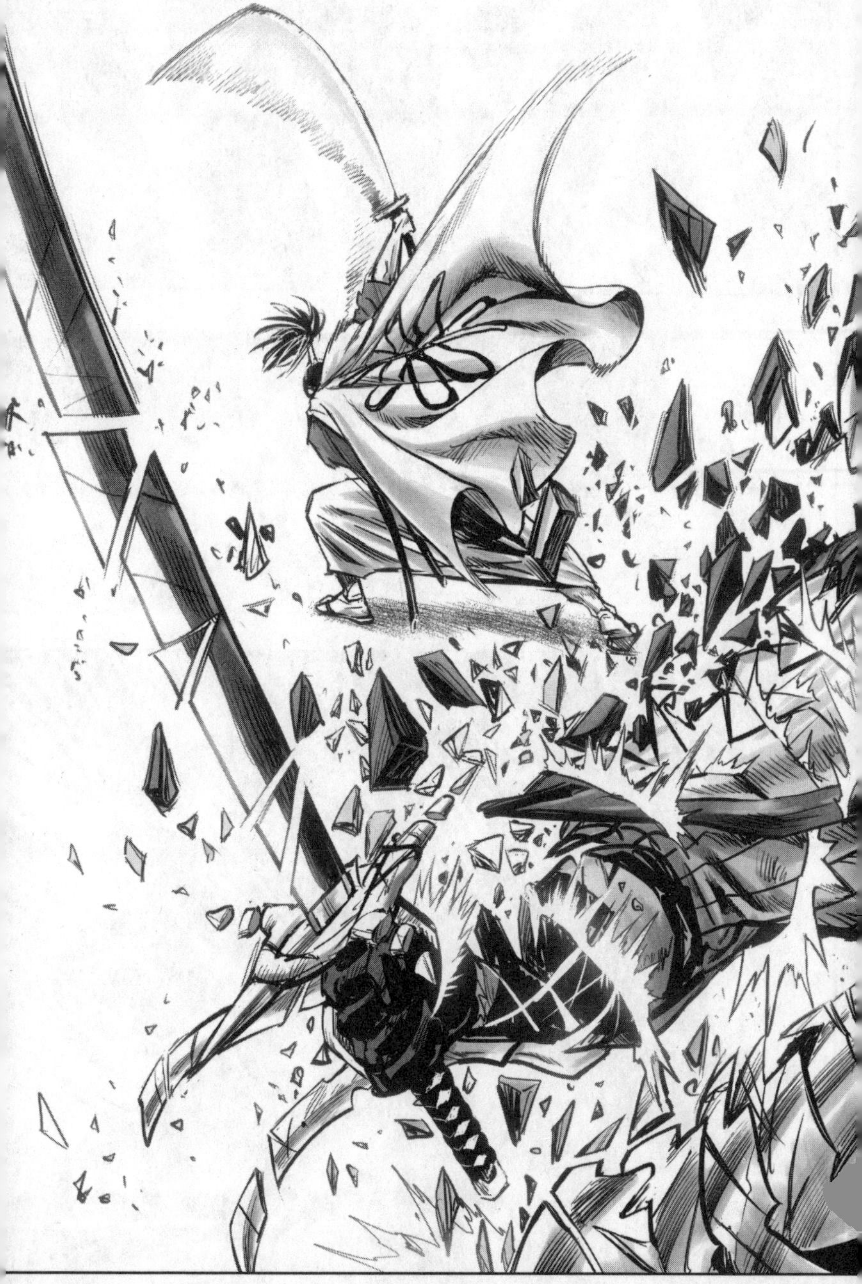

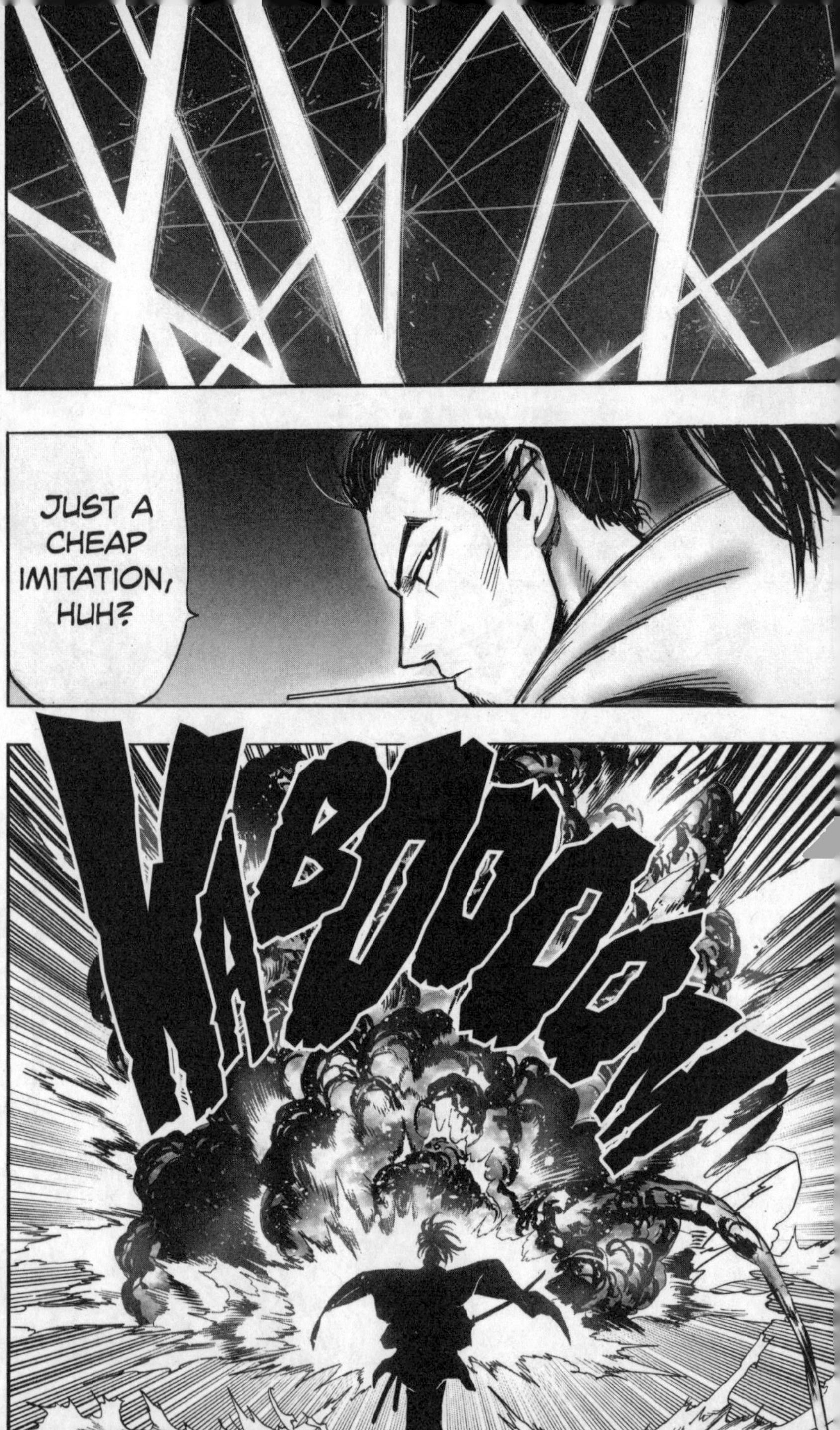
JUST A CHEAP IMITATION, HUH?
KABOOOM

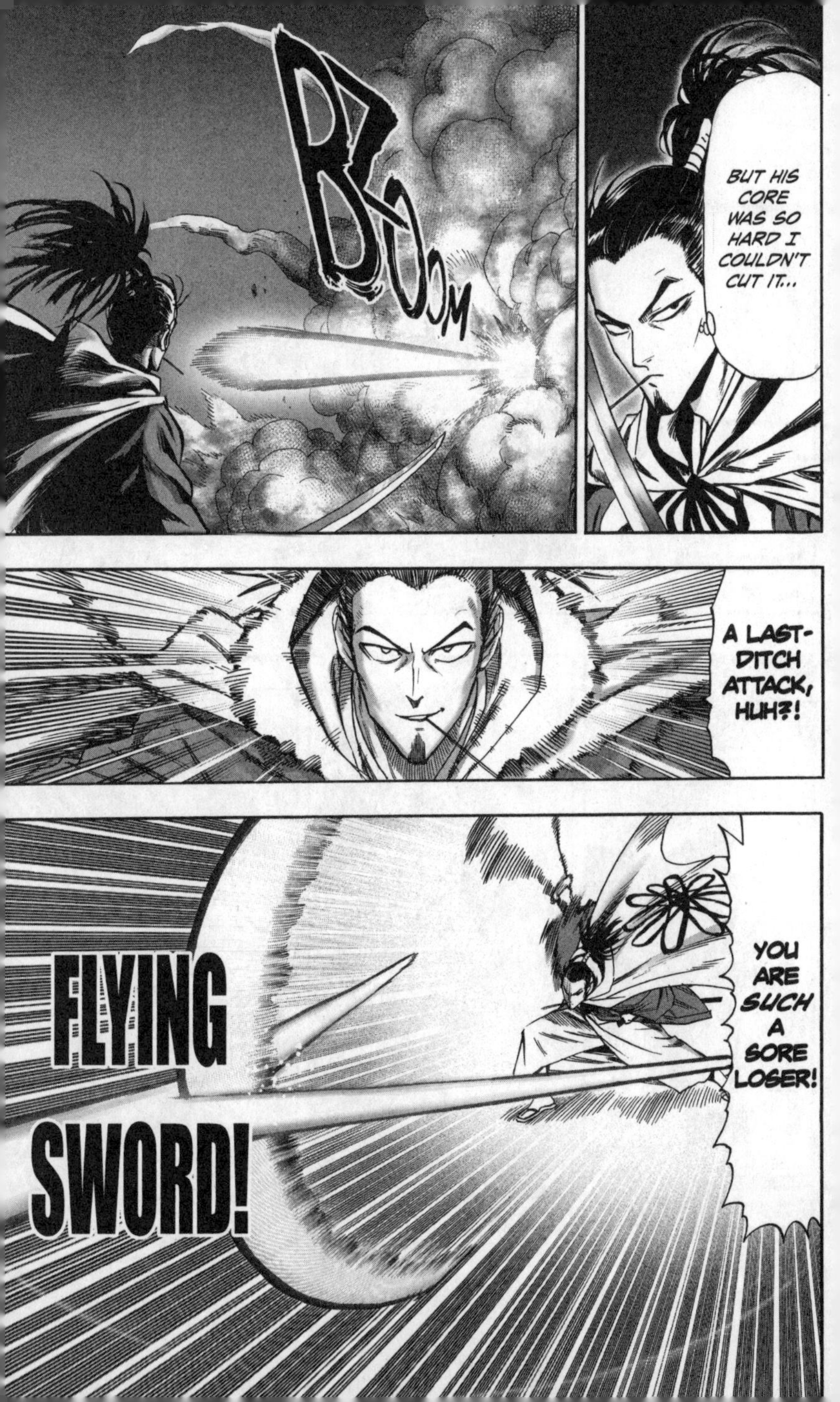
BUT HIS CORE WAS SO HARD I COULDN'T CUT IT...
BOOM
A LAST-DITCH ATTACK, HUH?!
YOU ARE SUCH A SORE LOSER!
FLYING SWORD!

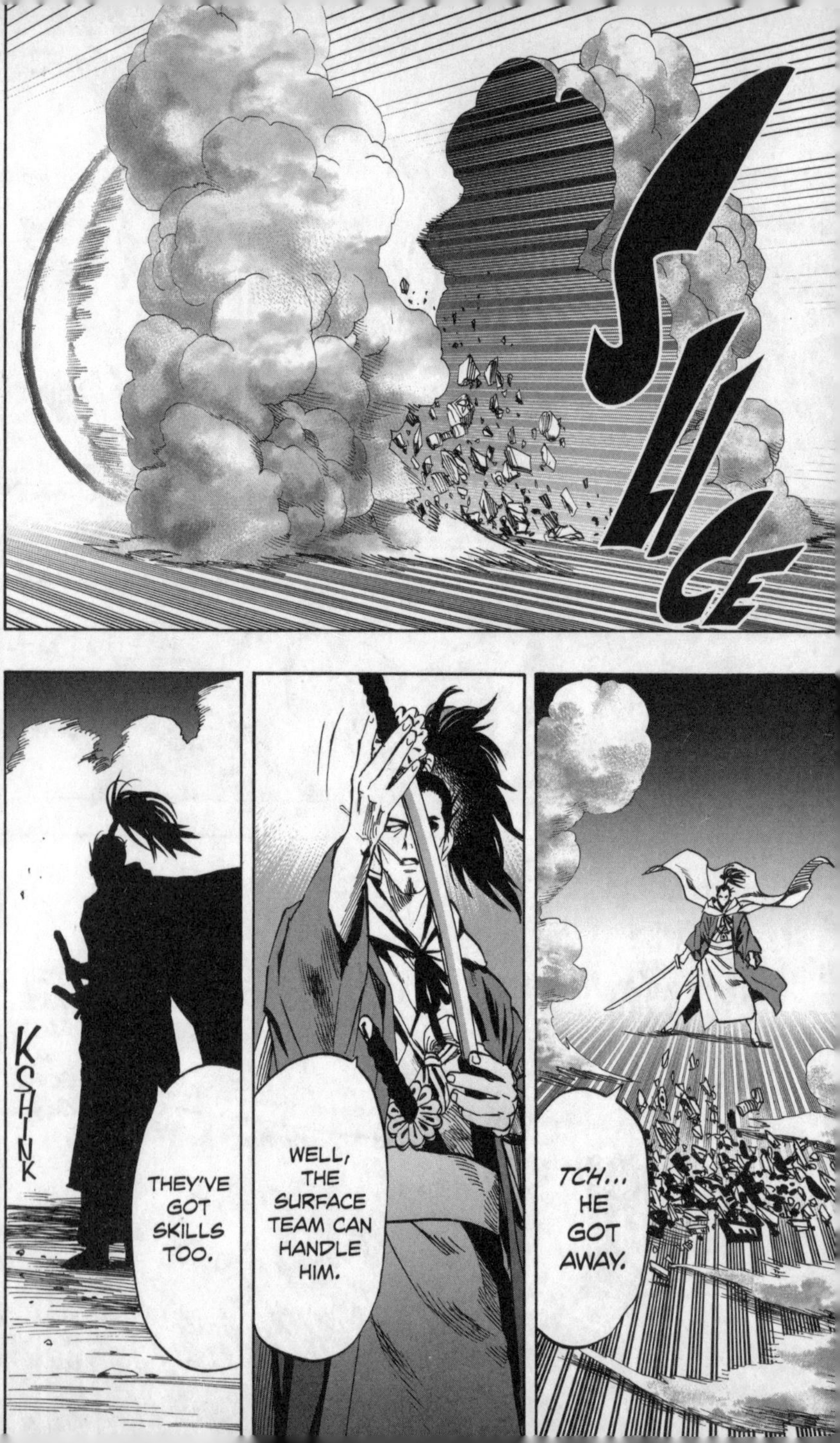
SLICE
TCH... HE GOT AWAY.
WELL, THE SURFACE TEAM CAN HANDLE HIM.
KSHINK
THEY'VE GOT SKILLS TOO.

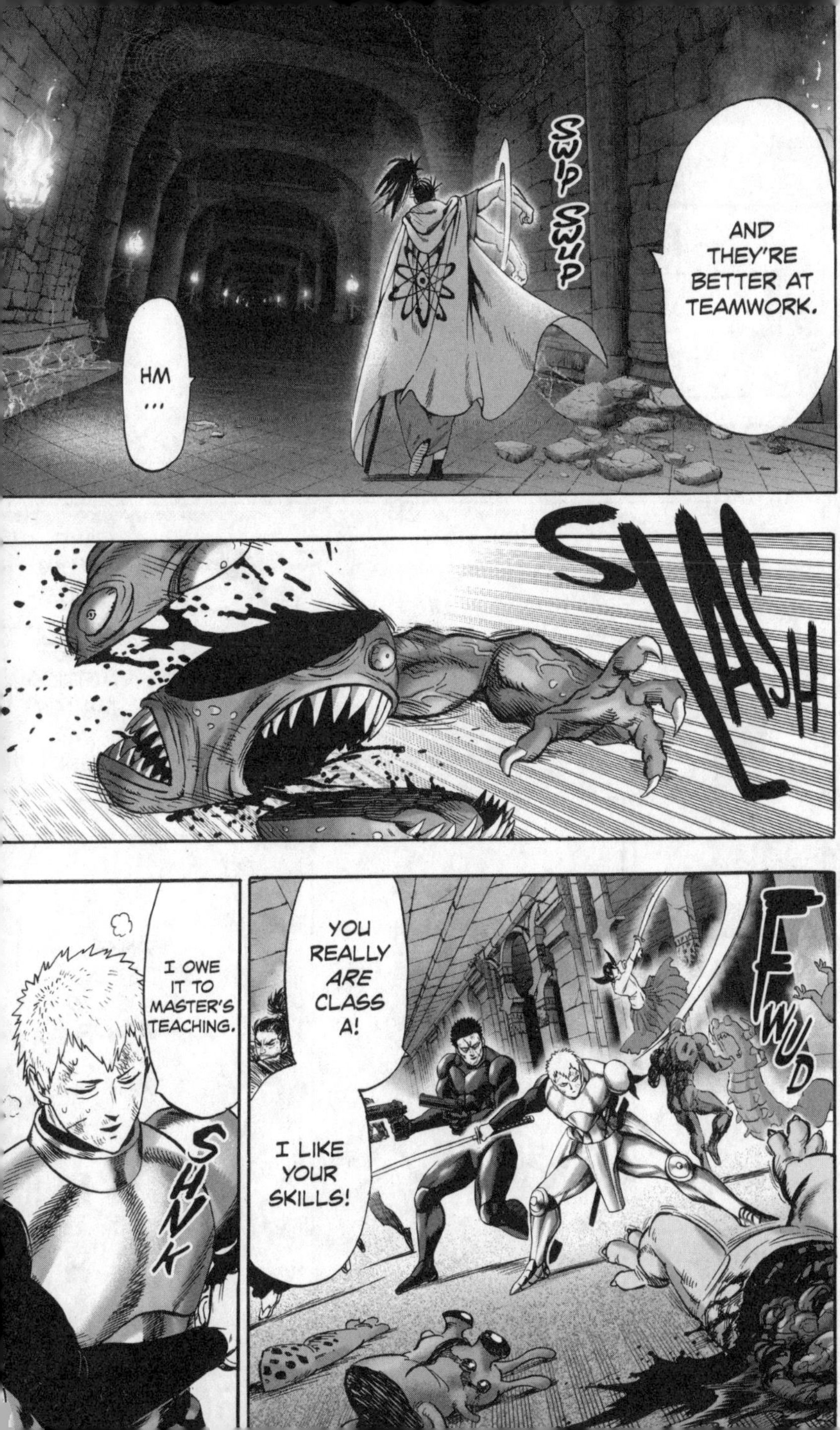
AND THEY'RE BETTER AT TEAMWORK.
SWIP SWUP
HM ...
SLASH
FWUD
YOU REALLY *ARE* CLASS A!
I LIKE YOUR SKILLS!
I OWE IT TO MASTER'S TEACHING.
SHNK

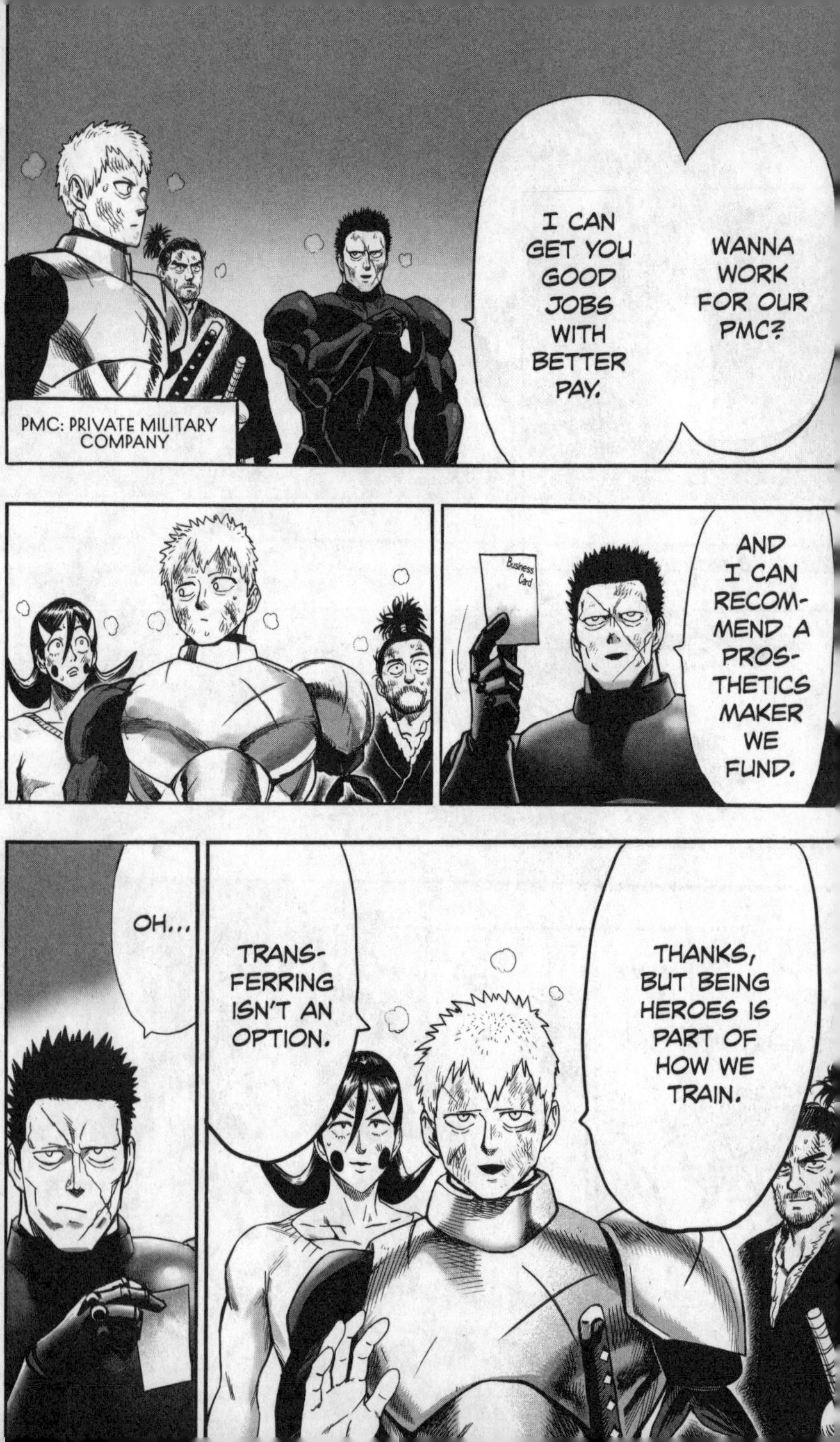
WANNA WORK FOR OUR PMC?
I CAN GET YOU GOOD JOBS WITH BETTER PAY.
PMC: PRIVATE MILITARY COMPANY
Business Card
AND I CAN RECOMMEND A PROSTHETICS MAKER WE FUND.
THANKS, BUT BEING HEROES IS PART OF HOW WE TRAIN.
TRANSFERRING ISN'T AN OPTION.
OH...

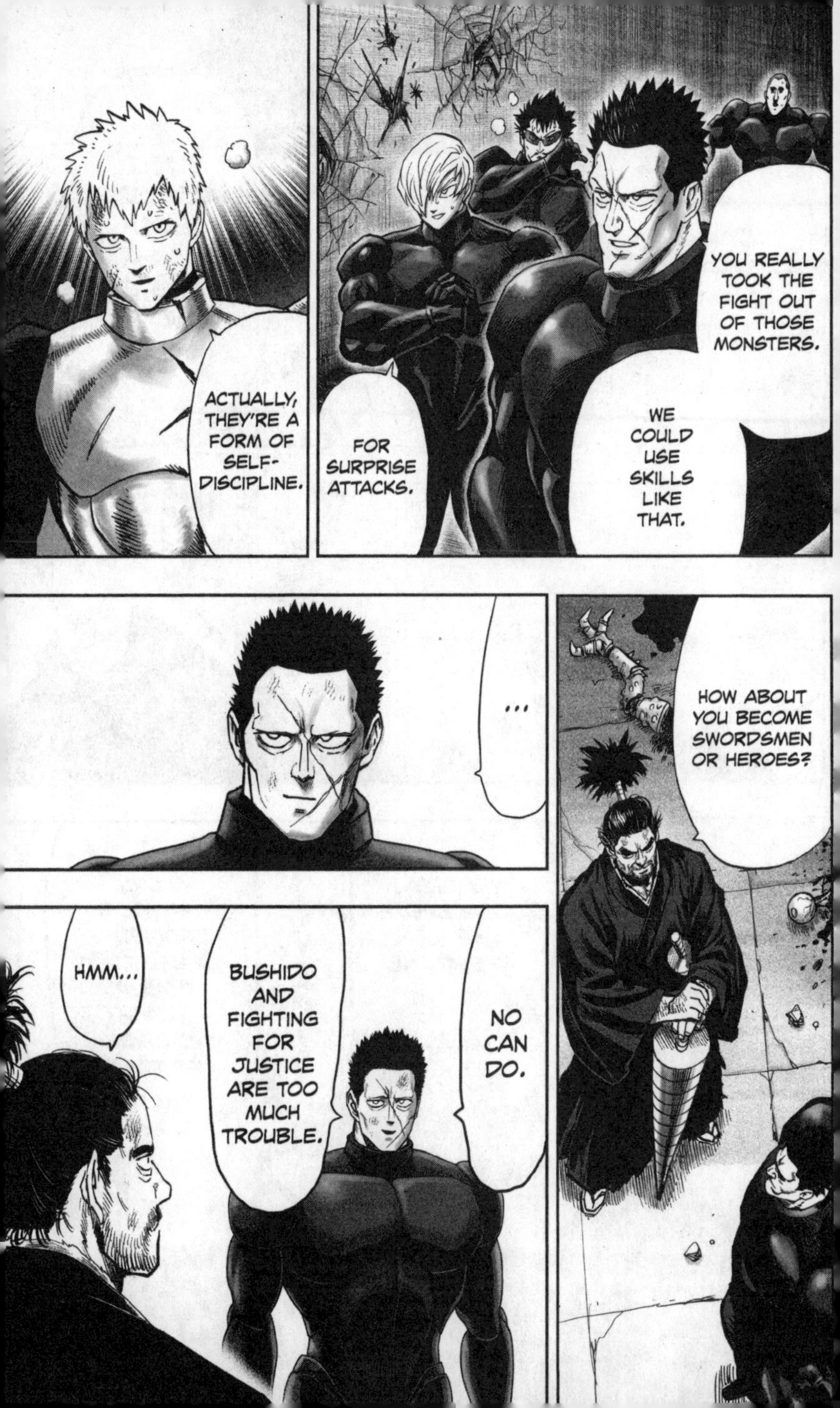
YOU REALLY TOOK THE FIGHT OUT OF THOSE MONSTERS.
WE COULD USE SKILLS LIKE THAT.
FOR SURPRISE ATTACKS.
ACTUALLY, THEY'RE A FORM OF SELF-DISCIPLINE.
HOW ABOUT YOU BECOME SWORDSMEN OR HEROES?
...
NO CAN DO.
BUSHIDO AND FIGHTING FOR JUSTICE ARE TOO MUCH TROUBLE.
HMM...

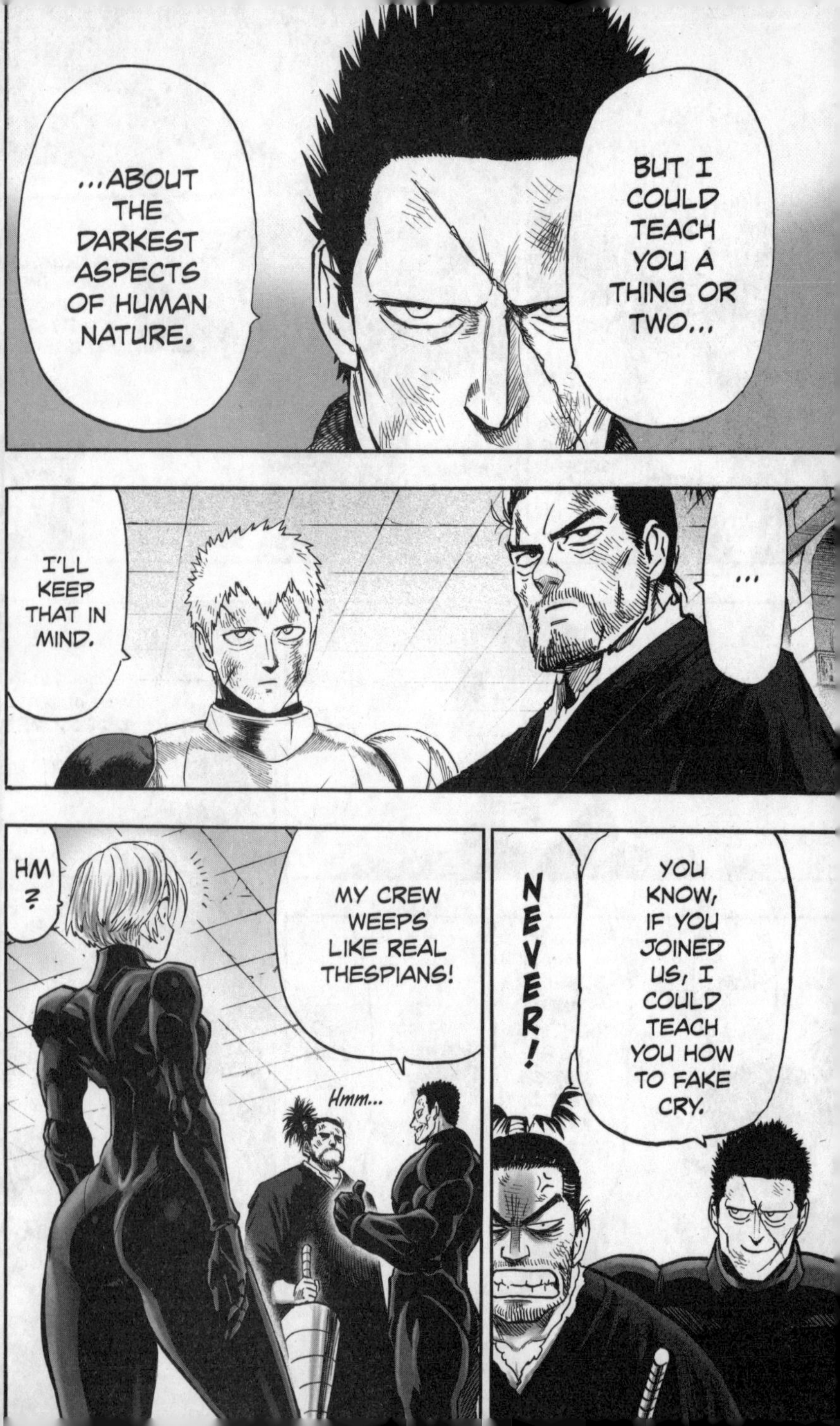
BUT I COULD TEACH YOU A THING OR TWO...
...ABOUT THE DARKEST ASPECTS OF HUMAN NATURE.
...
I'LL KEEP THAT IN MIND.
YOU KNOW, IF YOU JOINED US, I COULD TEACH YOU HOW TO FAKE CRY.
NEVER!
MY CREW WEEPS LIKE REAL THESPIANS!
Hmm...
HM?

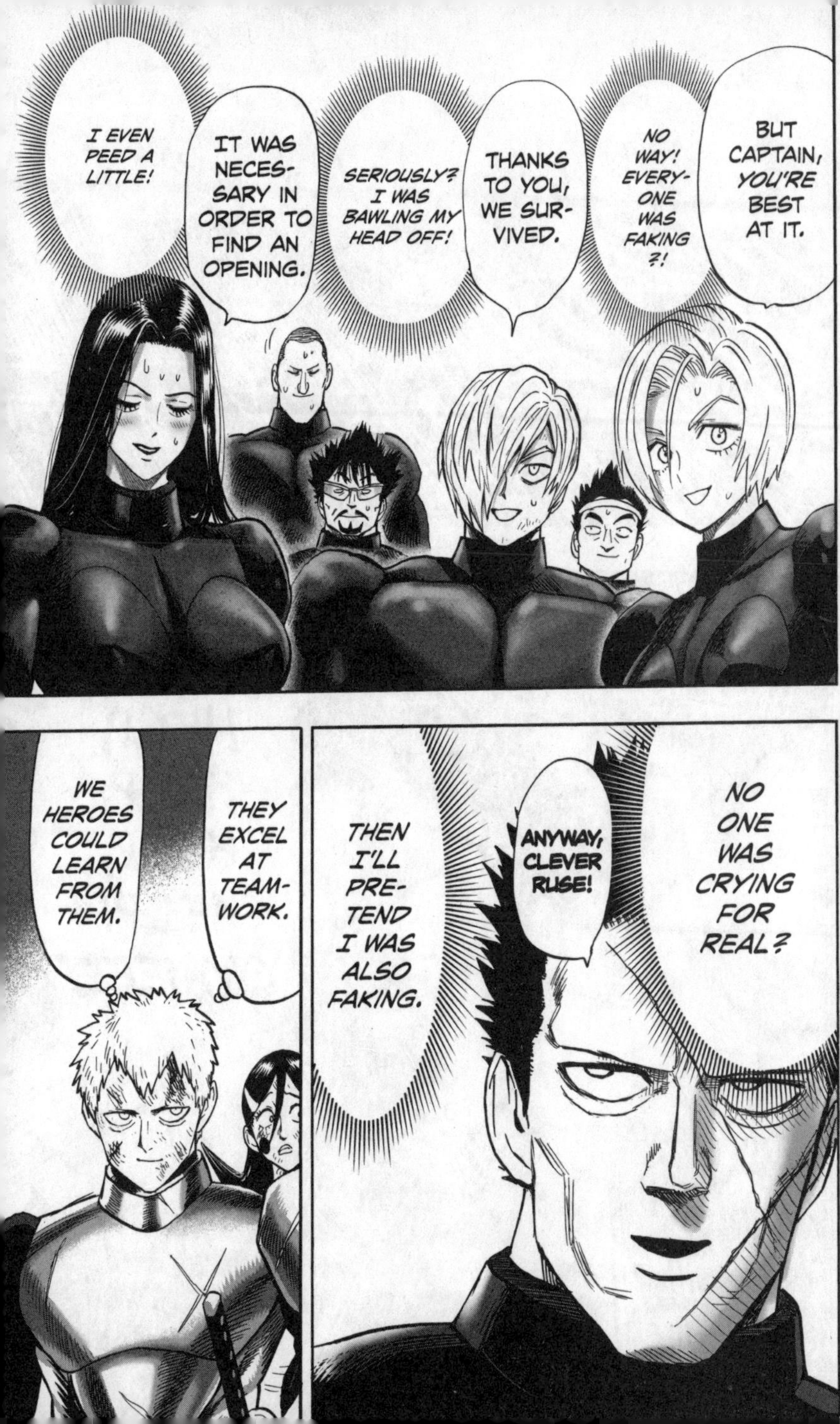

BUT CAPTAIN, YOU'RE BEST AT IT.
NO WAY! EVERY-ONE WAS FAKING?!
THANKS TO YOU, WE SUR-VIVED.
SERIOUSLY? I WAS BAWLING MY HEAD OFF!
IT WAS NECES-SARY IN ORDER TO FIND AN OPENING.
I EVEN PEED A LITTLE!
NO ONE WAS CRYING FOR REAL?
ANYWAY, CLEVER RUSE!
THEN I'LL PRE-TEND I WAS ALSO FAKING.
THEY EXCEL AT TEAM-WORK.
WE HEROES COULD LEARN FROM THEM.

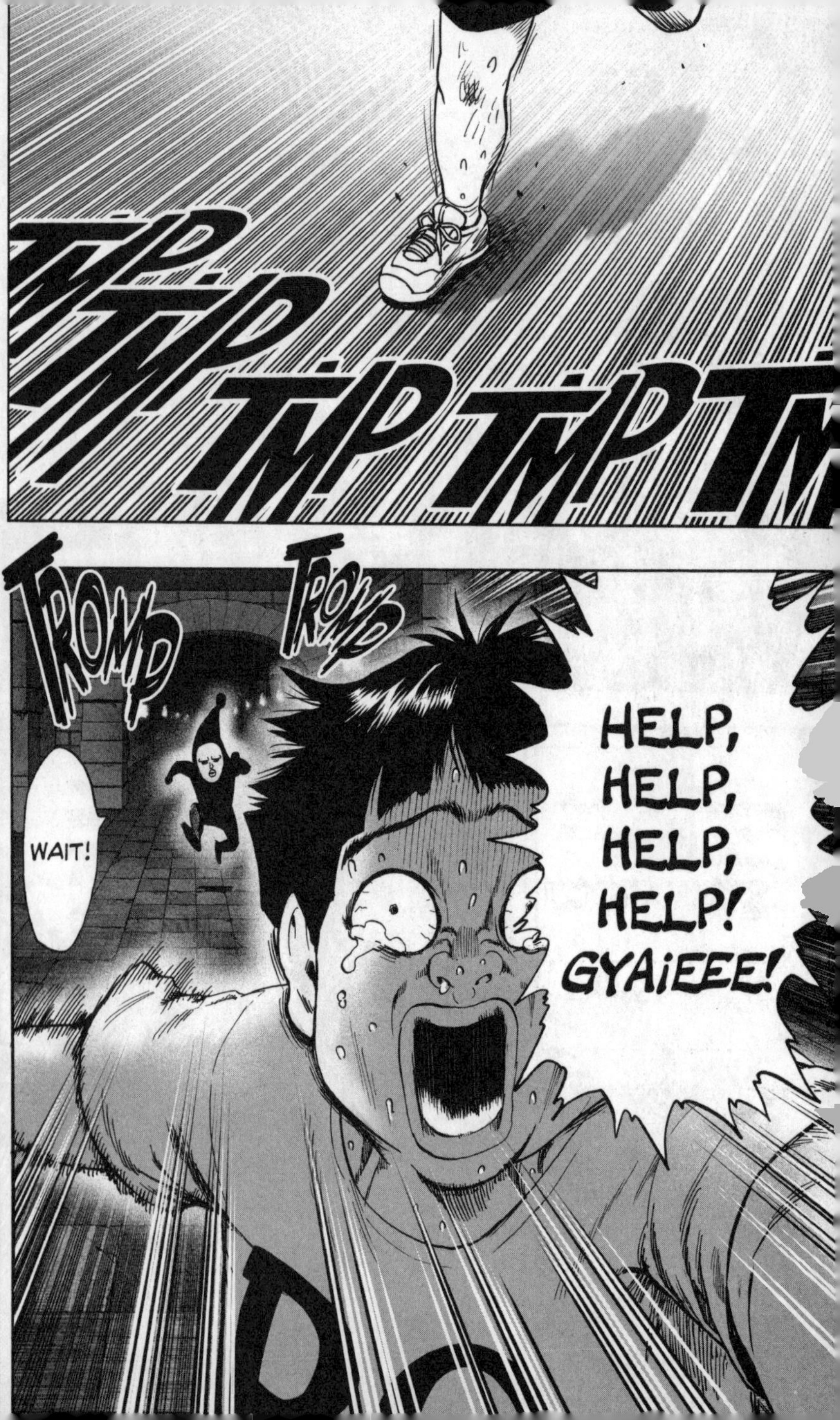
TMP TMP TMP TMP
TROMP TROMP
HELP, HELP, HELP, HELP! GYAiEEE!
WAIT!

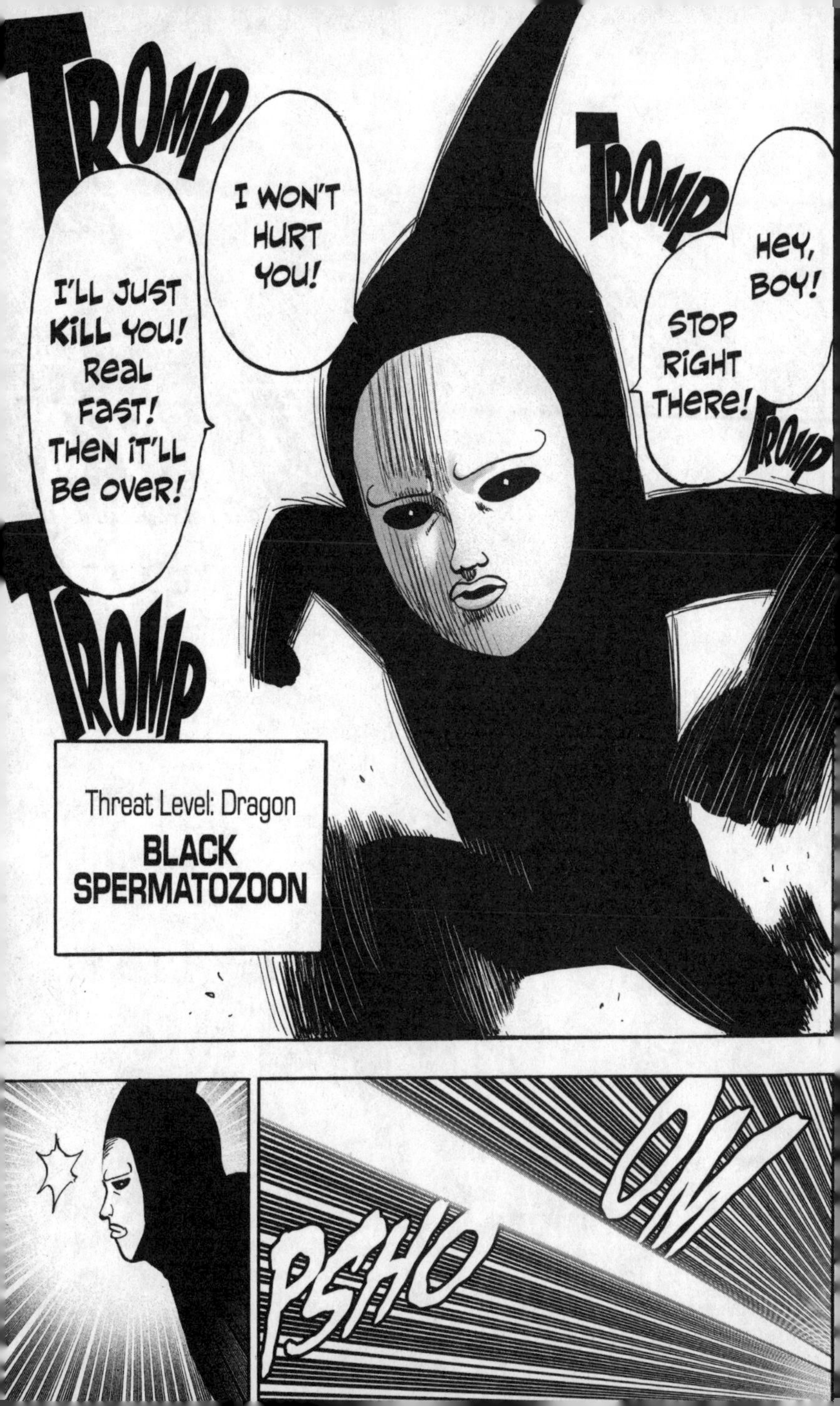
TROMP
HEY, BOY! STOP RIGHT THERE!
TROMP
I WON'T HURT YOU!
TROMP
I'LL JUST KILL YOU! REAL FAST! THEN IT'LL BE OVER!
TROMP
Threat Level: Dragon
BLACK SPERMATOZOON
PSHOOM

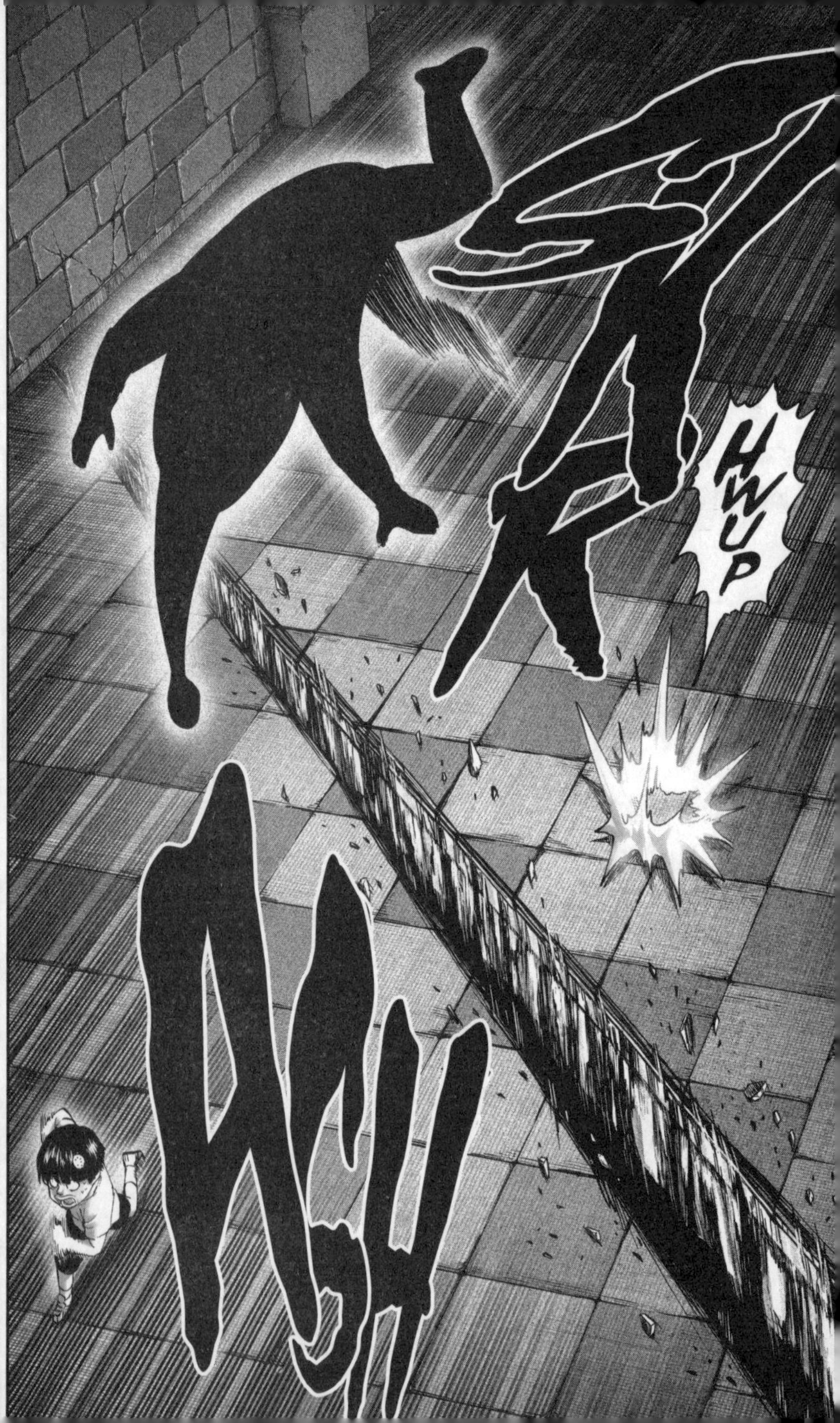
HWUP

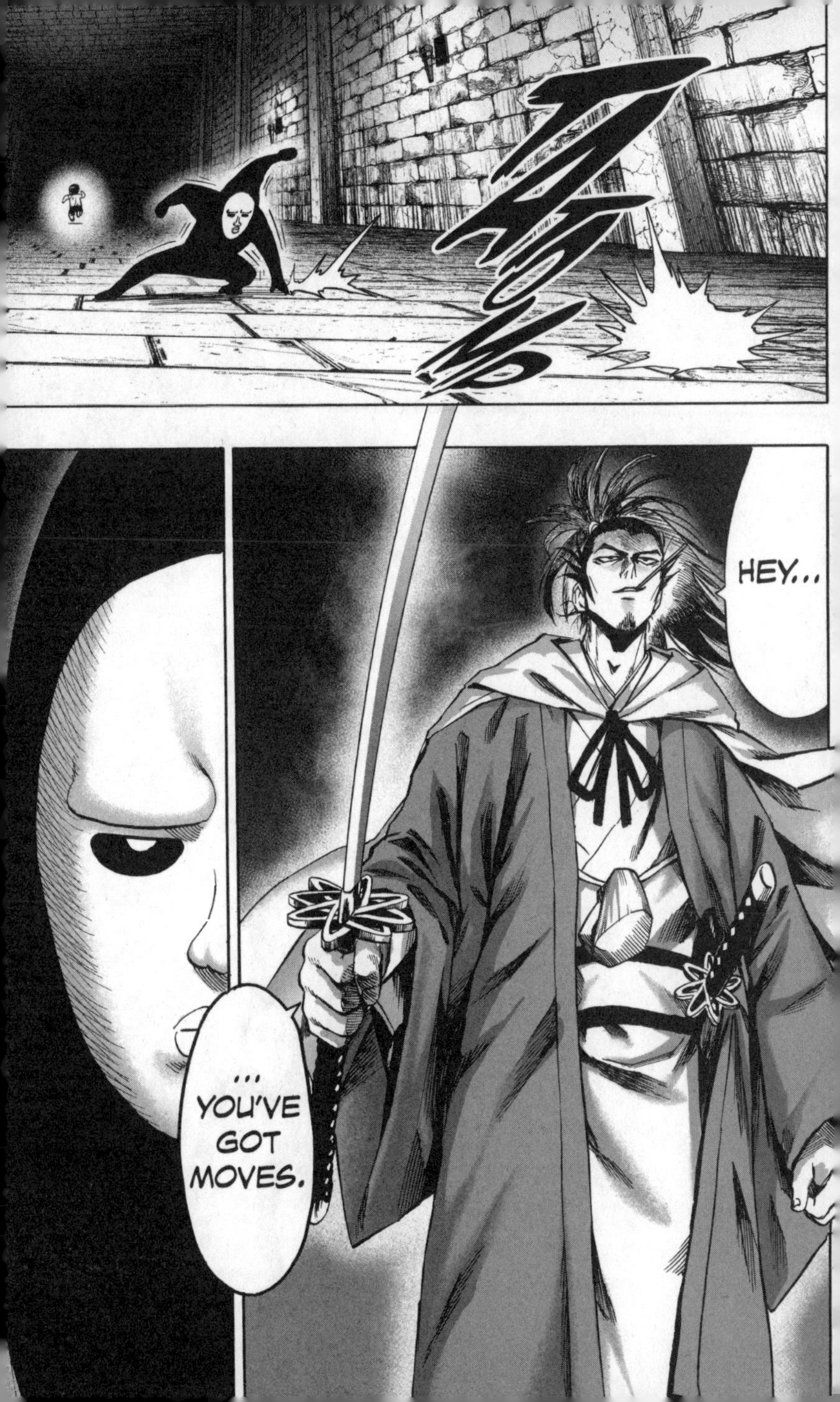
HEY...
... YOU'VE GOT MOVES.

PUNCH 109:
A DANGEROUS MULTIPLYING MONSTER

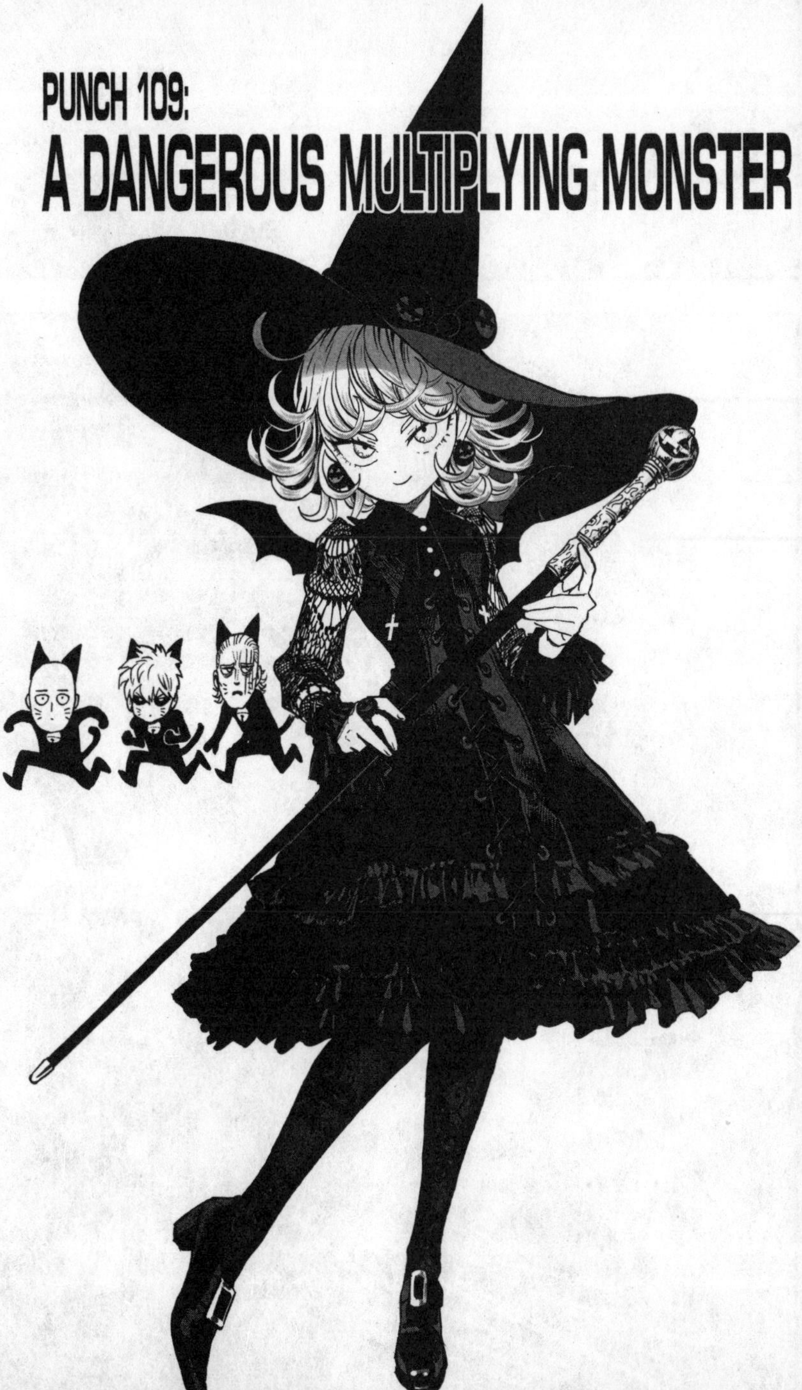

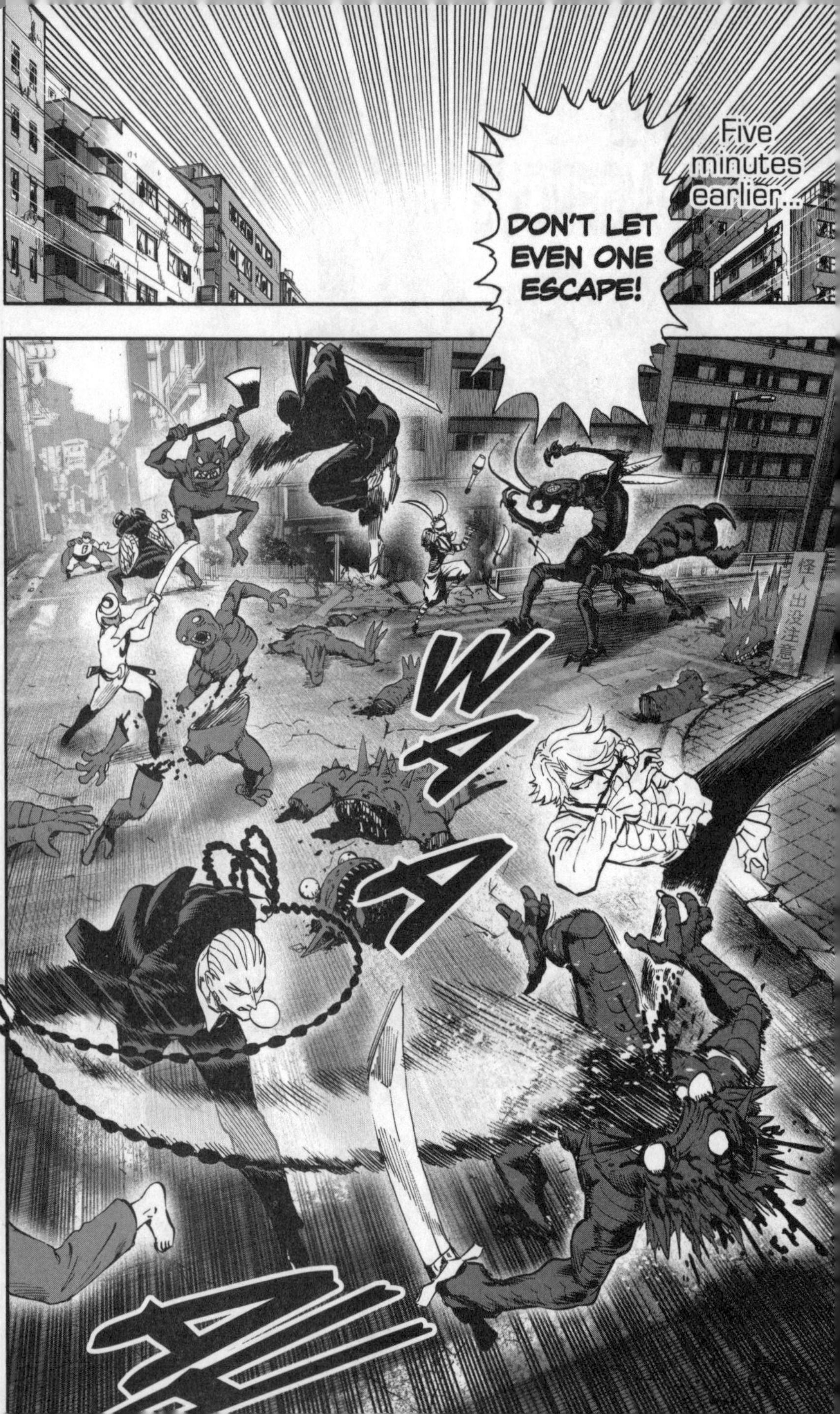
Five minutes earlier...
DON'T LET EVEN ONE ESCAPE!
怪人出没注意
WAAAH

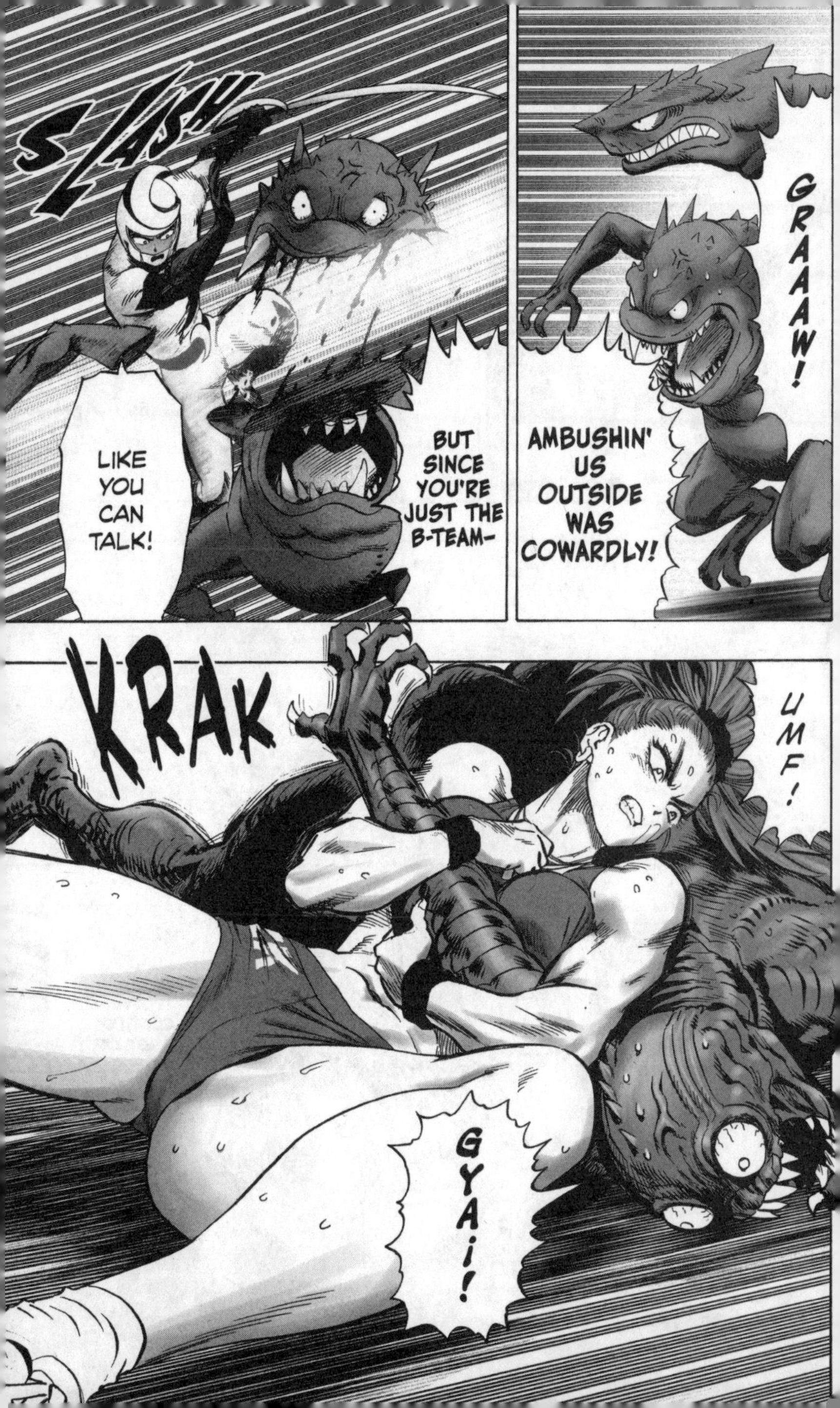
GRAAAAW!
AMBUSHIN' US OUTSIDE WAS COWARDLY!
SLASH
BUT SINCE YOU'RE JUST THE B-TEAM-
LIKE YOU CAN TALK!
UMF!
KRAK
GYA!!

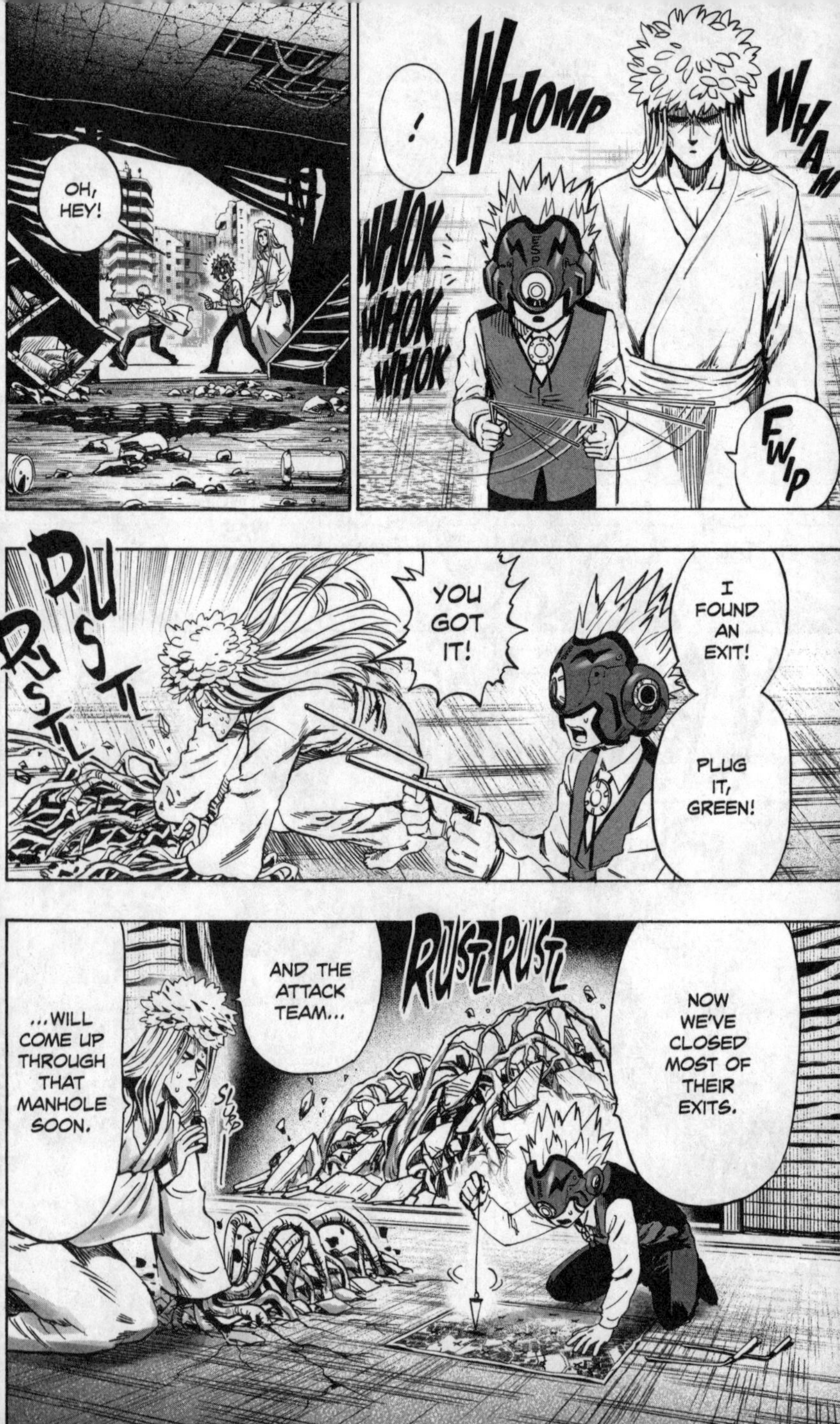
WHAM
WHOMP
!
FWIP
WHOK WHOK WHOK WHOK
OH, HEY!
I FOUND AN EXIT!
PLUG IT, GREEN!
YOU GOT IT!
RUSTL RUSTL
NOW WE'VE CLOSED MOST OF THEIR EXITS.
RUSTL RUSTL
AND THE ATTACK TEAM...
...WILL COME UP THROUGH THAT MANHOLE SOON.
SLURP

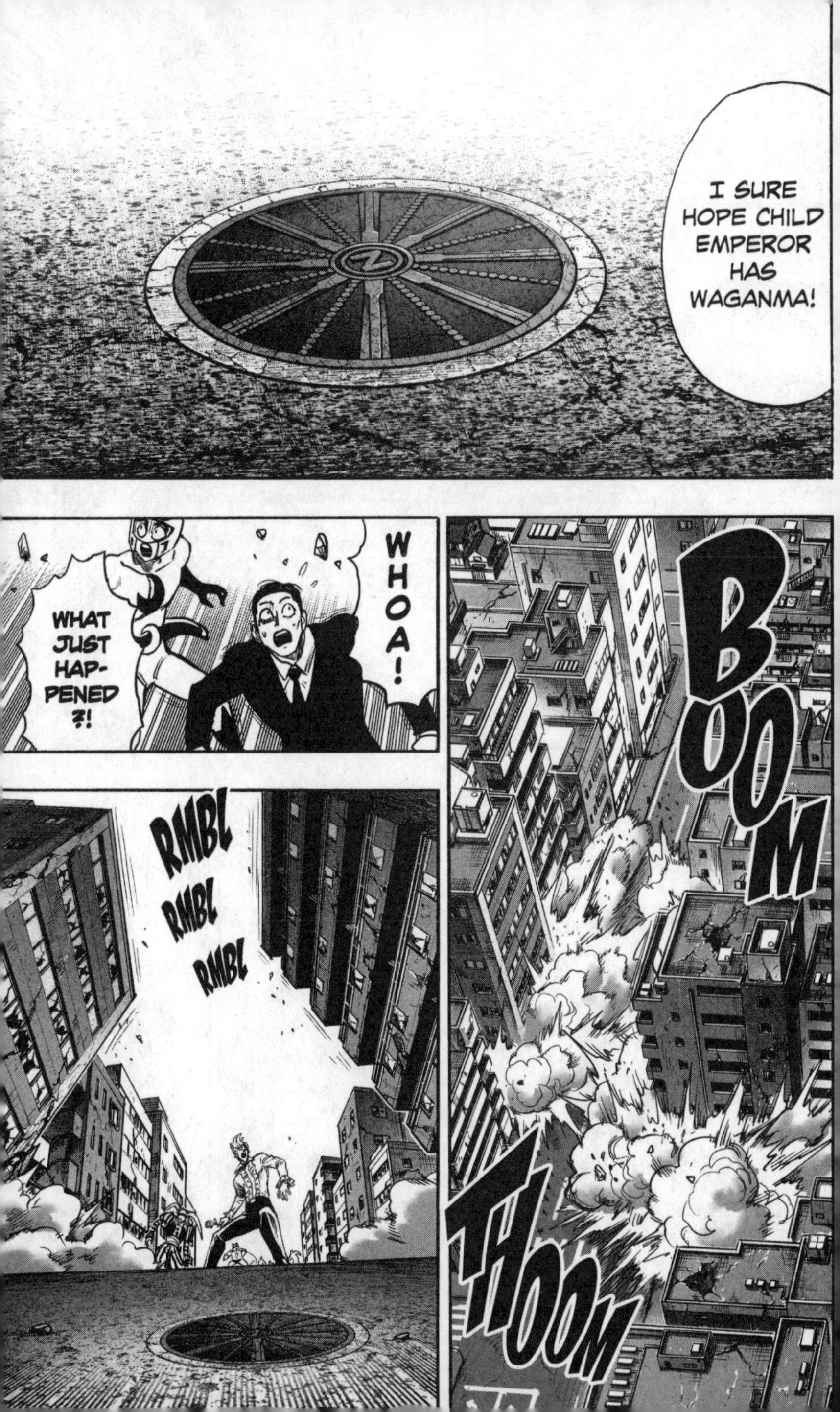
I SURE HOPE CHILD EMPEROR HAS WAGANMA!
BOOM
THOOM
WHOA!
WHAT JUST HAP-PENED?!
RMBL RMBL RMBL

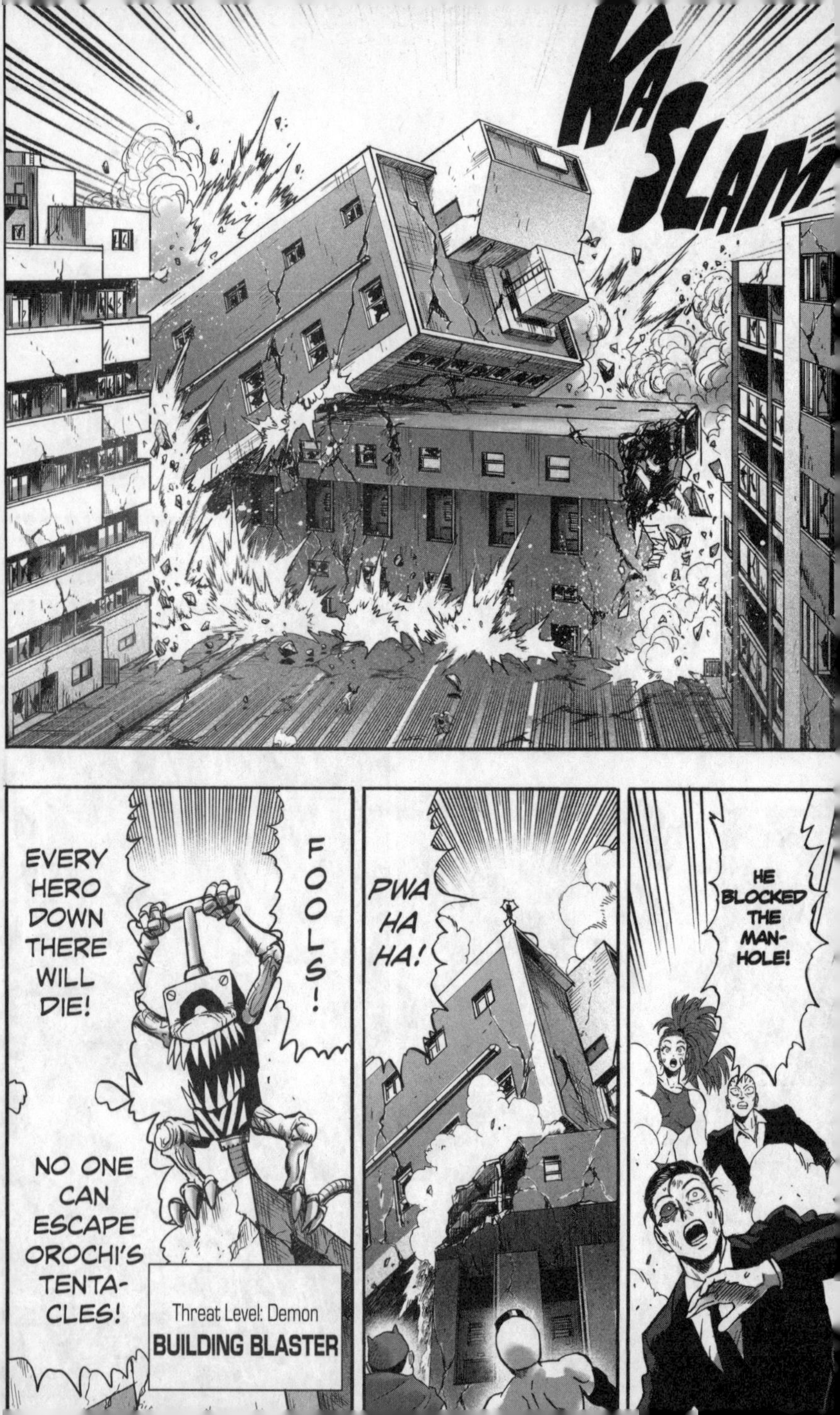
KA-SLAM
HE BLOCKED THE MAN-HOLE!
PWA HA HA!
FOOLS!
EVERY HERO DOWN THERE WILL DIE!
NO ONE CAN ESCAPE OROCHI'S TENTA-CLES!
Threat Level: Demon
BUILDING BLASTER

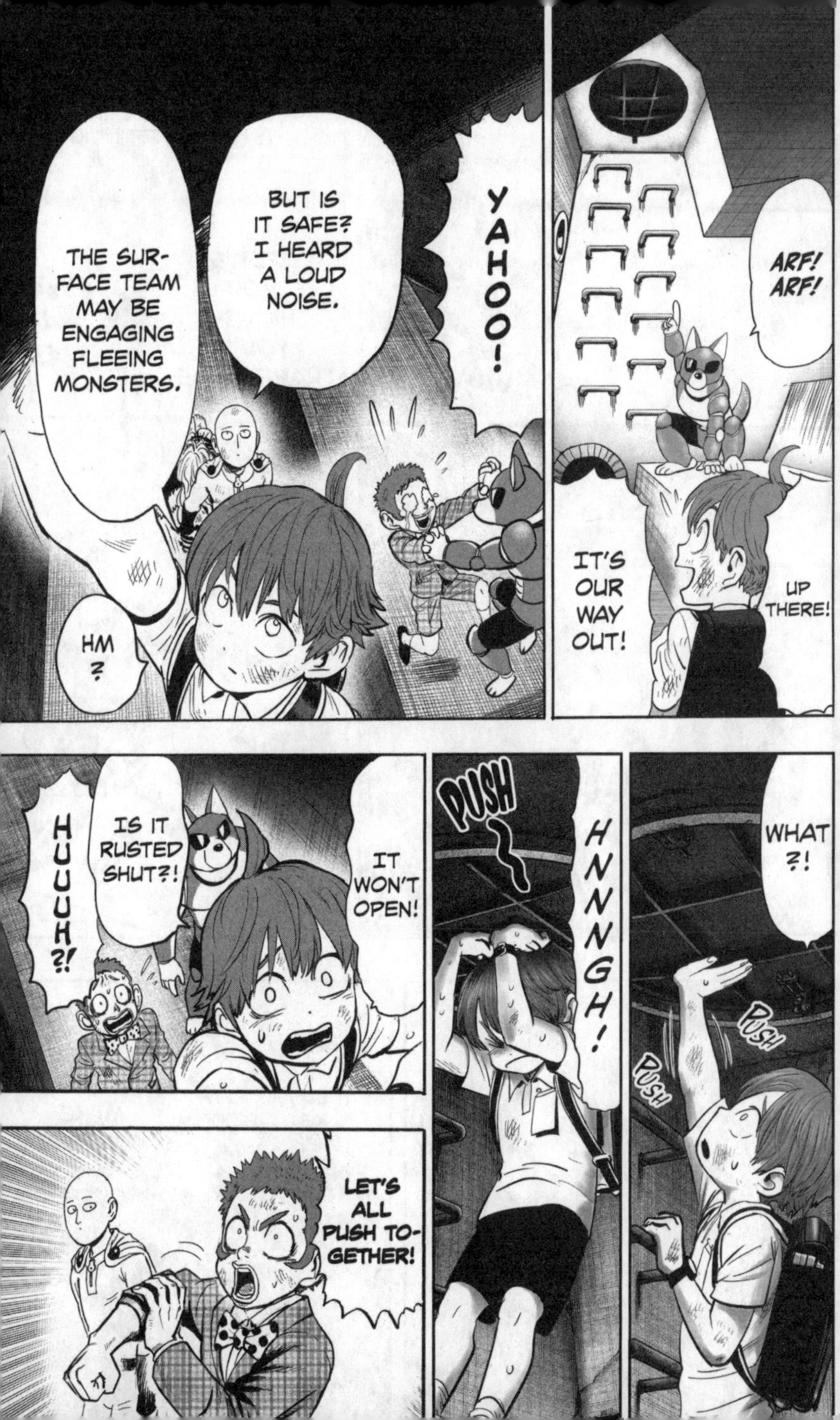
ARF! ARF!
UP THERE!
IT'S OUR WAY OUT!
YAHOO!
BUT IS IT SAFE? I HEARD A LOUD NOISE.
THE SURFACE TEAM MAY BE ENGAGING FLEEING MONSTERS.
HM?
WHAT?!
PUSH
PUSH
PUSH~
HNNNGH!
IT WON'T OPEN!
IS IT RUSTED SHUT?!
HUUUH?!
LET'S ALL PUSH TOGETHER!

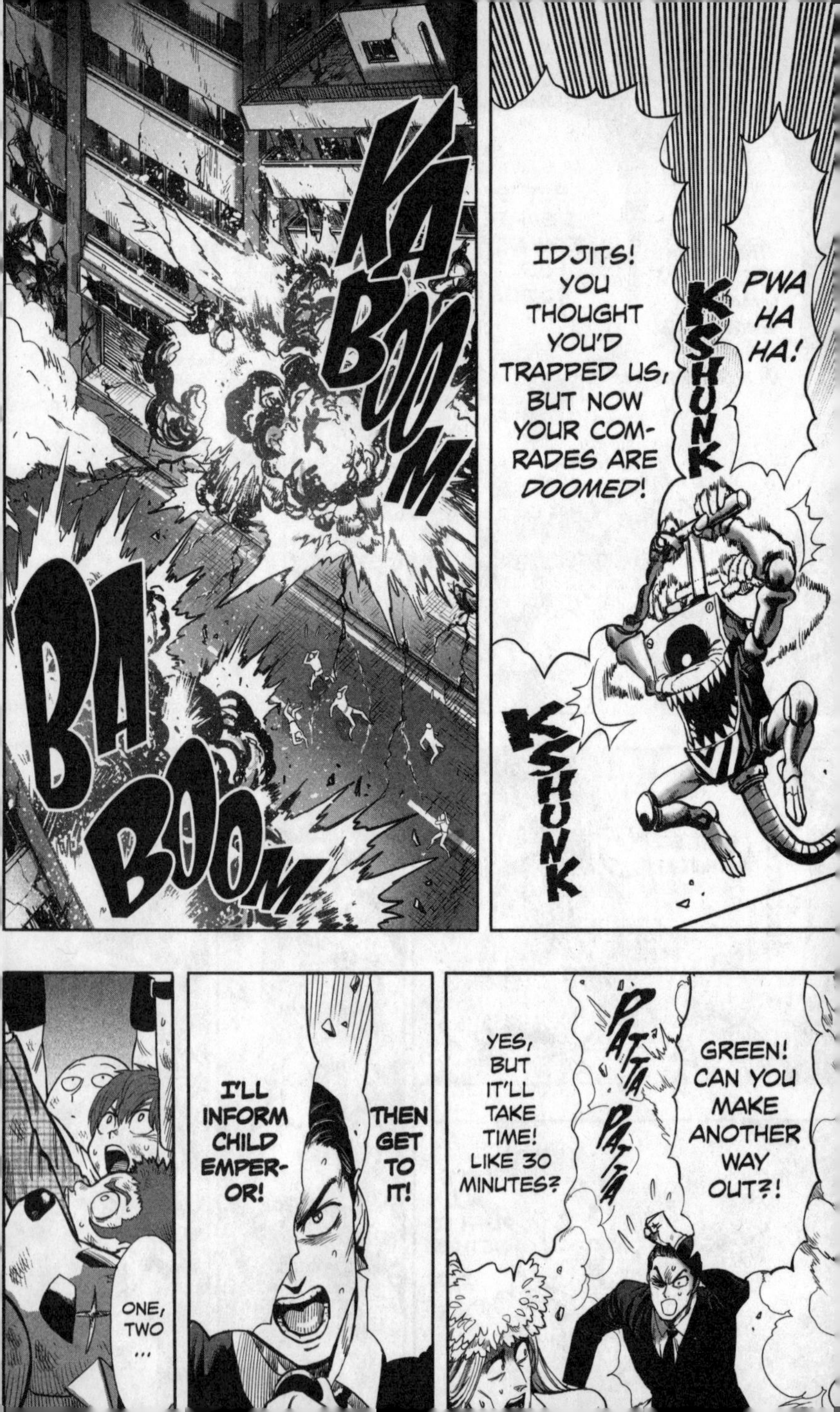
PWA HA HA!
IDJITS! YOU THOUGHT YOU'D TRAPPED US, BUT NOW YOUR COM-RADES ARE *DOOMED*!
KSHUNK
KSHUNK
KABOOM
BA BOOM
GREEN! CAN YOU MAKE ANOTHER WAY OUT?!
PATTA PATTA
YES, BUT IT'LL TAKE TIME! LIKE 30 MINUTES?
THEN GET TO IT!
I'LL INFORM CHILD EMPER-OR!
ONE, TWO ...

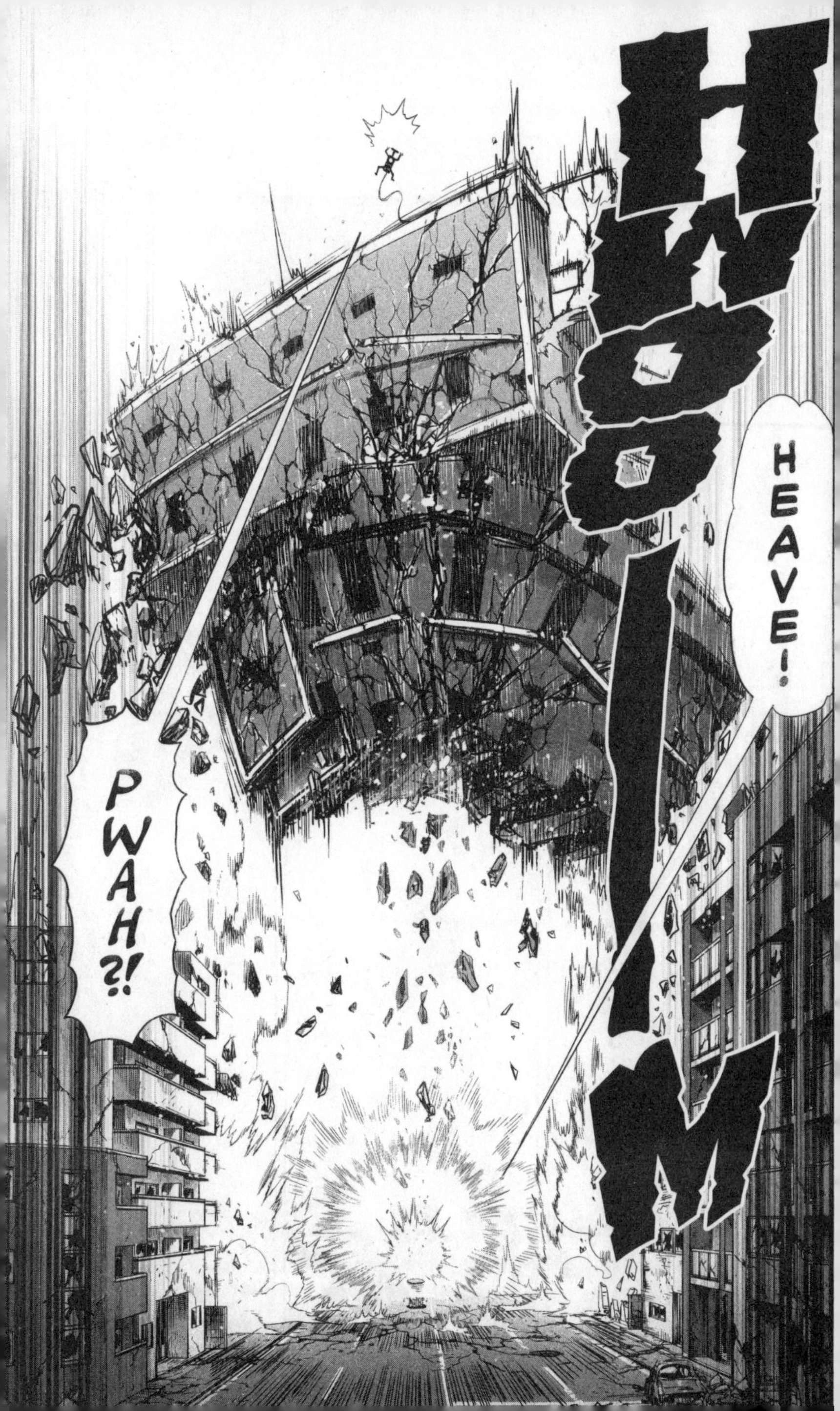
HWOOM
HEAVE!
PWAH?!

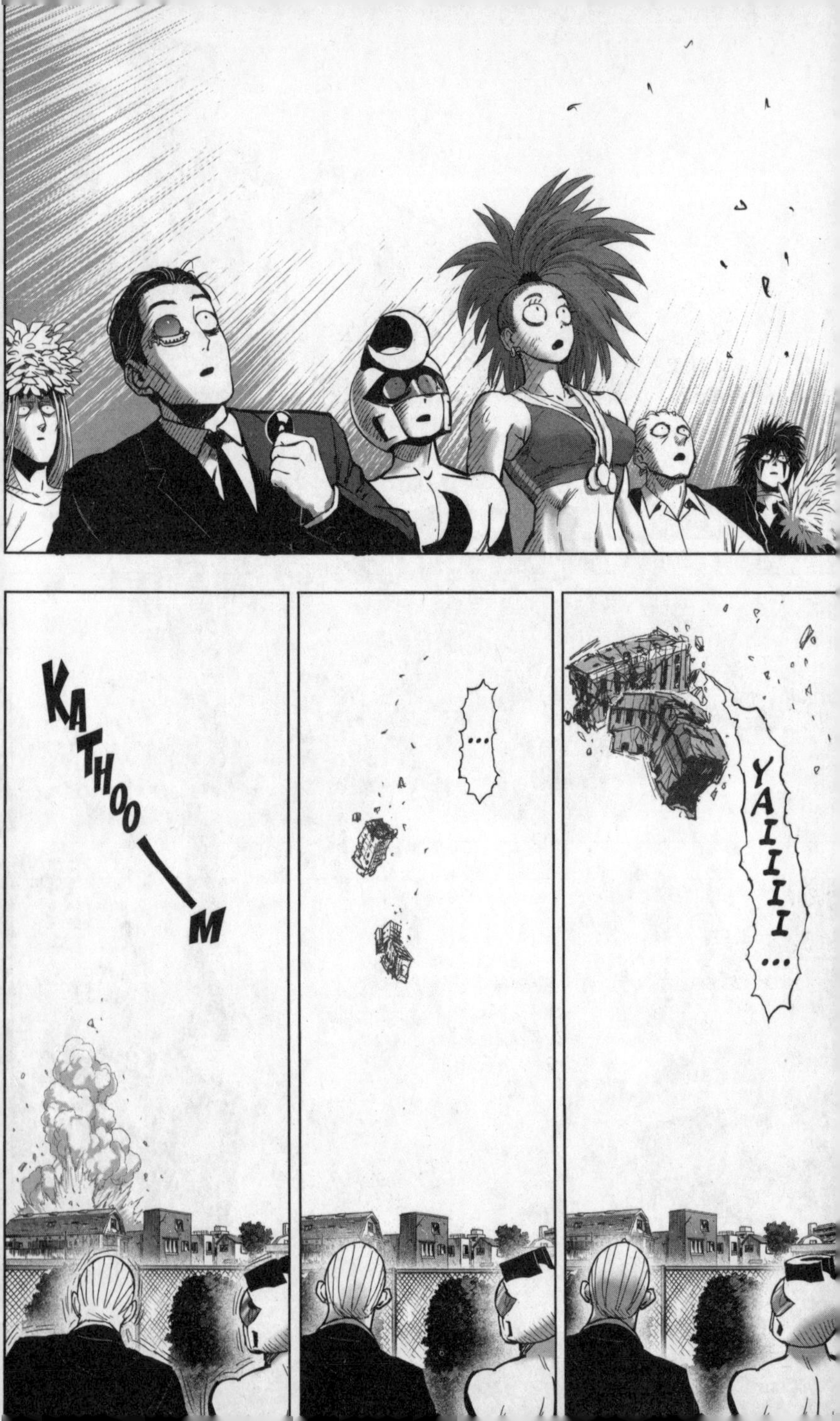
YAIIIII...
...
KATHOO—M

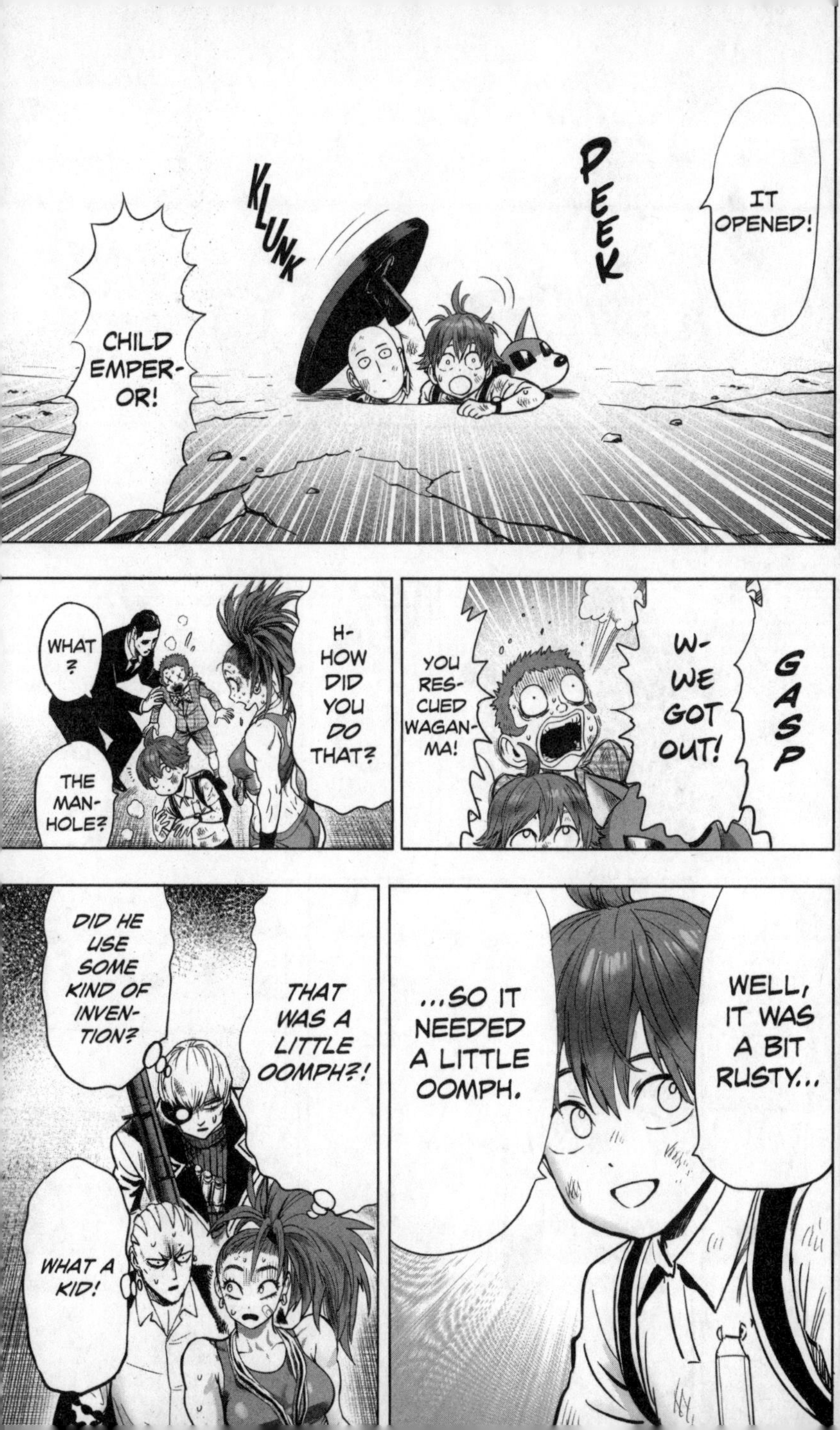

IT OPENED!
PEEK
KLUNK
CHILD EMPEROR!
GASP
W- WE GOT OUT!
YOU RESCUED WAGANMA!
H- HOW DID YOU DO THAT?
WHAT?
THE MANHOLE?
WELL, IT WAS A BIT RUSTY...
...SO IT NEEDED A LITTLE OOMPH.
THAT WAS A LITTLE OOMPH?!
DID HE USE SOME KIND OF INVENTION?
WHAT A KID!

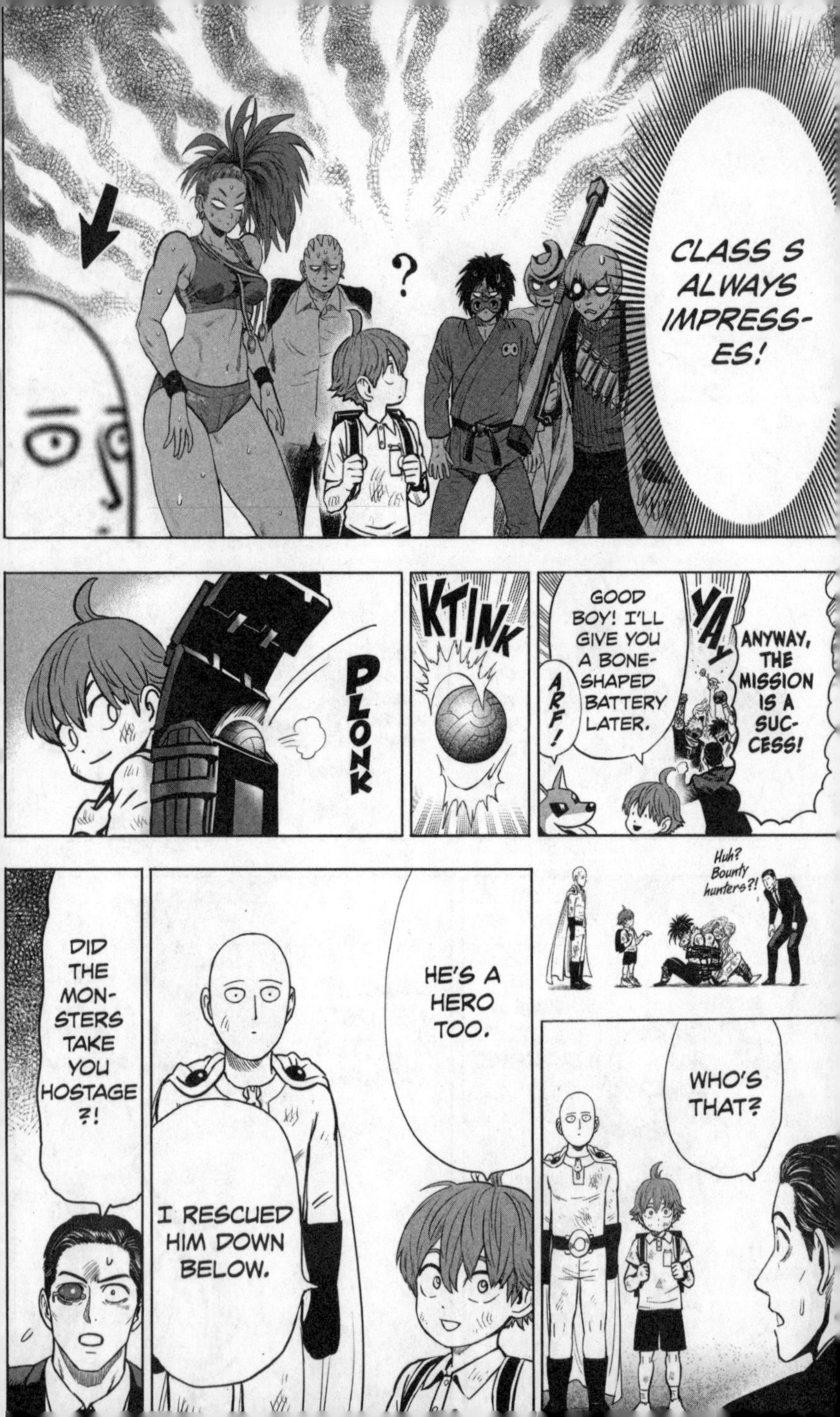
CLASS S ALWAYS IMPRESS-ES!
?
ANYWAY, THE MISSION IS A SUC-CESS!
YAY
GOOD BOY! I'LL GIVE YOU A BONE-SHAPED BATTERY LATER.
ARF!
KTINK
PLONK
Huh? Bounty hunters?!
WHO'S THAT?
HE'S A HERO TOO.
I RESCUED HIM DOWN BELOW.
DID THE MON-STERS TAKE YOU HOSTAGE?!

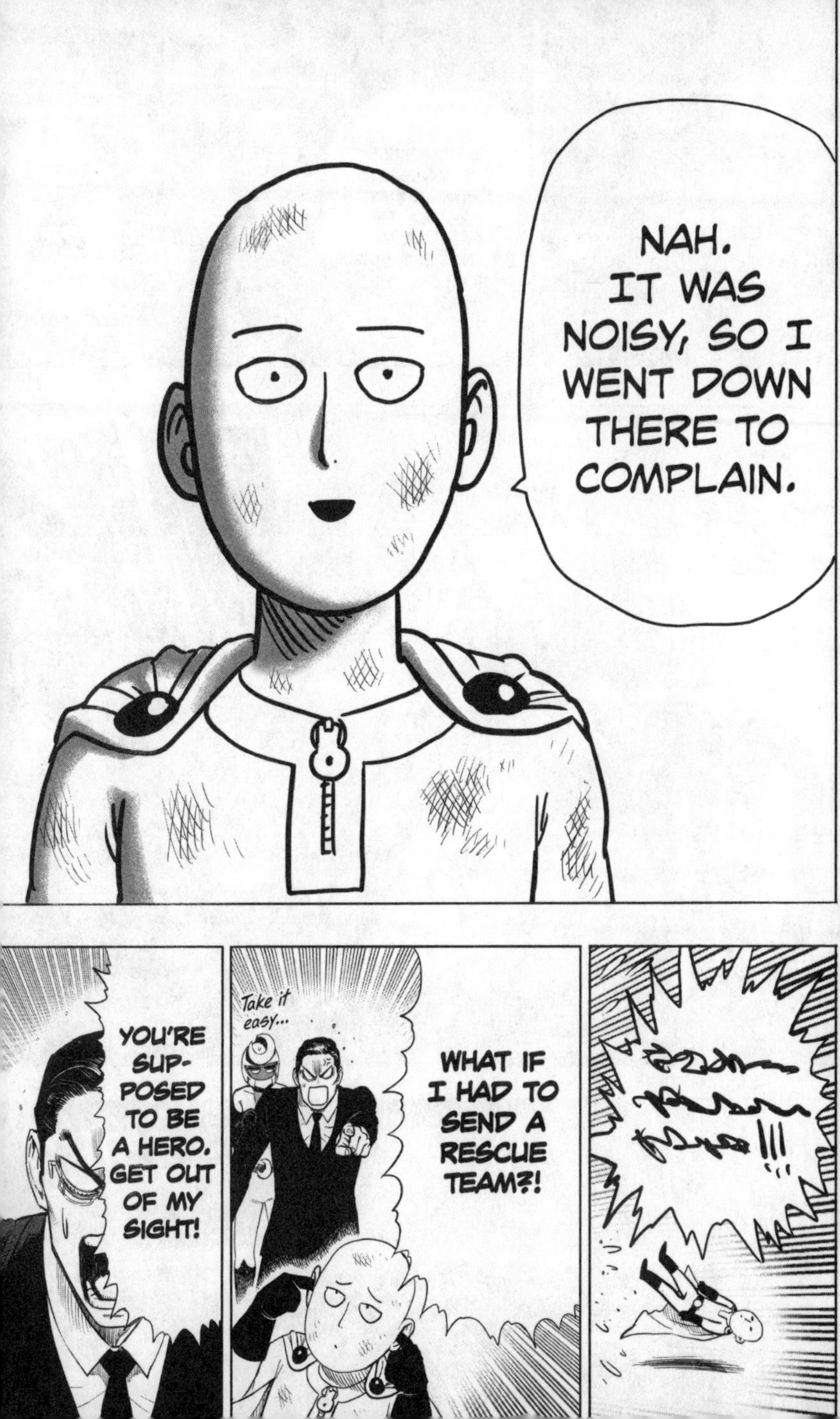
NAH. IT WAS NOISY, SO I WENT DOWN THERE TO COMPLAIN.
WHAT IF I HAD TO SEND A RESCUE TEAM?!
Take it easy...
YOU'RE SUP-POSED TO BE A HERO. GET OUT OF MY SIGHT!

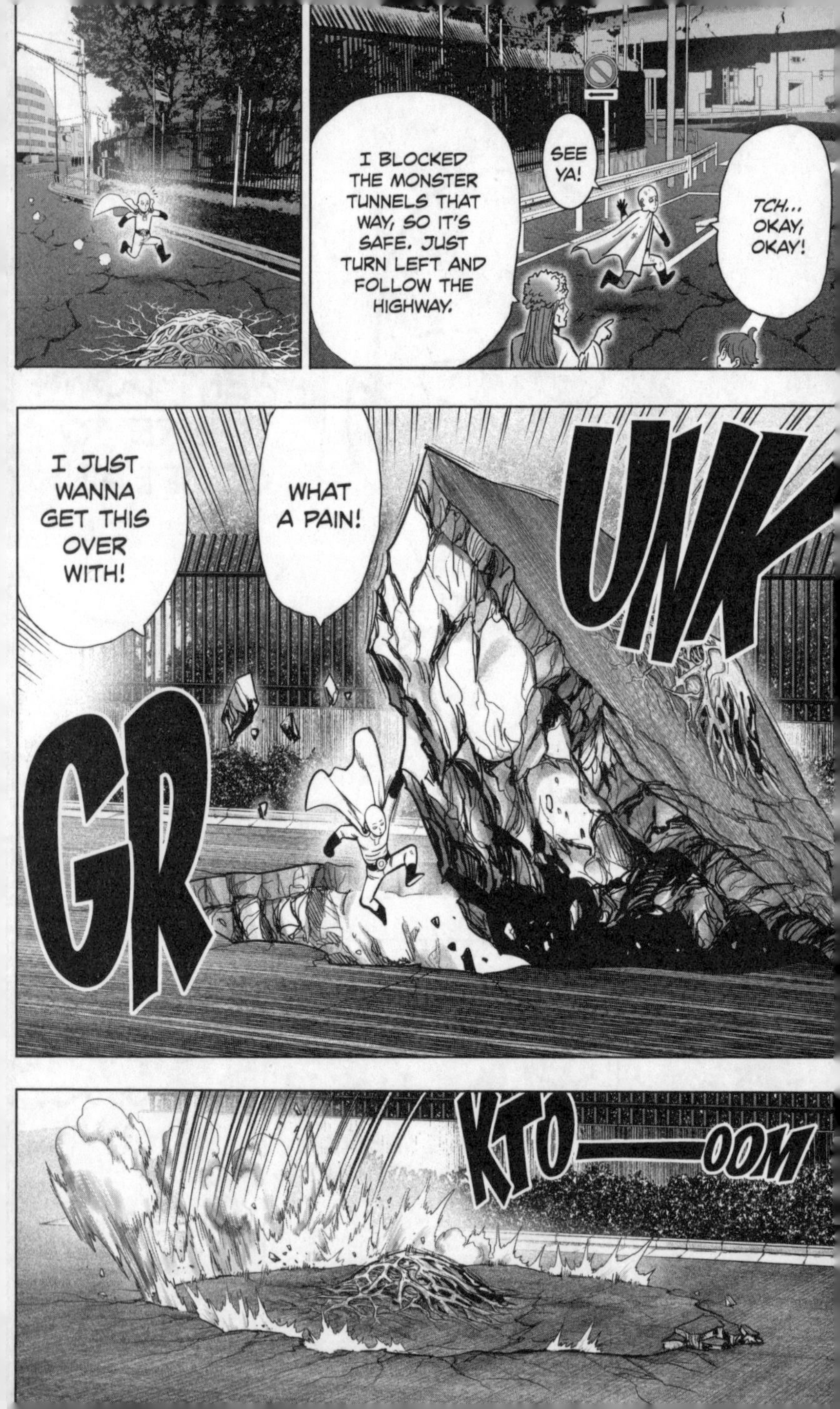
TCH... OKAY, OKAY!
SEE YA!
I BLOCKED THE MONSTER TUNNELS THAT WAY, SO IT'S SAFE. JUST TURN LEFT AND FOLLOW THE HIGHWAY.
UNK
WHAT A PAIN!
I JUST WANNA GET THIS OVER WITH!
GR
KTO——OOM

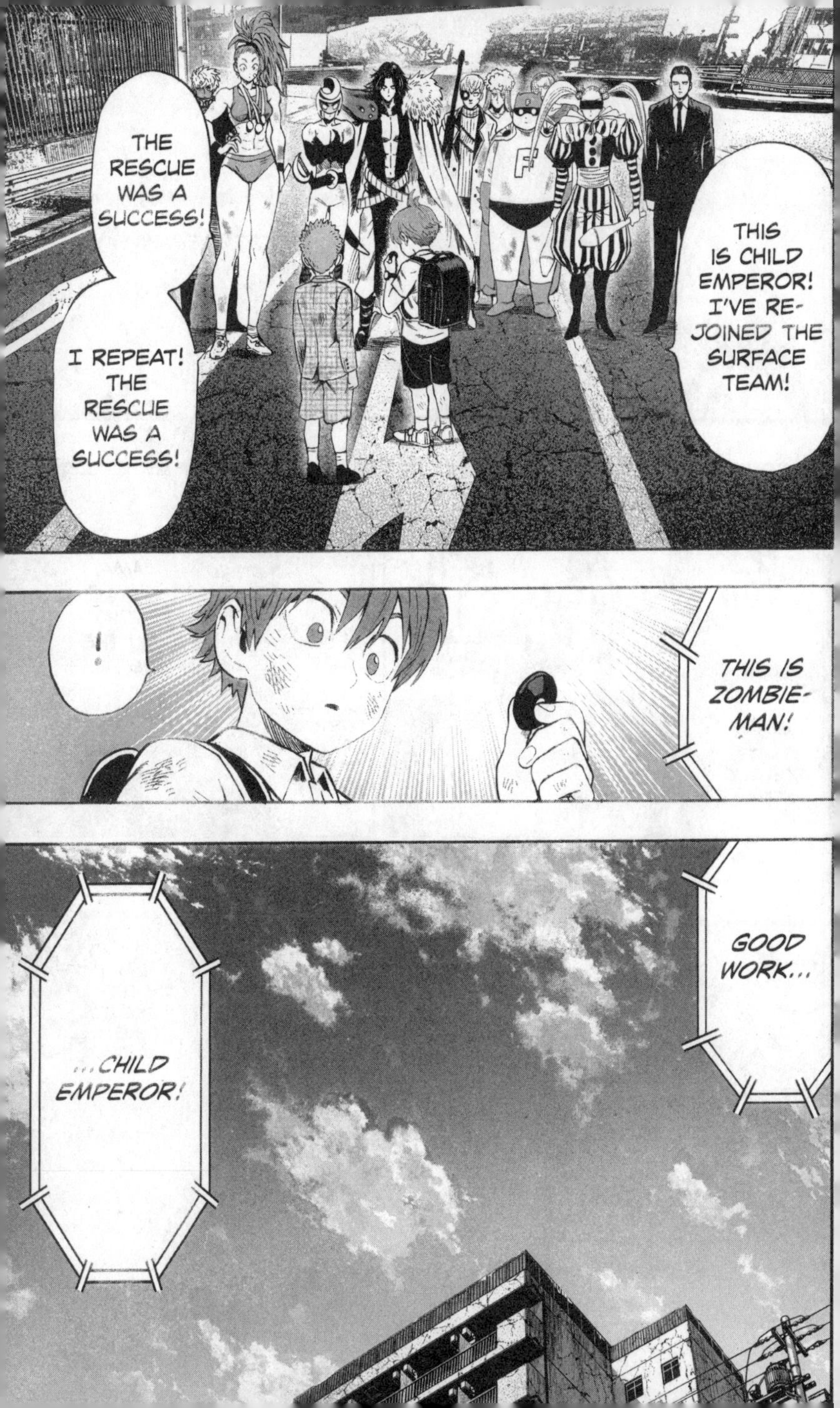
THIS IS CHILD EMPEROR! I'VE RE-JOINED THE SURFACE TEAM!
THE RESCUE WAS A SUCCESS!
I REPEAT! THE RESCUE WAS A SUCCESS!
THIS IS ZOMBIE-MAN!
!
GOOD WORK...
...CHILD EMPEROR!

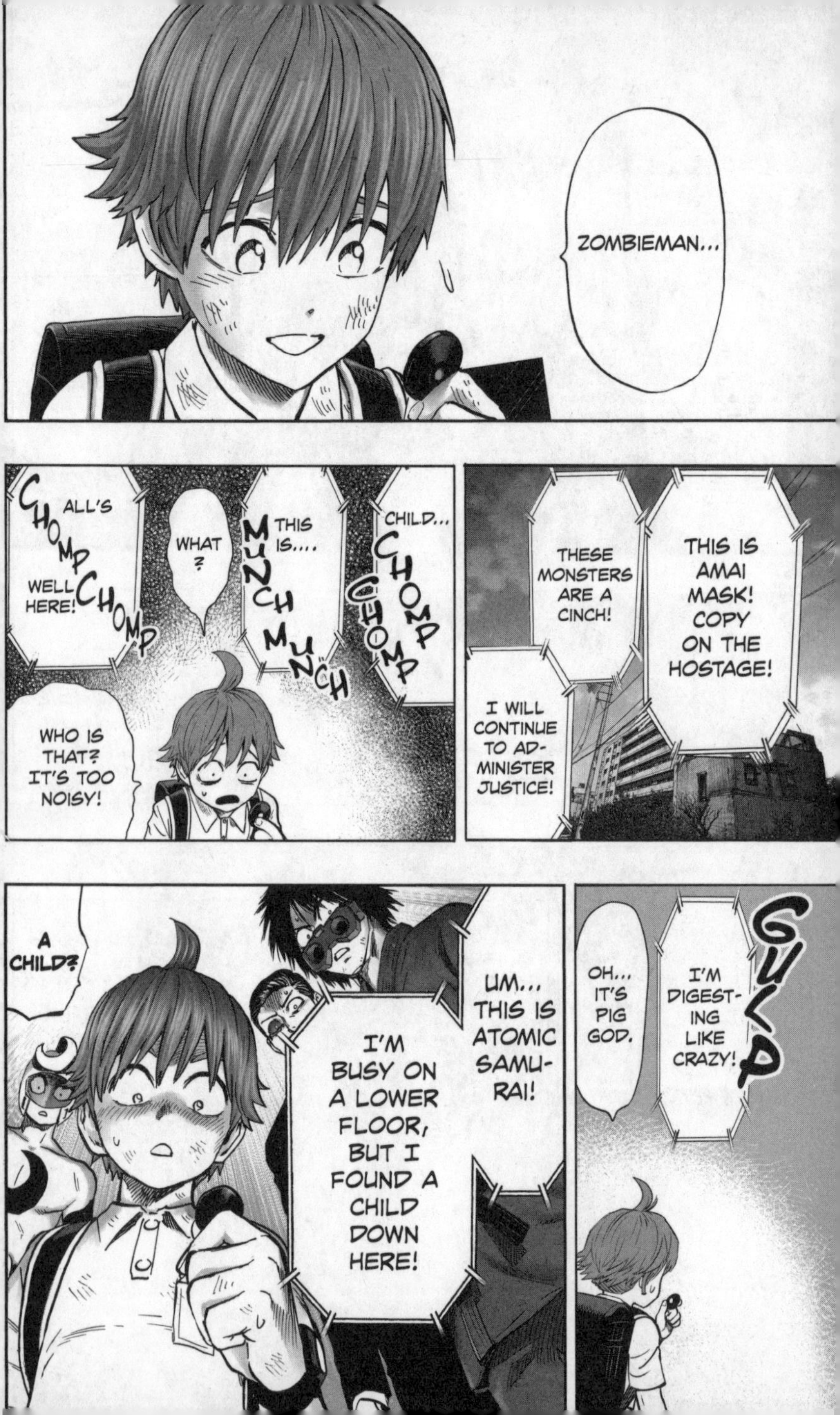

ZOMBIEMAN...
THIS IS AMAI MASK! COPY ON THE HOSTAGE!
THESE MONSTERS ARE A CINCH!
I WILL CONTINUE TO AD-MINISTER JUSTICE!
CHILD...
CHOMP CHOMP
THIS IS....
MUNCH MUNCH
WHAT?
ALL'S WELL HERE!
CHOMP CHOMP
WHO IS THAT? IT'S TOO NOISY!
I'M DIGEST-ING LIKE CRAZY!
GULP
OH... IT'S PIG GOD.
UM... THIS IS ATOMIC SAMU-RAI!
I'M BUSY ON A LOWER FLOOR, BUT I FOUND A CHILD DOWN HERE!
A CHILD?

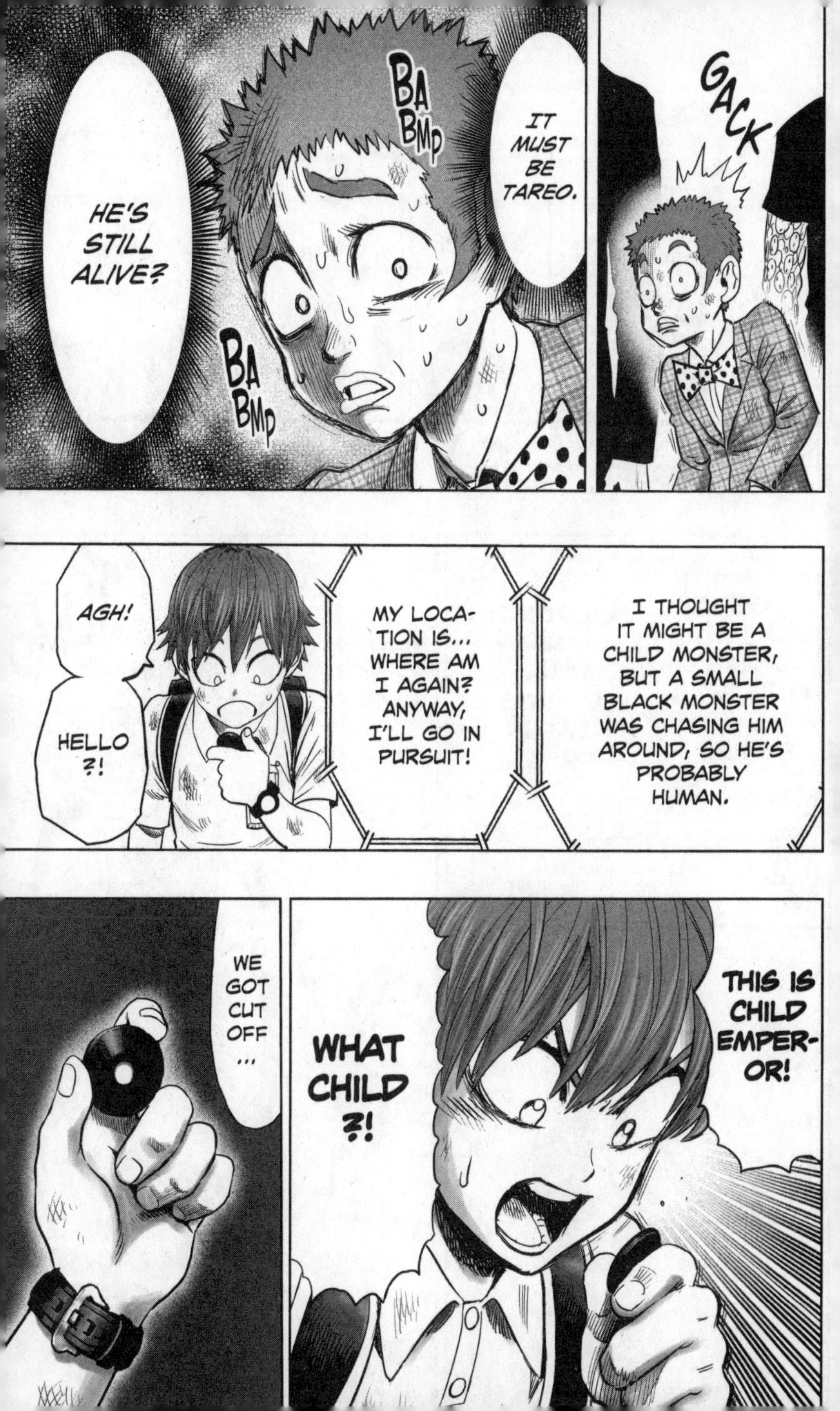
GACK
IT MUST BE TAREO.
BA BMP
HE'S STILL ALIVE?
BA BMP
I THOUGHT IT MIGHT BE A CHILD MONSTER, BUT A SMALL BLACK MONSTER WAS CHASING HIM AROUND, SO HE'S PROBABLY HUMAN.
MY LOCATION IS... WHERE AM I AGAIN? ANYWAY, I'LL GO IN PURSUIT!
AGH!
HELLO?!
THIS IS CHILD EMPEROR!
WHAT CHILD?!
WE GOT CUT OFF...

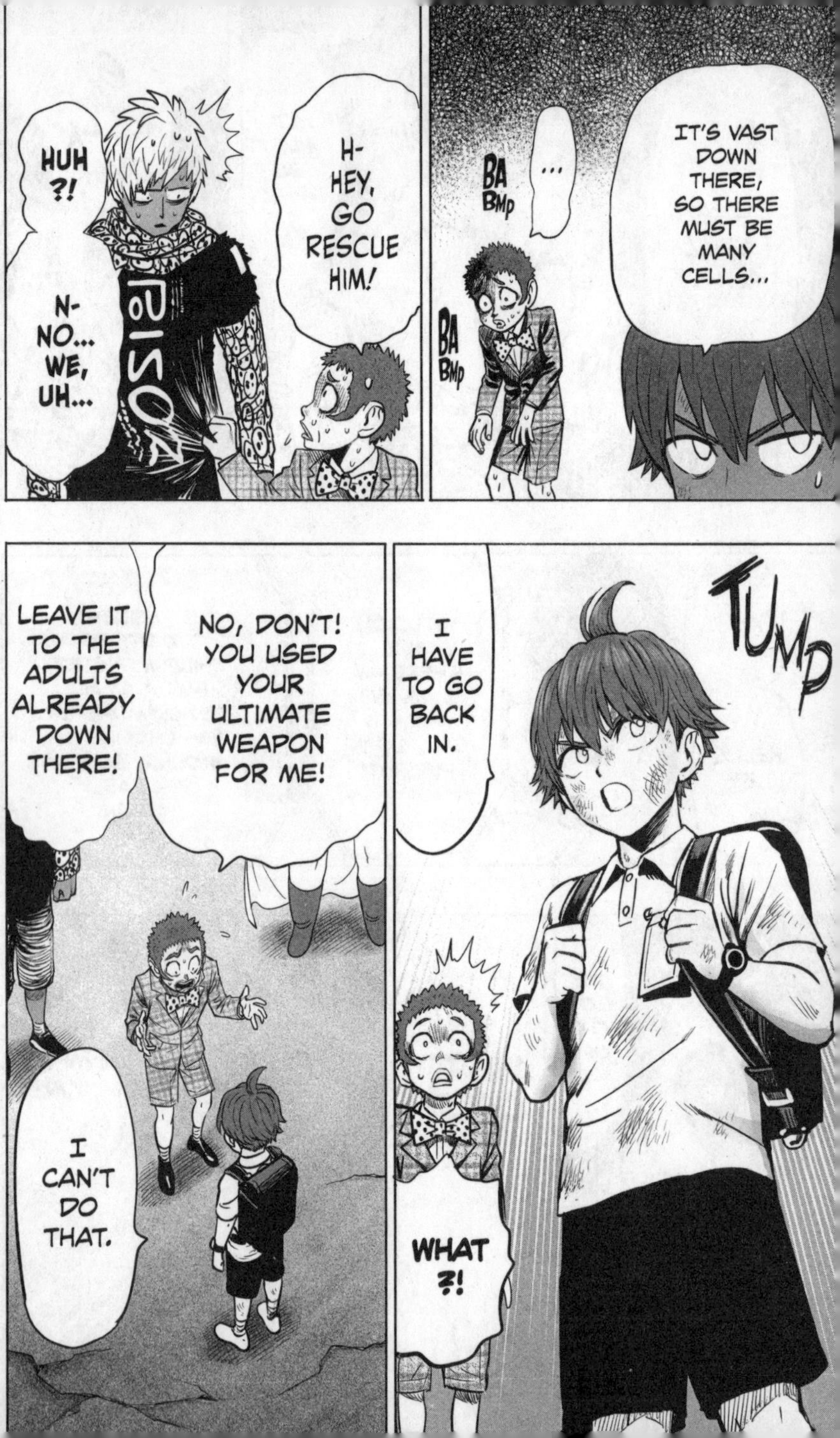
IT'S VAST DOWN THERE, SO THERE MUST BE MANY CELLS...
...
BA BMP
BA BMP
H- HEY, GO RESCUE HIM!
HUH ?!
N- NO... WE, UH...
TUMP
I HAVE TO GO BACK IN.
WHAT ?!
NO, DON'T! YOU USED YOUR ULTIMATE WEAPON FOR ME!
LEAVE IT TO THE ADULTS ALREADY DOWN THERE!
I CAN'T DO THAT.

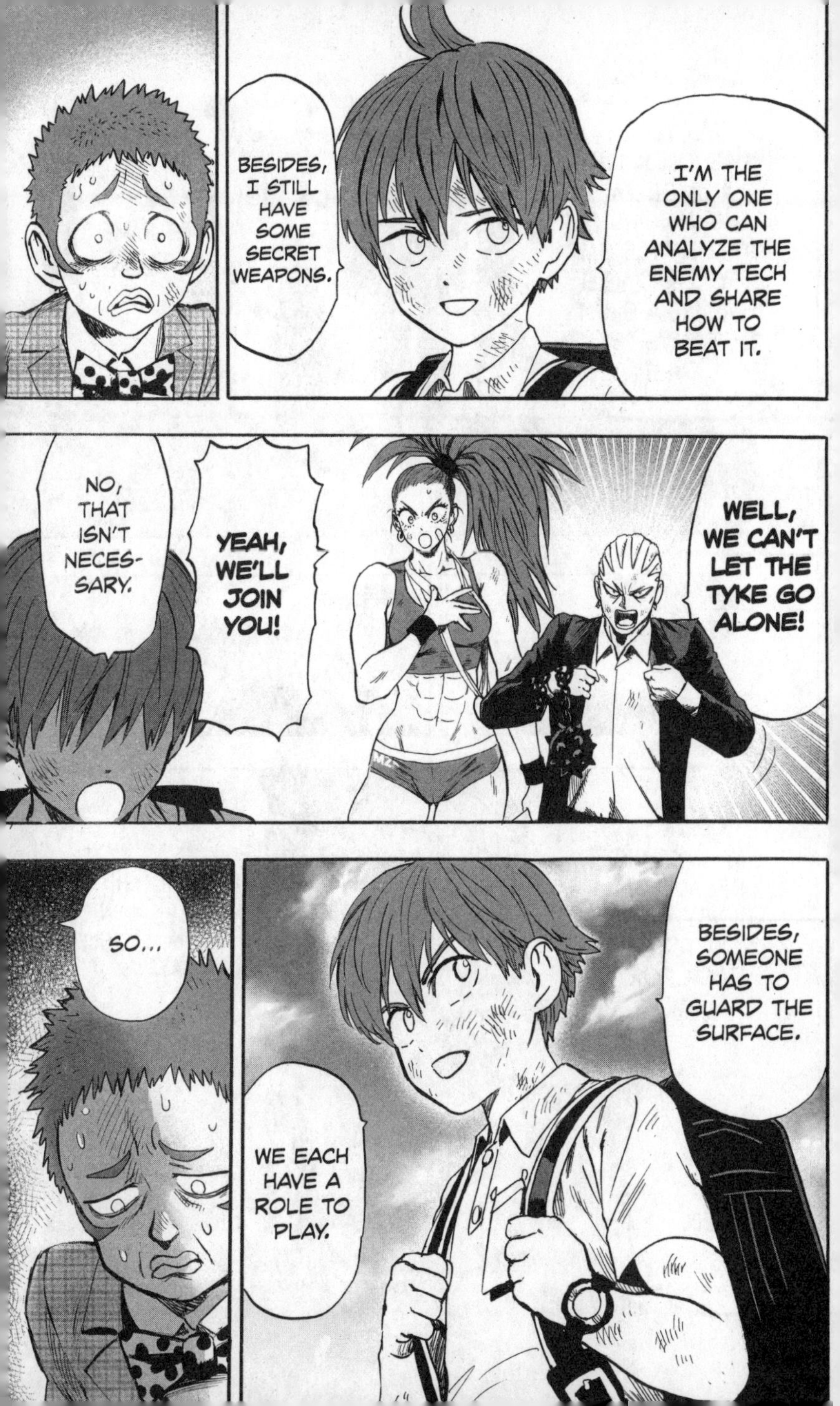
I'M THE ONLY ONE WHO CAN ANALYZE THE ENEMY TECH AND SHARE HOW TO BEAT IT.
BESIDES, I STILL HAVE SOME SECRET WEAPONS.
WELL, WE CAN'T LET THE TYKE GO ALONE!
YEAH, WE'LL JOIN YOU!
NO, THAT ISN'T NECES- SARY.
BESIDES, SOMEONE HAS TO GUARD THE SURFACE.
WE EACH HAVE A ROLE TO PLAY.
SO...

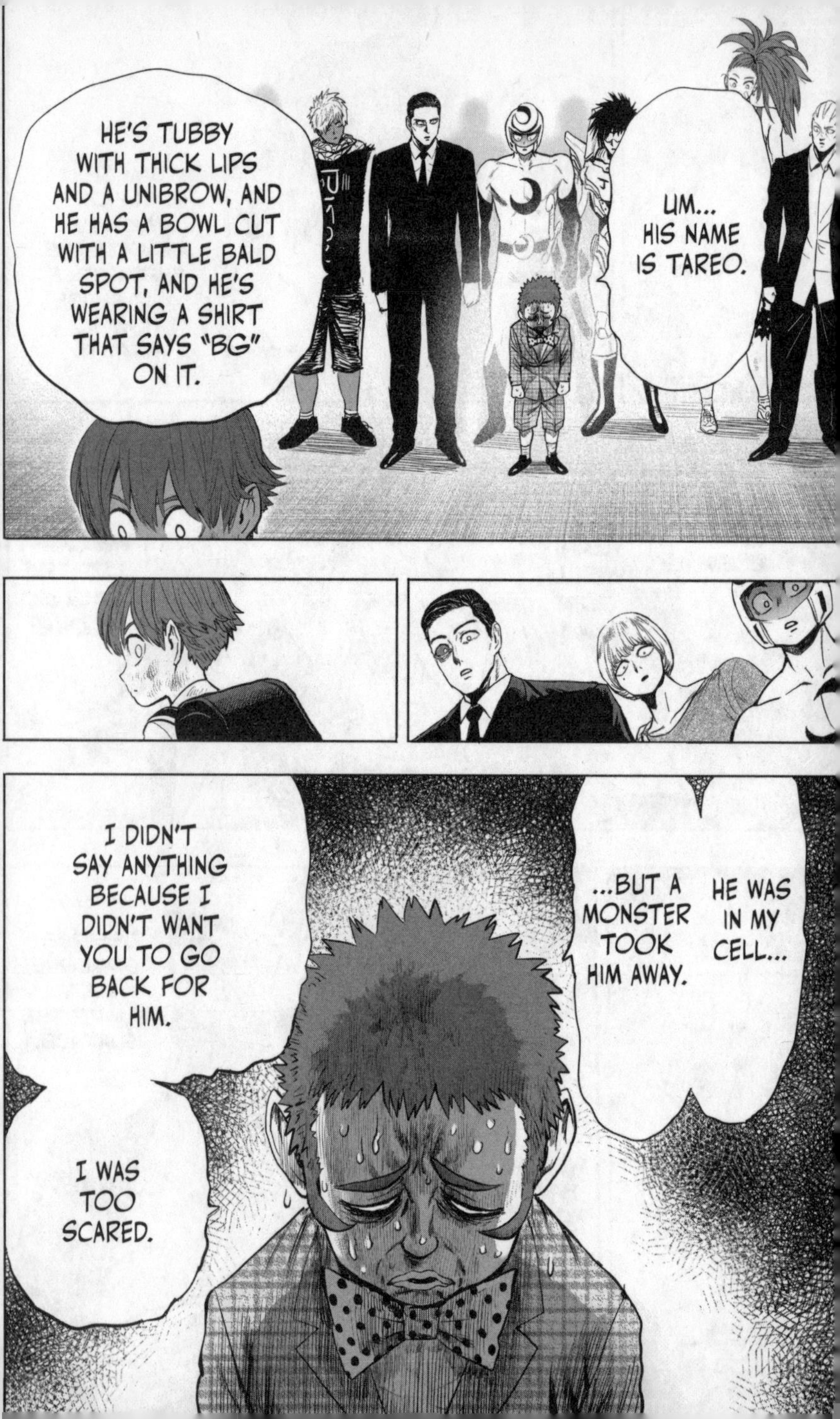
UM... HIS NAME IS TAREO.
HE'S TUBBY WITH THICK LIPS AND A UNIBROW, AND HE HAS A BOWL CUT WITH A LITTLE BALD SPOT, AND HE'S WEARING A SHIRT THAT SAYS "BG" ON IT.
HE WAS IN MY CELL...
...BUT A MONSTER TOOK HIM AWAY.
I DIDN'T SAY ANYTHING BECAUSE I DIDN'T WANT YOU TO GO BACK FOR HIM.
I WAS TOO SCARED.

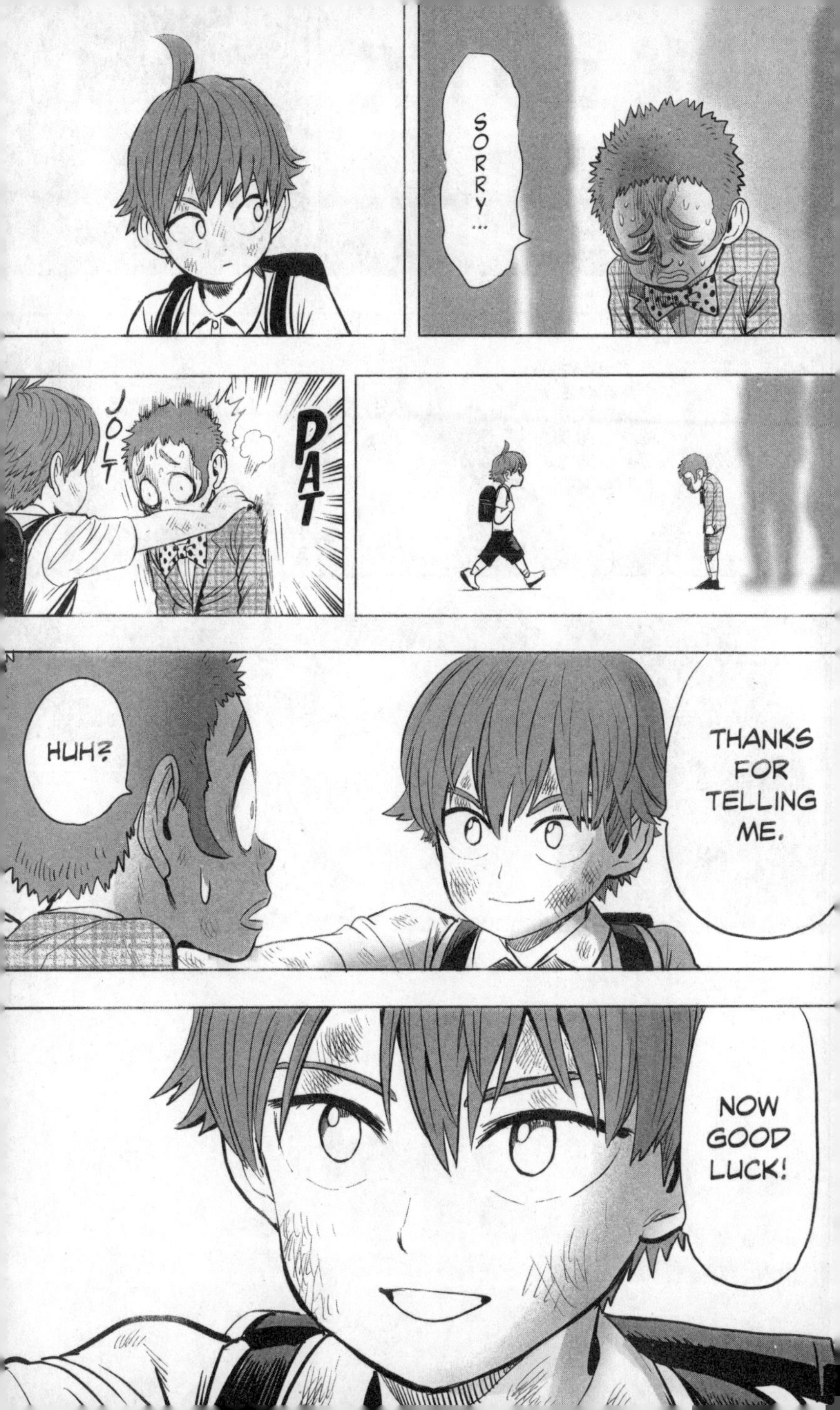
SORRY...
PAT
JOLT
THANKS FOR TELLING ME.
HUH?
NOW GOOD LUCK!

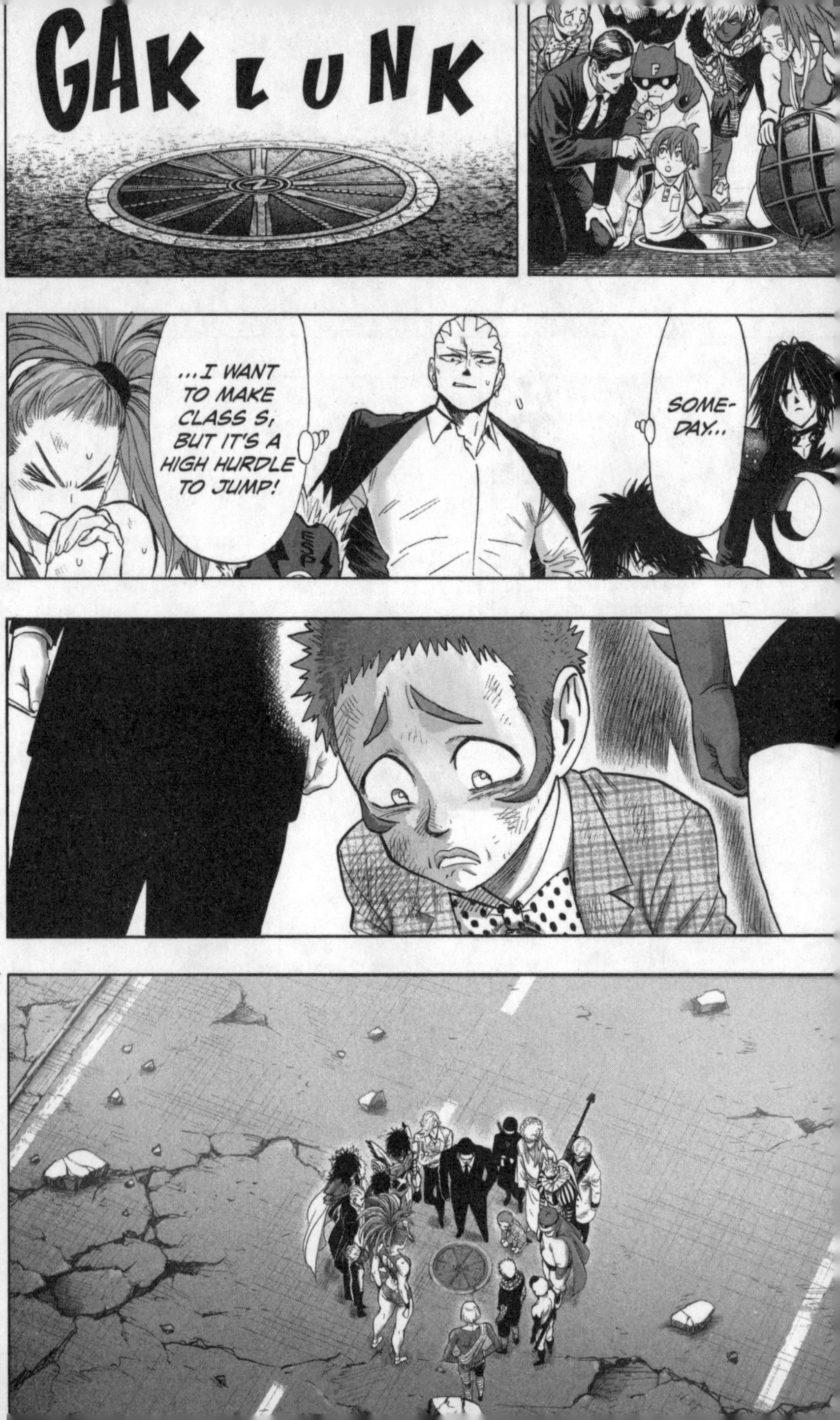
GAKLUNK
SOME-DAY...
...I WANT TO MAKE CLASS S, BUT IT'S A HIGH HURDLE TO JUMP!

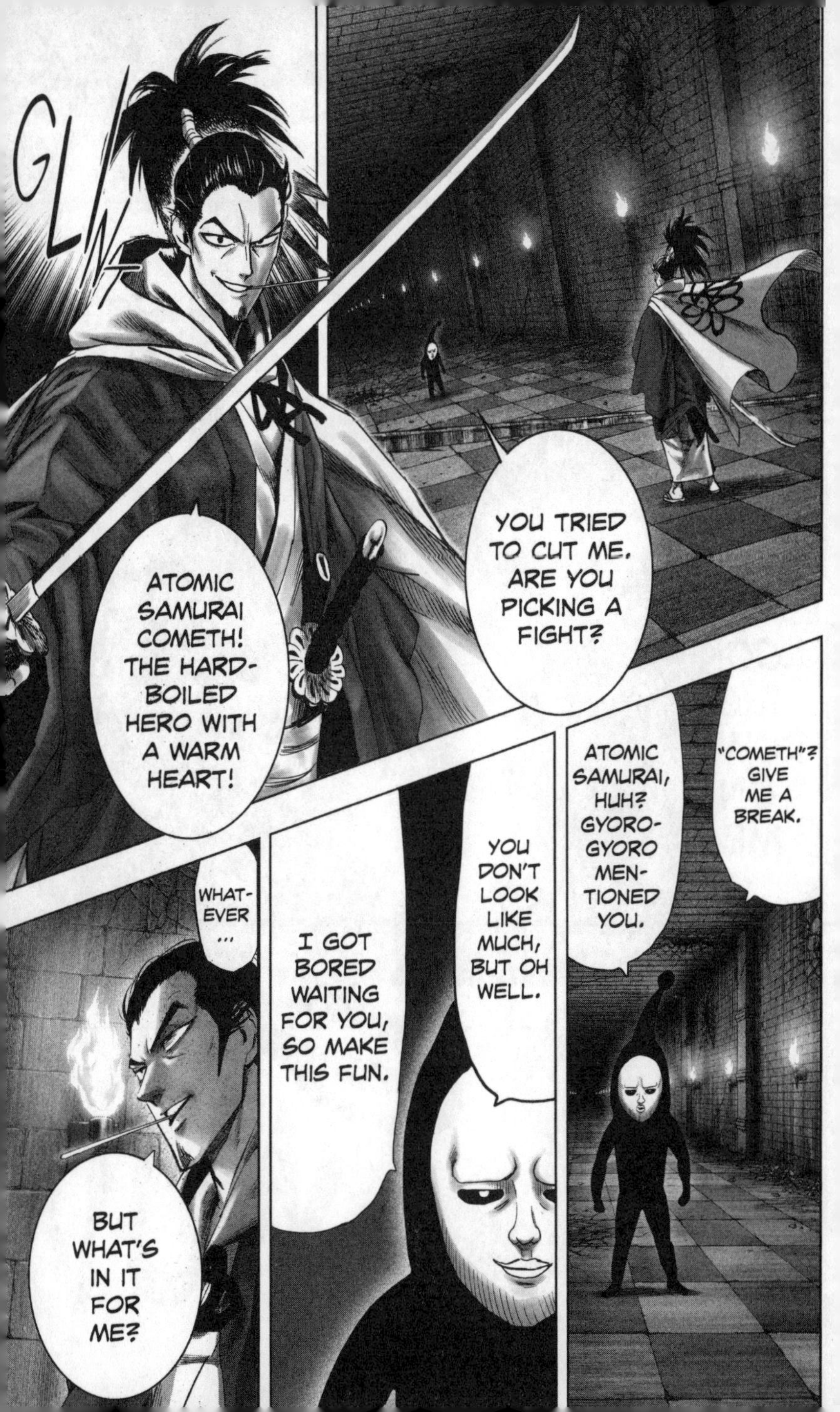

YOU TRIED TO CUT ME. ARE YOU PICKING A FIGHT?
GLINT
ATOMIC SAMURAI COMETH! THE HARD-BOILED HERO WITH A WARM HEART!
"COMETH"? GIVE ME A BREAK.
ATOMIC SAMURAI, HUH? GYORO-GYORO MENTIONED YOU.
YOU DON'T LOOK LIKE MUCH, BUT OH WELL.
I GOT BORED WAITING FOR YOU, SO MAKE THIS FUN.
WHAT-EVER ...
BUT WHAT'S IN IT FOR ME?

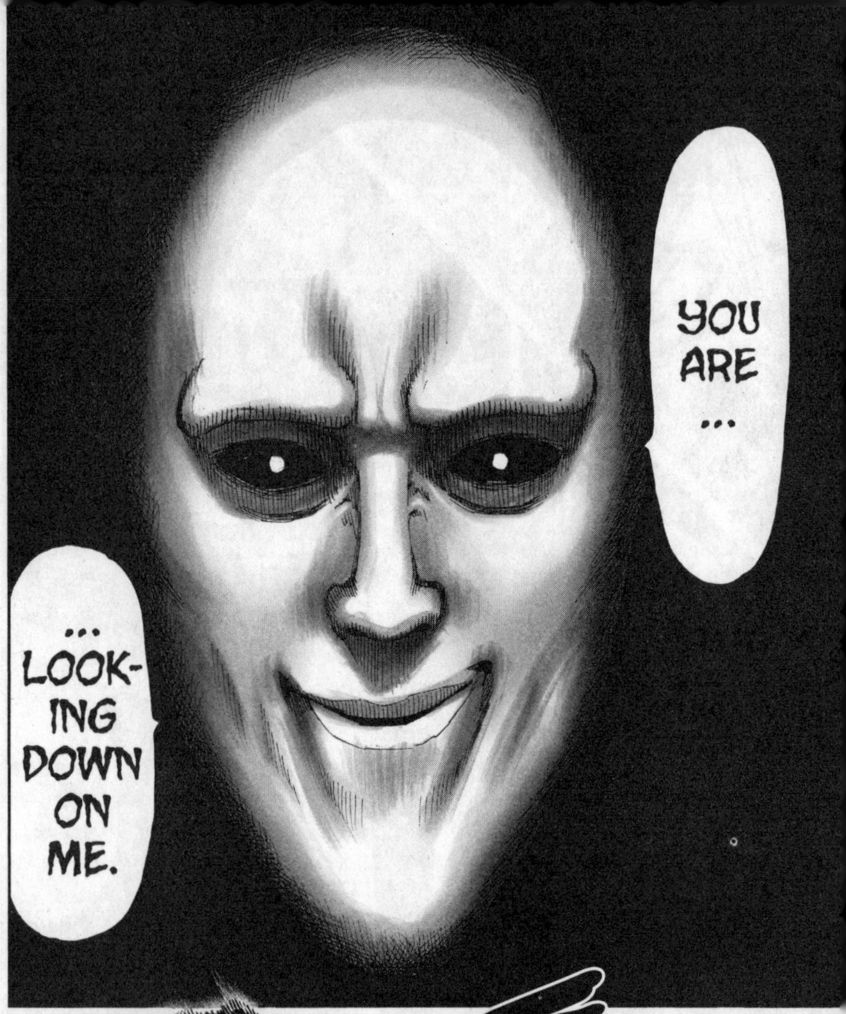
YOU ARE ...
... LOOKING DOWN ON ME.
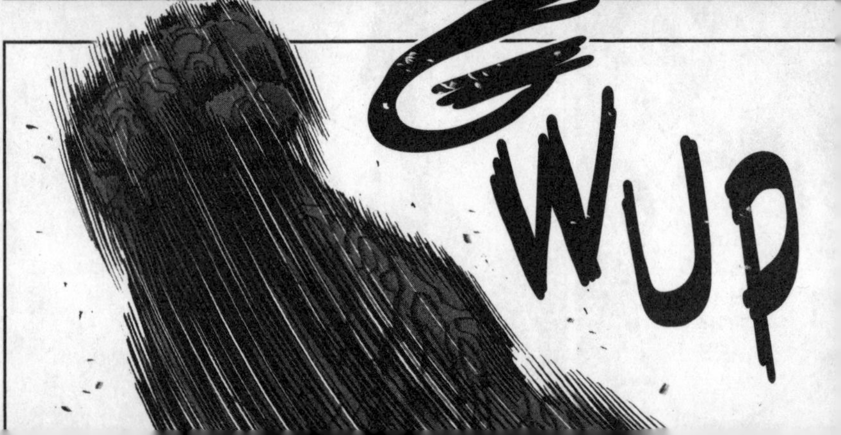
GWUP

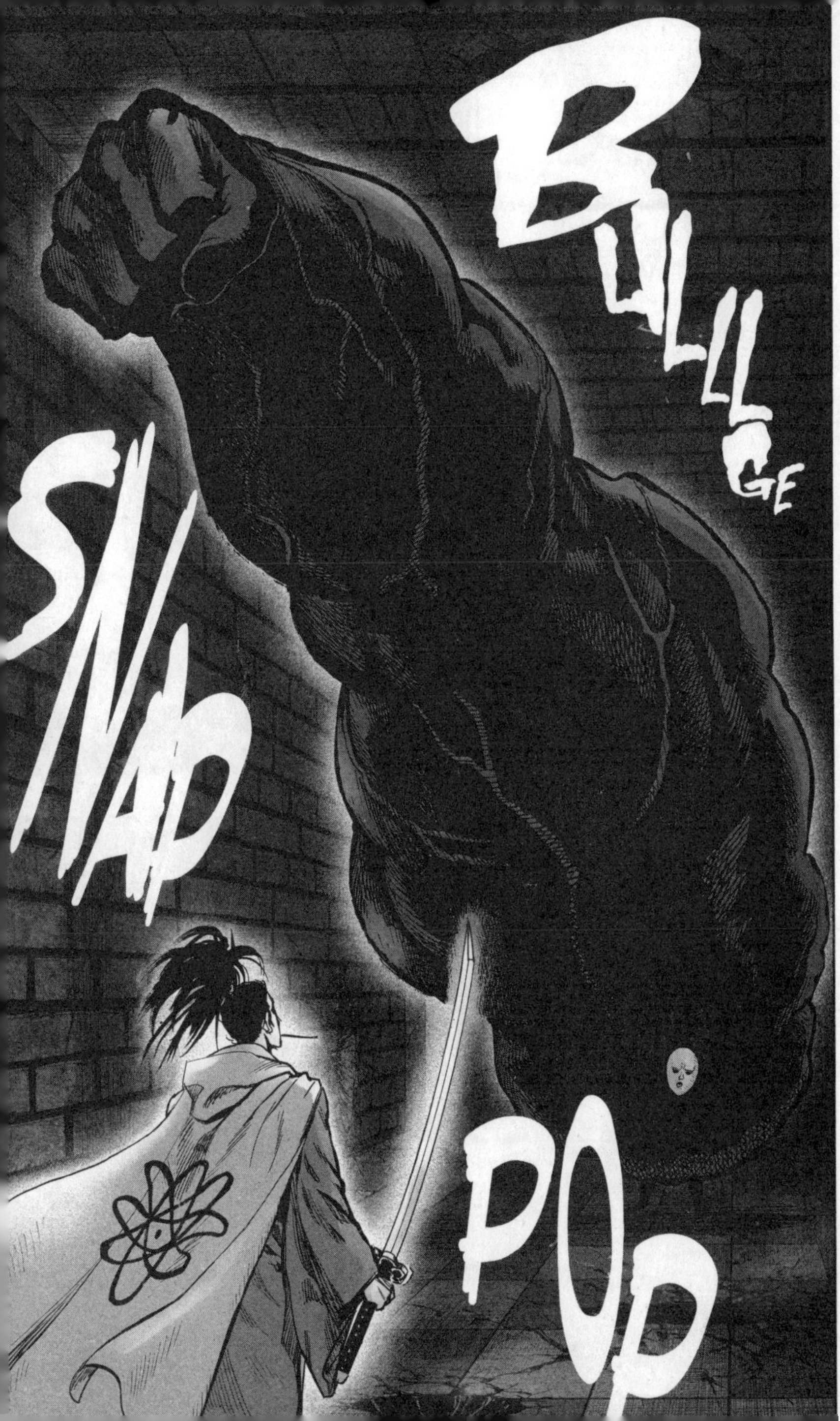
BULLLGE
SNAP
POP

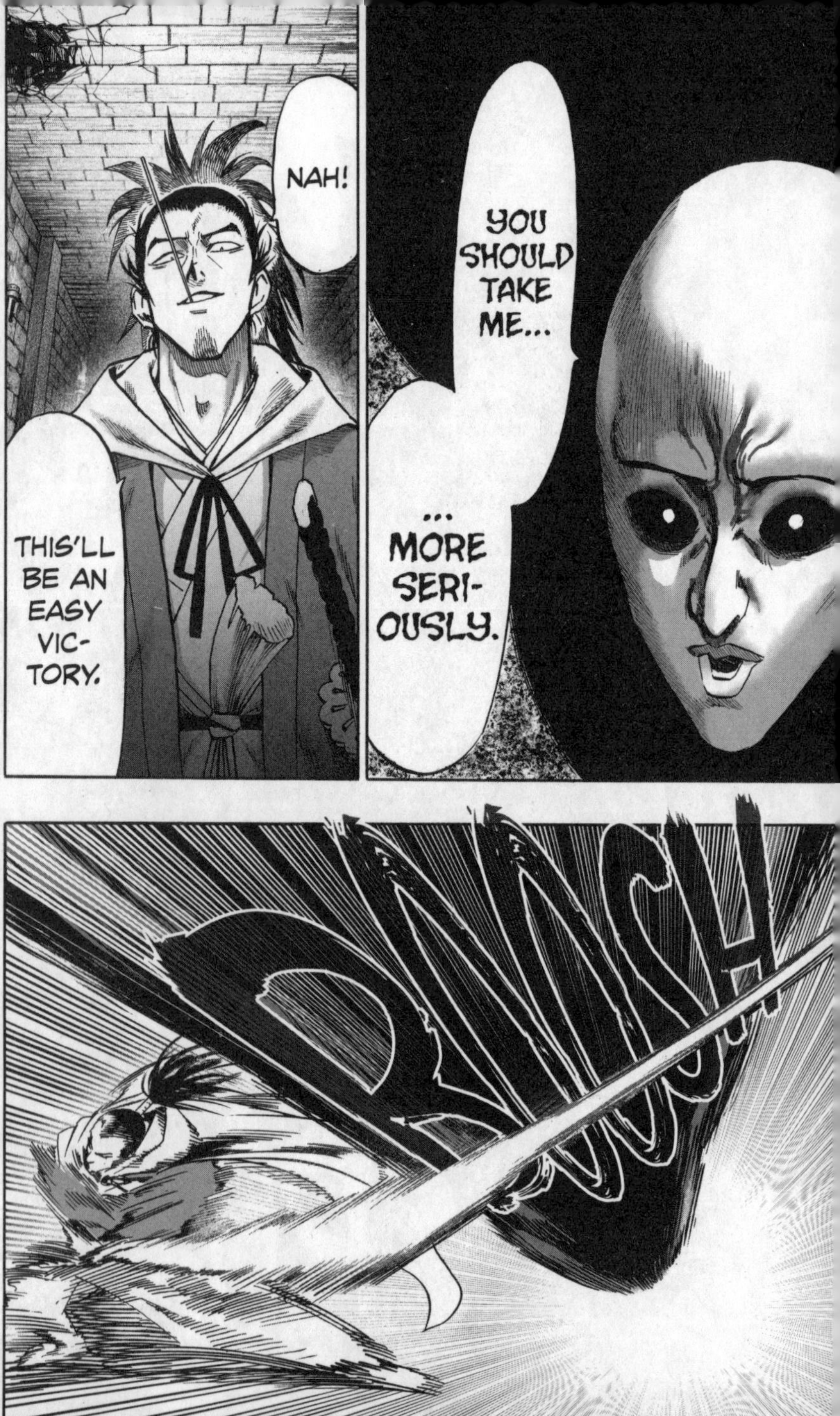
YOU SHOULD TAKE ME...
... MORE SERI-OUSLY.
NAH!
THIS'LL BE AN EASY VIC-TORY.

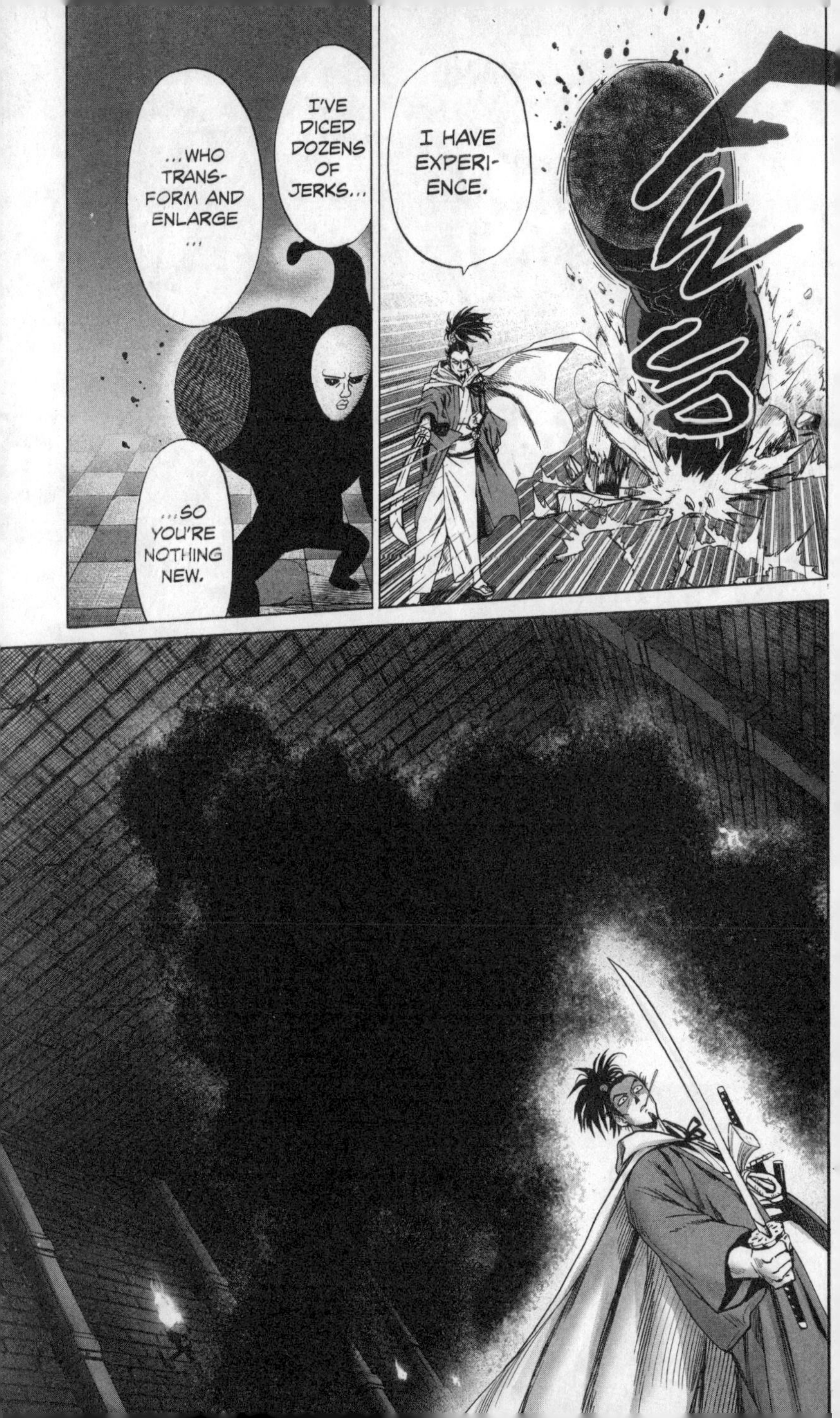
I HAVE EXPERIENCE.
I'VE DICED DOZENS OF JERKS...
...WHO TRANSFORM AND ENLARGE...
...SO YOU'RE NOTHING NEW.

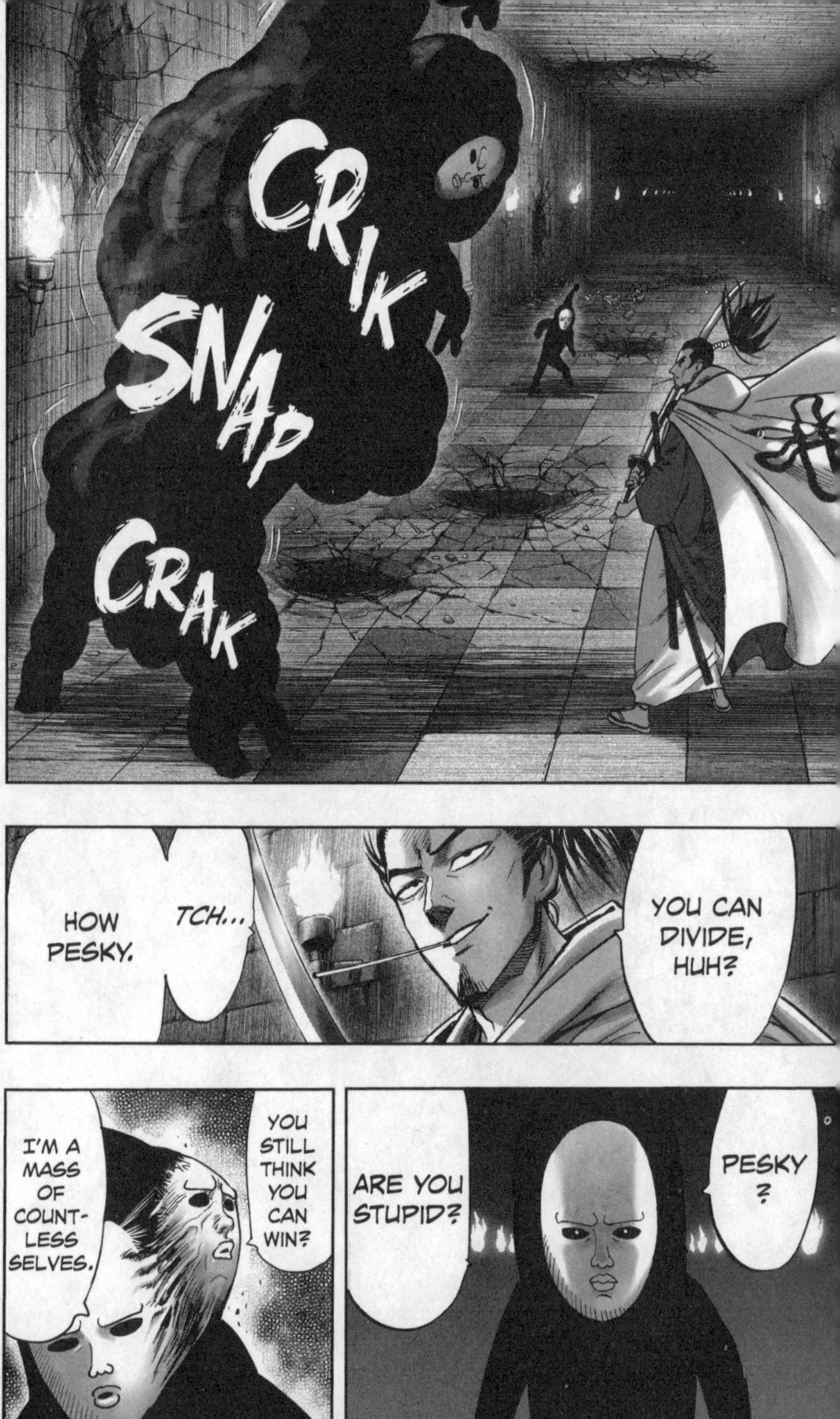
CRIK
SNAP
CRAK
YOU CAN DIVIDE, HUH?
TCH...
HOW PESKY.
PESKY?
ARE YOU STUPID?
YOU STILL THINK YOU CAN WIN?
I'M A MASS OF COUNT-LESS SELVES.

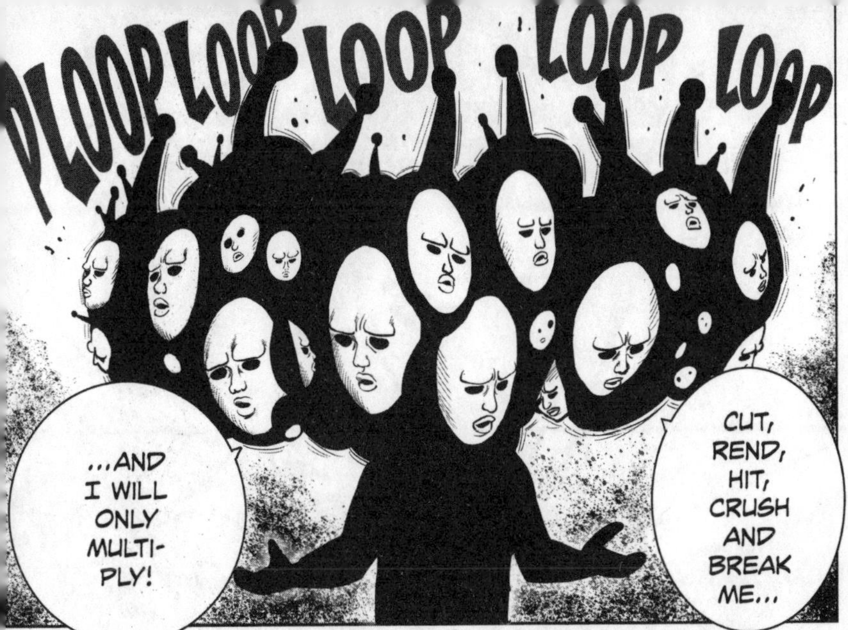
PLOOP LOOP LOOP LOOP LOOP
CUT, REND, HIT, CRUSH AND BREAK ME...
...AND I WILL ONLY MULTI-PLY!
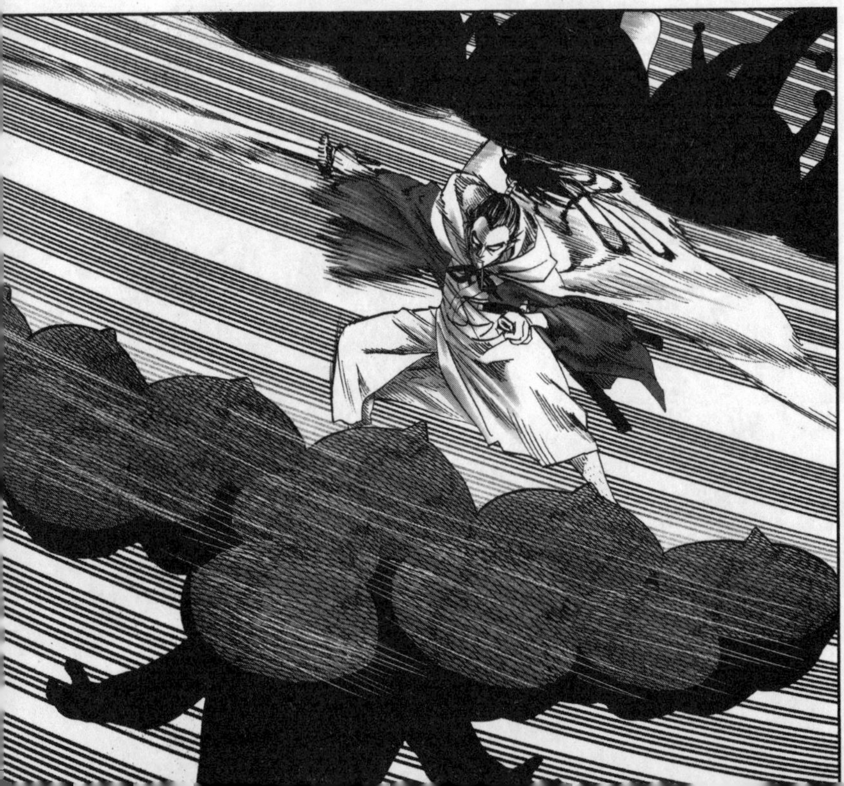

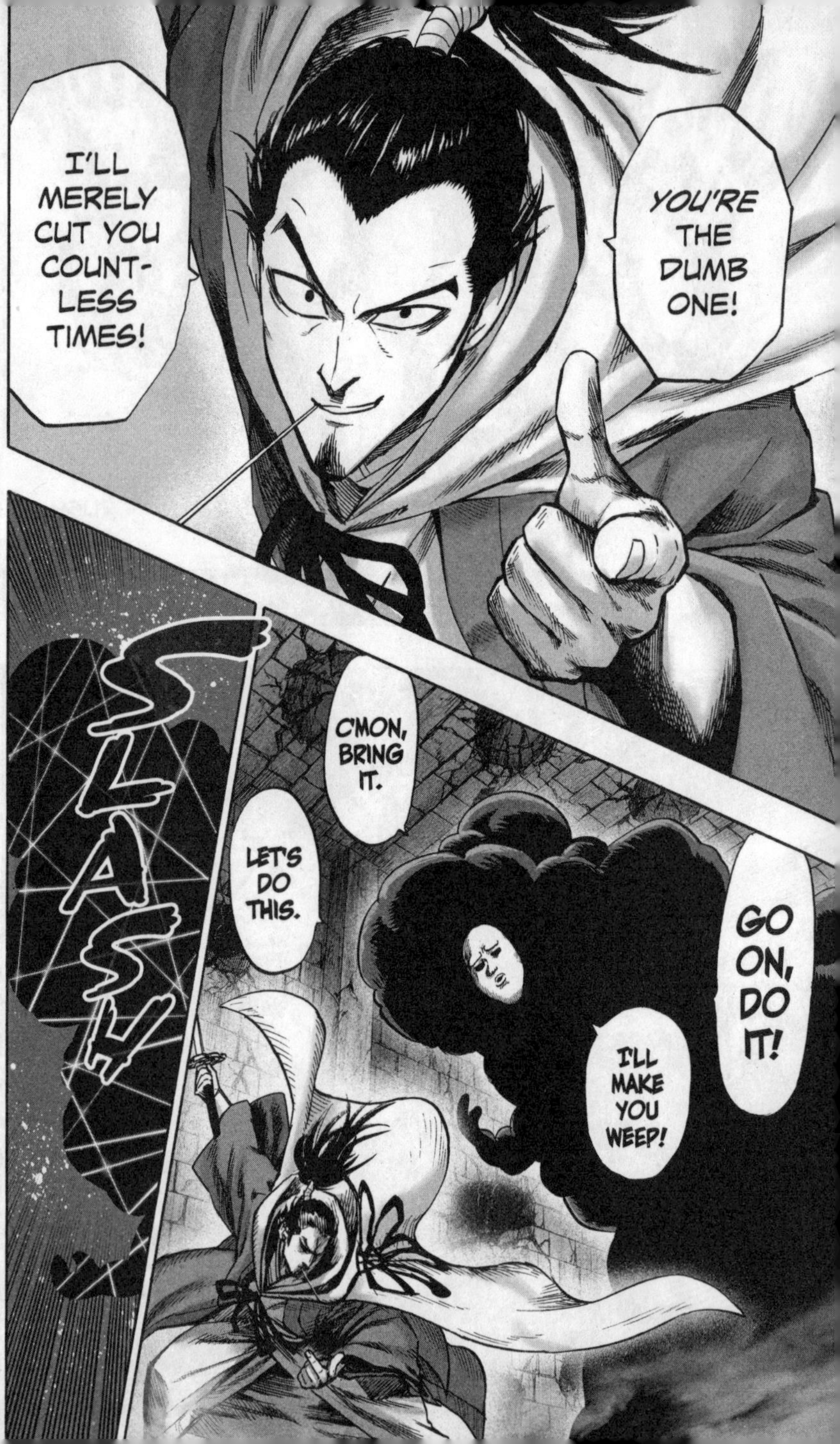
YOU'RE THE DUMB ONE!
I'LL MERELY CUT YOU COUNTLESS TIMES!
GO ON, DO IT!
I'LL MAKE YOU WEEP!
C'MON, BRING IT.
LET'S DO THIS.
SLASH

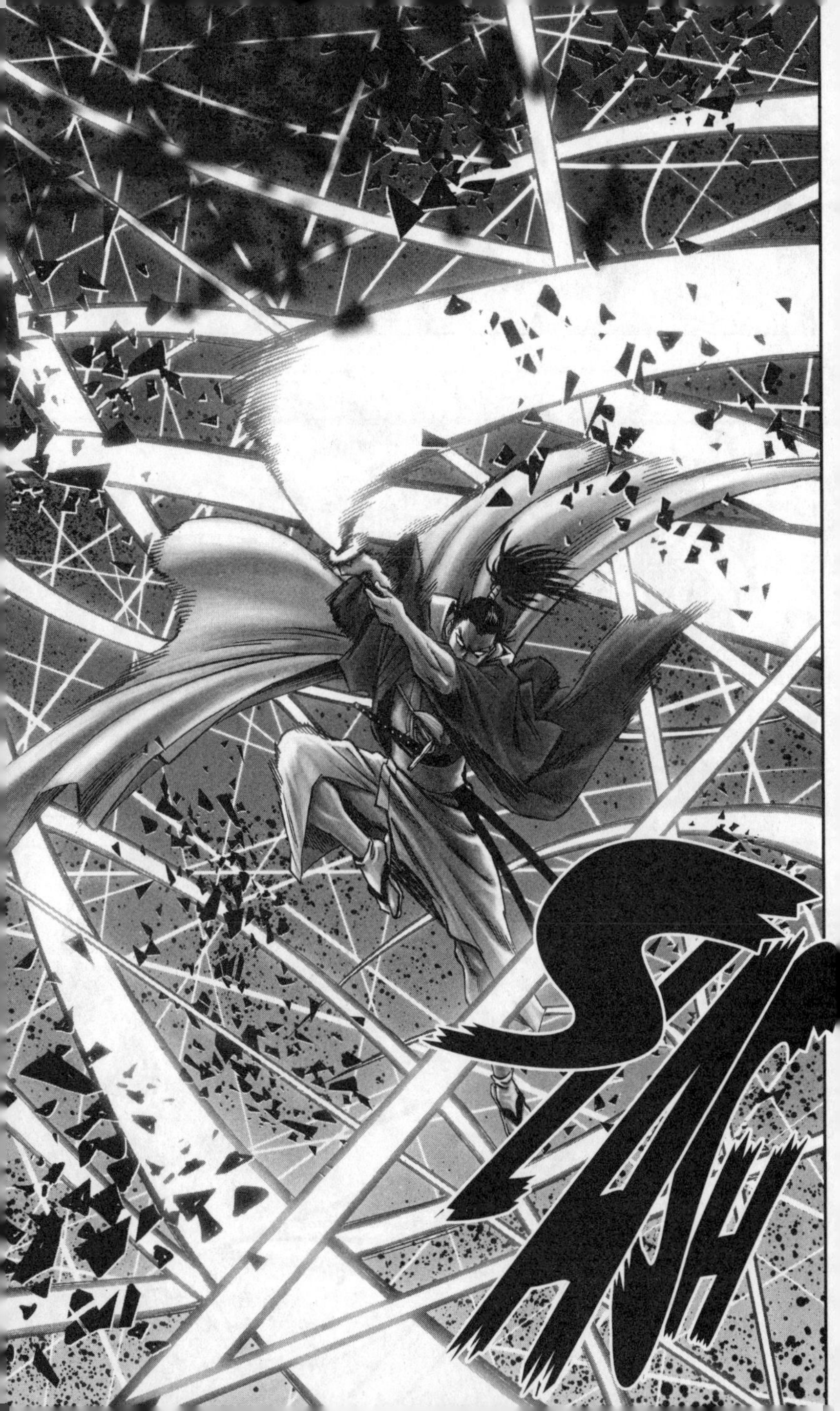
SHA

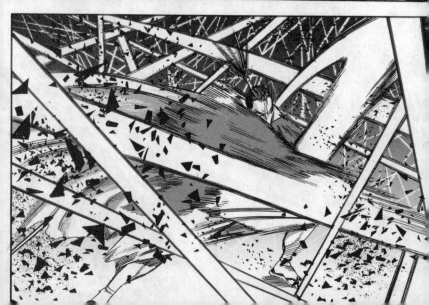

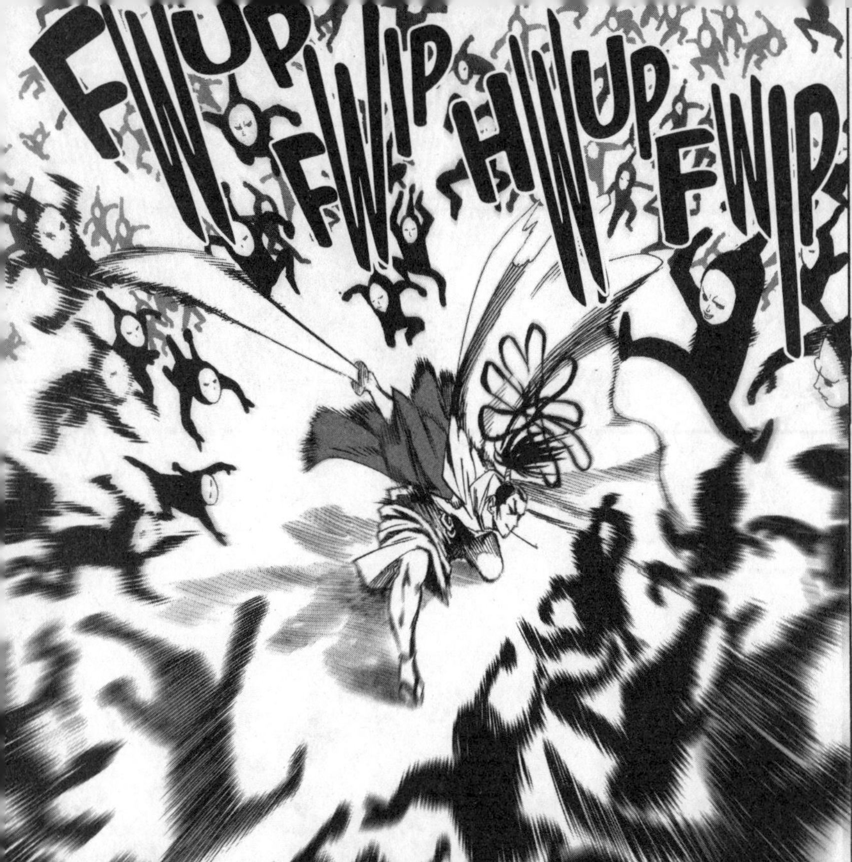
FWIP
HWUP
FWIP
FWIP
FWUP
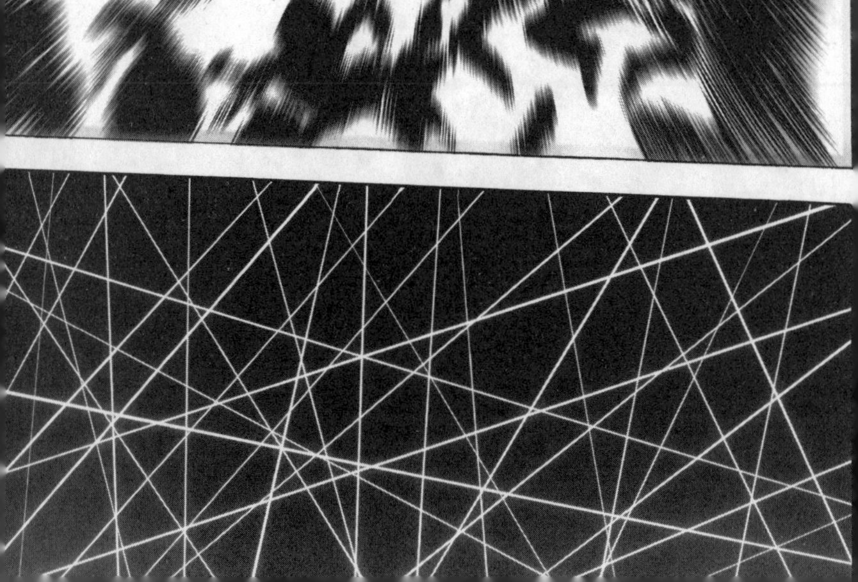

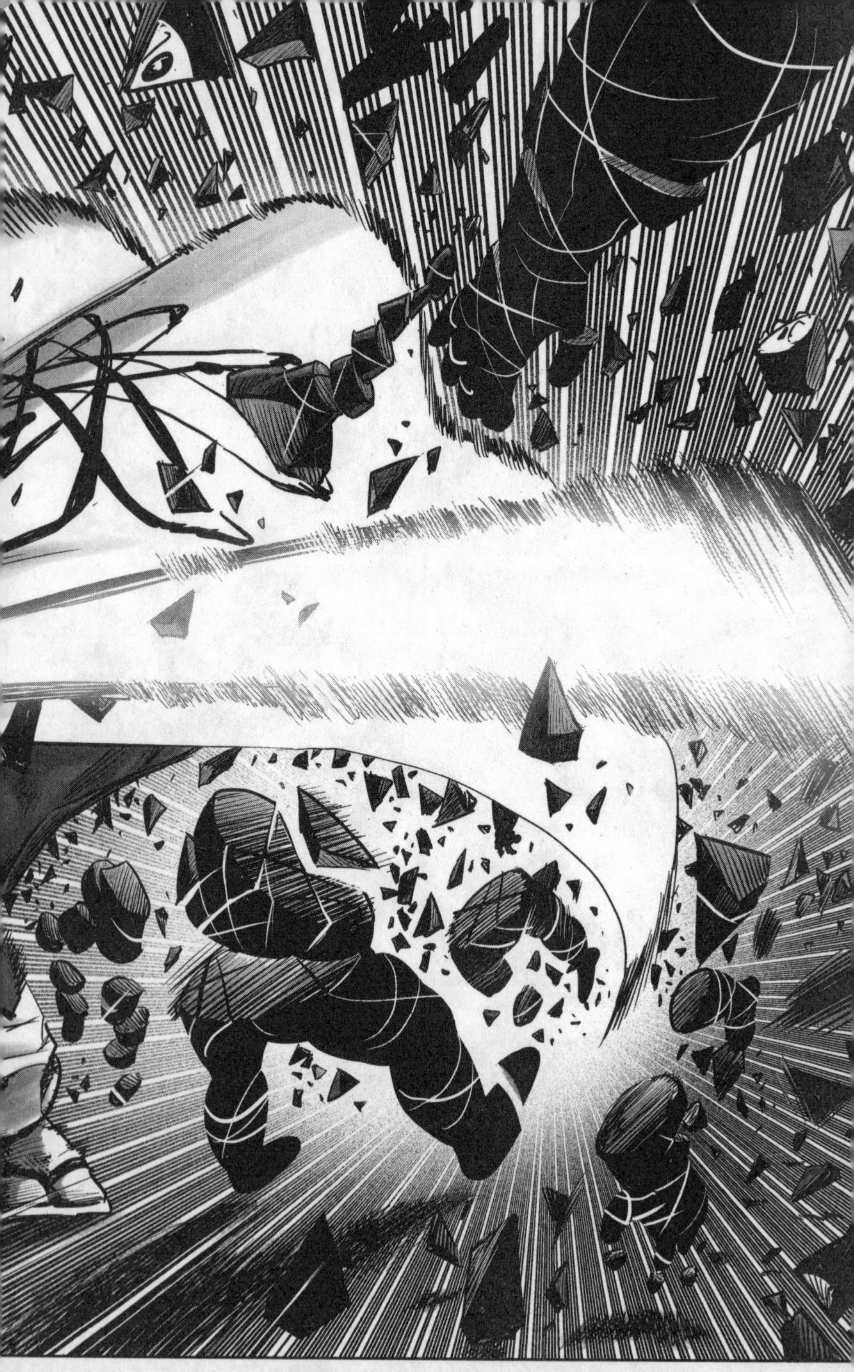

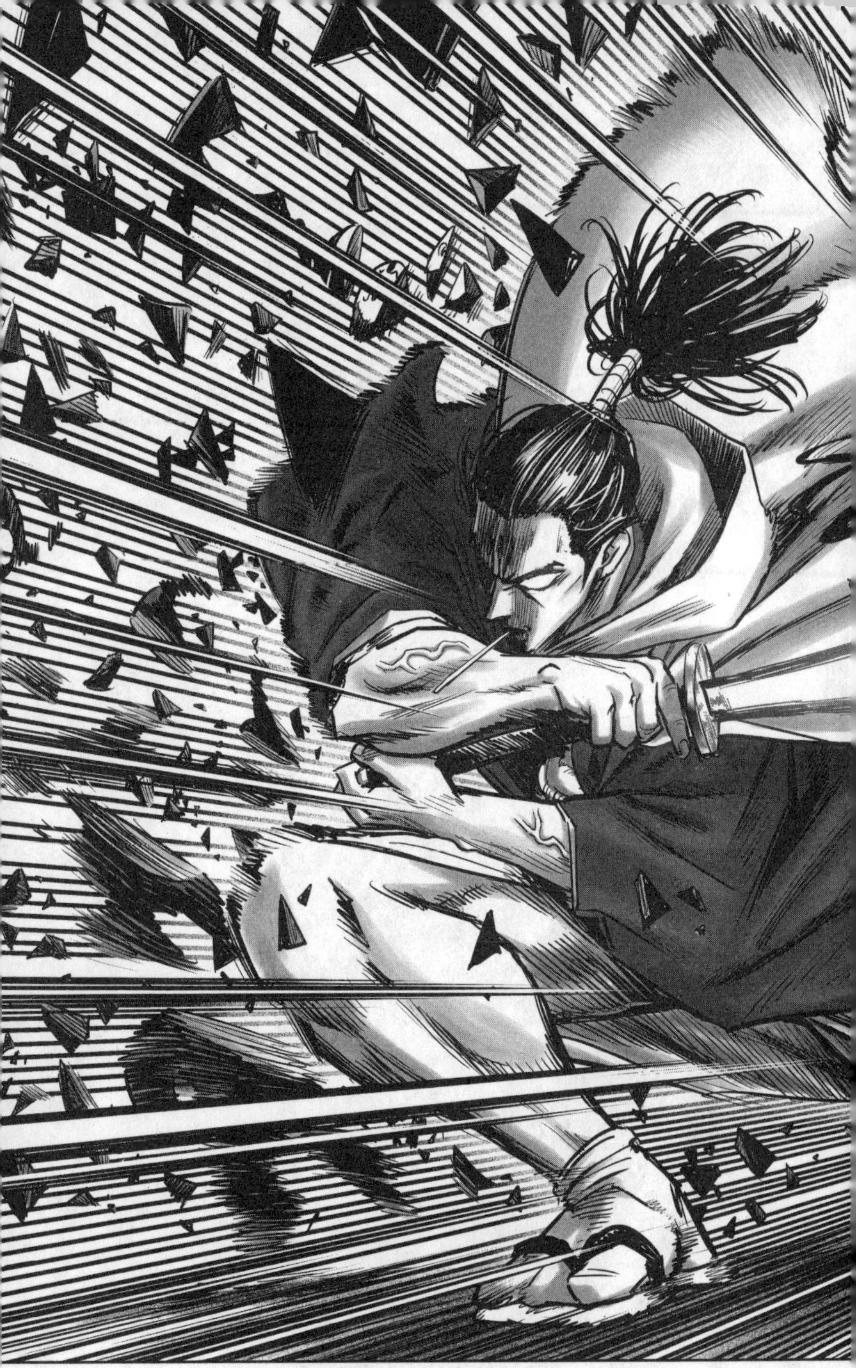

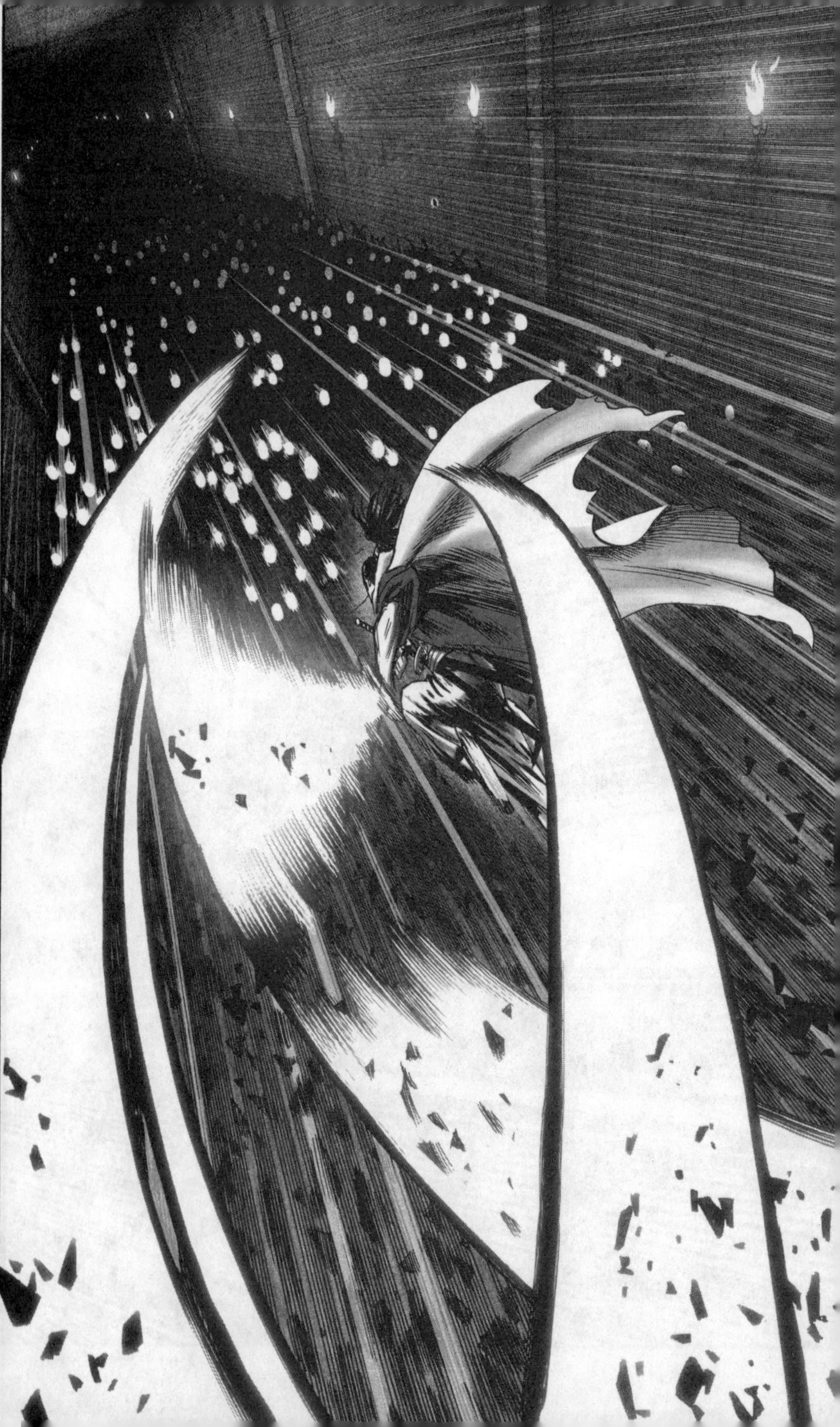

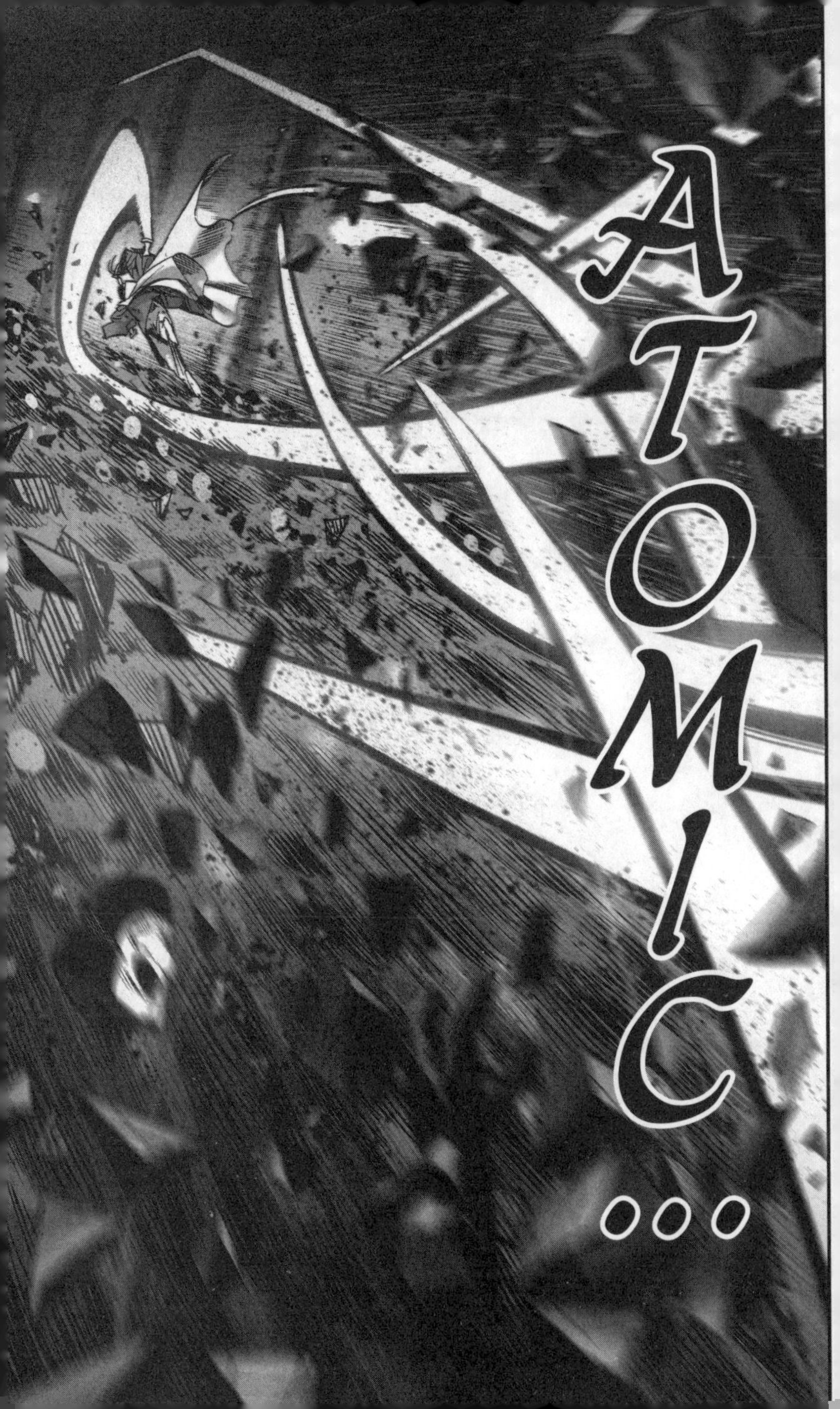
ATOMIC...

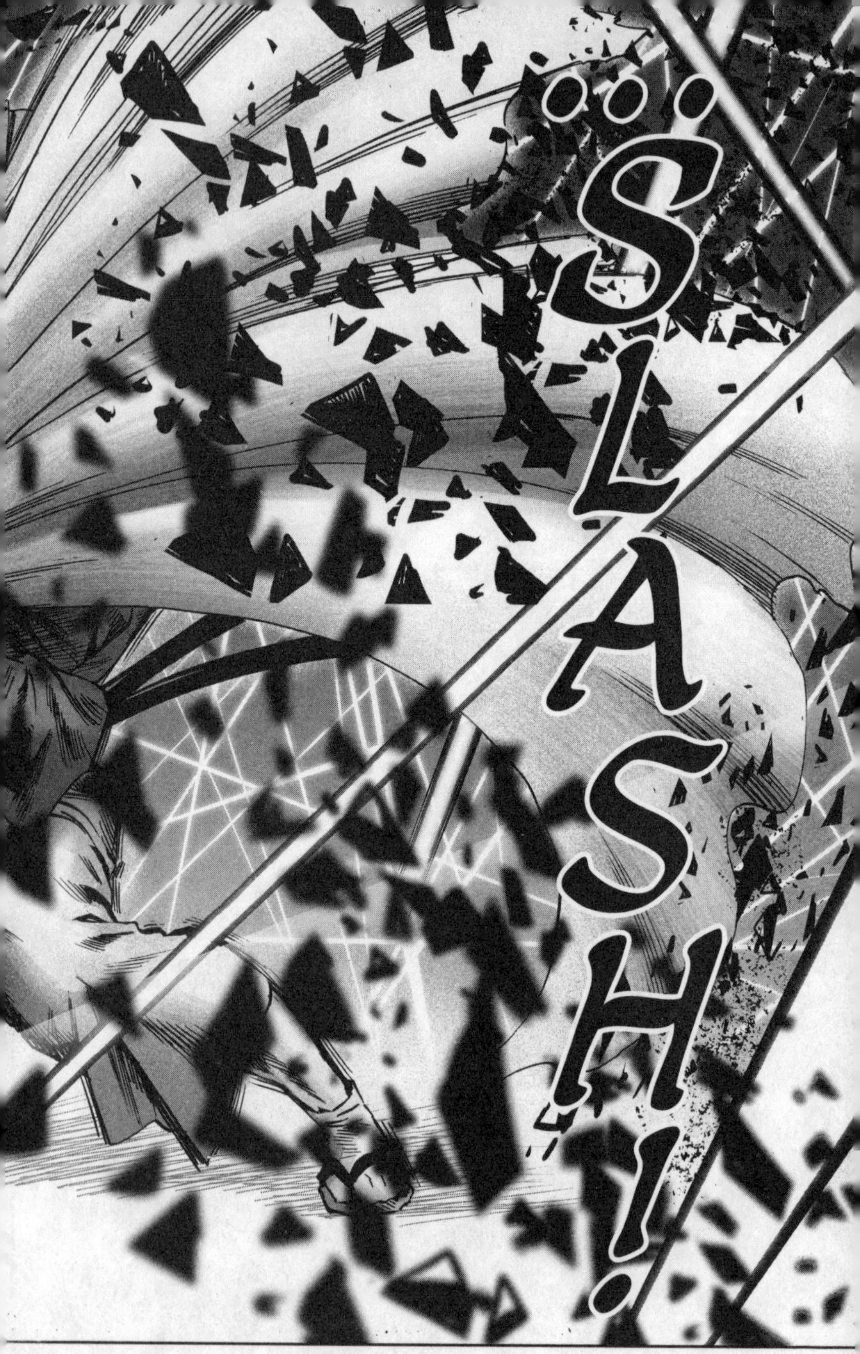
SLASH!

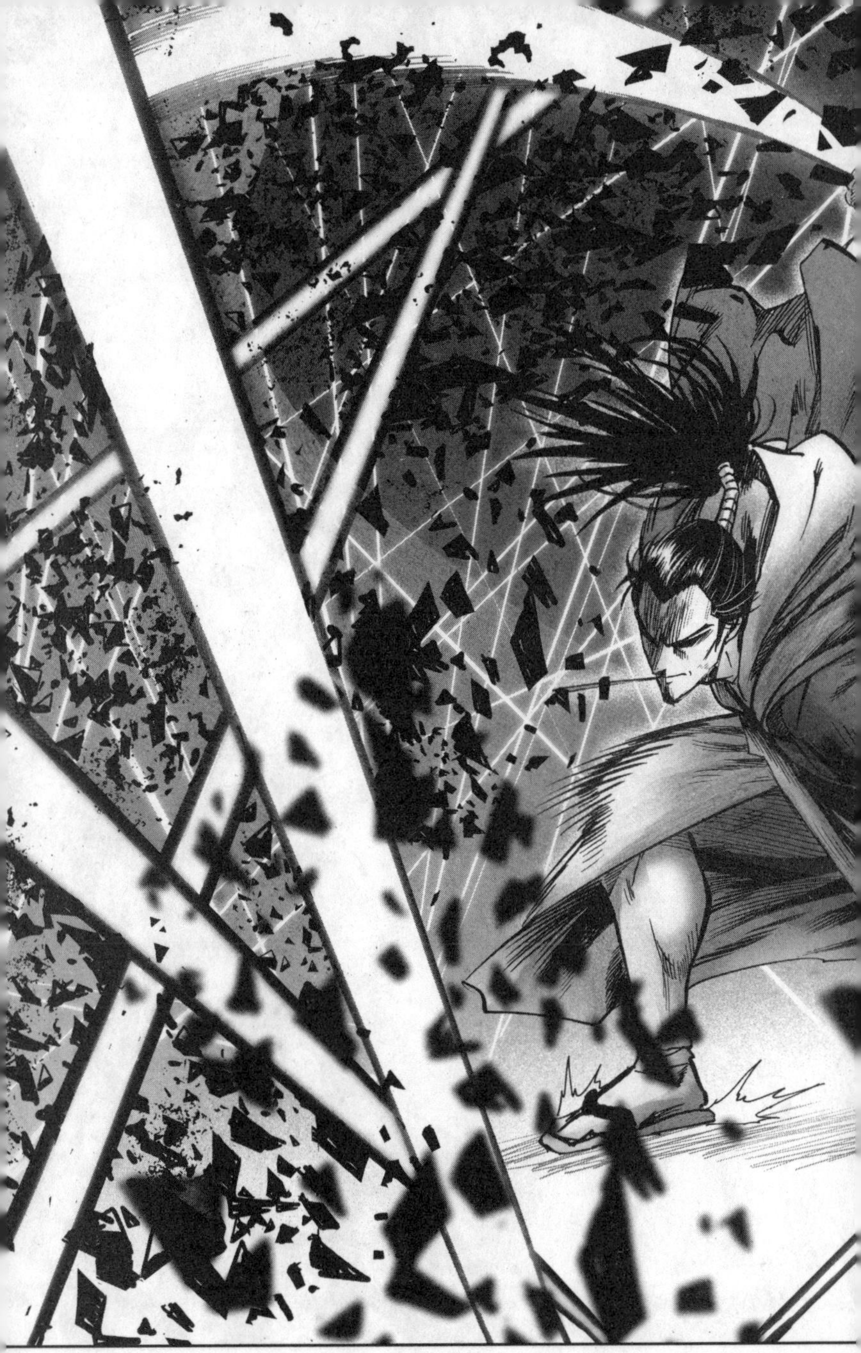

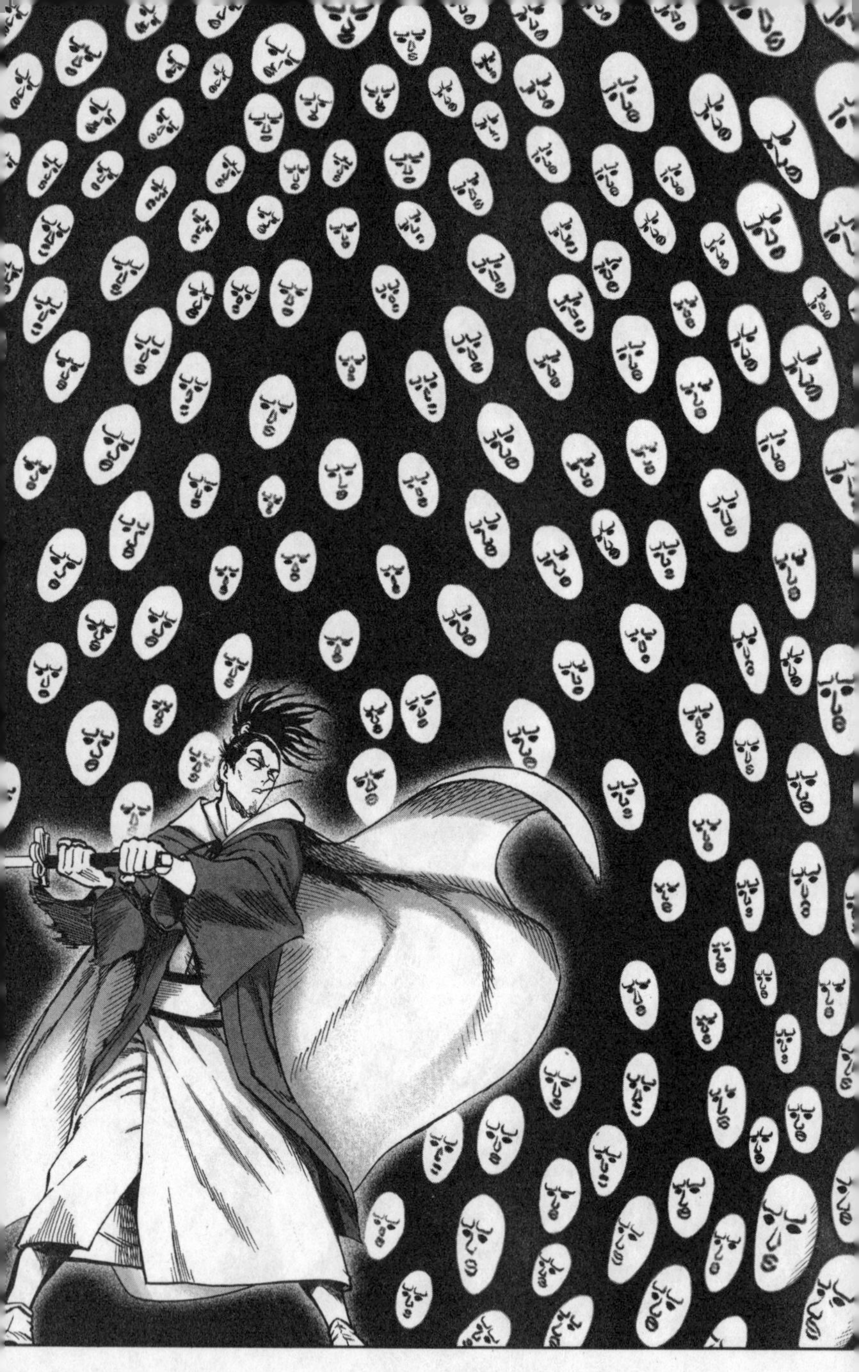

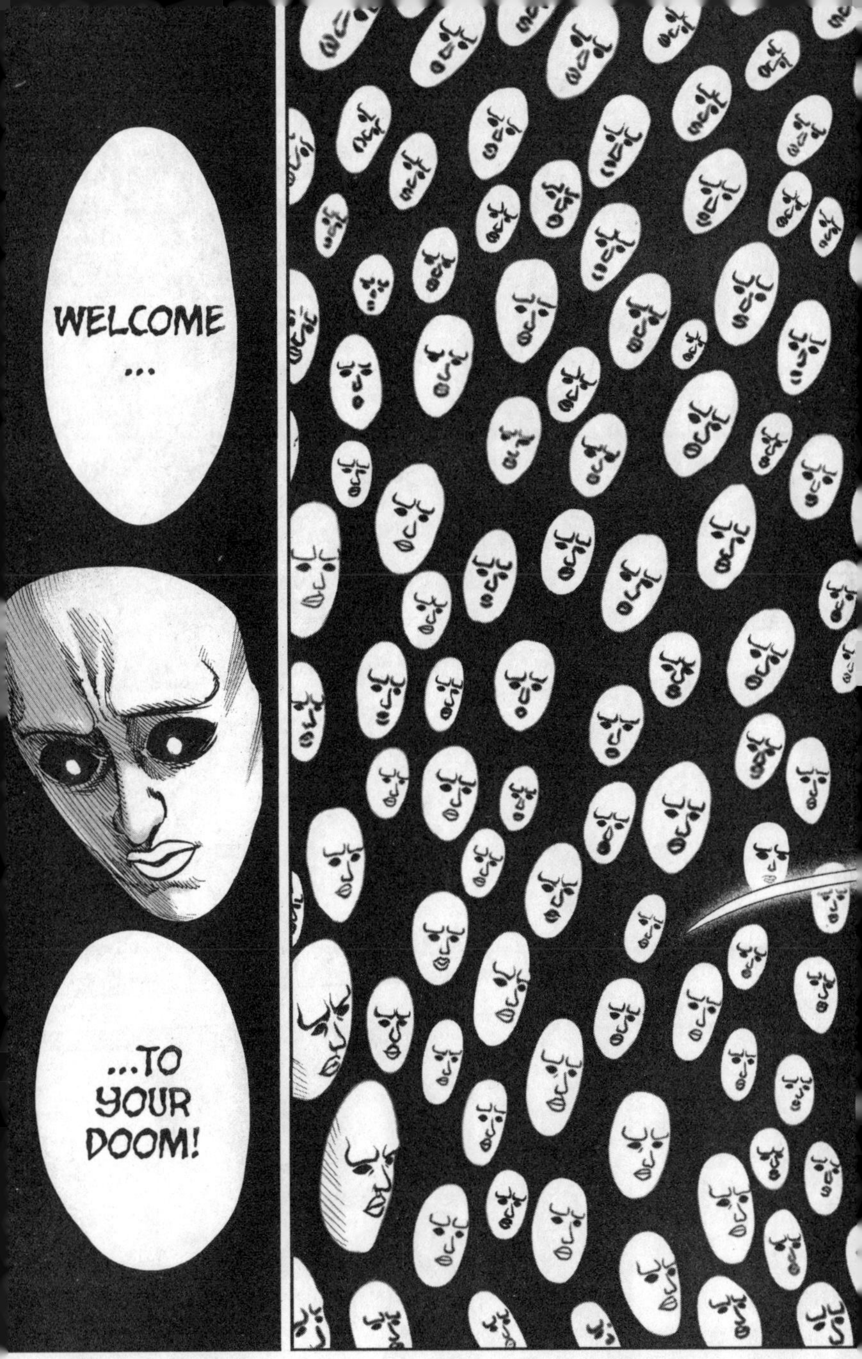
WELCOME ...
...TO YOUR DOOM!

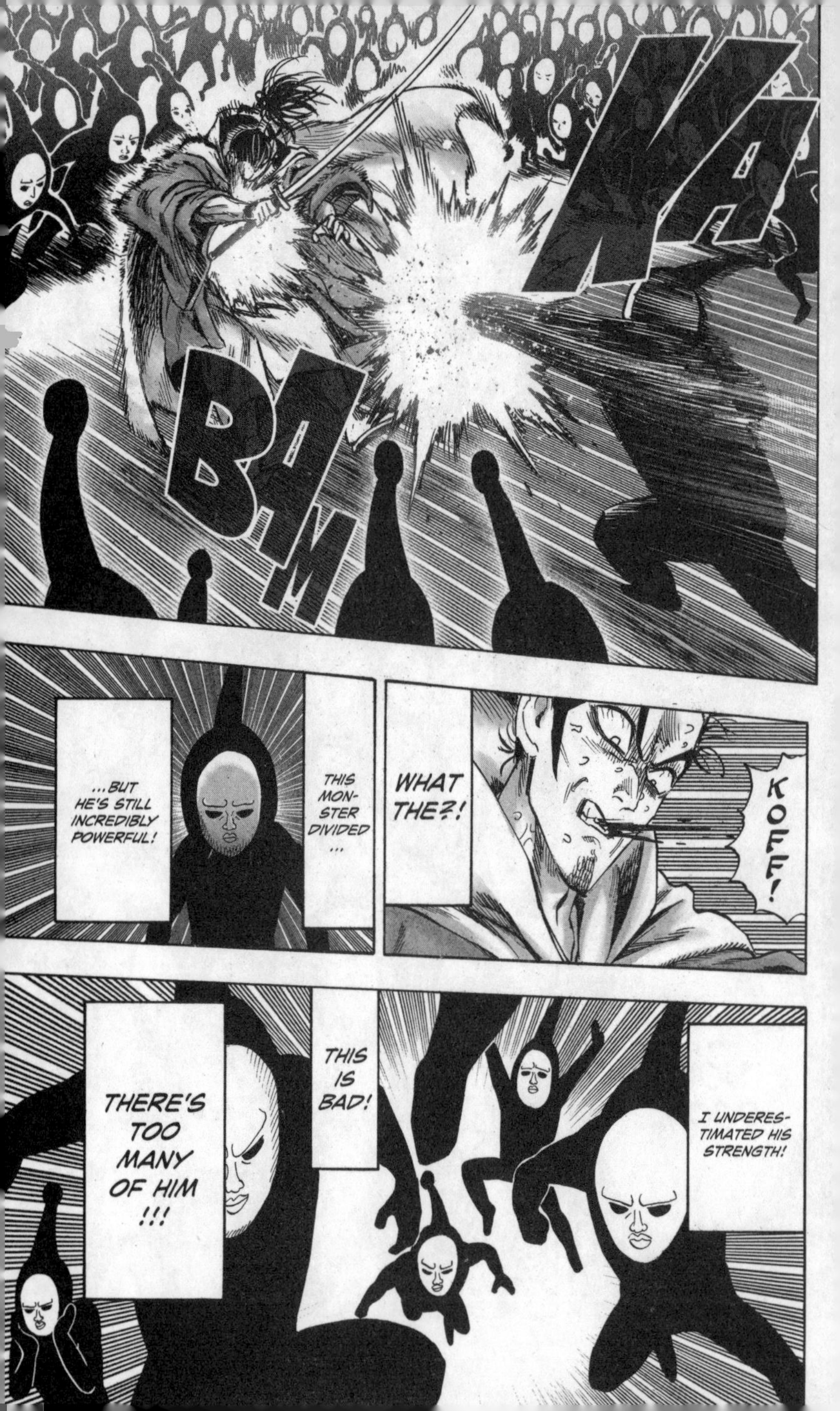
KA
BAM
WHAT THE?!
KOFF!
THIS MONSTER DIVIDED...
...BUT HE'S STILL INCREDIBLY POWERFUL!
I UNDERESTIMATED HIS STRENGTH!
THIS IS BAD!
THERE'S TOO MANY OF HIM!!!

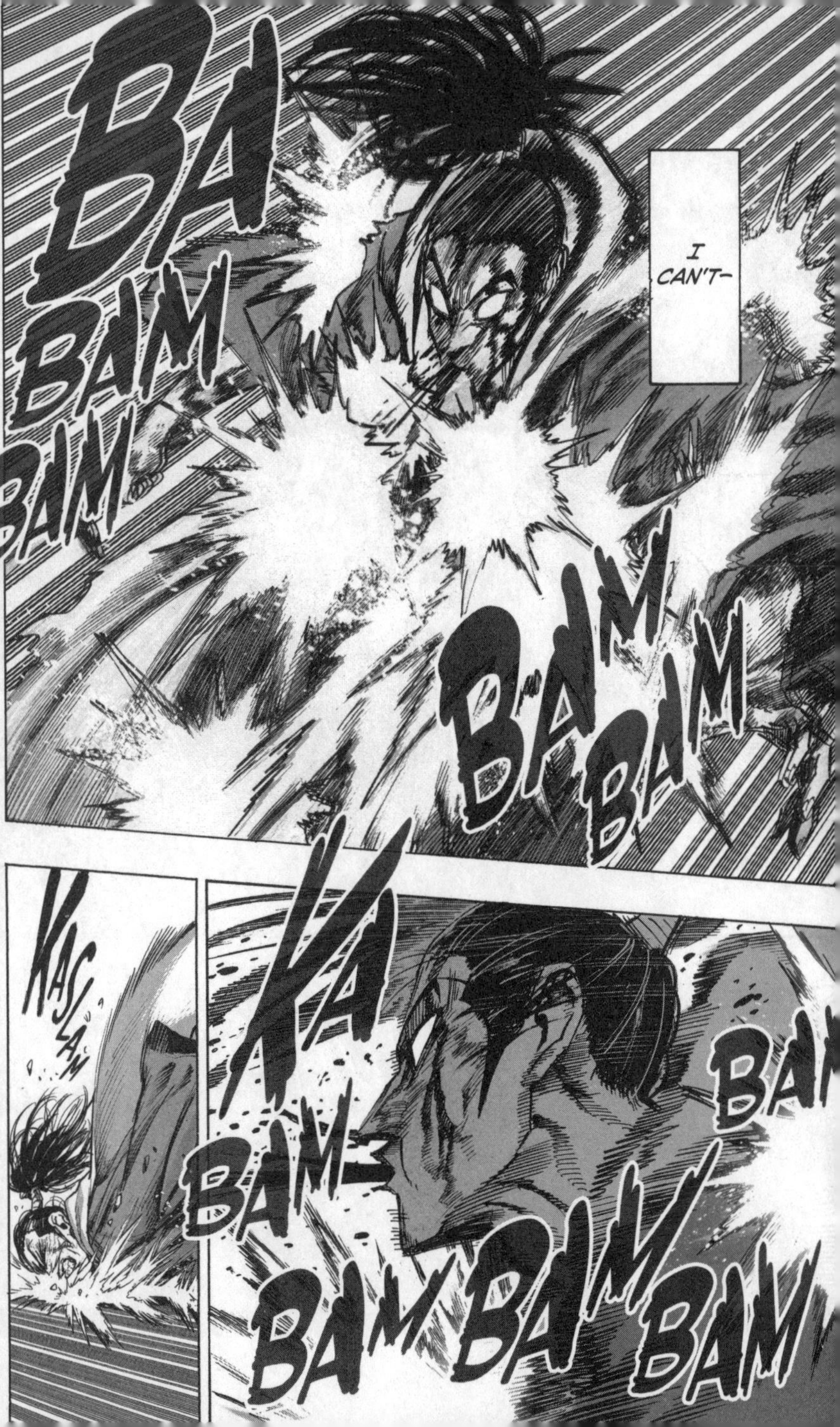
I CAN'T—
BA
BAM
BAM
BAM
BAM
BAM
BAM
KA
BAM
BAM
BAM
BAM
KASLAM

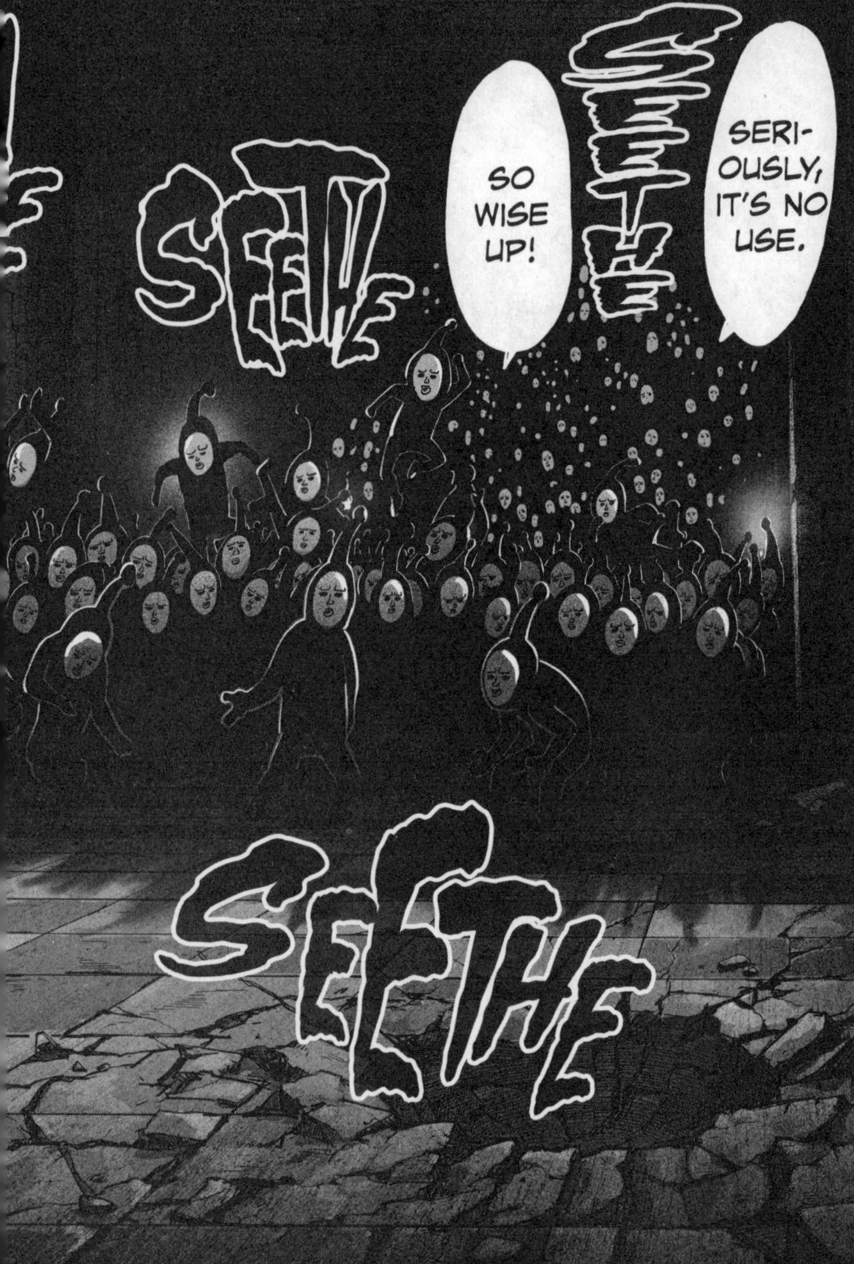
SERI-
OUSLY,
IT'S NO
USE.
SEETHE
SO
WISE
UP!
SEETHE
SEETHE

WE'RE THE WORST TYPE OF OPPONENT FOR YOU!
GYORO-GYORO FIGURED THAT OUT ALREADY!

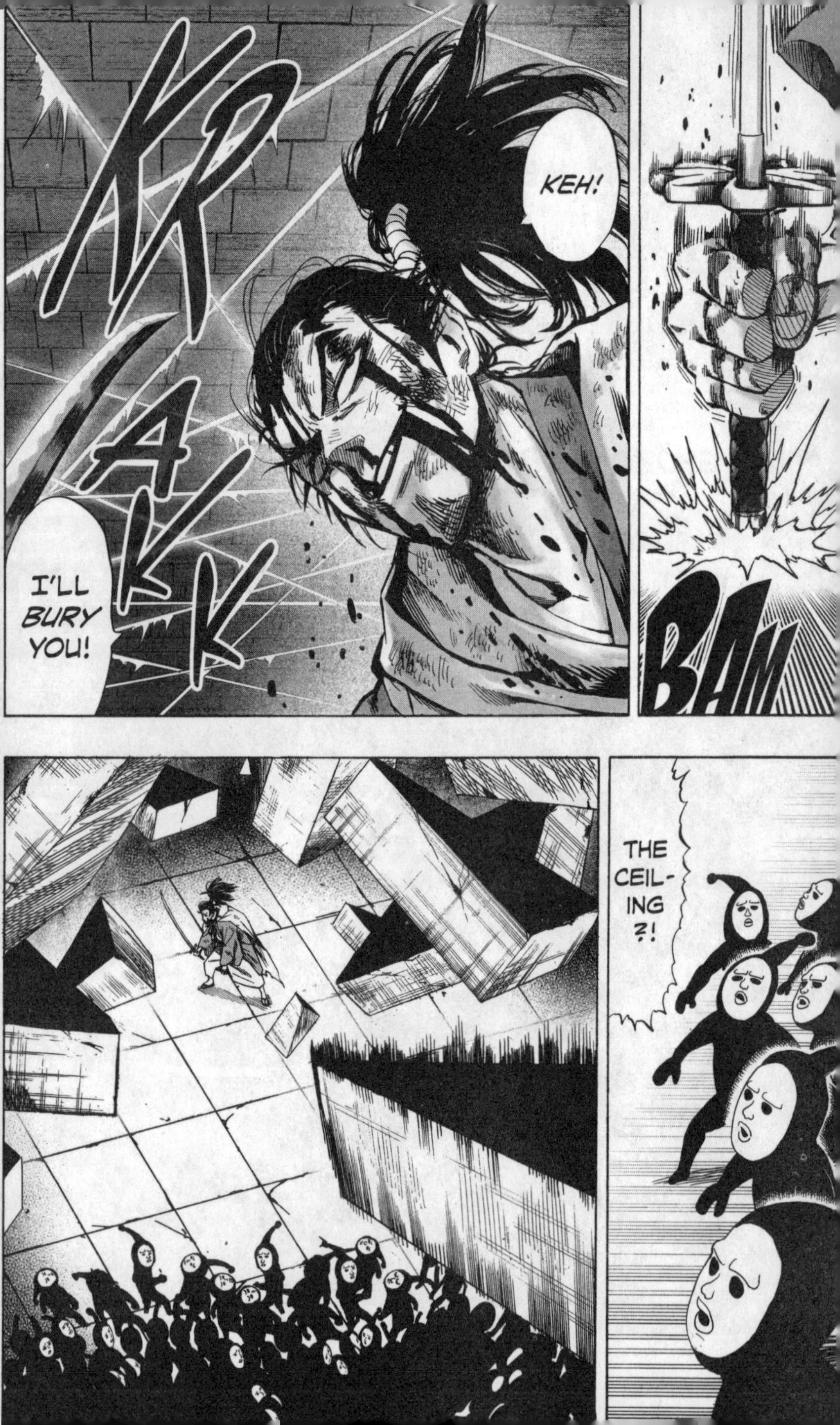
BAM
KEH!
KRAKK
I'LL BURY YOU!
THE CEIL-ING?!

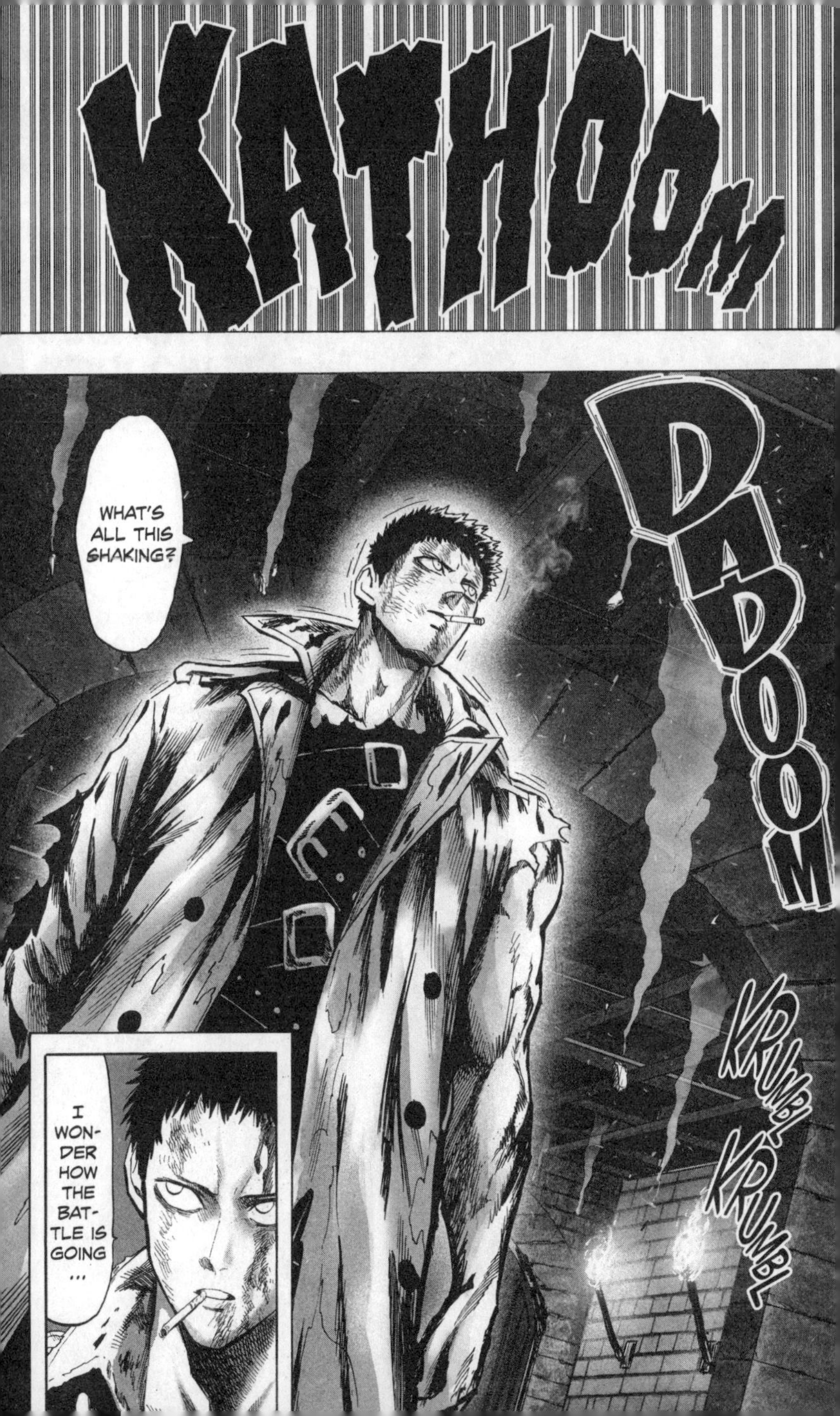
KATHOOM
DADOOM
WHAT'S ALL THIS SHAKING?
KRUMBL KRUMBL
I WONDER HOW THE BATTLE IS GOING...

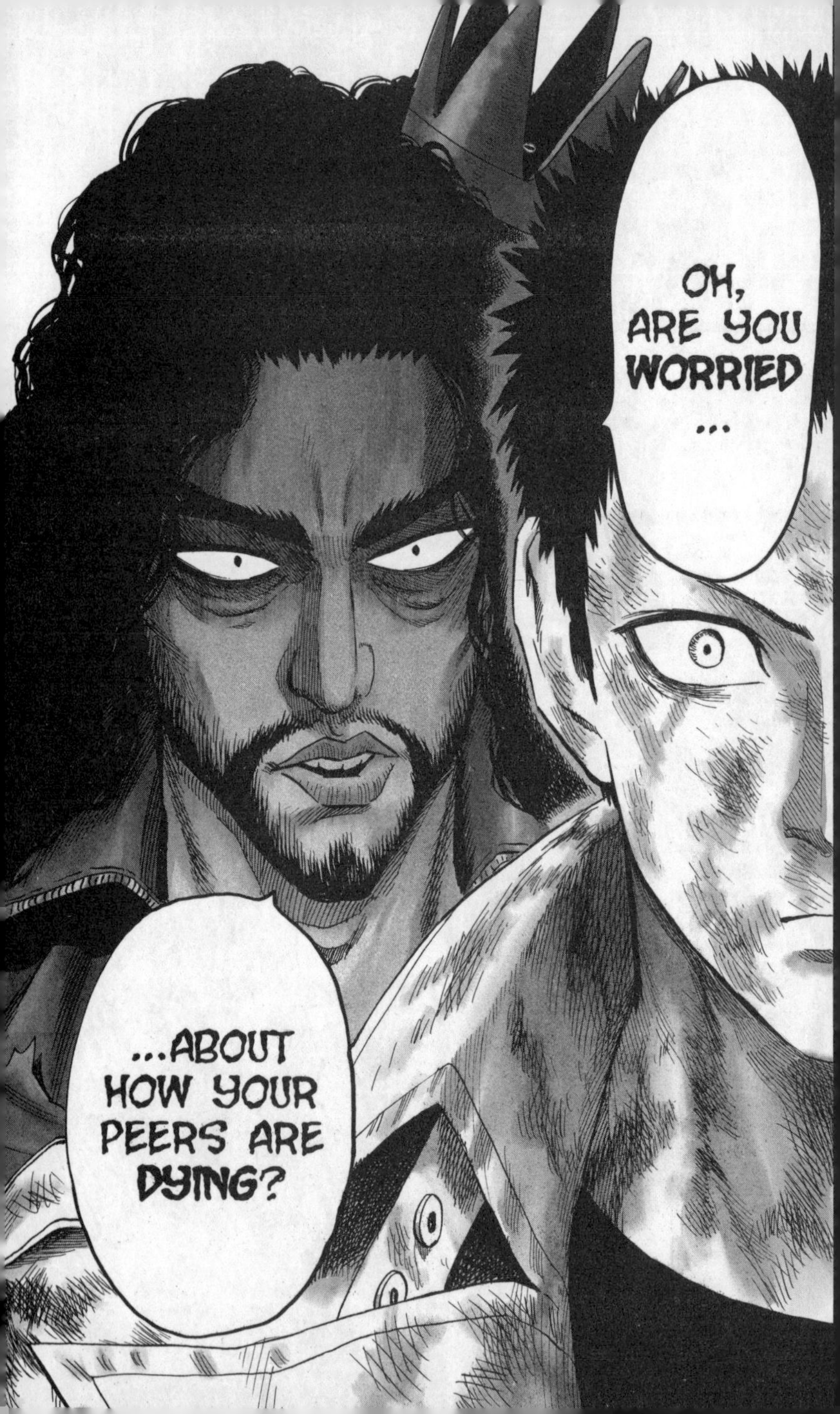
OH, ARE YOU WORRIED ...
...ABOUT HOW YOUR PEERS ARE DYING?

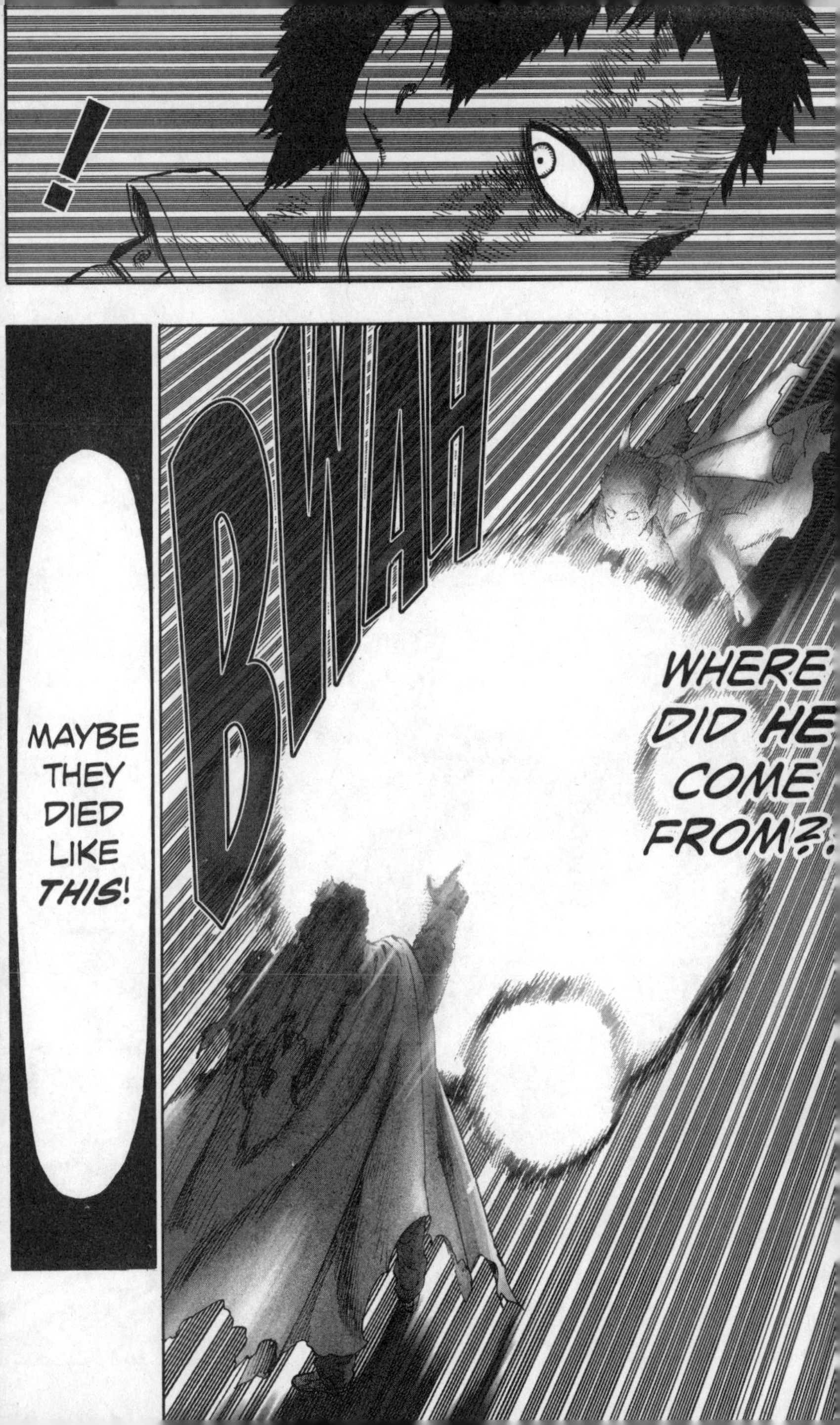
!
WHERE DID HE COME FROM?!
BWAH
MAYBE THEY DIED LIKE *THIS*!

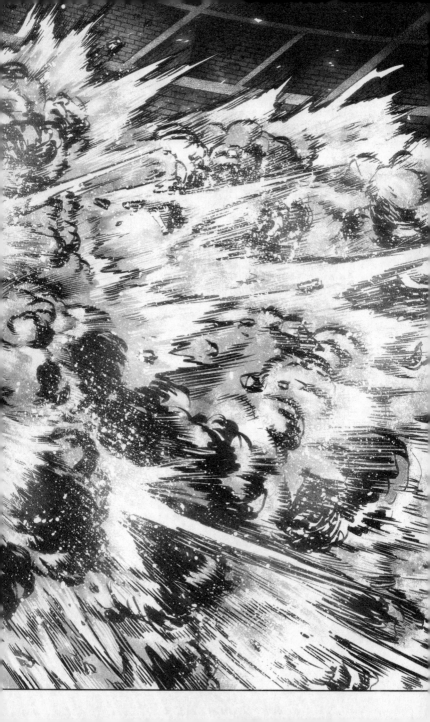

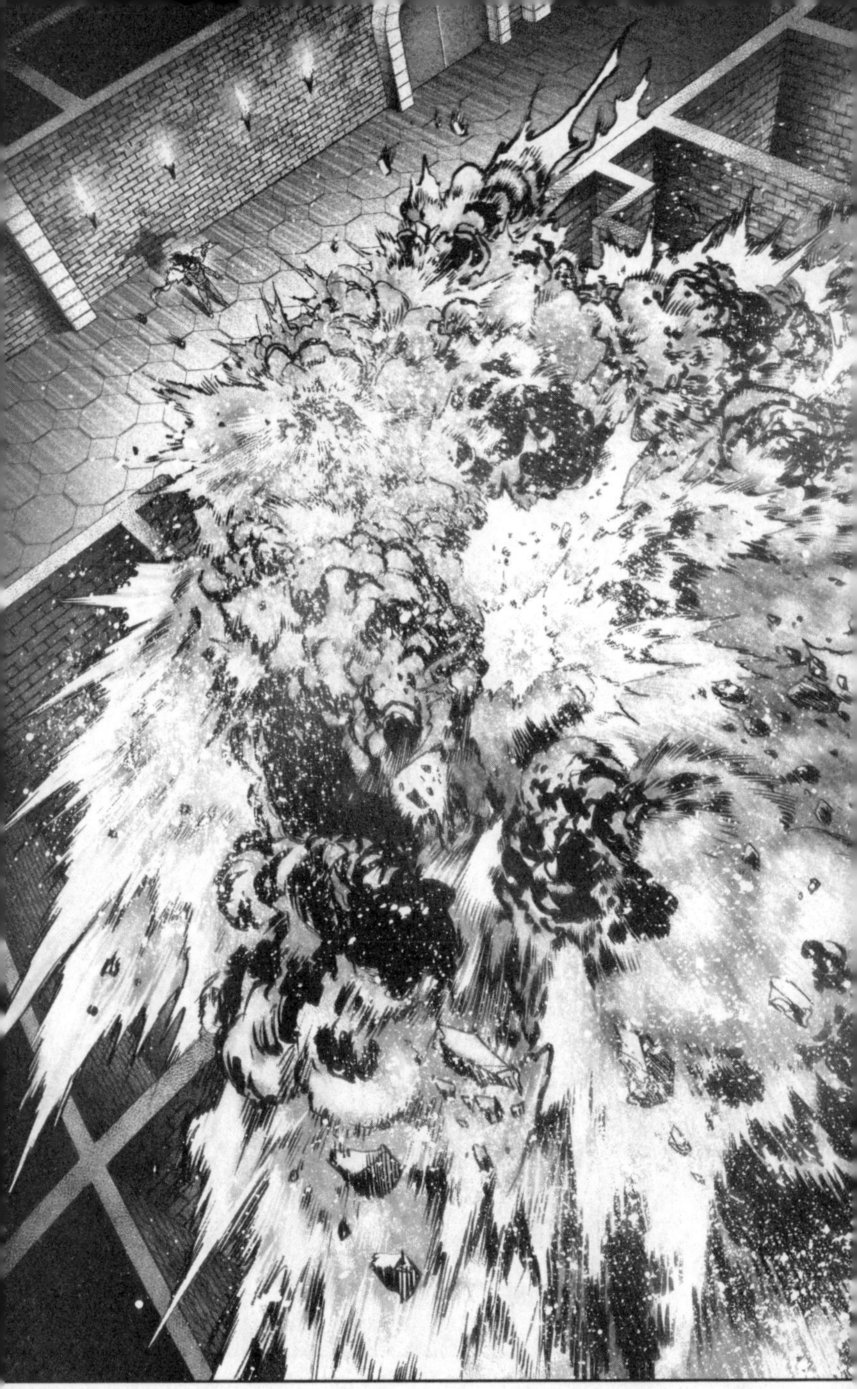

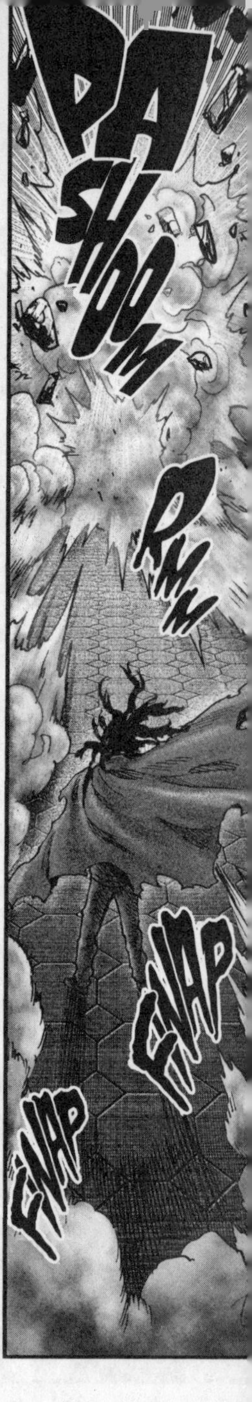
DA
SHOOM
RMMM
FWAP
FWAP
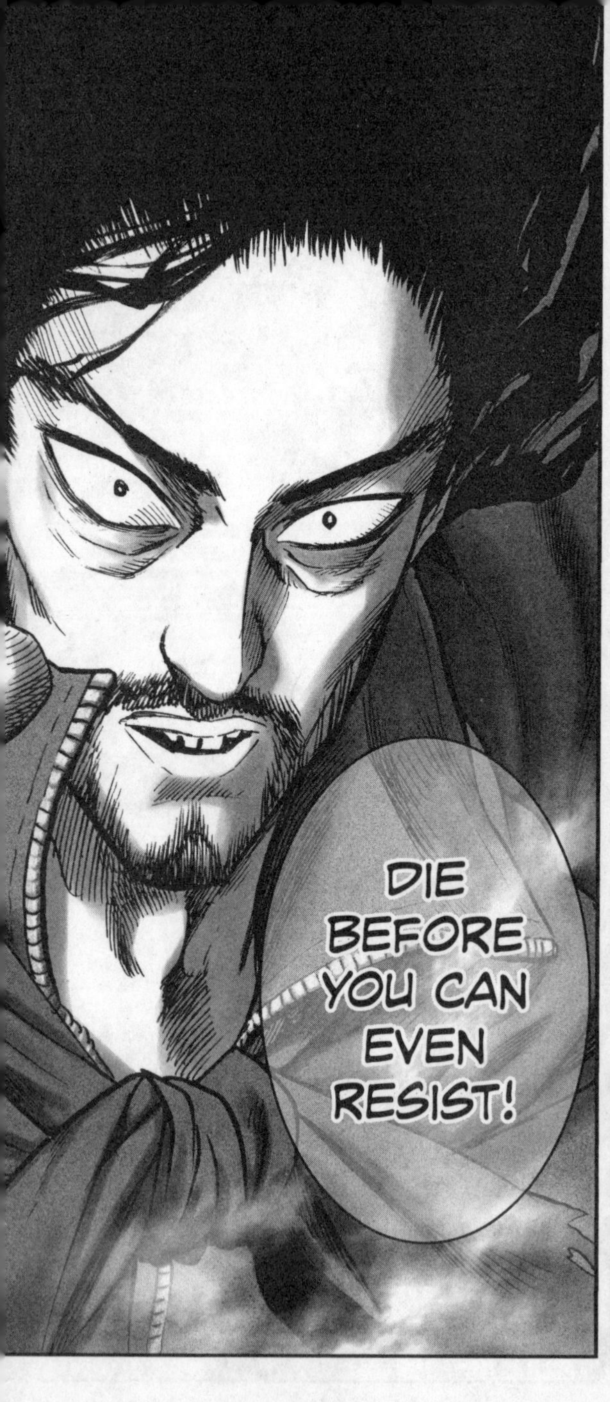
DIE BEFORE YOU CAN EVEN RESIST!

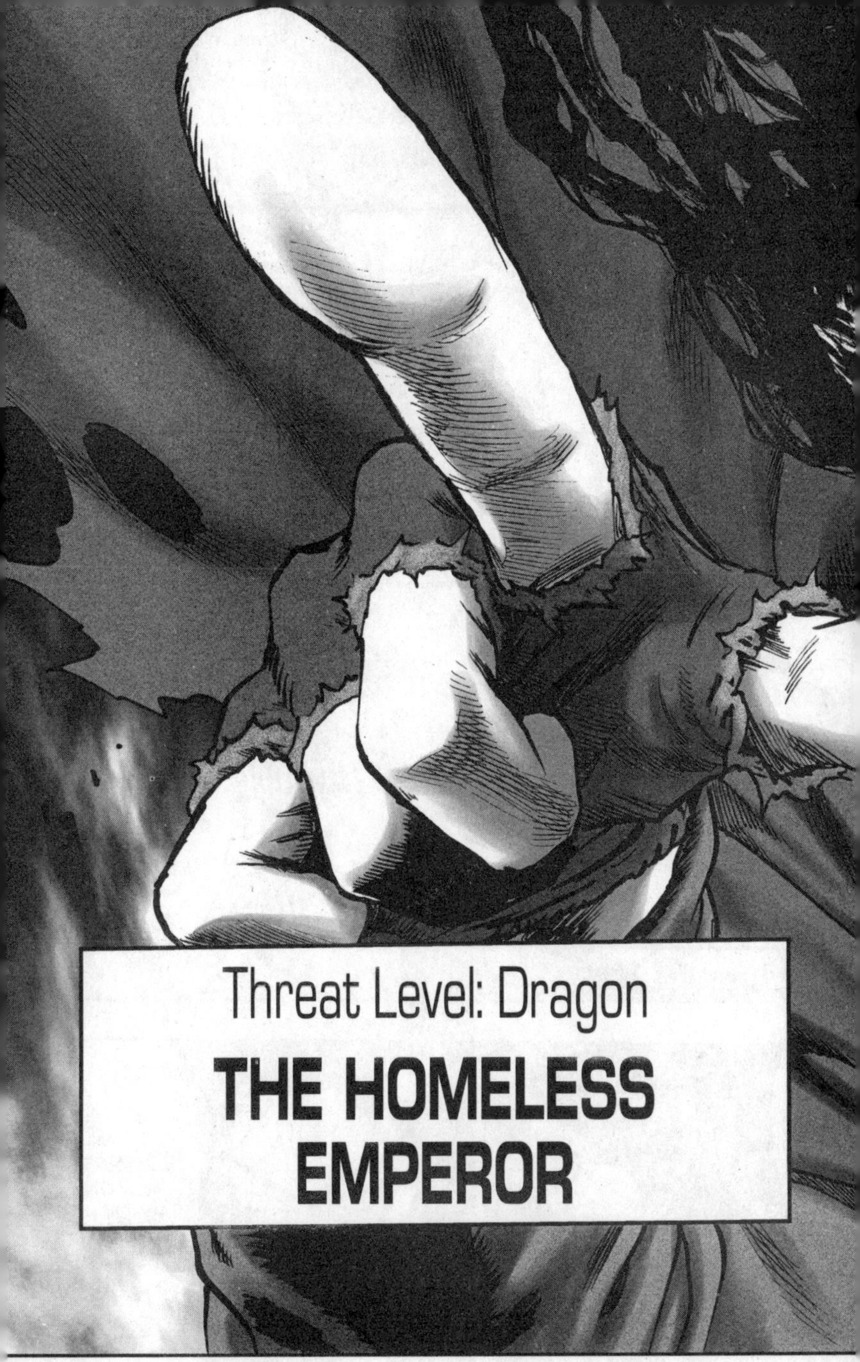
Threat Level: Dragon
THE HOMELESS EMPEROR

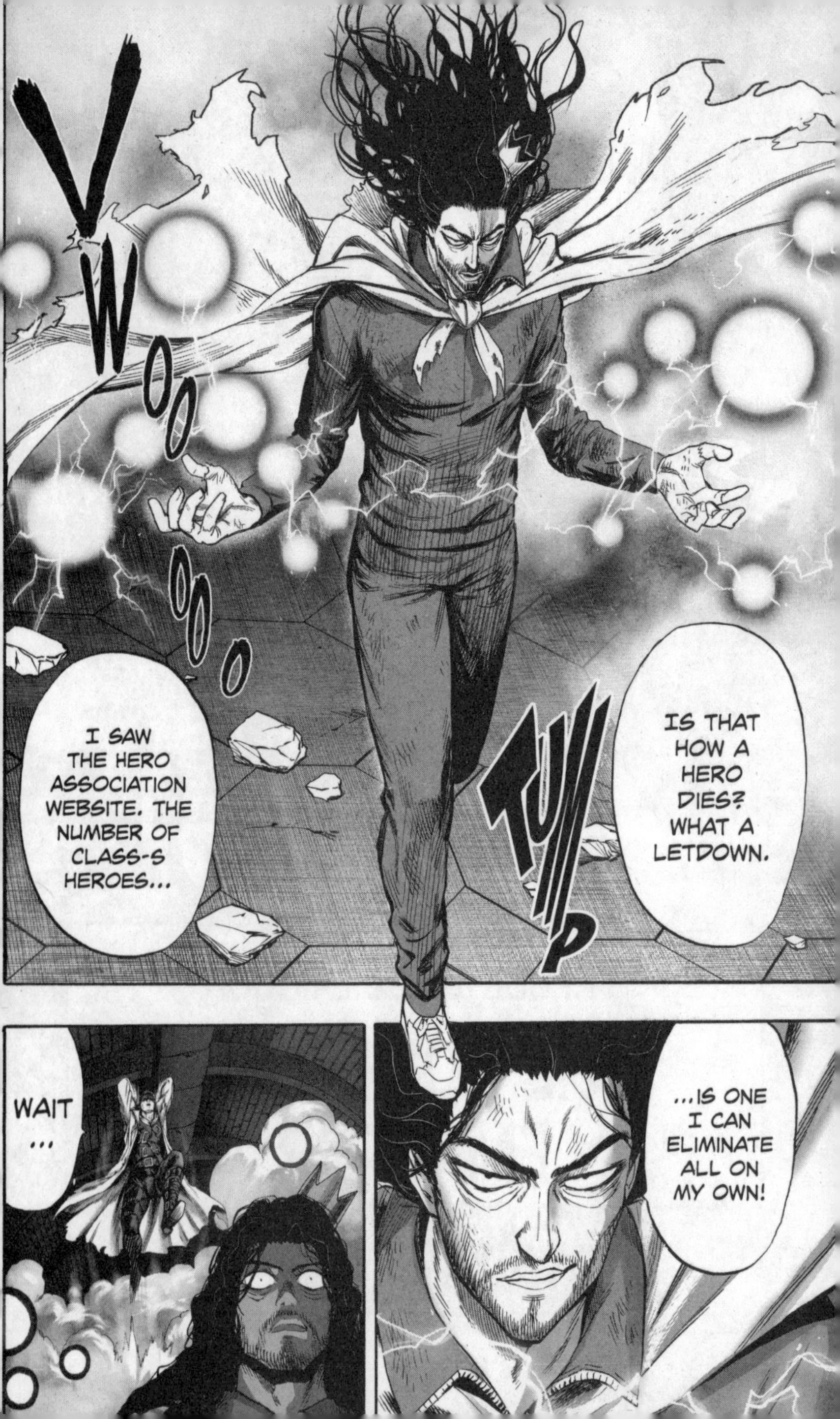
VWOOOOOO
IS THAT HOW A HERO DIES? WHAT A LETDOWN.
TUMP
I SAW THE HERO ASSOCIATION WEBSITE. THE NUMBER OF CLASS-S HEROES...
...IS ONE I CAN ELIMINATE ALL ON MY OWN!
WAIT ...

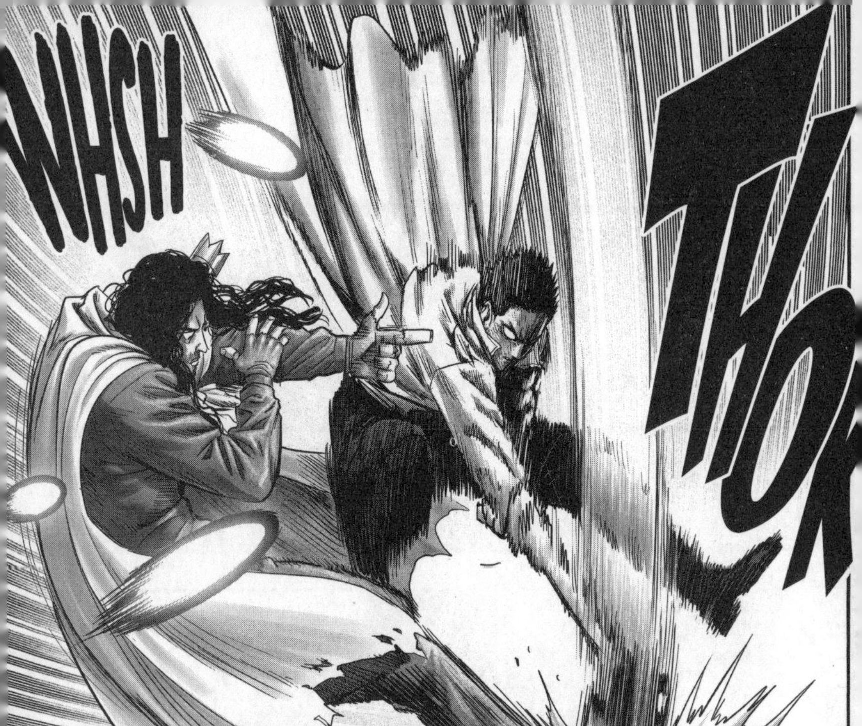
THOK
WHSH
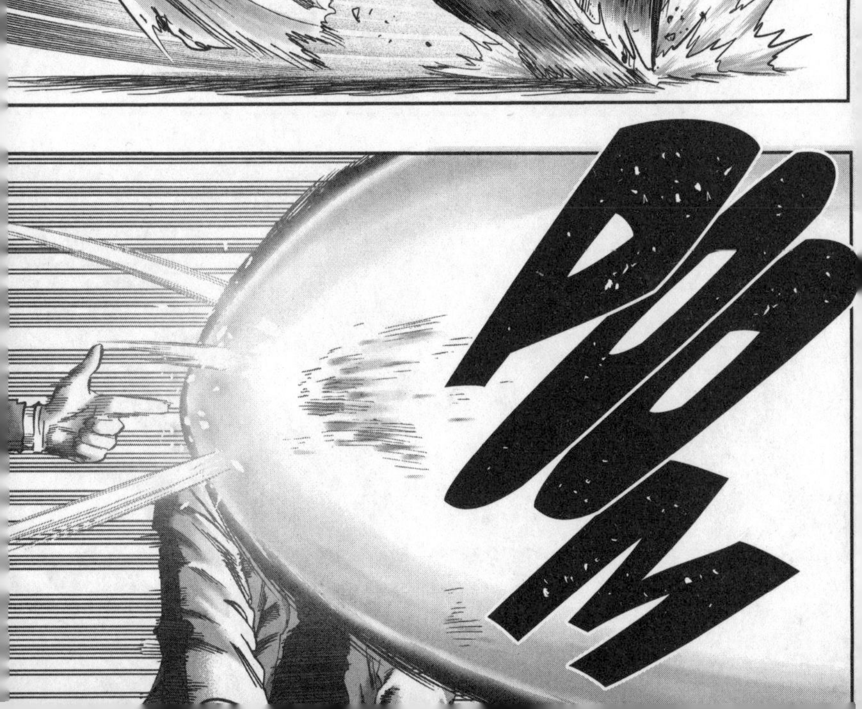

FUMP

!

KLICK

BA DOOM

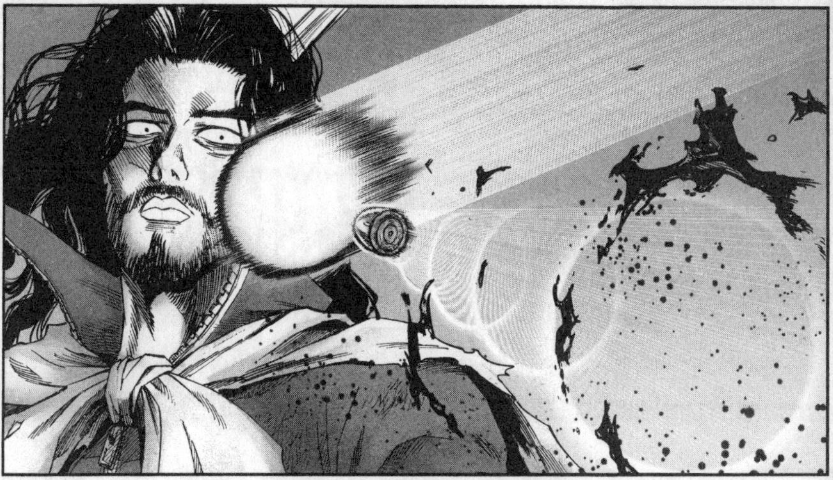

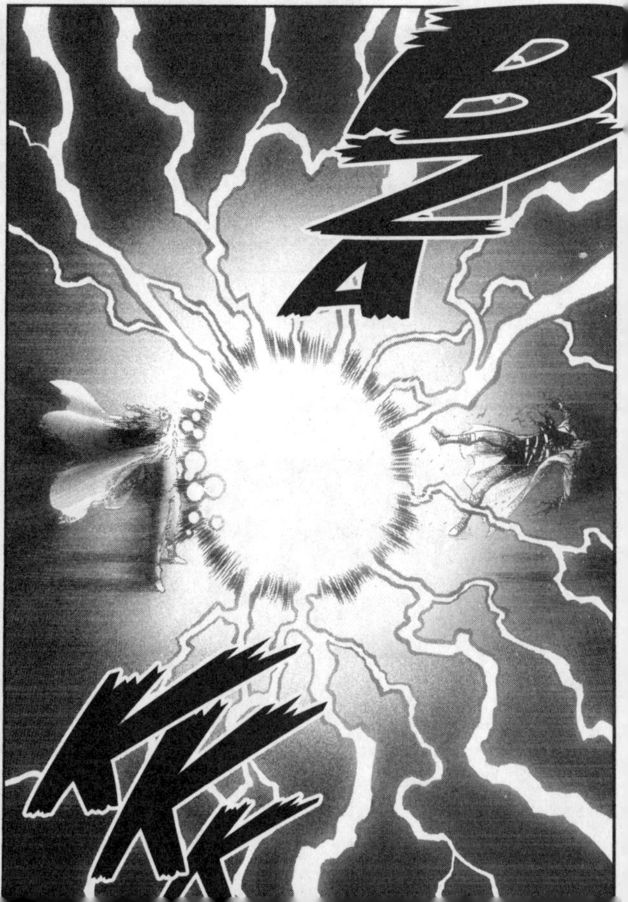
BZA
KKKK

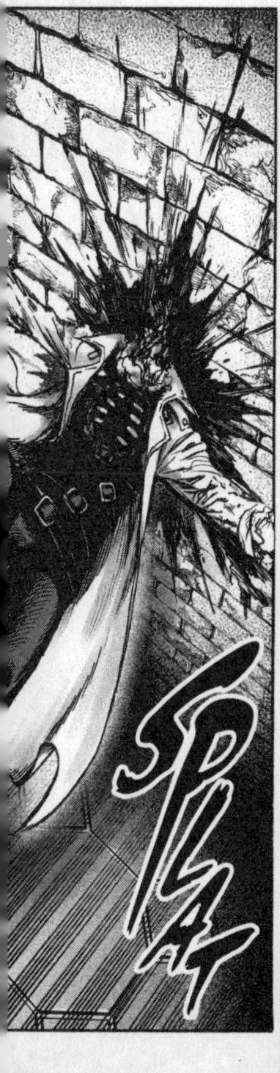
SPLAT

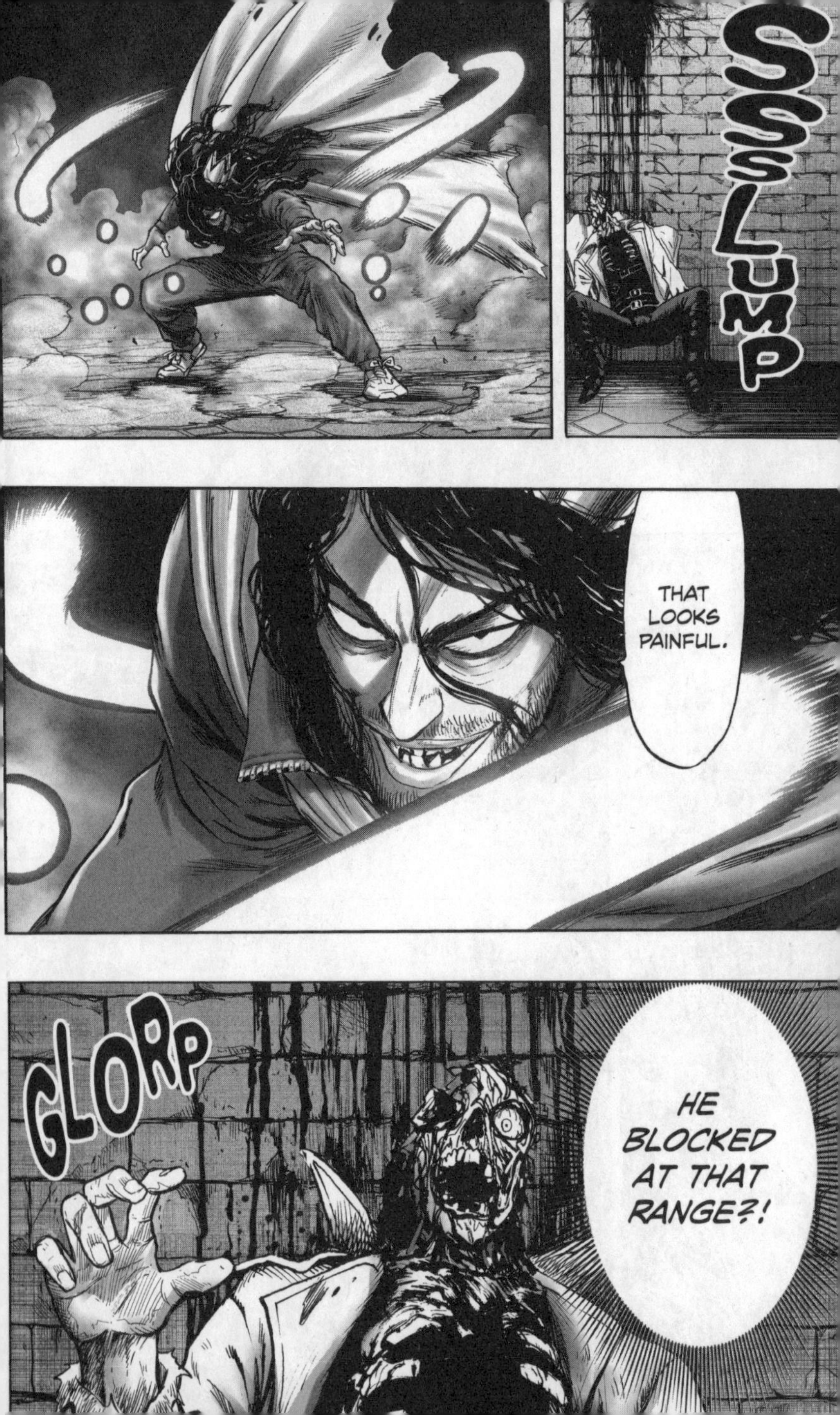
SSSLUMP
THAT LOOKS PAINFUL.
HE BLOCKED AT THAT RANGE?!
GLORP

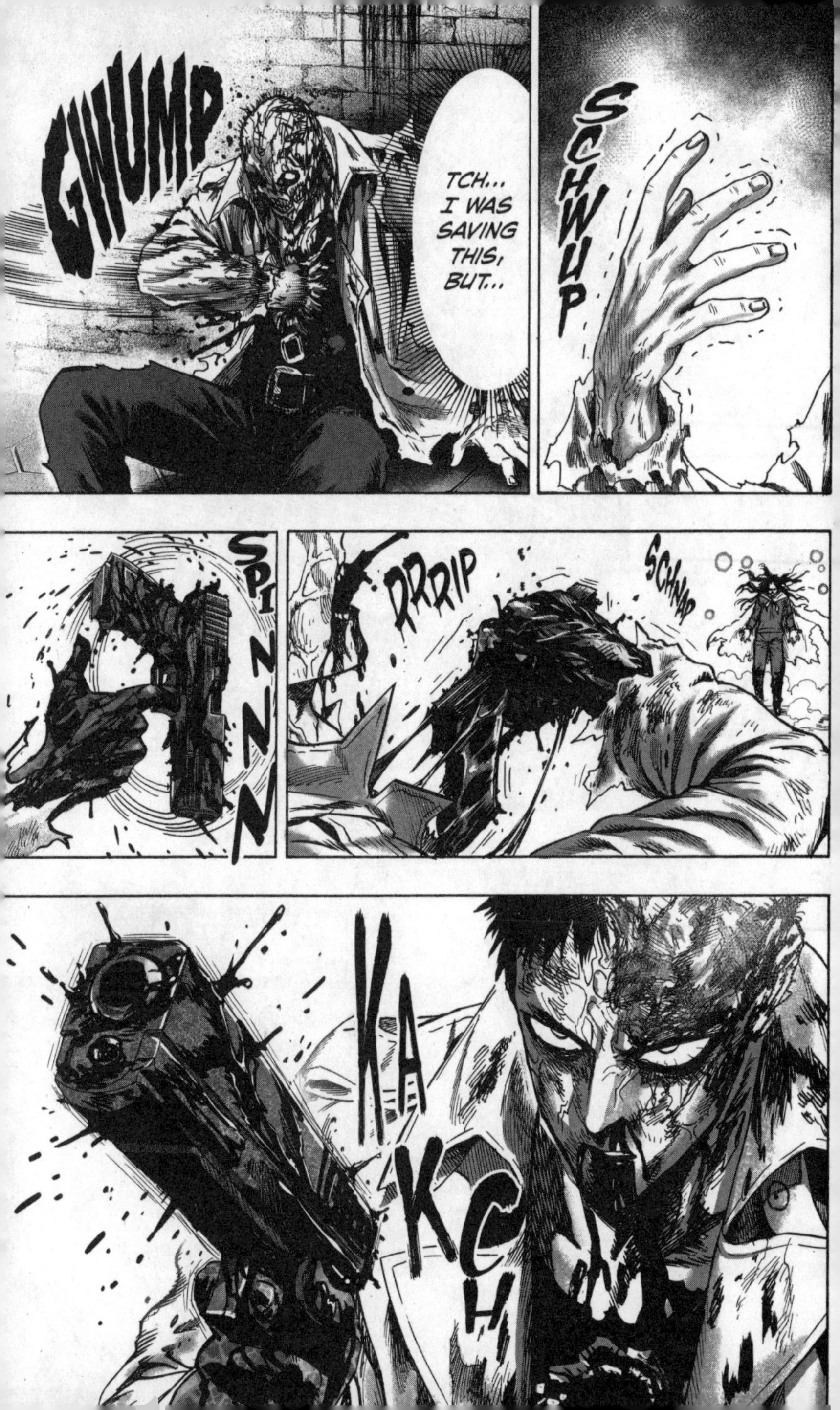
SCHWUP
TCH... I WAS SAVING THIS, BUT...
GWUMP
SCHNAP
DRRIP
SPINNNN
KAKCH

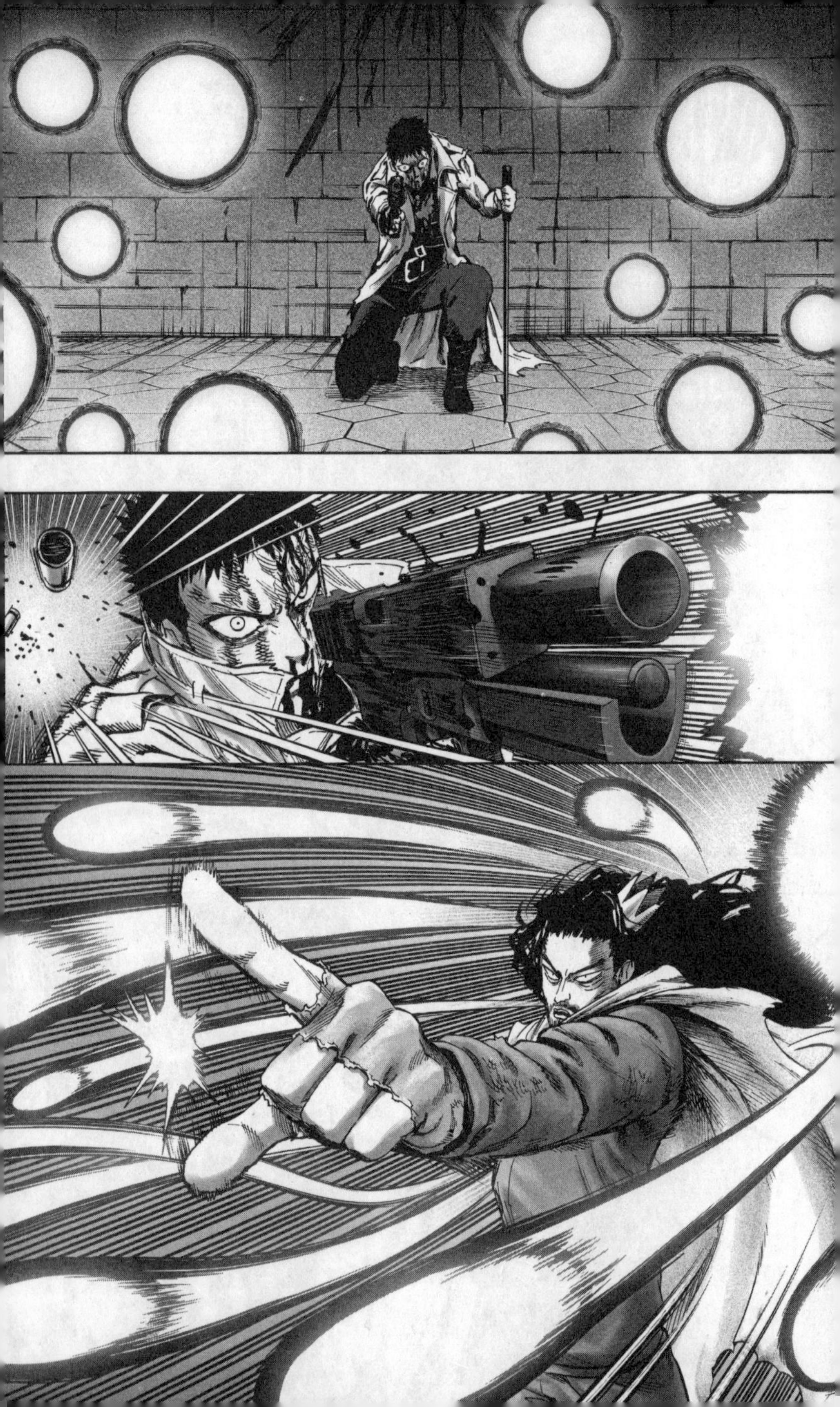

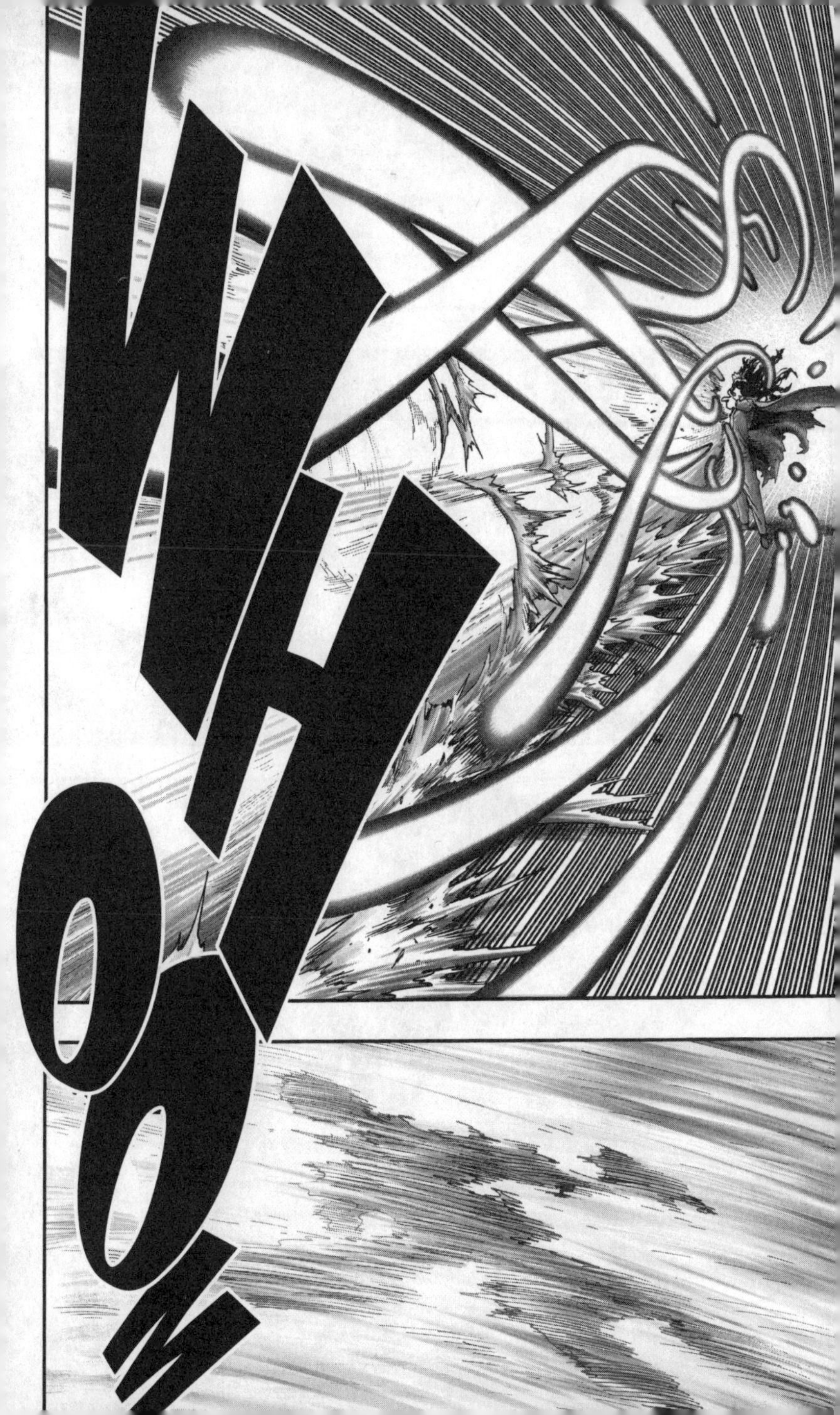
WHOOM

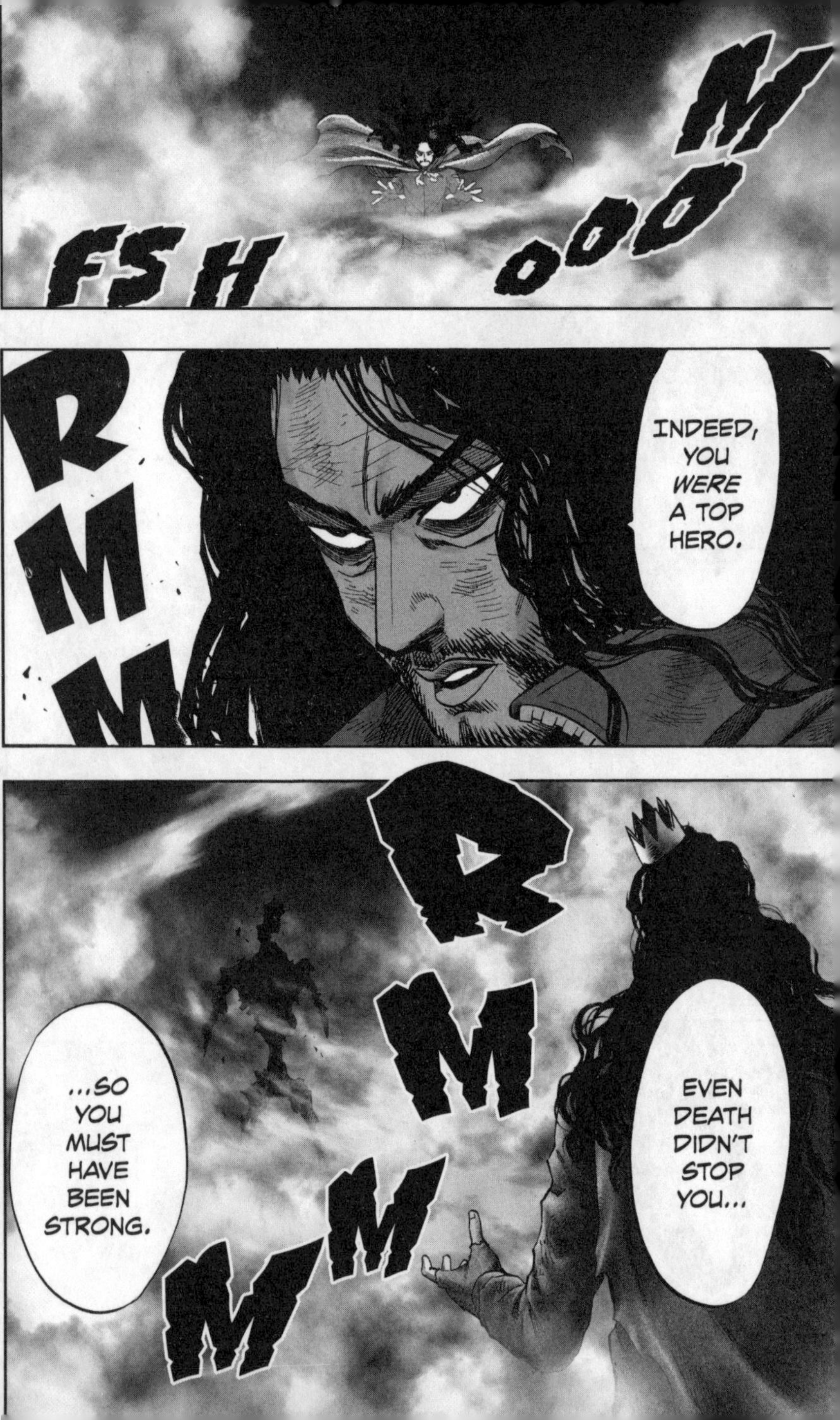
FSHOOOOM
INDEED, YOU WERE A TOP HERO.
RMMM
EVEN DEATH DIDN'T STOP YOU...
...SO YOU MUST HAVE BEEN STRONG.
RMMM

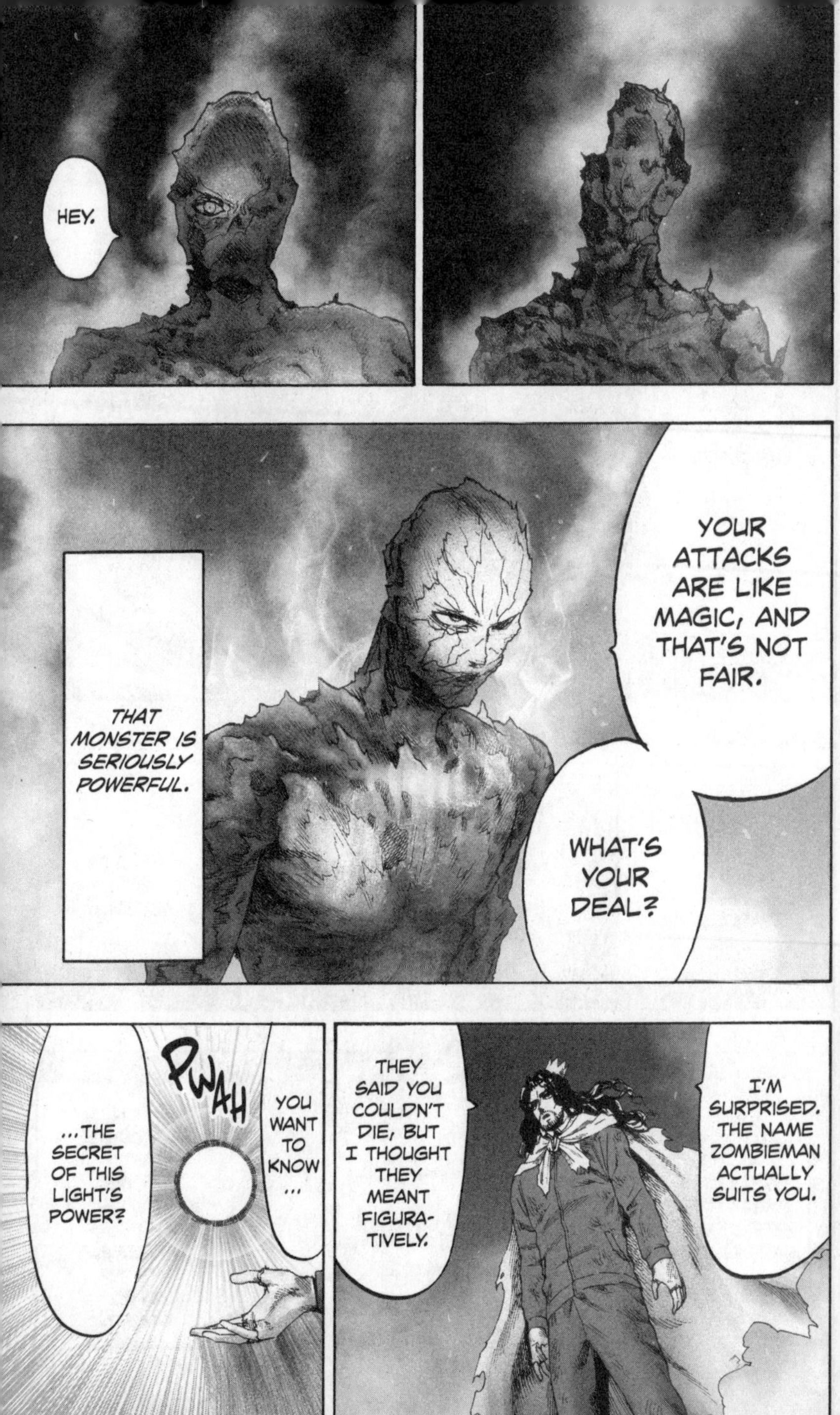
HEY.
YOUR ATTACKS ARE LIKE MAGIC, AND THAT'S NOT FAIR.
WHAT'S YOUR DEAL?
THAT MONSTER IS SERIOUSLY POWERFUL.
I'M SURPRISED. THE NAME ZOMBIEMAN ACTUALLY SUITS YOU.
THEY SAID YOU COULDN'T DIE, BUT I THOUGHT THEY MEANT FIGURATIVELY.
YOU WANT TO KNOW...
PWAH
...THE SECRET OF THIS LIGHT'S POWER?

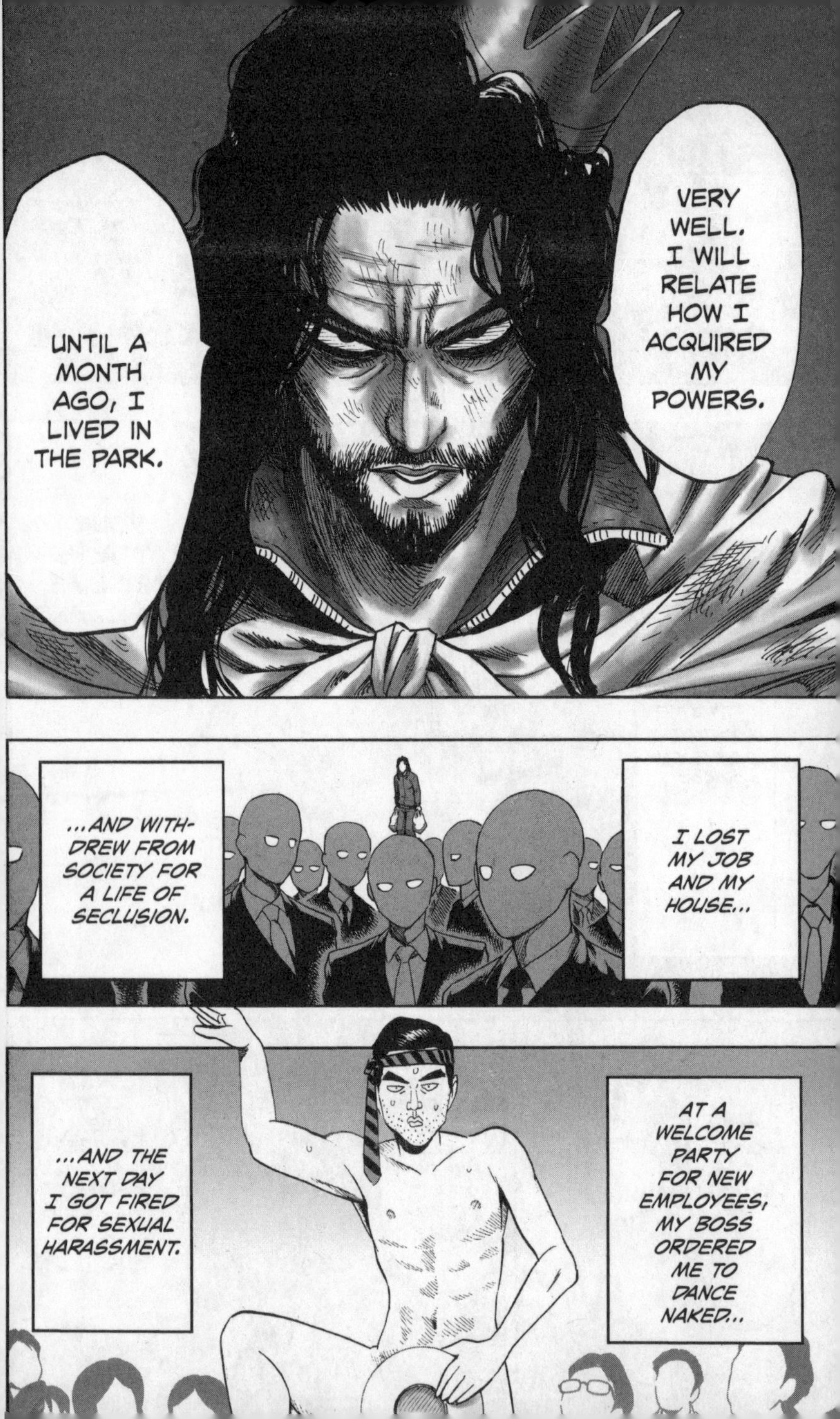
VERY WELL. I WILL RELATE HOW I ACQUIRED MY POWERS.
UNTIL A MONTH AGO, I LIVED IN THE PARK.
I LOST MY JOB AND MY HOUSE...
...AND WITH-DREW FROM SOCIETY FOR A LIFE OF SECLUSION.
AT A WELCOME PARTY FOR NEW EMPLOYEES, MY BOSS ORDERED ME TO DANCE NAKED...
...AND THE NEXT DAY I GOT FIRED FOR SEXUAL HARASSMENT.

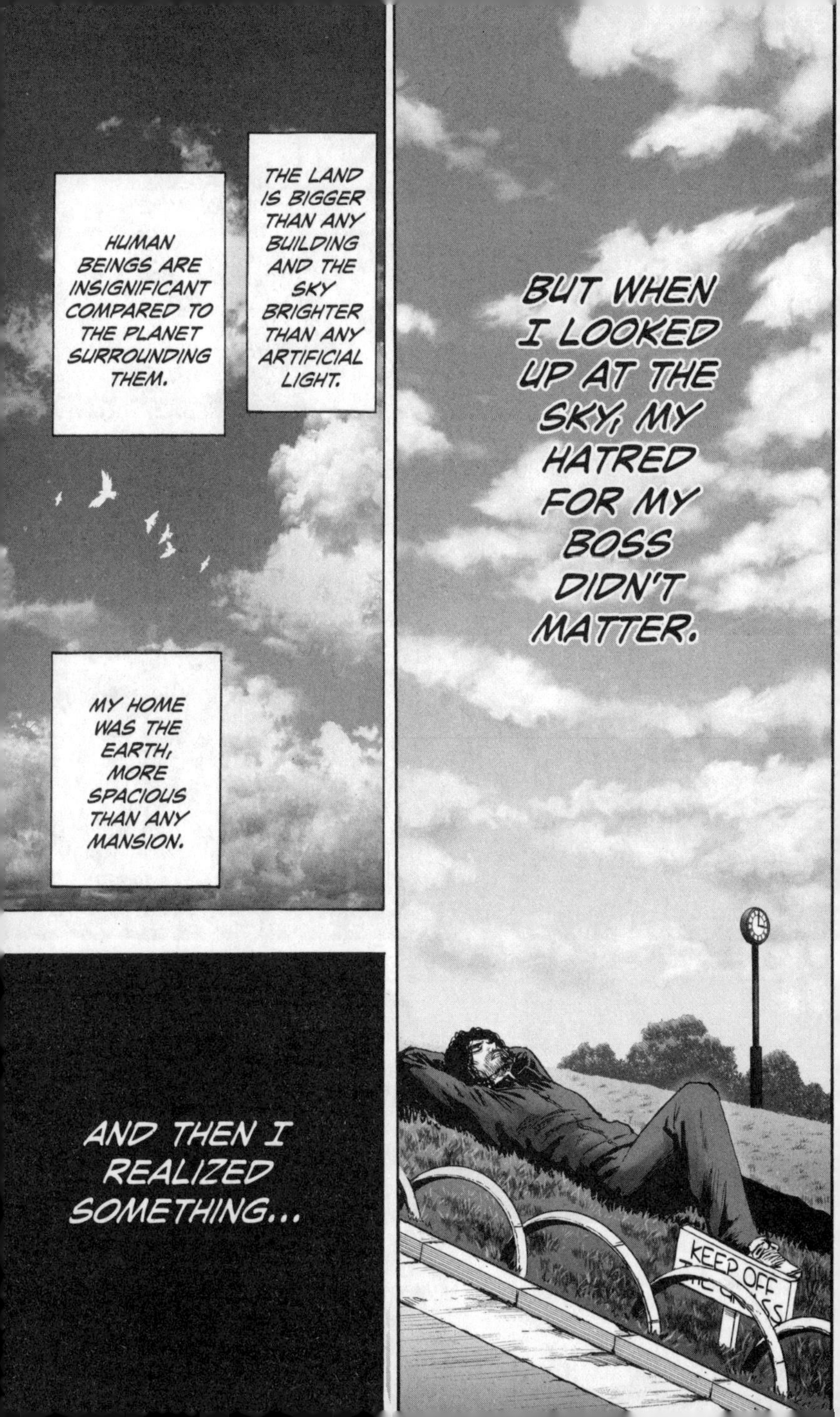
BUT WHEN I LOOKED UP AT THE SKY, MY HATRED FOR MY BOSS DIDN'T MATTER.
KEEP OFF
THE LAND IS BIGGER THAN ANY BUILDING AND THE SKY BRIGHTER THAN ANY ARTIFICIAL LIGHT.
HUMAN BEINGS ARE INSIGNIFICANT COMPARED TO THE PLANET SURROUNDING THEM.
MY HOME WAS THE EARTH, MORE SPACIOUS THAN ANY MANSION.
AND THEN I REALIZED SOMETHING...

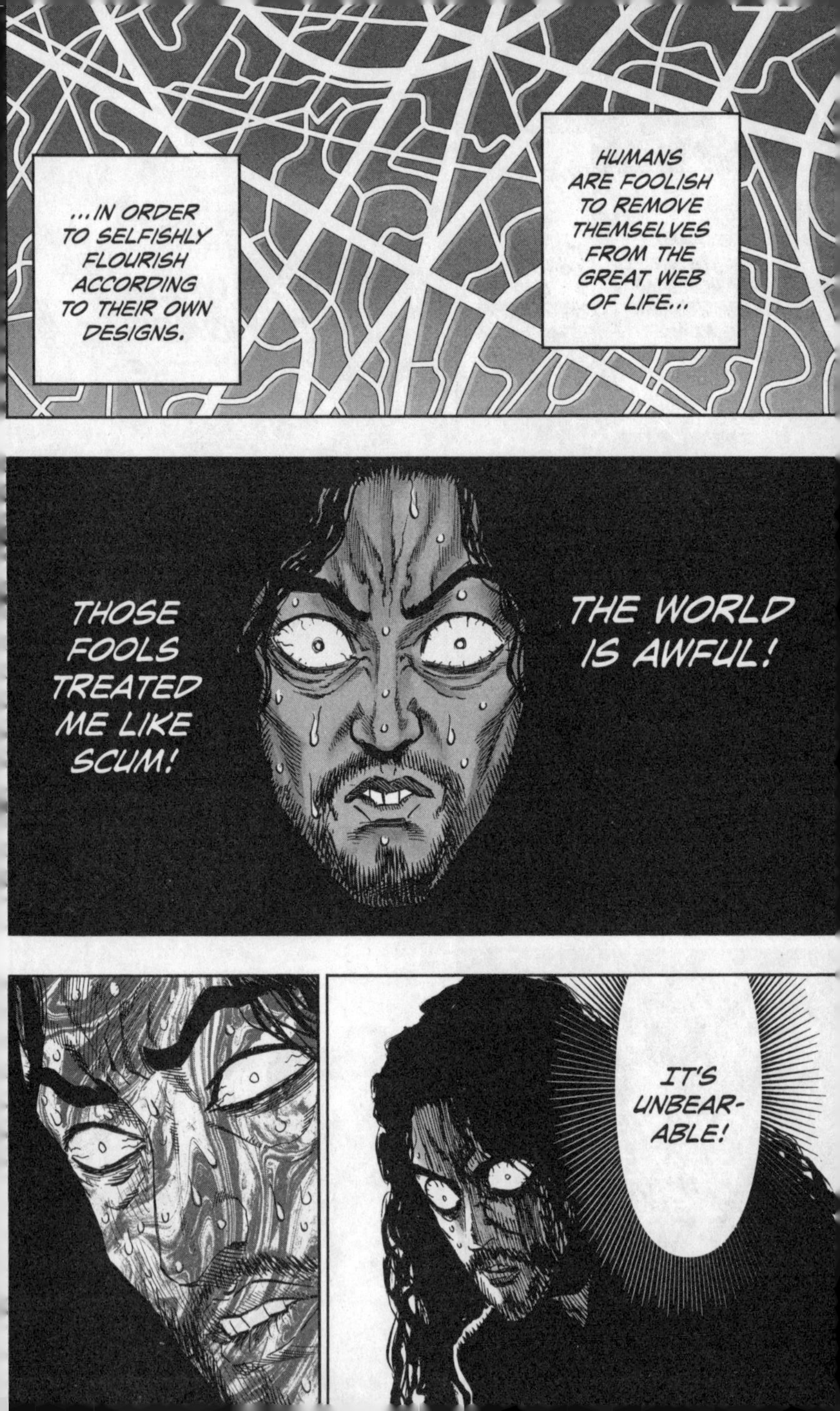
HUMANS ARE FOOLISH TO REMOVE THEMSELVES FROM THE GREAT WEB OF LIFE...
...IN ORDER TO SELFISHLY FLOURISH ACCORDING TO THEIR OWN DESIGNS.
THE WORLD IS AWFUL!
THOSE FOOLS TREATED ME LIKE SCUM!
IT'S UNBEAR-ABLE!

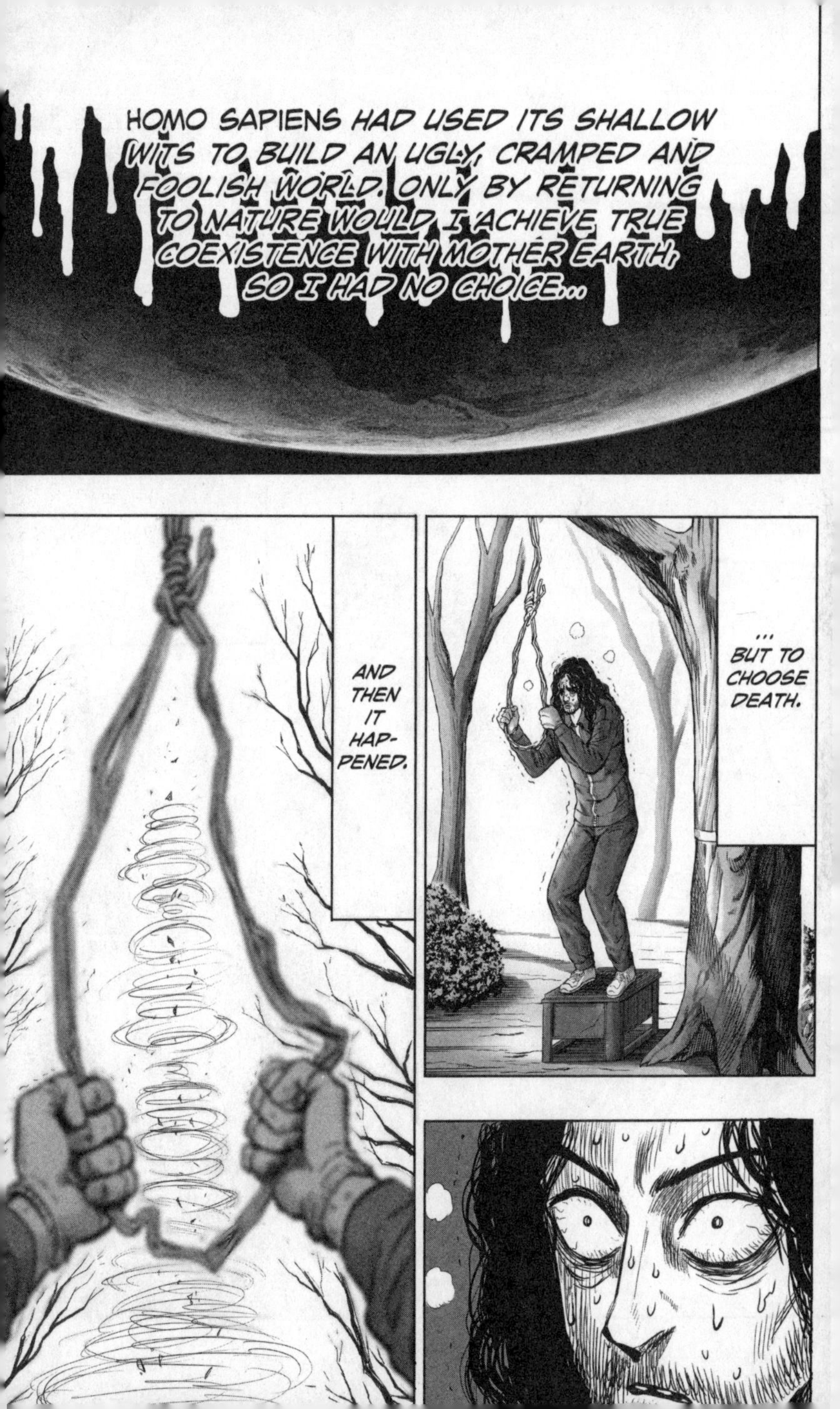
HOMO SAPIENS HAD USED ITS SHALLOW WITS TO BUILD AN UGLY, CRAMPED AND FOOLISH WORLD. ONLY BY RETURNING TO NATURE WOULD I ACHIEVE TRUE COEXISTENCE WITH MOTHER EARTH, SO I HAD NO CHOICE...
... BUT TO CHOOSE DEATH.
AND THEN IT HAP-PENED.

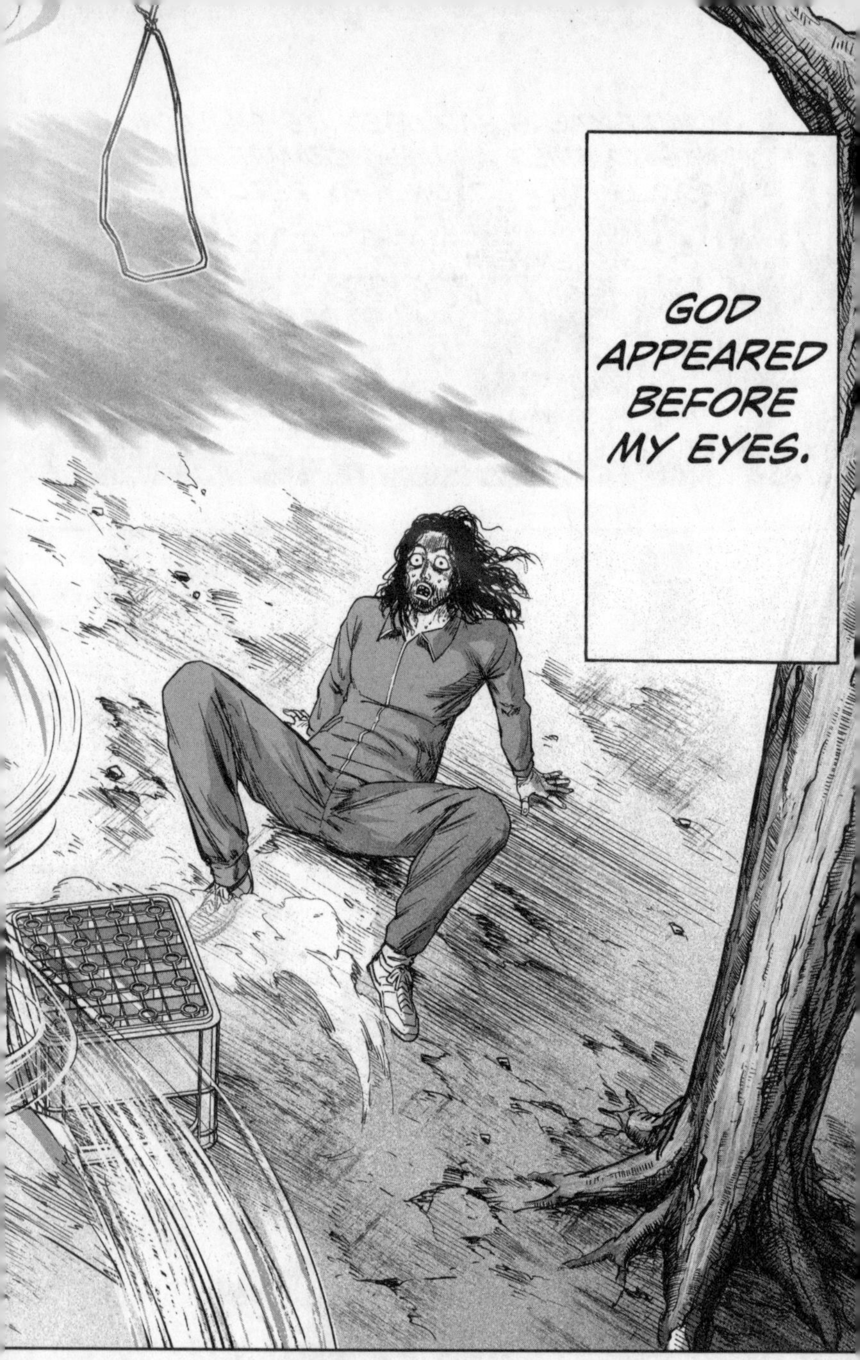
GOD APPEARED BEFORE MY EYES.

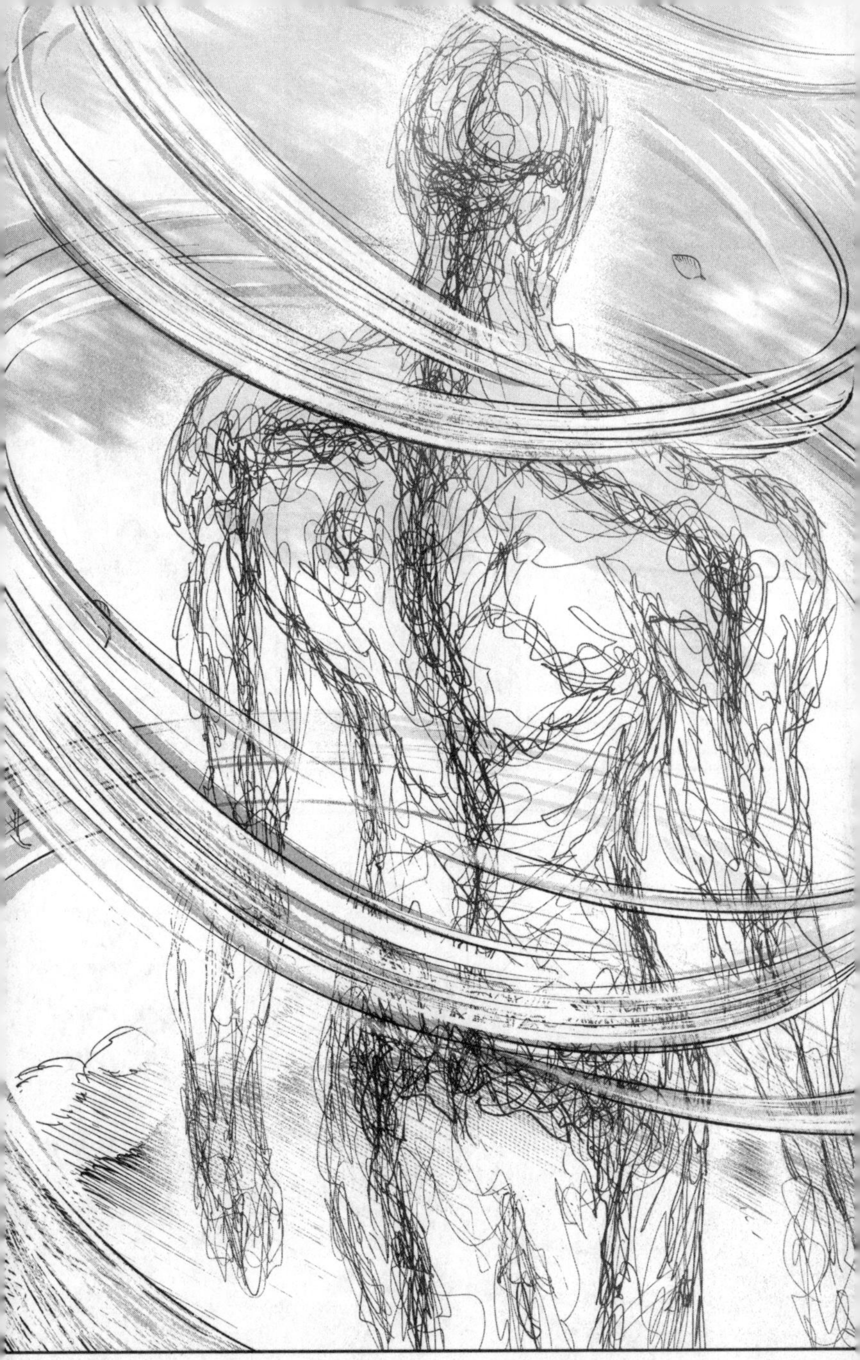

YOU ARE CORRECT.
HUMAN BEINGS ARE FOOLS.
BUT YOU DO NOT NEED TO DIE.
I WILL GRANT YOU POWER!
AND YOU KNOW WHAT YOU SHOULD DO...
...WITH THAT POWER.

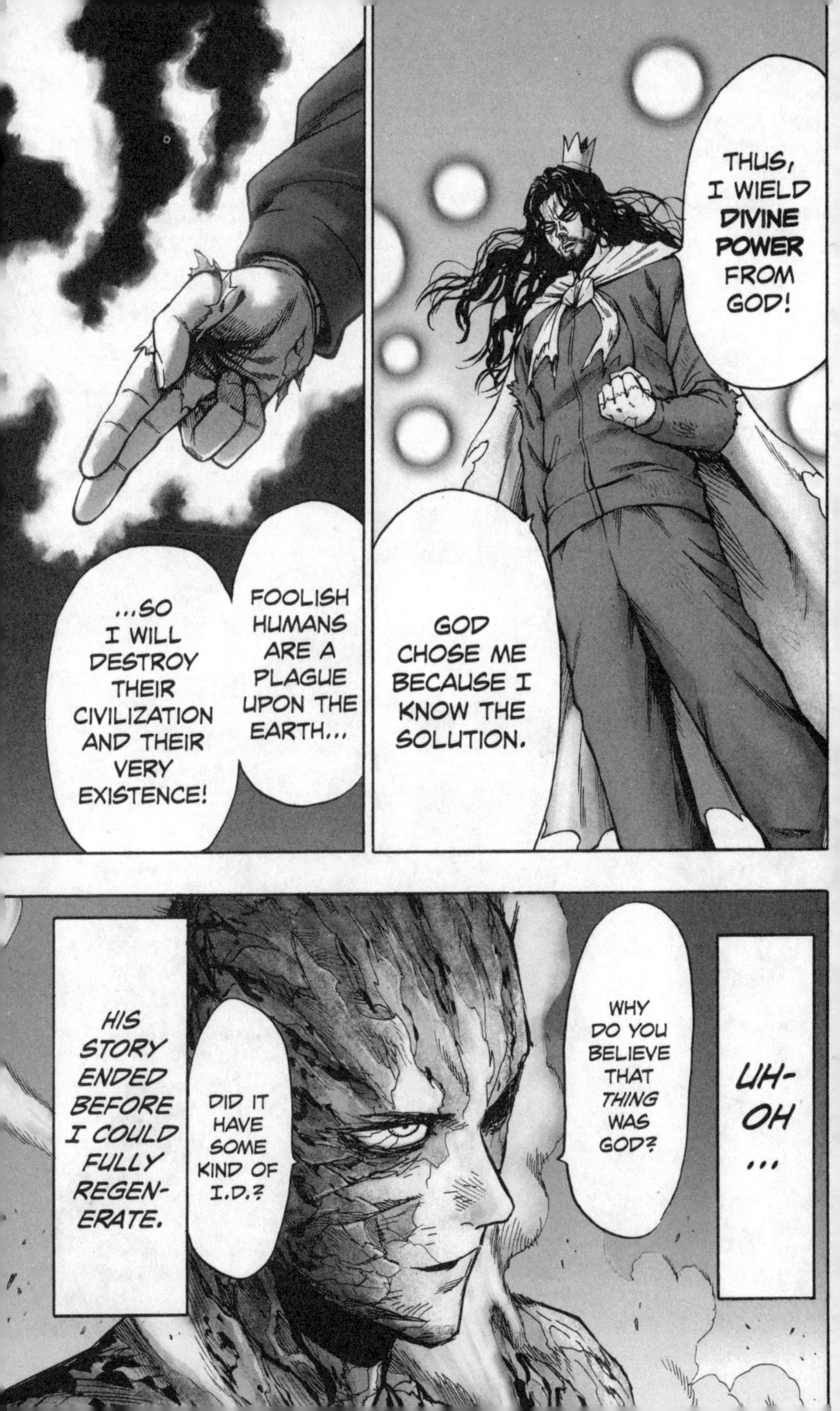
THUS, I WIELD DIVINE POWER FROM GOD!
GOD CHOSE ME BECAUSE I KNOW THE SOLUTION.
FOOLISH HUMANS ARE A PLAGUE UPON THE EARTH...
...SO I WILL DESTROY THEIR CIVILIZATION AND THEIR VERY EXISTENCE!
UH-OH...
WHY DO YOU BELIEVE THAT THING WAS GOD?
DID IT HAVE SOME KIND OF I.D.?
HIS STORY ENDED BEFORE I COULD FULLY REGENERATE.

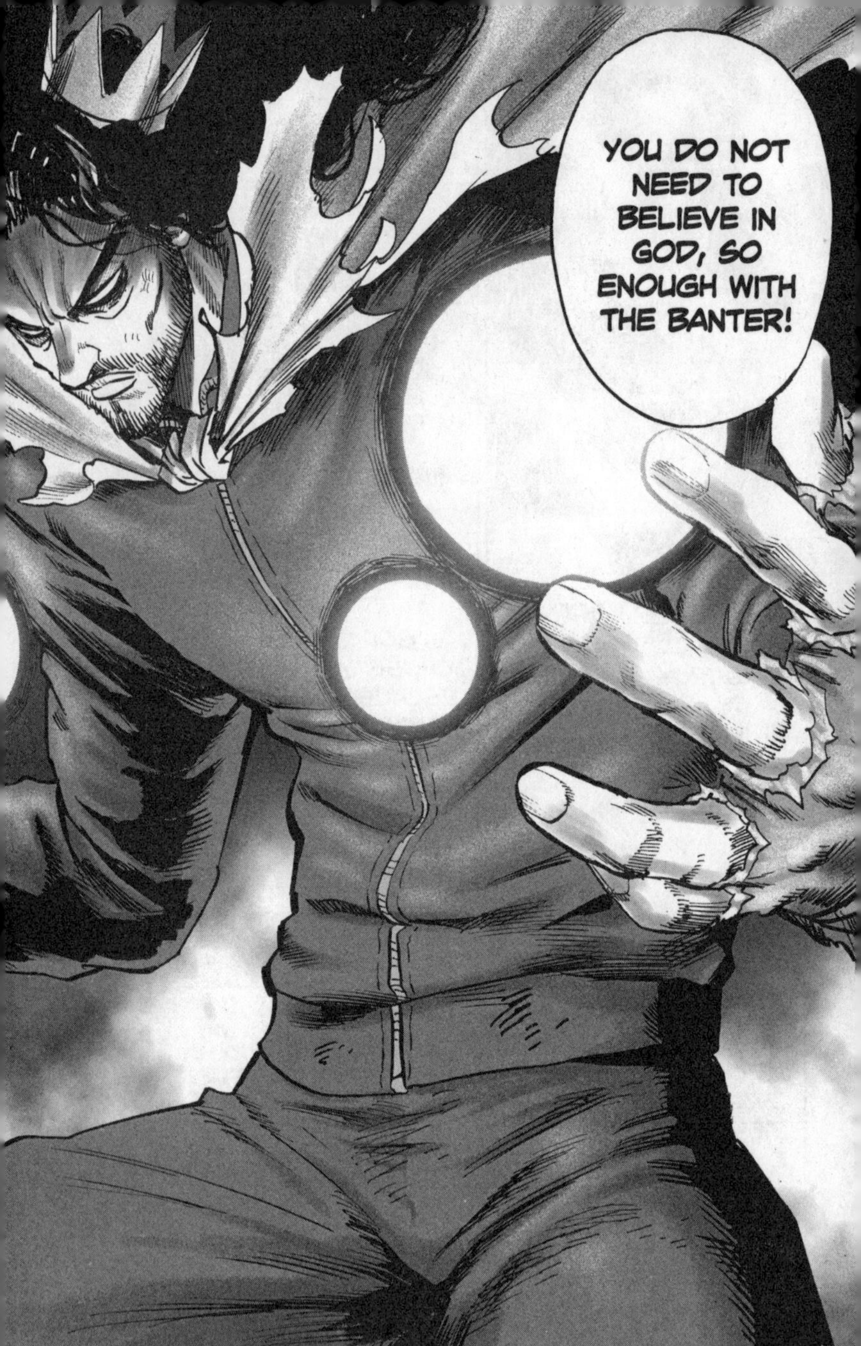
YOU DO NOT NEED TO BELIEVE IN GOD, SO ENOUGH WITH THE BANTER!

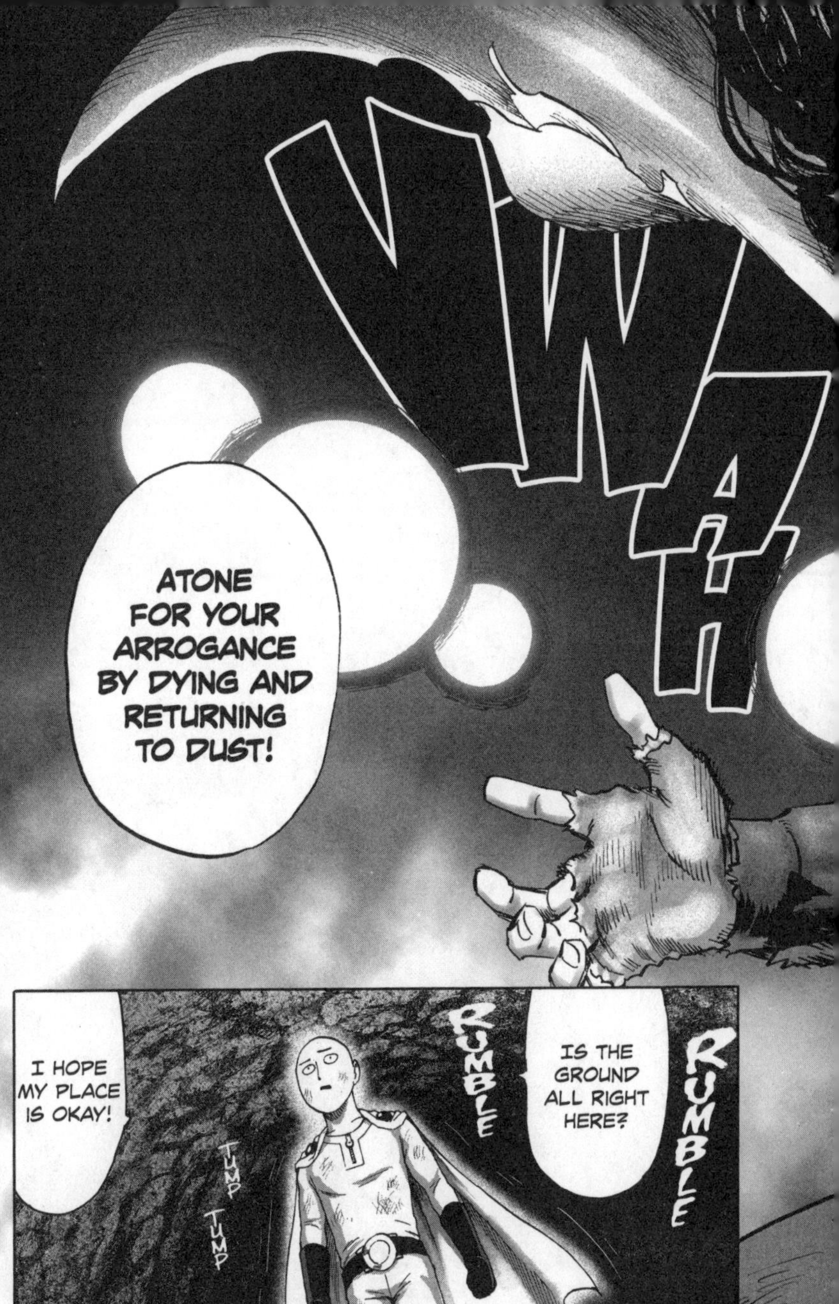
VWAH
ATONE FOR YOUR ARROGANCE BY DYING AND RETURNING TO DUST!
RUMBLE
IS THE GROUND ALL RIGHT HERE?
RUMBLE
TUMP TUMP
I HOPE MY PLACE IS OKAY!

PUNCH 110: LOVE EVOLUTIO

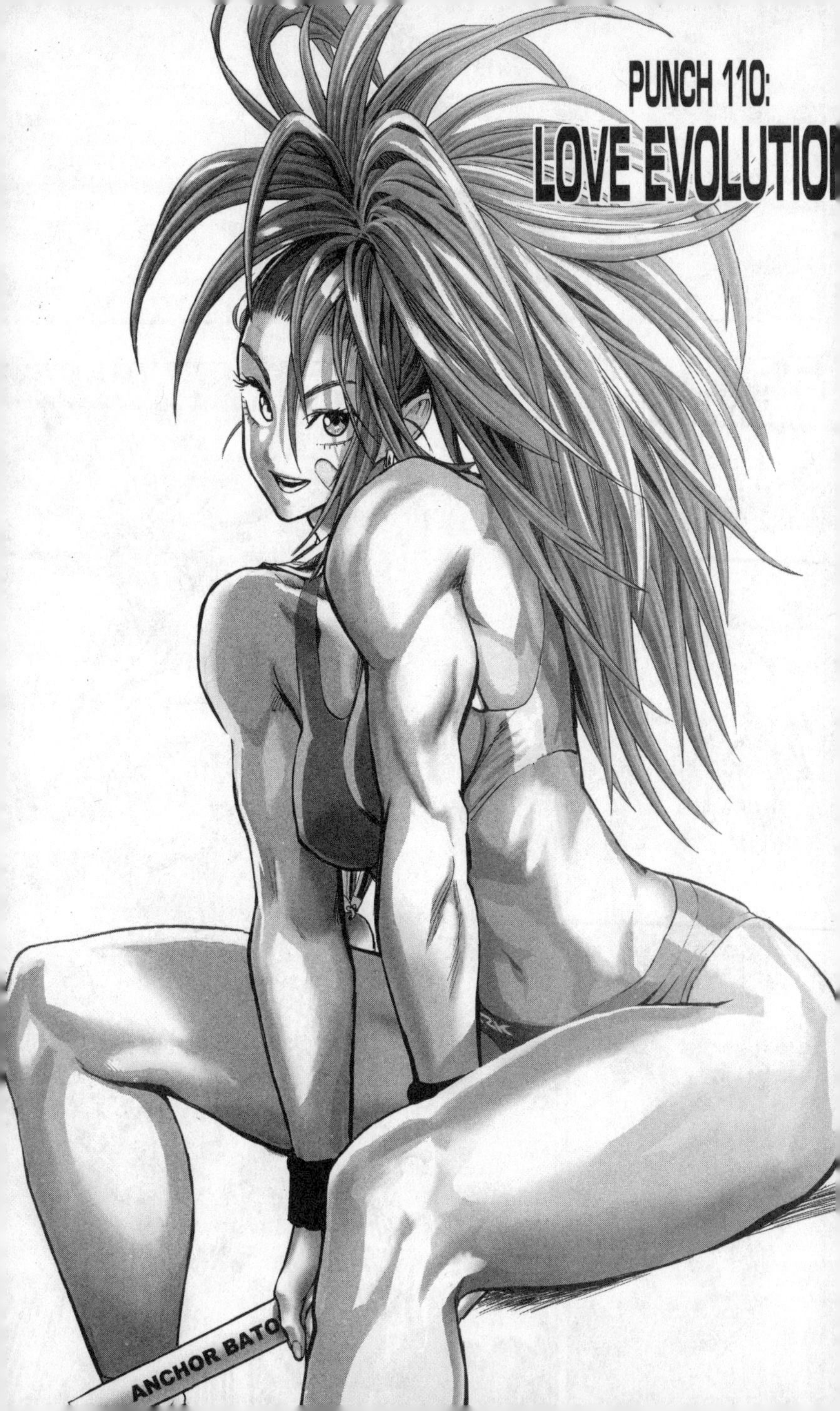
ANCHOR BATO

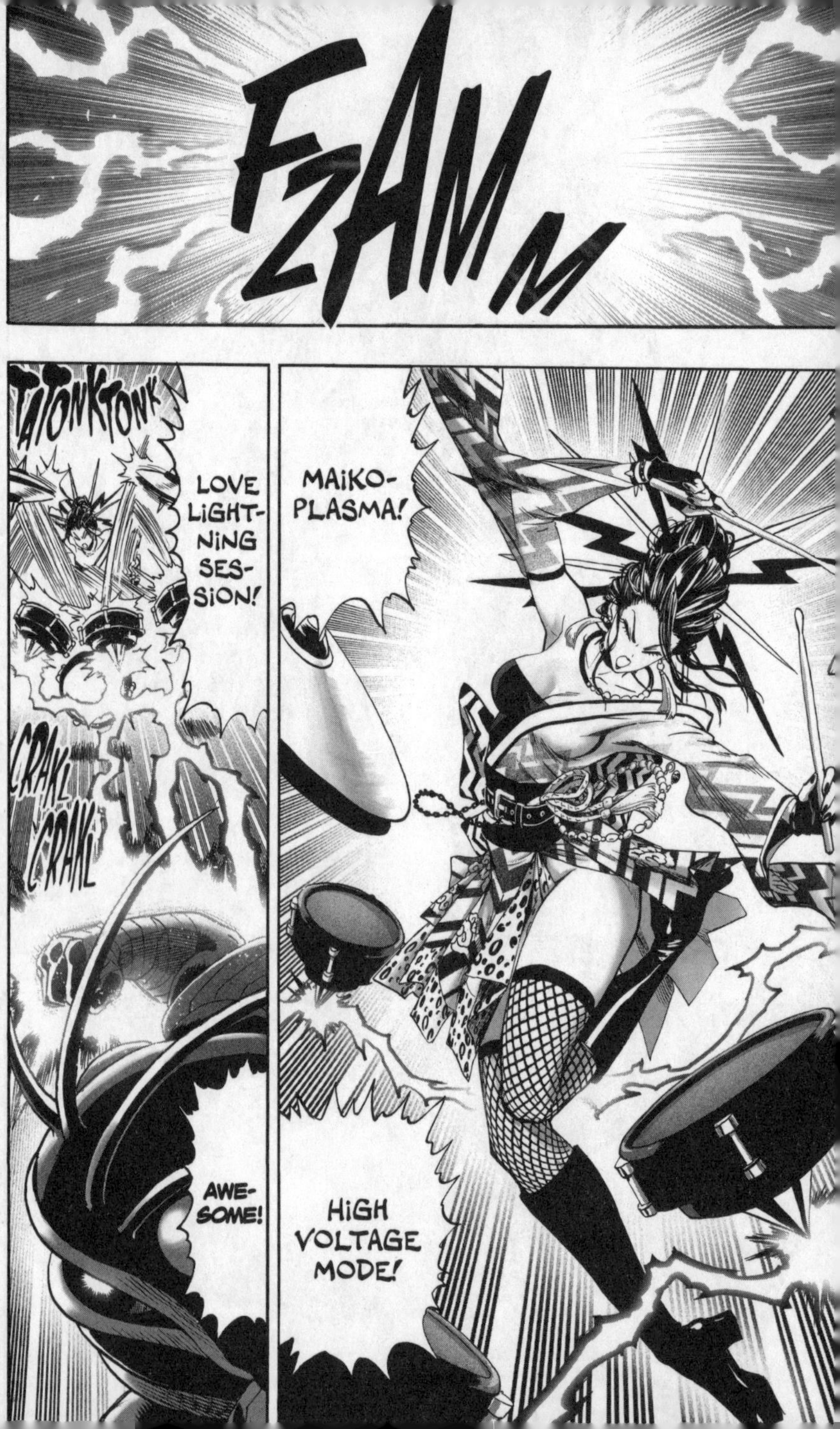
FZAMM
MAIKO-PLASMA!
HIGH VOLTAGE MODE!
TATONKTONK
LOVE LIGHTNING SESSION!
CRAKL CRAKL CRAKL
AWESOME!

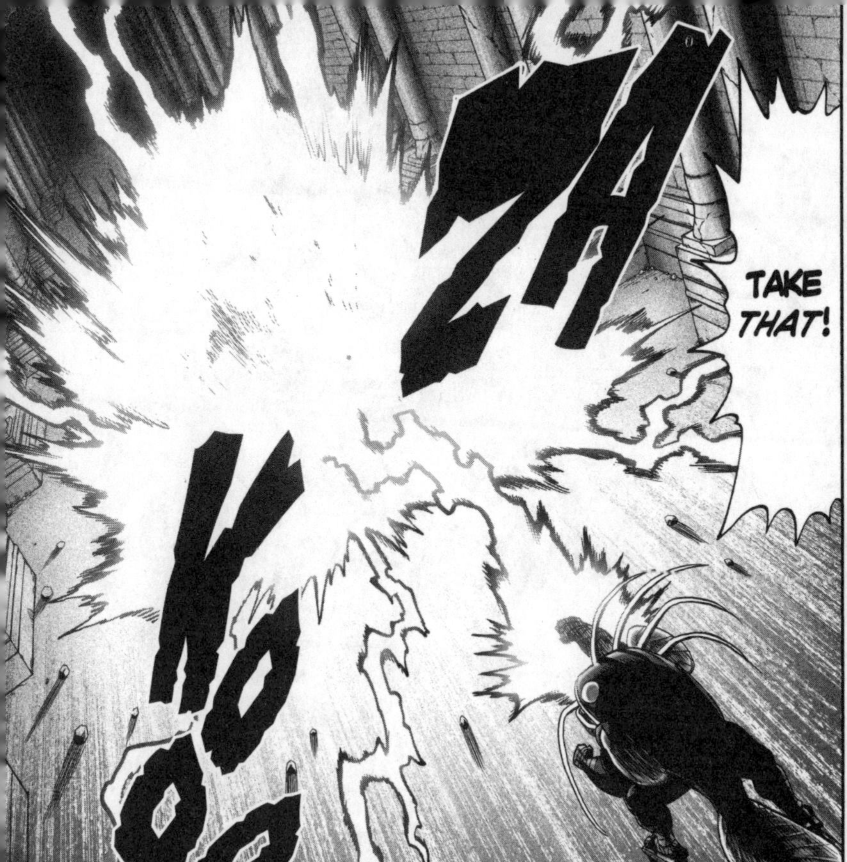
ZA
KOOOM
TAKE *THAT!*

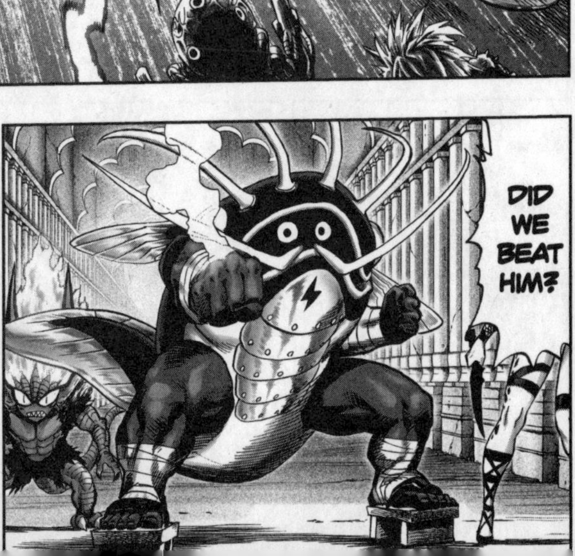
DID WE BEAT HIM?

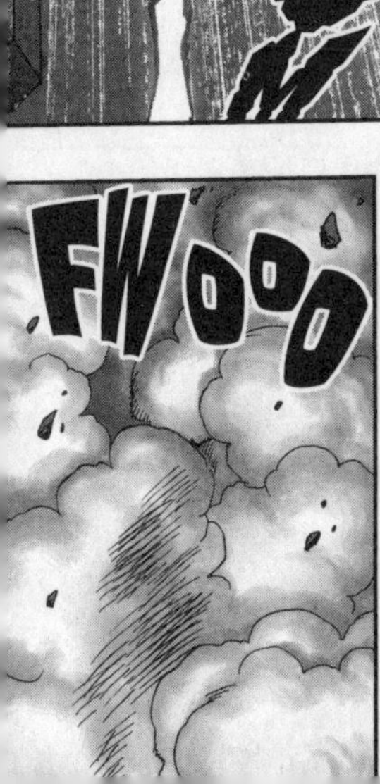
FWOOO

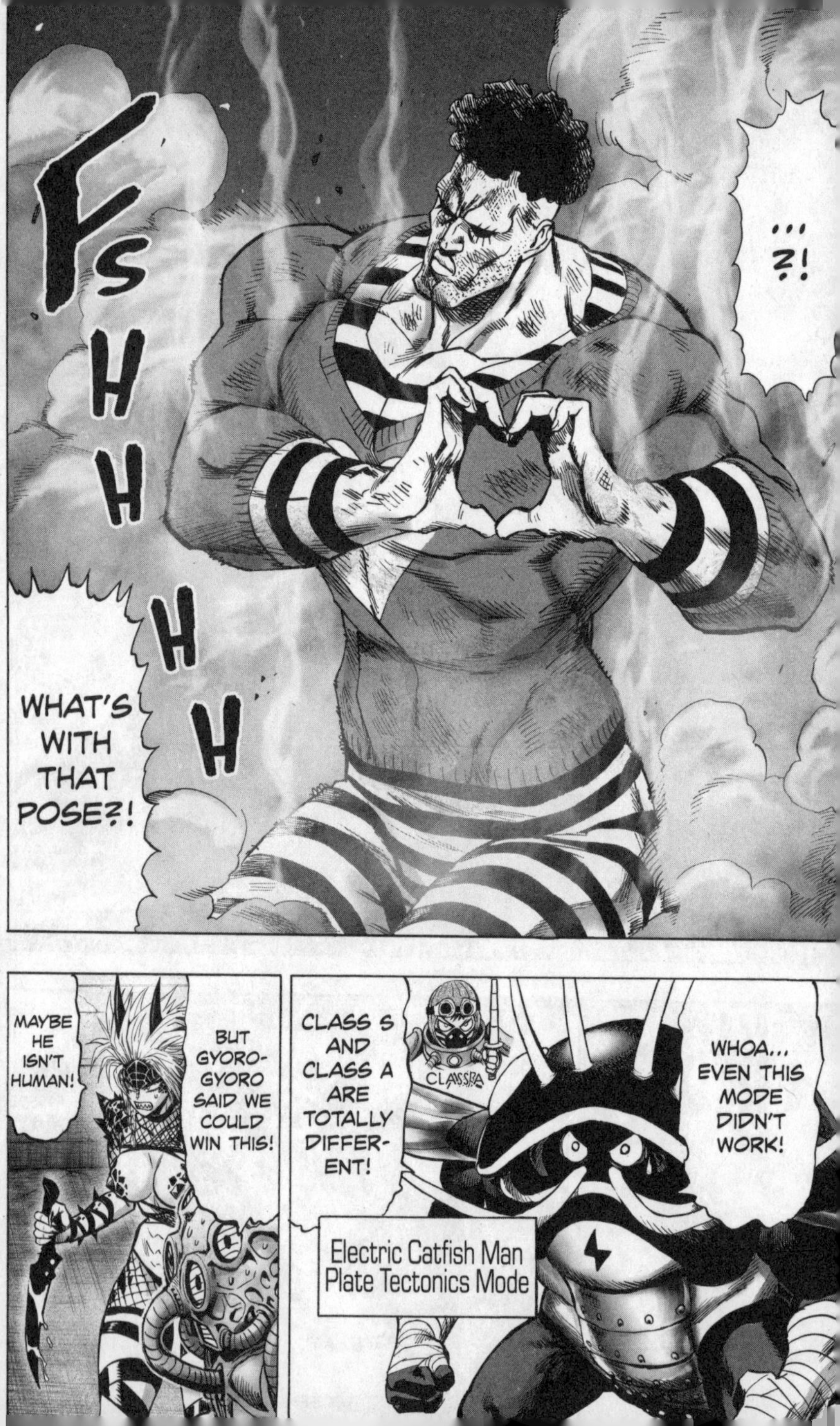

...?!
FSHHHH
WHAT'S WITH THAT POSE?!
WHOA... EVEN THIS MODE DIDN'T WORK!
CLASS S AND CLASS A ARE TOTALLY DIFFER-ENT!
Electric Catfish Man Plate Tectonics Mode
BUT GYORO-GYORO SAID WE COULD WIN THIS!
MAYBE HE ISN'T HUMAN!

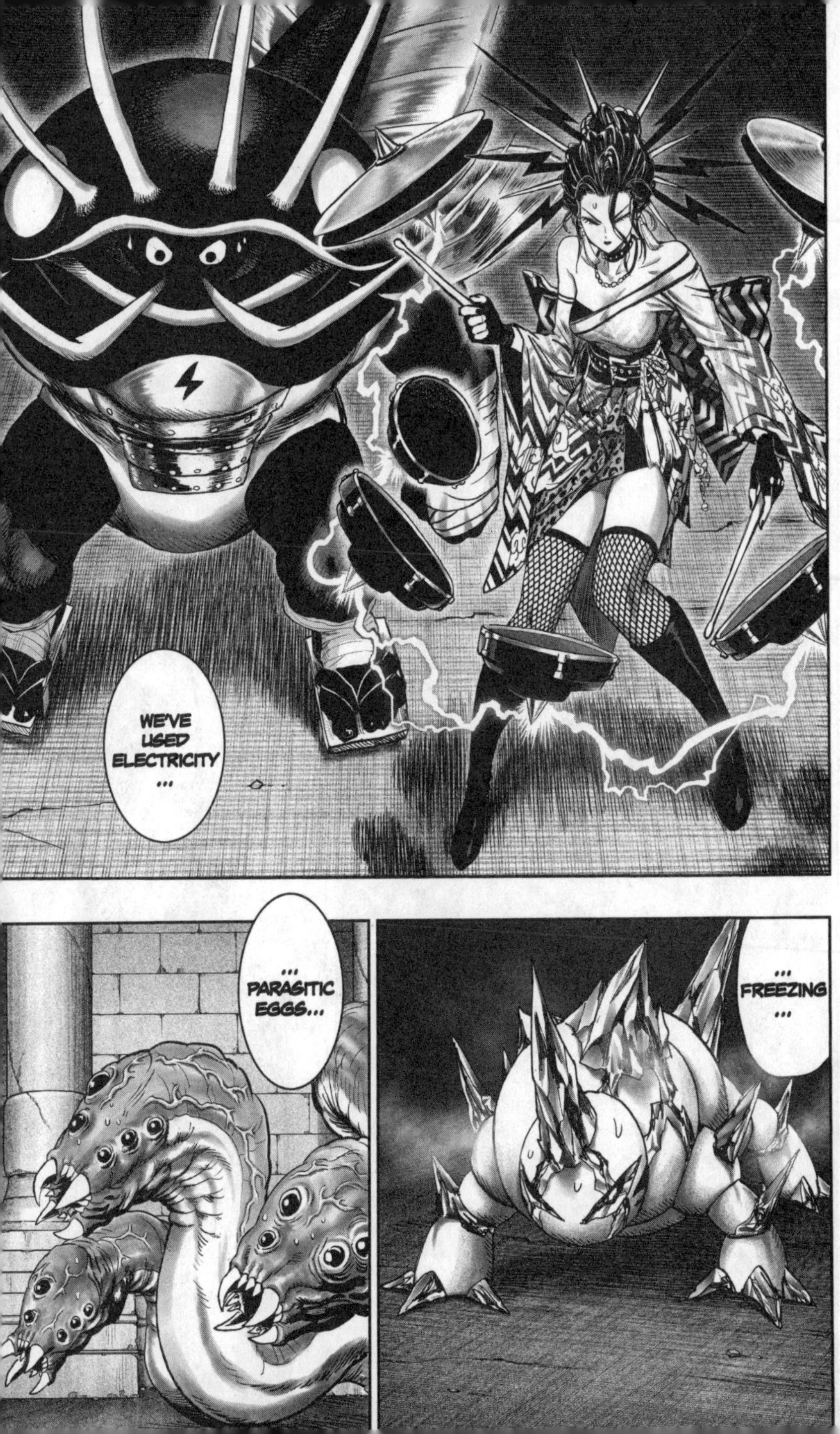
WE'VE USED ELECTRICITY ...
... FREEZING ...
... PARASITIC EGGS...

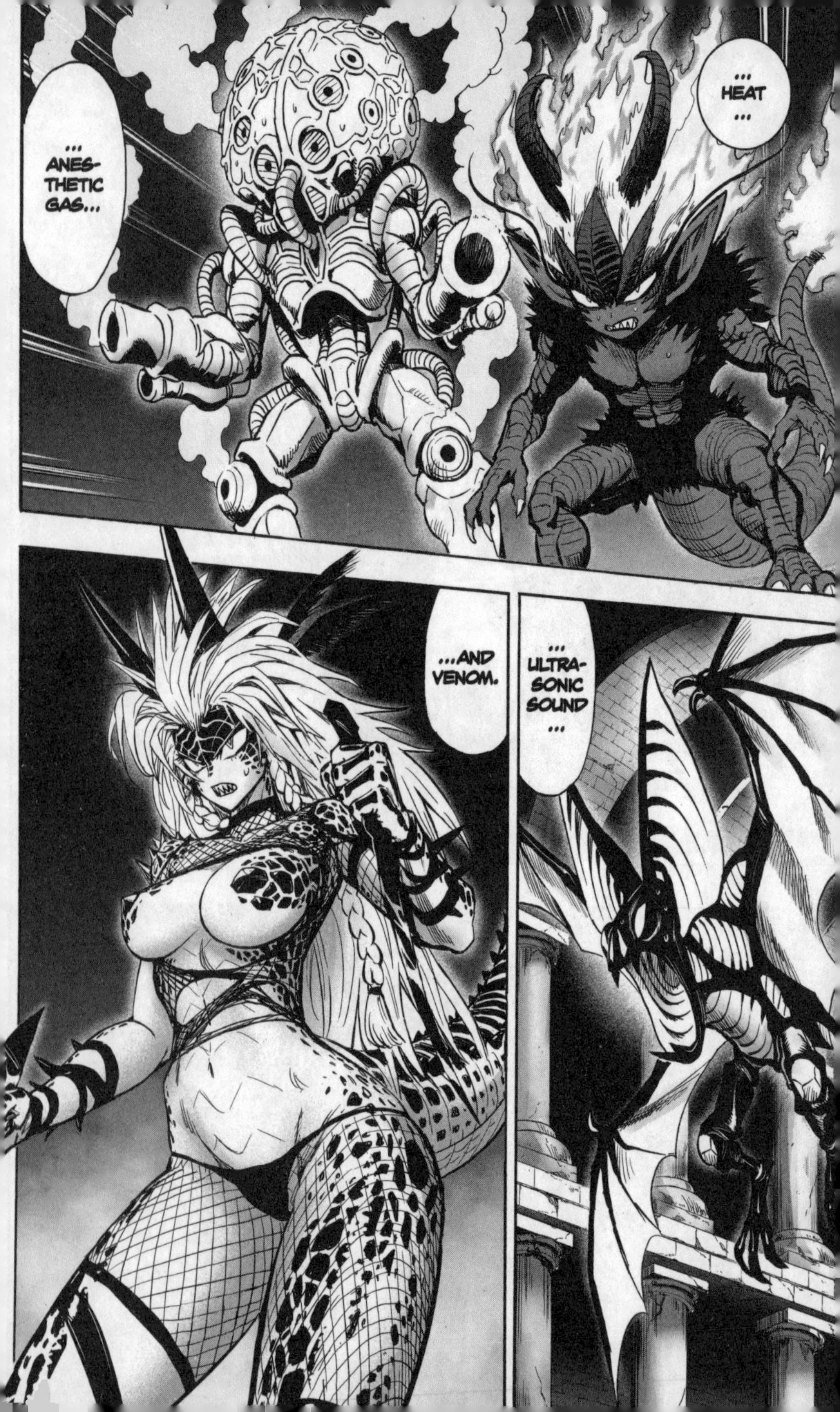
... HEAT ...
... ANES-THETIC GAS...
... ULTRA-SONIC SOUND ...
...AND VENOM.

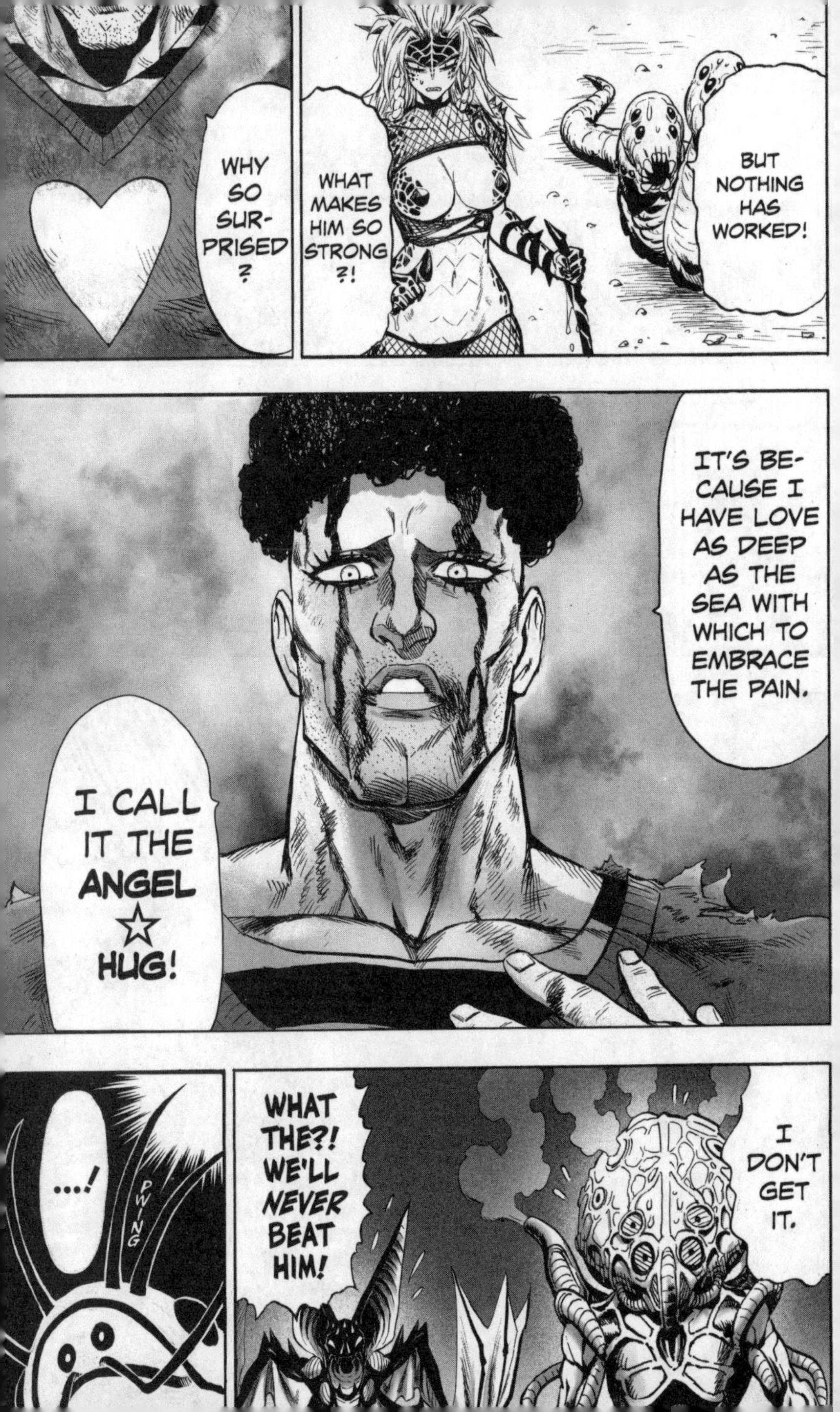
BUT NOTHING HAS WORKED!
WHAT MAKES HIM SO STRONG?!
WHY SO SURPRISED?
IT'S BECAUSE I HAVE LOVE AS DEEP AS THE SEA WITH WHICH TO EMBRACE THE PAIN.
I CALL IT THE ANGEL☆HUG!
I DON'T GET IT.
WHAT THE?! WE'LL NEVER BEAT HIM!
PWING
...!

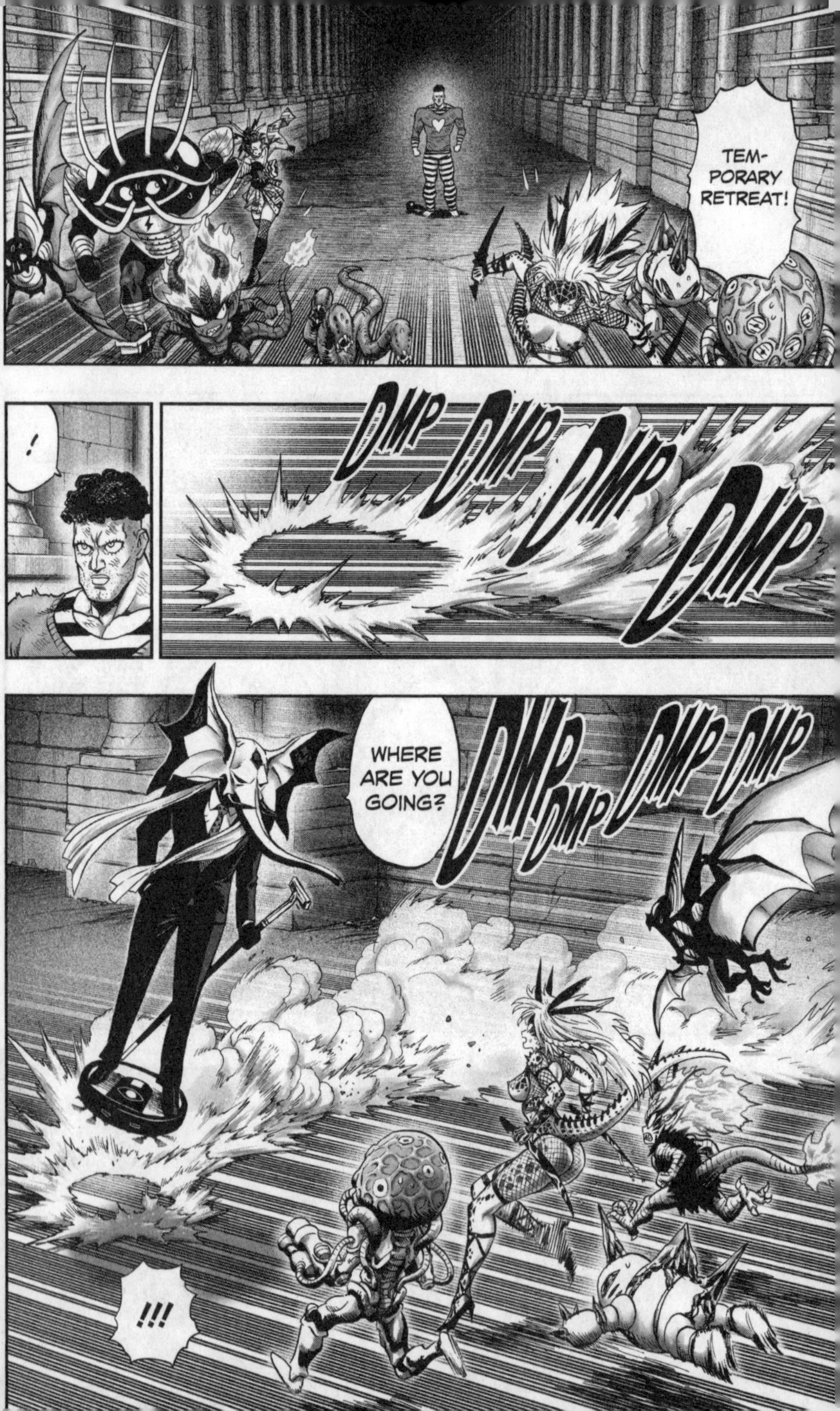
TEM-PORARY RETREAT!
DMP DMP DMP DMP
!
DMP DMP DMP DMP DMP
WHERE ARE YOU GOING?
!!!

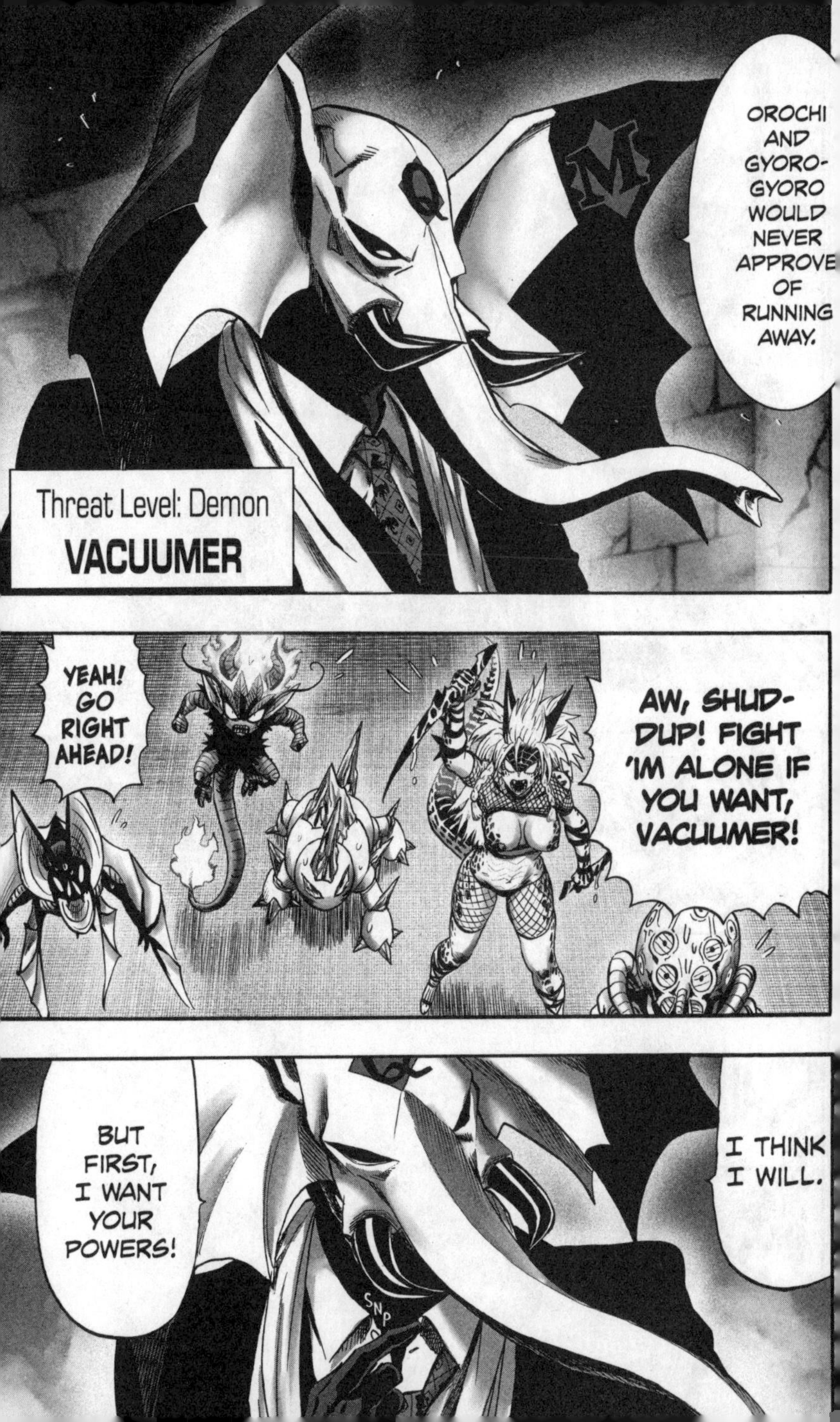
OROCHI AND GYORO-GYORO WOULD NEVER APPROVE OF RUNNING AWAY.
Threat Level: Demon
VACUUMER
AW, SHUD-DUP! FIGHT 'IM ALONE IF YOU WANT, VACUUMER!
YEAH! GO RIGHT AHEAD!
I THINK I WILL.
BUT FIRST, I WANT YOUR POWERS!
SNP

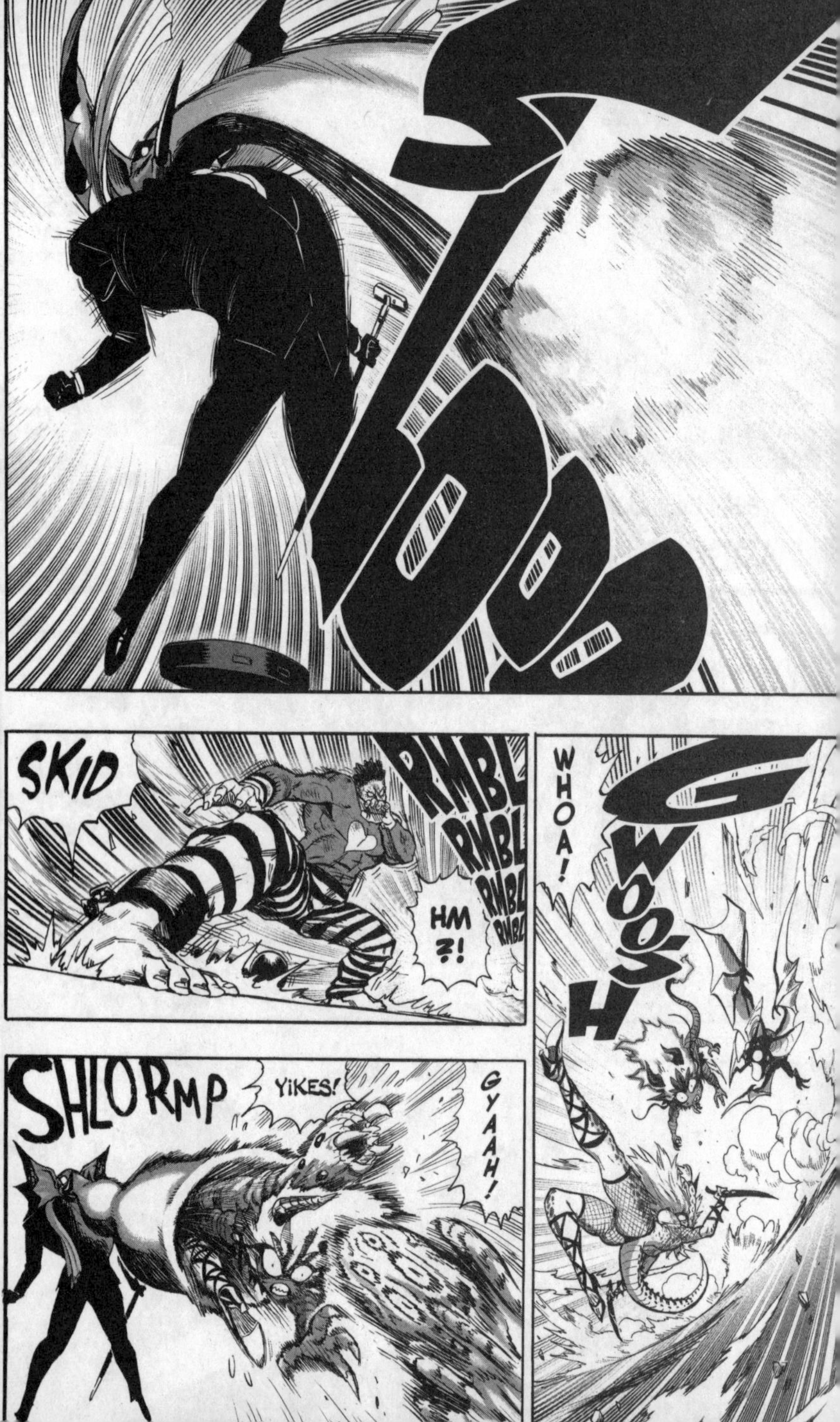
WHOA!
GWOOSH
SKID
RMBL RMBL RMBL RMBL
HM ?!
SHLORMP
YIKES!
GYAAH!

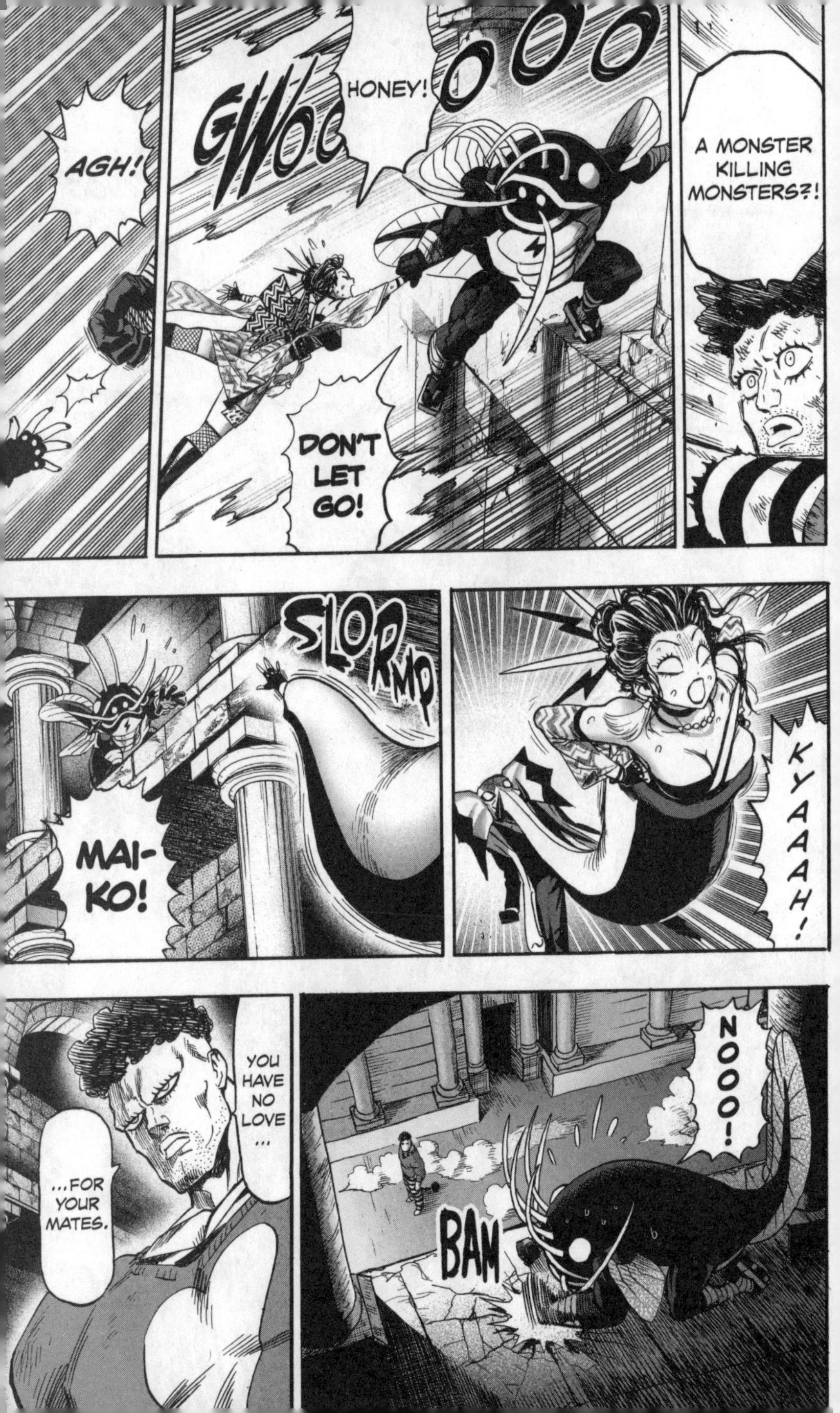
A MONSTER KILLING MONSTERS?!
HONEY!
GWOOOOO
DON'T LET GO!
AGH!
KYAAAH!
SLORMP
MAI-KO!
NOOOO!
BAM
YOU HAVE NO LOVE...
...FOR YOUR MATES.

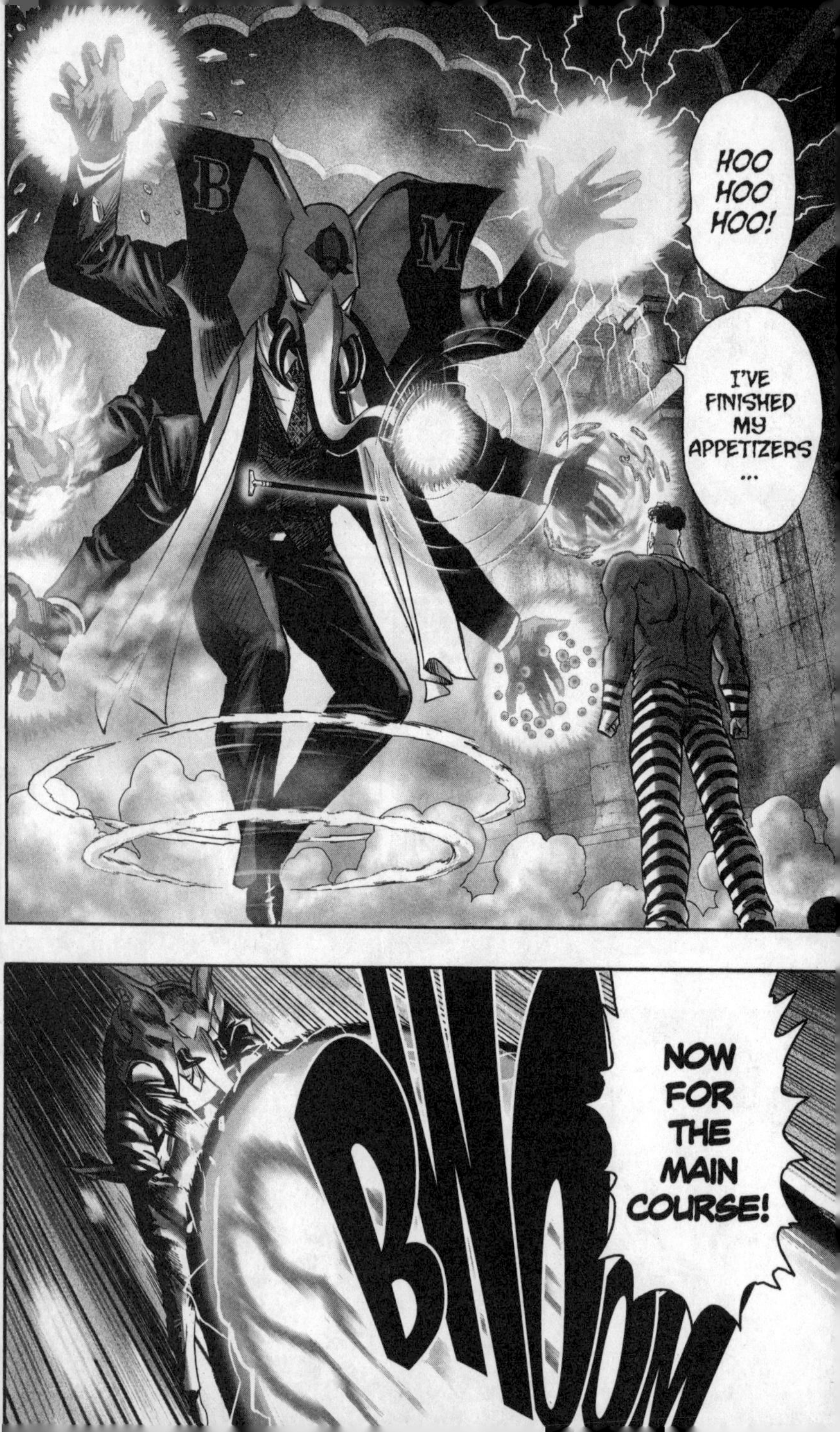
HOO HOO HOO!
I'VE FINISHED MY APPETIZERS...
NOW FOR THE MAIN COURSE!
BWOOOM

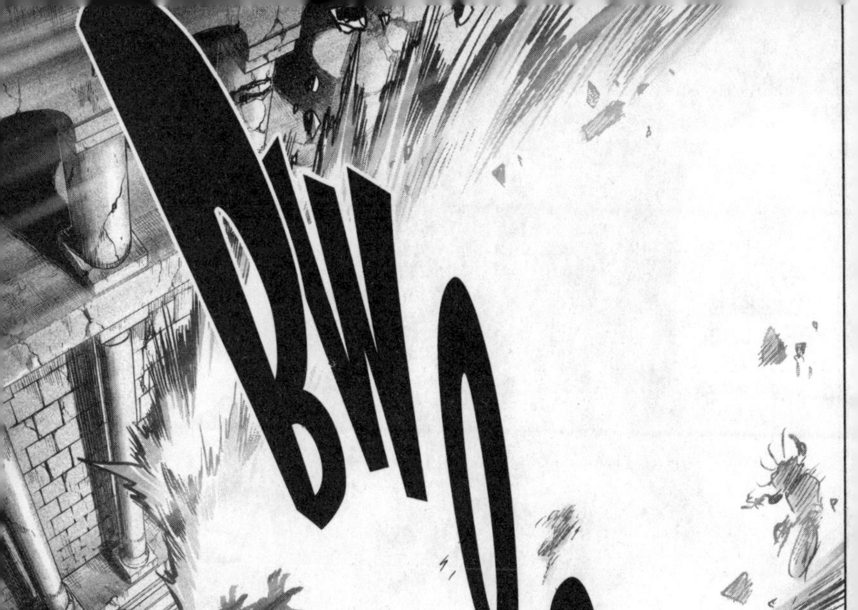
BWOOOOM

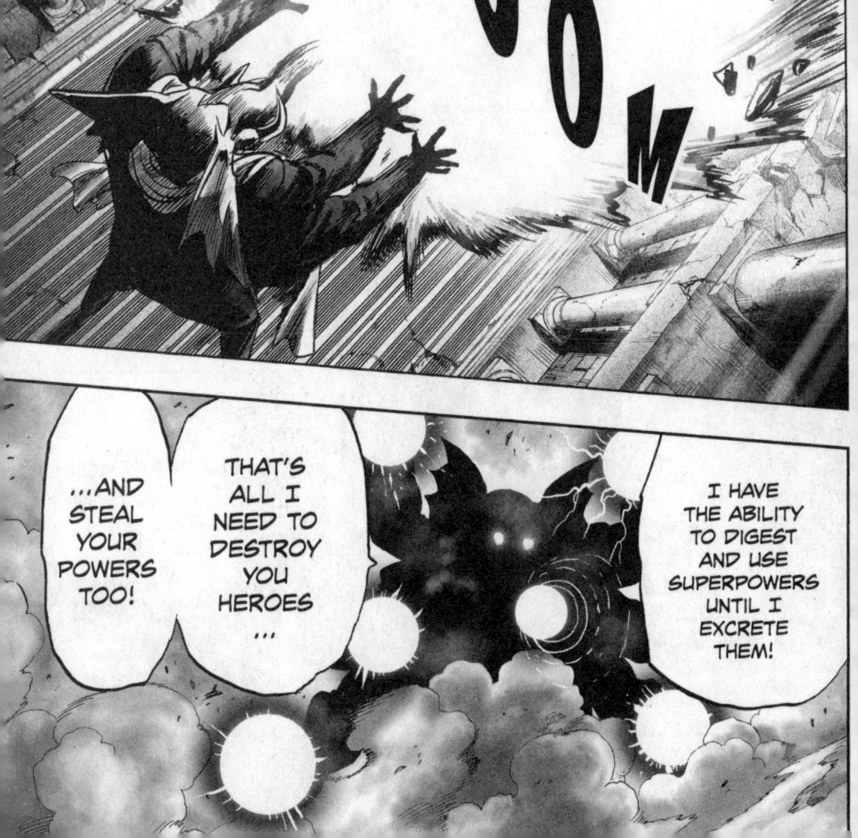
I HAVE THE ABILITY TO DIGEST AND USE SUPERPOWERS UNTIL I EXCRETE THEM!
THAT'S ALL I NEED TO DESTROY YOU HEROES ...
...AND STEAL YOUR POWERS TOO!

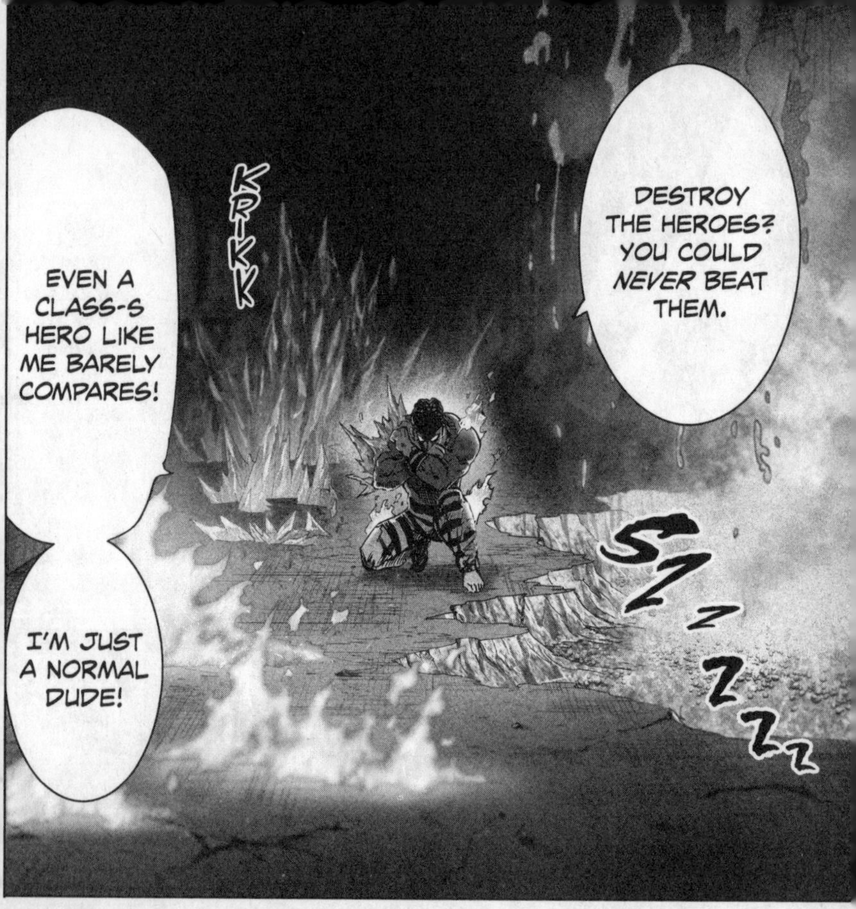
DESTROY THE HEROES? YOU COULD *NEVER* BEAT THEM.
KRIKK
EVEN A CLASS-S HERO LIKE ME BARELY COMPARES!
SZZZZ
I'M JUST A NORMAL DUDE!

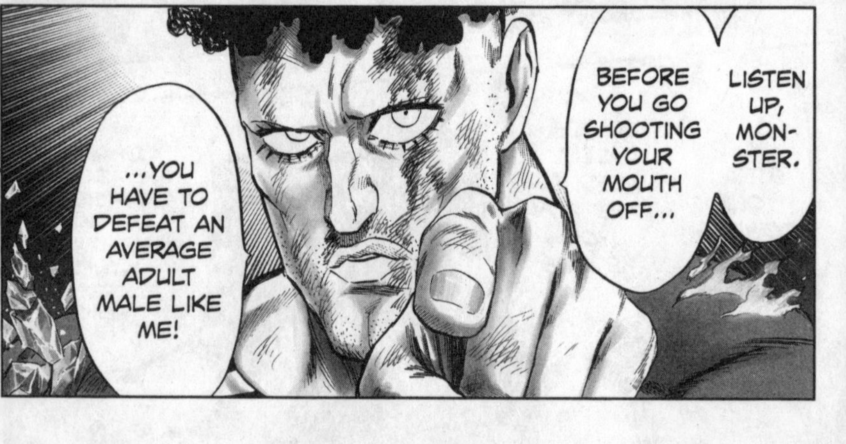
LISTEN UP, MON-STER.
BEFORE YOU GO SHOOTING YOUR MOUTH OFF...
...YOU HAVE TO DEFEAT AN AVERAGE ADULT MALE LIKE ME!

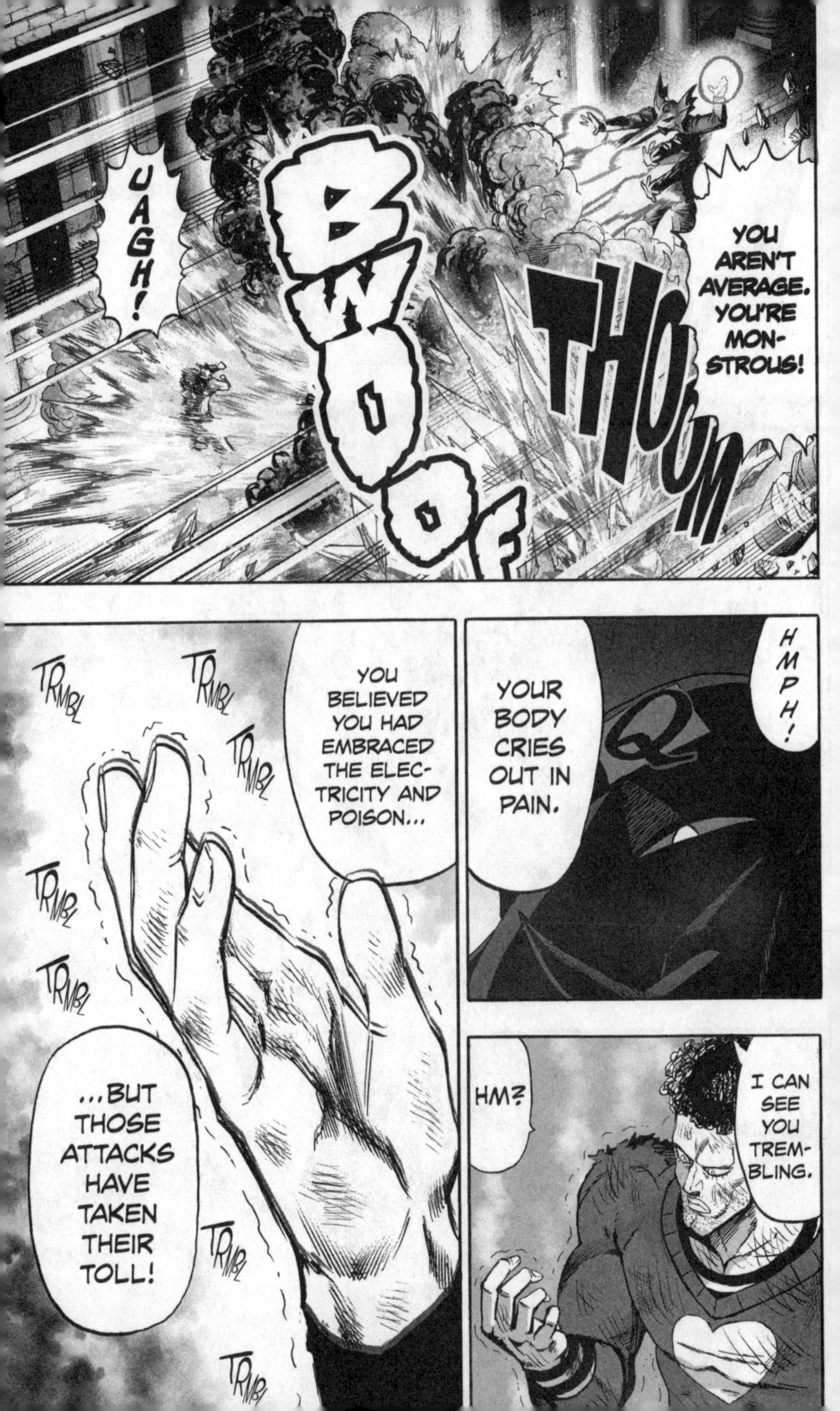
YOU AREN'T AVERAGE. YOU'RE MON-STROUS!
THOOOM
BWOOOF
UAGH!
HMPH!
YOUR BODY CRIES OUT IN PAIN.
I CAN SEE YOU TREM-BLING.
HM?
YOU BELIEVED YOU HAD EMBRACED THE ELEC-TRICITY AND POISON...
TRMBL
TRMBL
TRMBL
TRMBL
...BUT THOSE ATTACKS HAVE TAKEN THEIR TOLL!
TRMBL
TRMBL
TRMBL

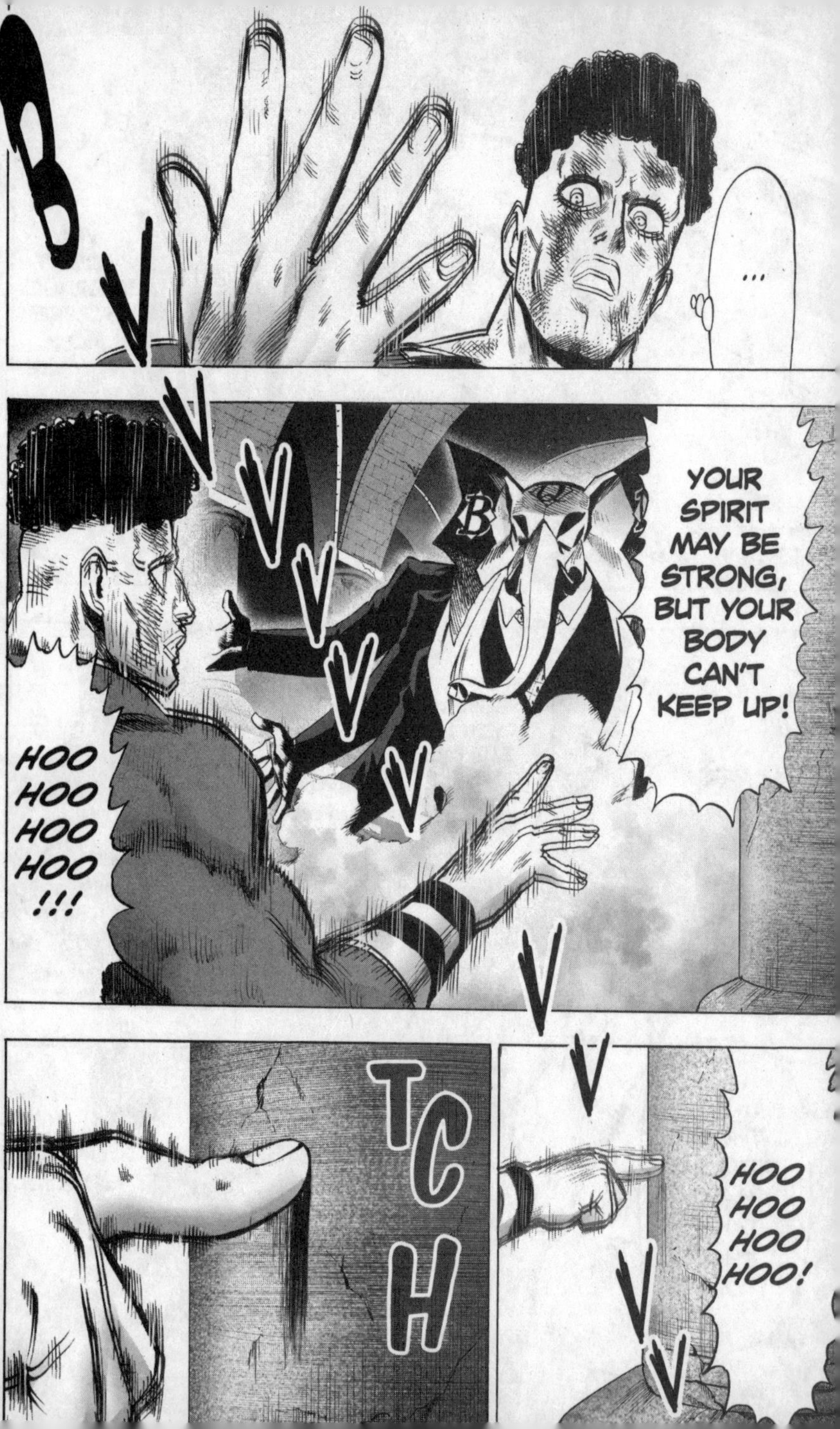
...
YOUR SPIRIT MAY BE STRONG, BUT YOUR BODY CAN'T KEEP UP!
HOO HOO HOO HOO !!!
HOO HOO HOO HOO!
TCH

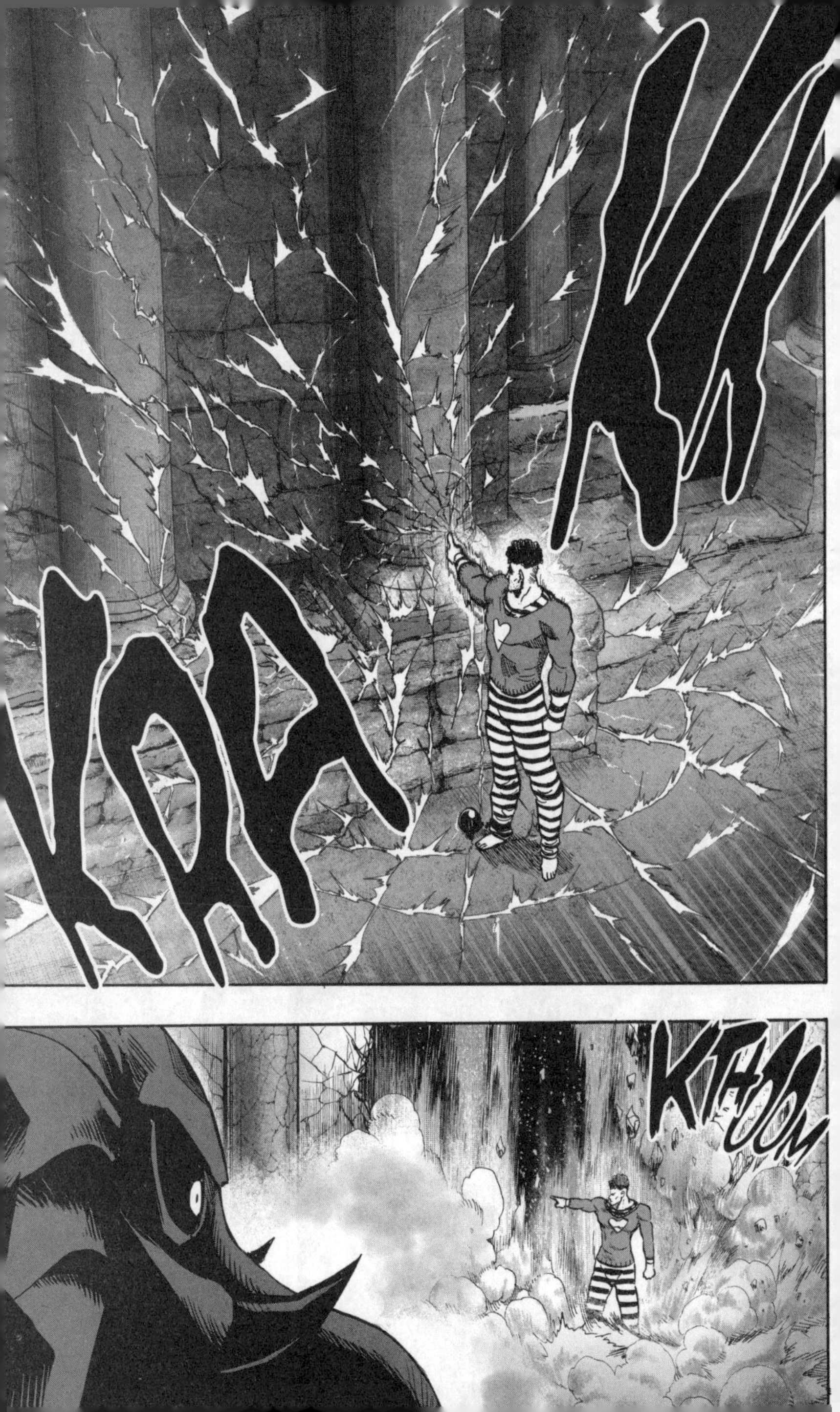
KTHOOM

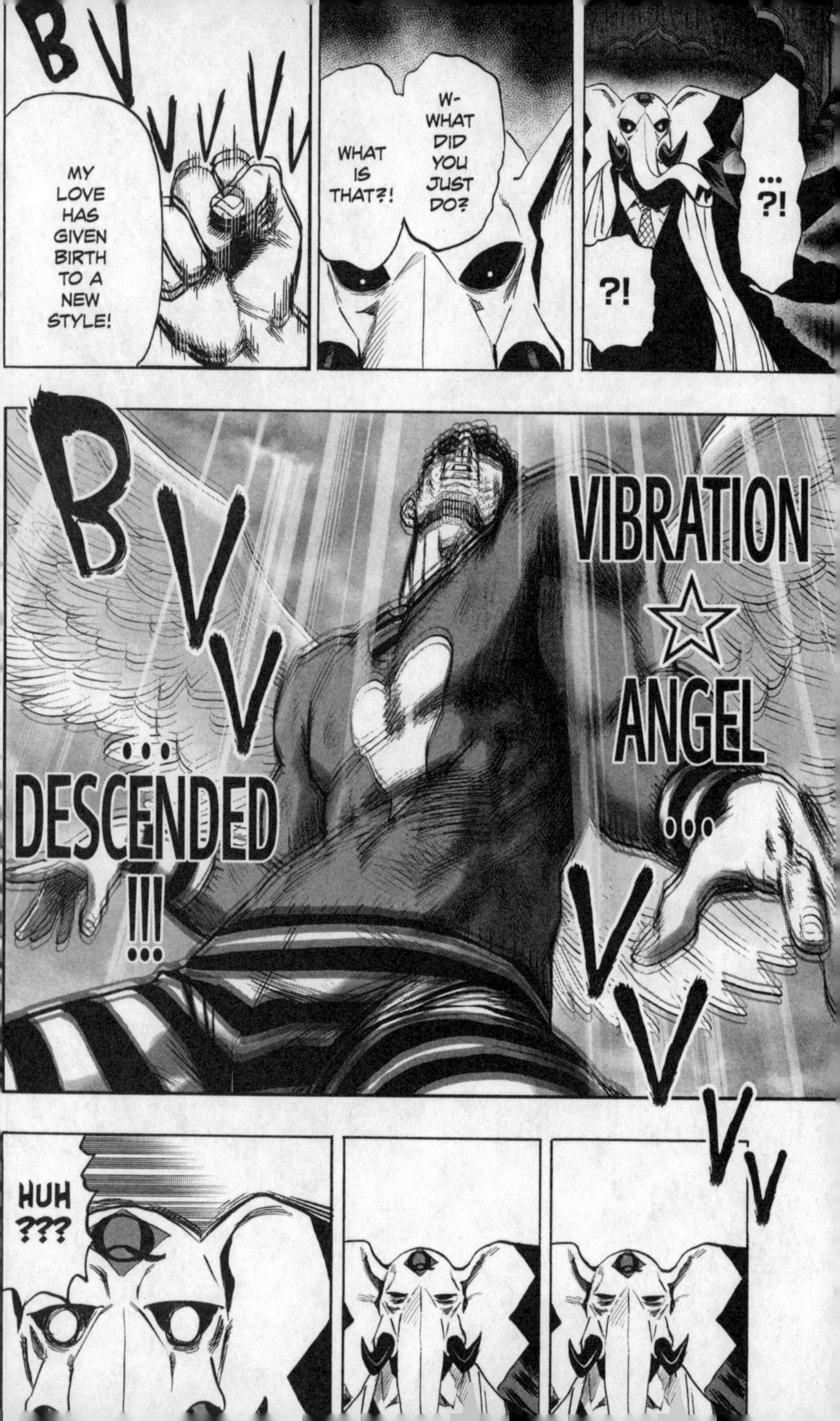
...?!
?!
W-WHAT DID YOU JUST DO?
WHAT IS THAT?!
BVVVVV
MY LOVE HAS GIVEN BIRTH TO A NEW STYLE!
VIBRATION ☆ ANGEL...
BVV
...DESCENDED!!!
VVVV
HUH ???

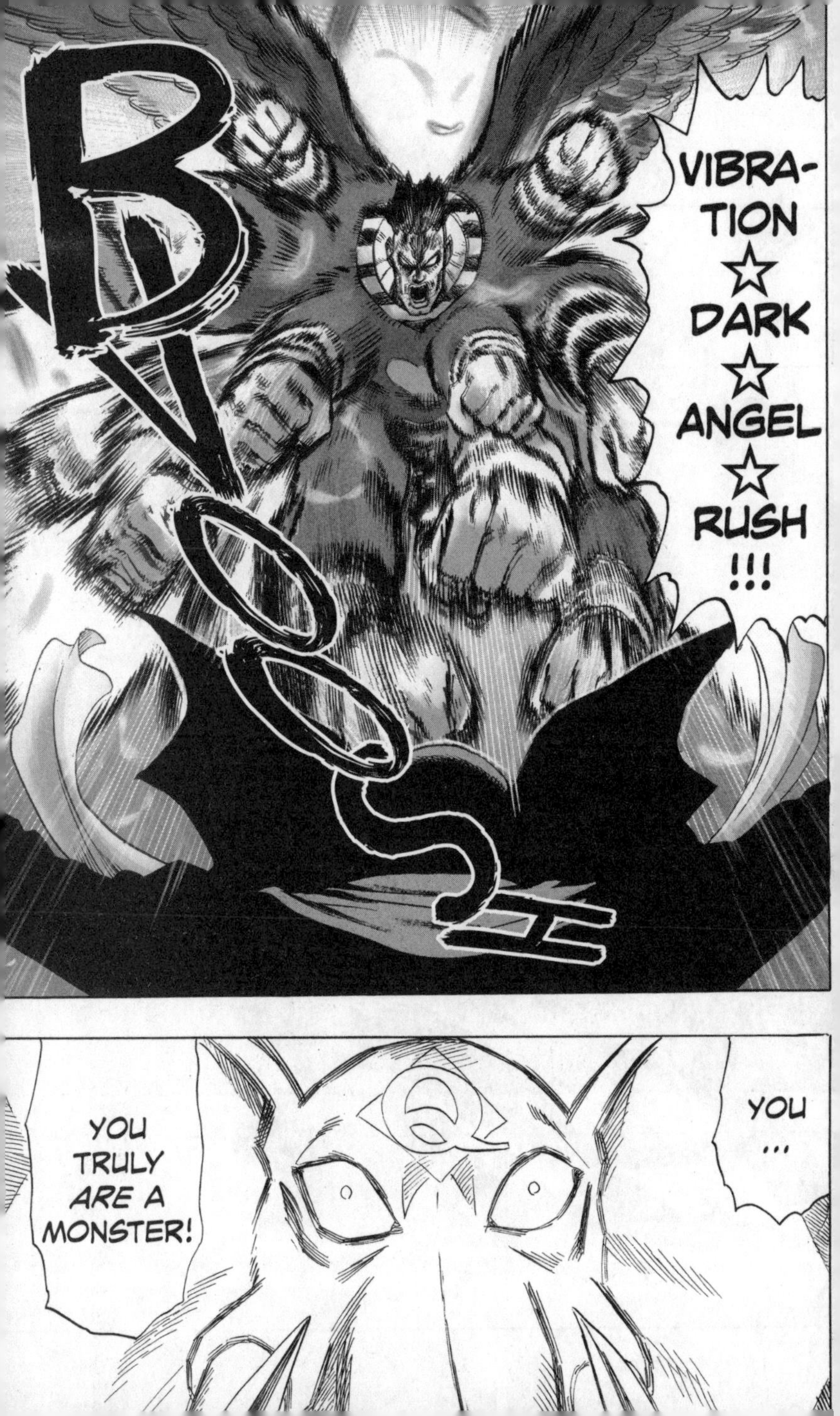
VIBRATION ☆ DARK ☆ ANGEL ☆ RUSH !!!
BDOOSH
YOU ...
YOU TRULY ARE A MONSTER!

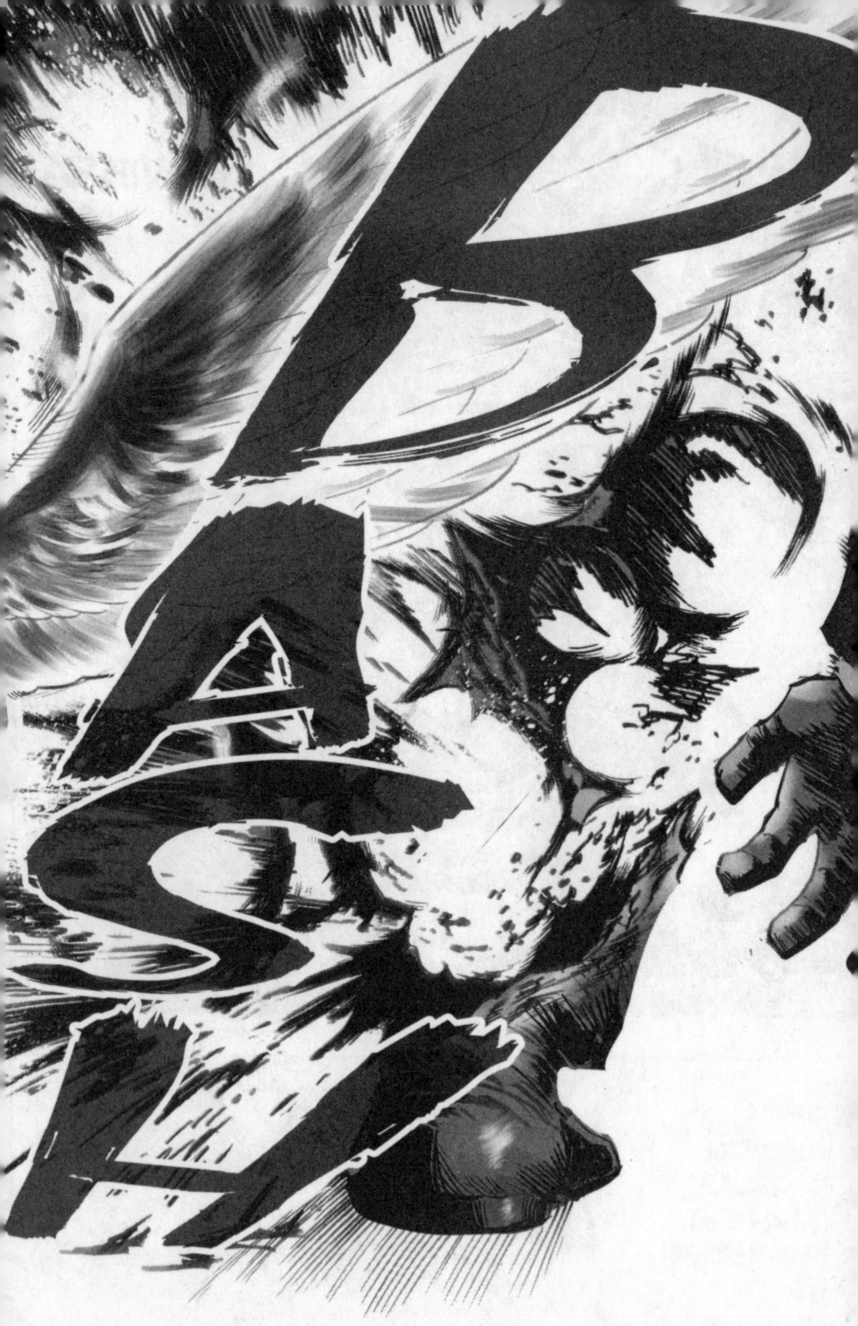

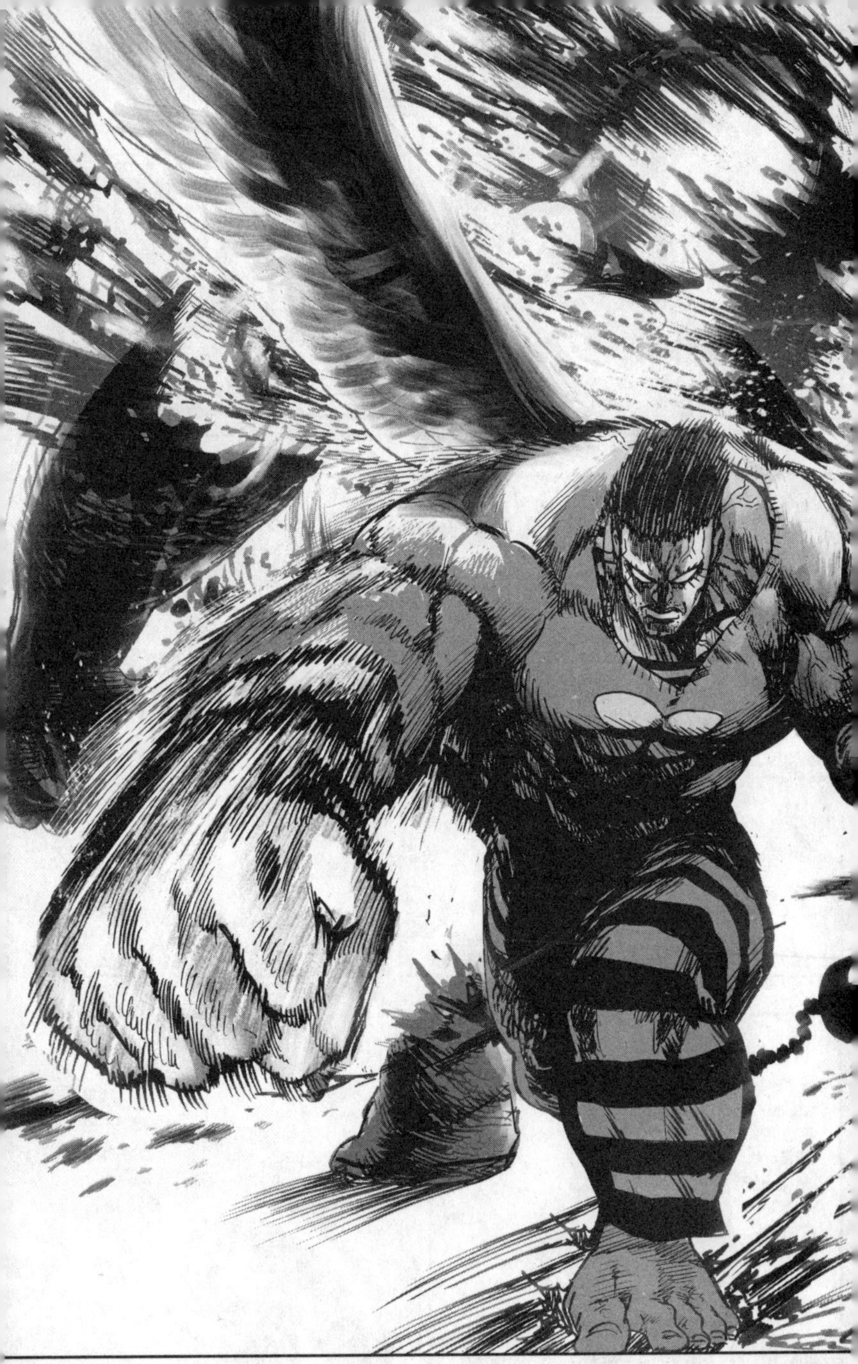

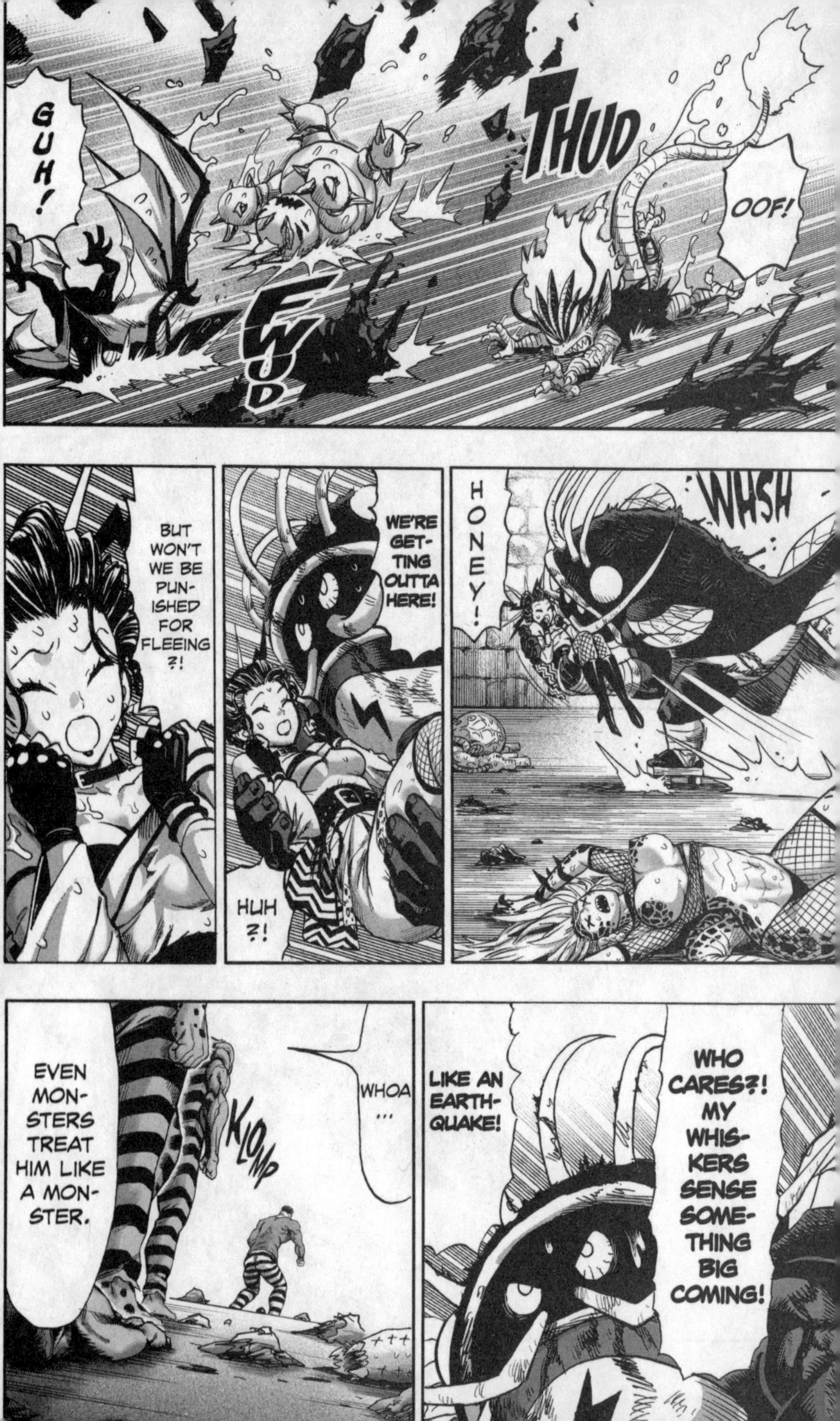
OOF!
THUD
GUH!
FWUD
WHSH
HONEY!
WE'RE GETTING OUTTA HERE!
HUH?!
BUT WON'T WE BE PUNISHED FOR FLEEING?!
WHO CARES?! MY WHISKERS SENSE SOMETHING BIG COMING!
LIKE AN EARTHQUAKE!
WHOA...
KLOMP
EVEN MONSTERS TREAT HIM LIKE A MONSTER.

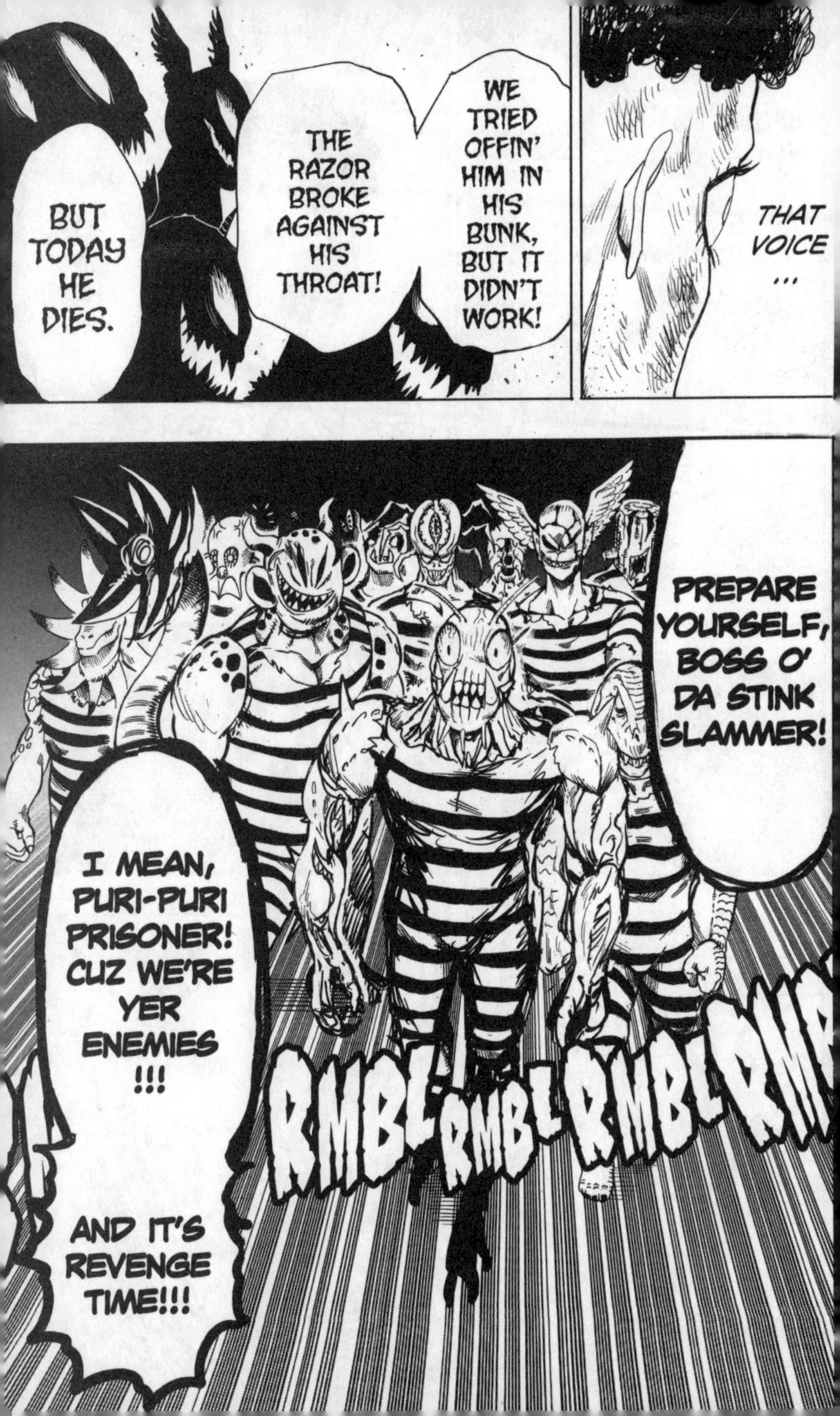
THAT VOICE ...
WE TRIED OFFIN' HIM IN HIS BUNK, BUT IT DIDN'T WORK!
THE RAZOR BROKE AGAINST HIS THROAT!
BUT TODAY HE DIES.
PREPARE YOURSELF, BOSS O' DA STINK SLAMMER!
I MEAN, PURI-PURI PRISONER! CUZ WE'RE YER ENEMIES!!!
AND IT'S REVENGE TIME!!!
RMBL RMBL RMBL RMB

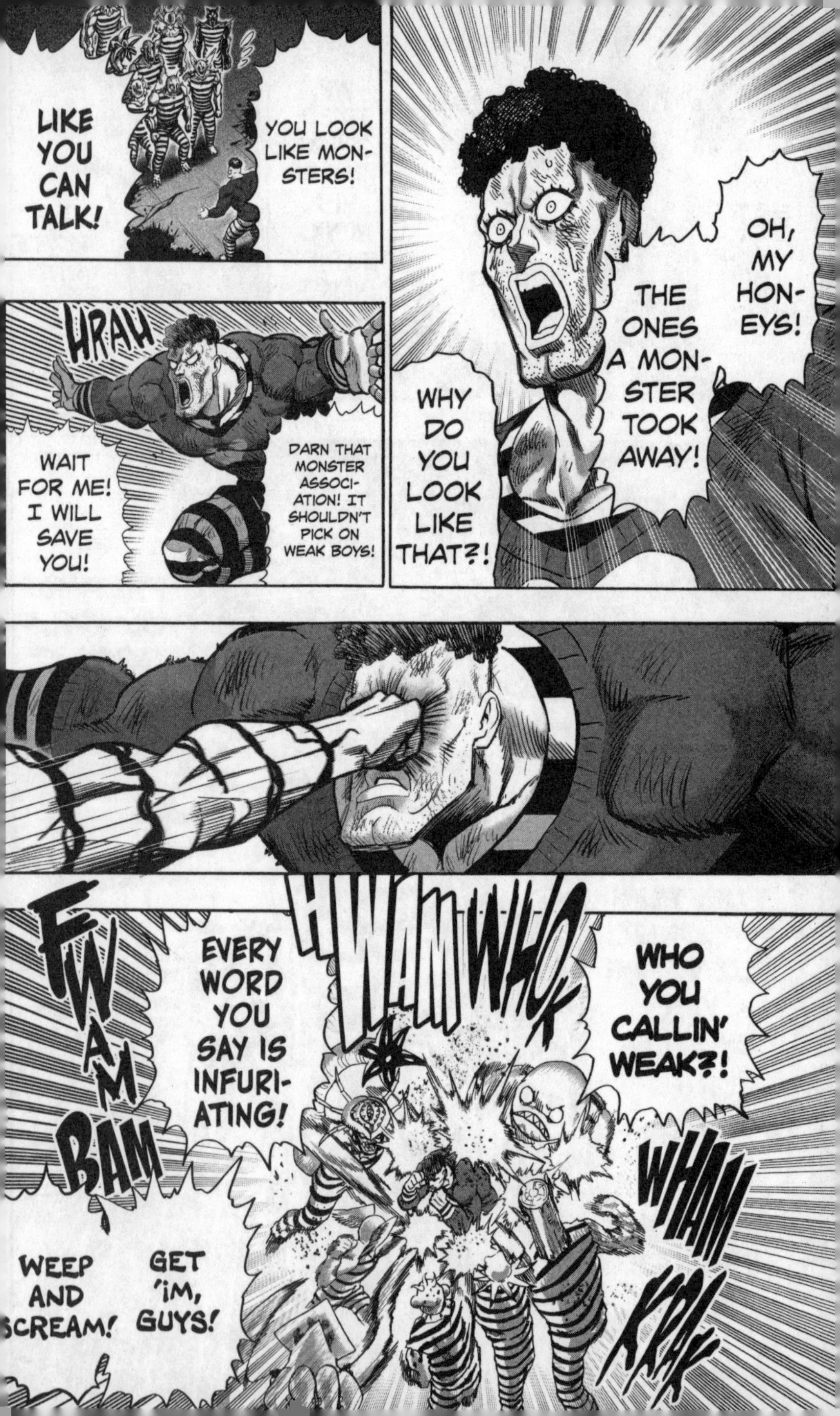
OH, MY HONEYS!
THE ONES A MONSTER TOOK AWAY!
WHY DO YOU LOOK LIKE THAT?!
YOU LOOK LIKE MONSTERS!
LIKE YOU CAN TALK!
HRAH
DARN THAT MONSTER ASSOCIATION! IT SHOULDN'T PICK ON WEAK BOYS!
WAIT FOR ME! I WILL SAVE YOU!
WHO YOU CALLIN' WEAK?!
WHOK
WAM
HWAM
EVERY WORD YOU SAY IS INFURIATING!
FWAM
BAM
WHAM
KRAK
GET 'IM, GUYS!
WEEP AND SCREAM!

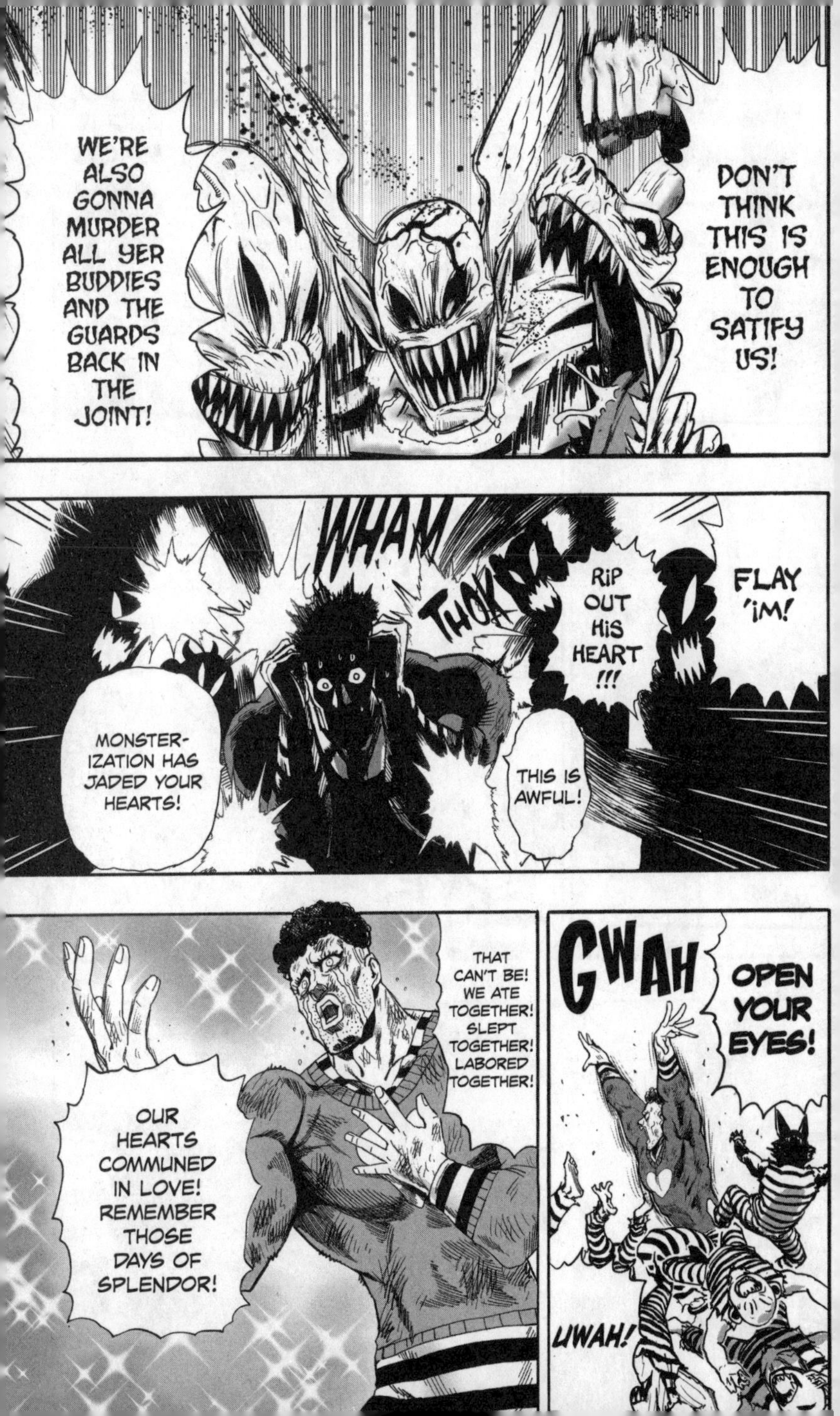
DON'T THINK THIS IS ENOUGH TO SATIFY US!
WE'RE ALSO GONNA MURDER ALL YER BUDDIES AND THE GUARDS BACK IN THE JOINT!
FLAY 'IM!
WHAM
RIP OUT HIS HEART!!!
THOK
THIS IS AWFUL!
MONSTER-IZATION HAS JADED YOUR HEARTS!
OPEN YOUR EYES!
GWAH
UWAH!
THAT CAN'T BE! WE ATE TOGETHER! SLEPT TOGETHER! LABORED TOGETHER!
OUR HEARTS COMMUNED IN LOVE! REMEMBER THOSE DAYS OF SPLENDOR!

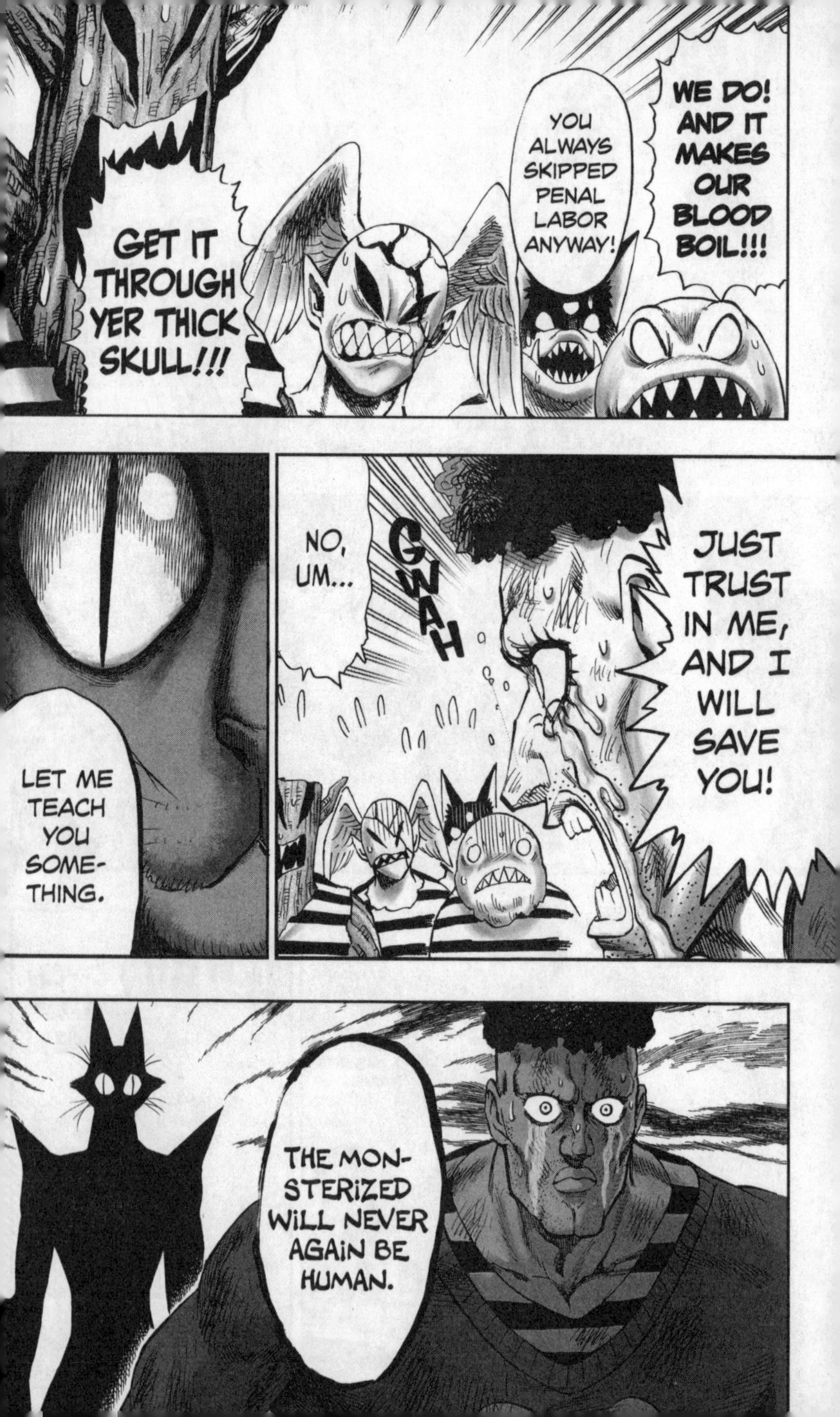
WE DO! AND IT MAKES OUR BLOOD BOIL!!!
YOU ALWAYS SKIPPED PENAL LABOR ANYWAY!
GET IT THROUGH YER THICK SKULL!!!
JUST TRUST IN ME, AND I WILL SAVE YOU!
GWAH
NO, UM...
LET ME TEACH YOU SOME-THING.
THE MON-STERIZED WILL NEVER AGAIN BE HUMAN.

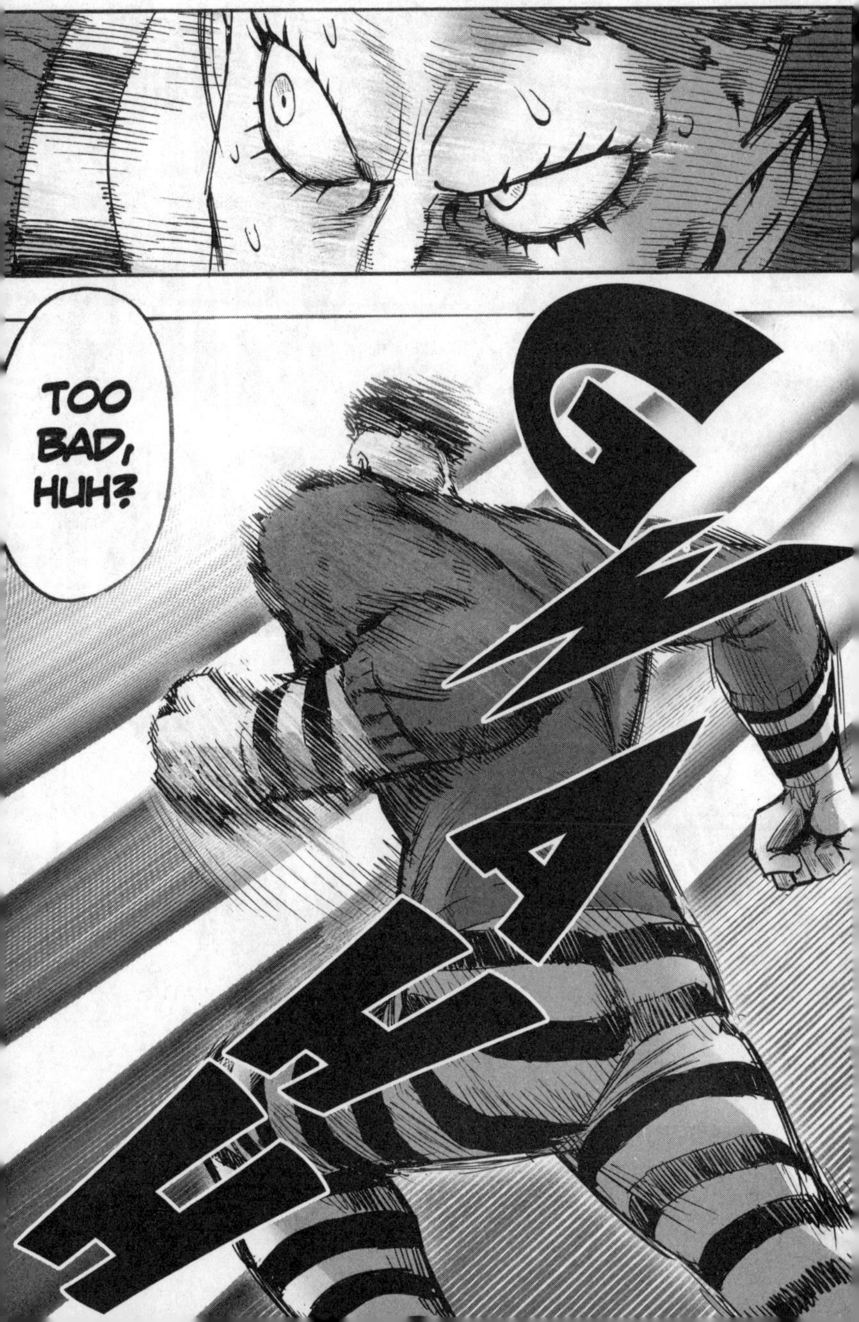
TOO BAD, HUH?

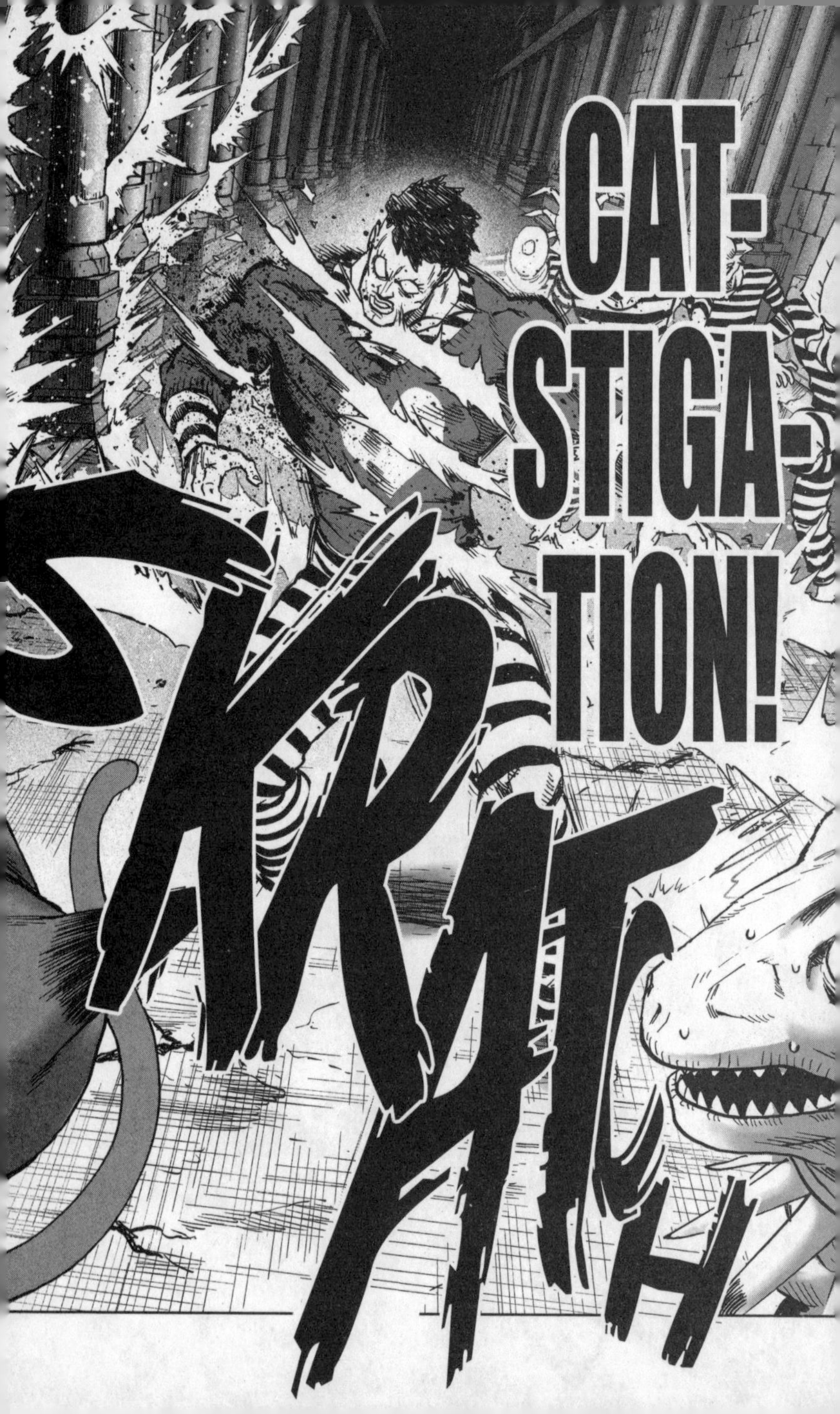
CAT-
STIGA-
TION!
SKRATCH

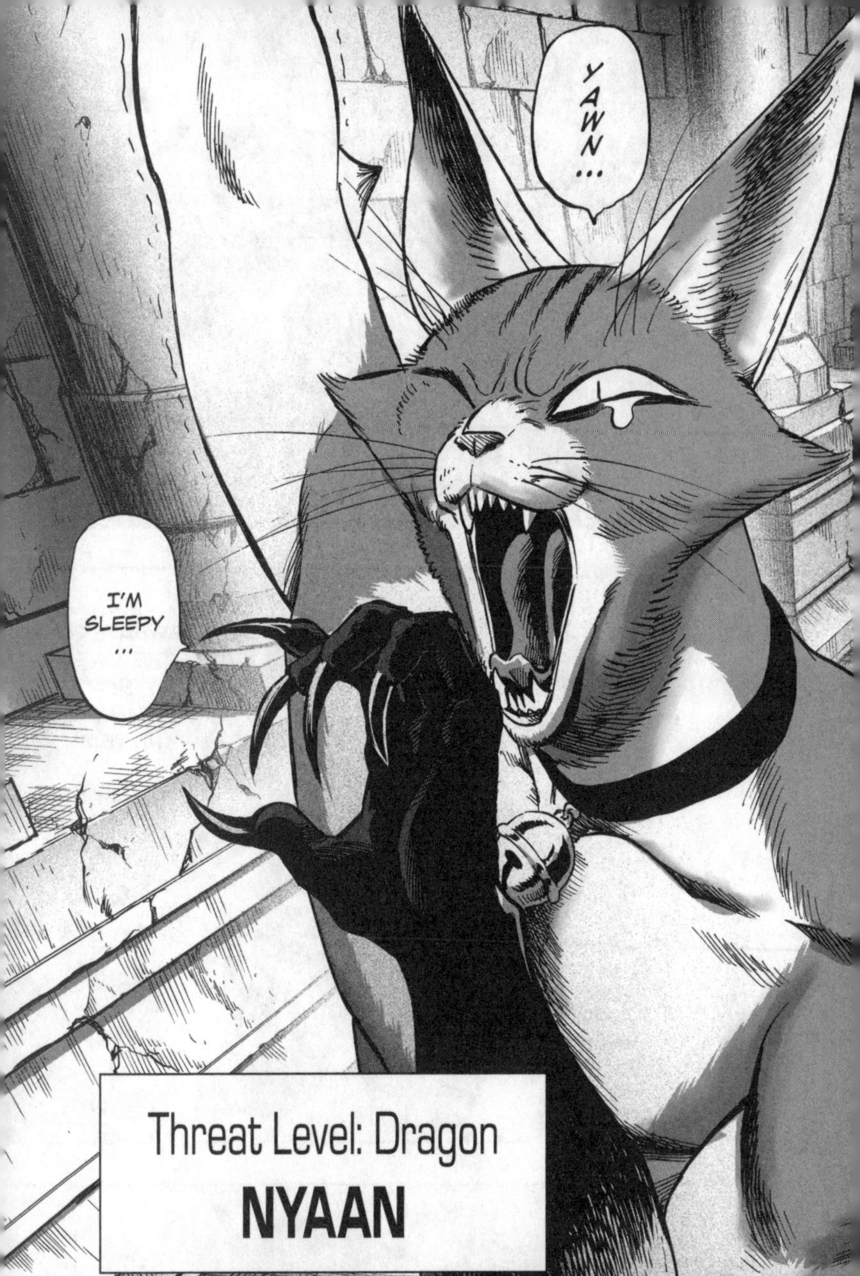
YAWN...
I'M SLEEPY...
Threat Level: Dragon
NYAAN

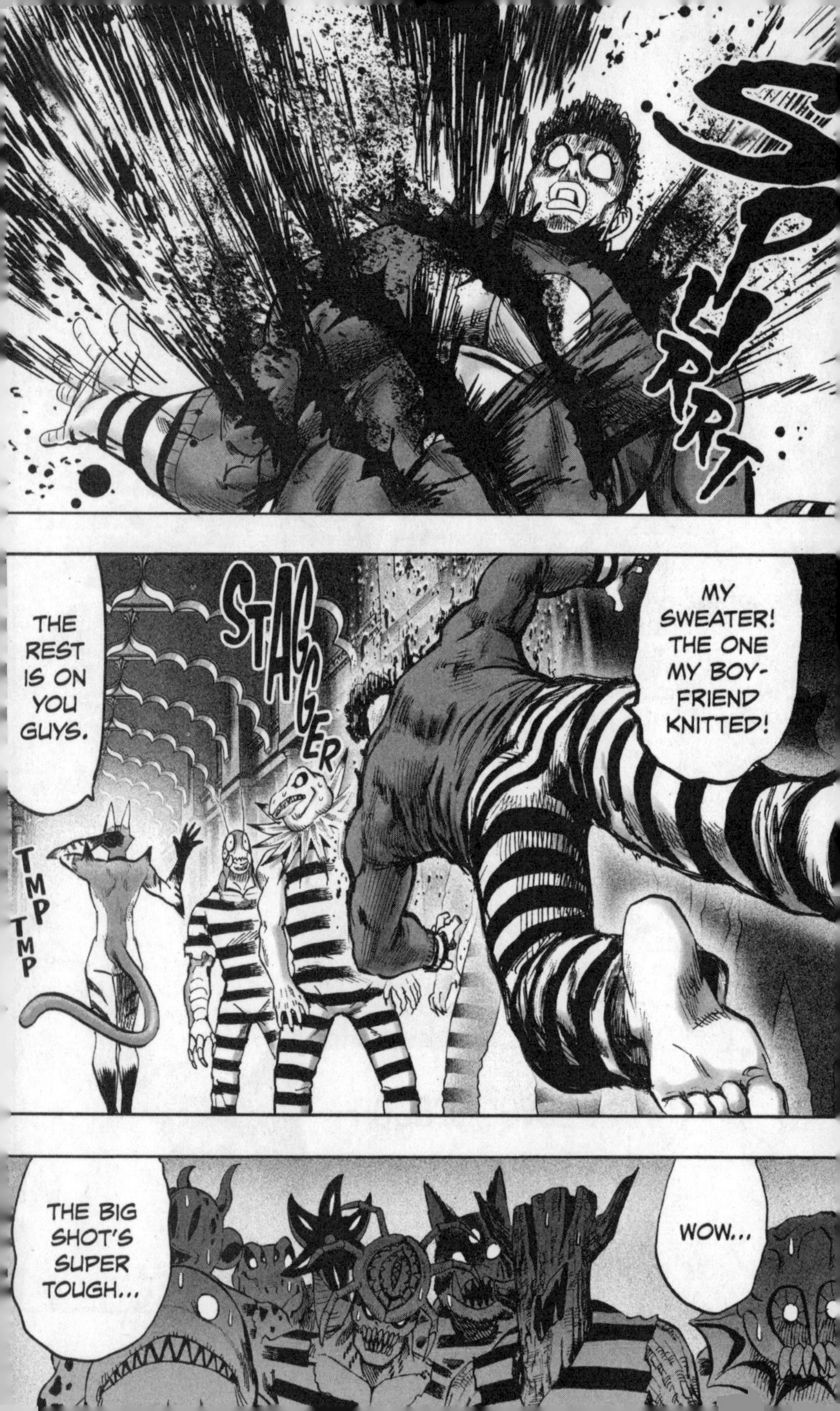
SPLURRRT
MY SWEATER! THE ONE MY BOY-FRIEND KNITTED!
STAGGER
THE REST IS ON YOU GUYS.
TMP TMP
WOW...
THE BIG SHOT'S SUPER TOUGH...

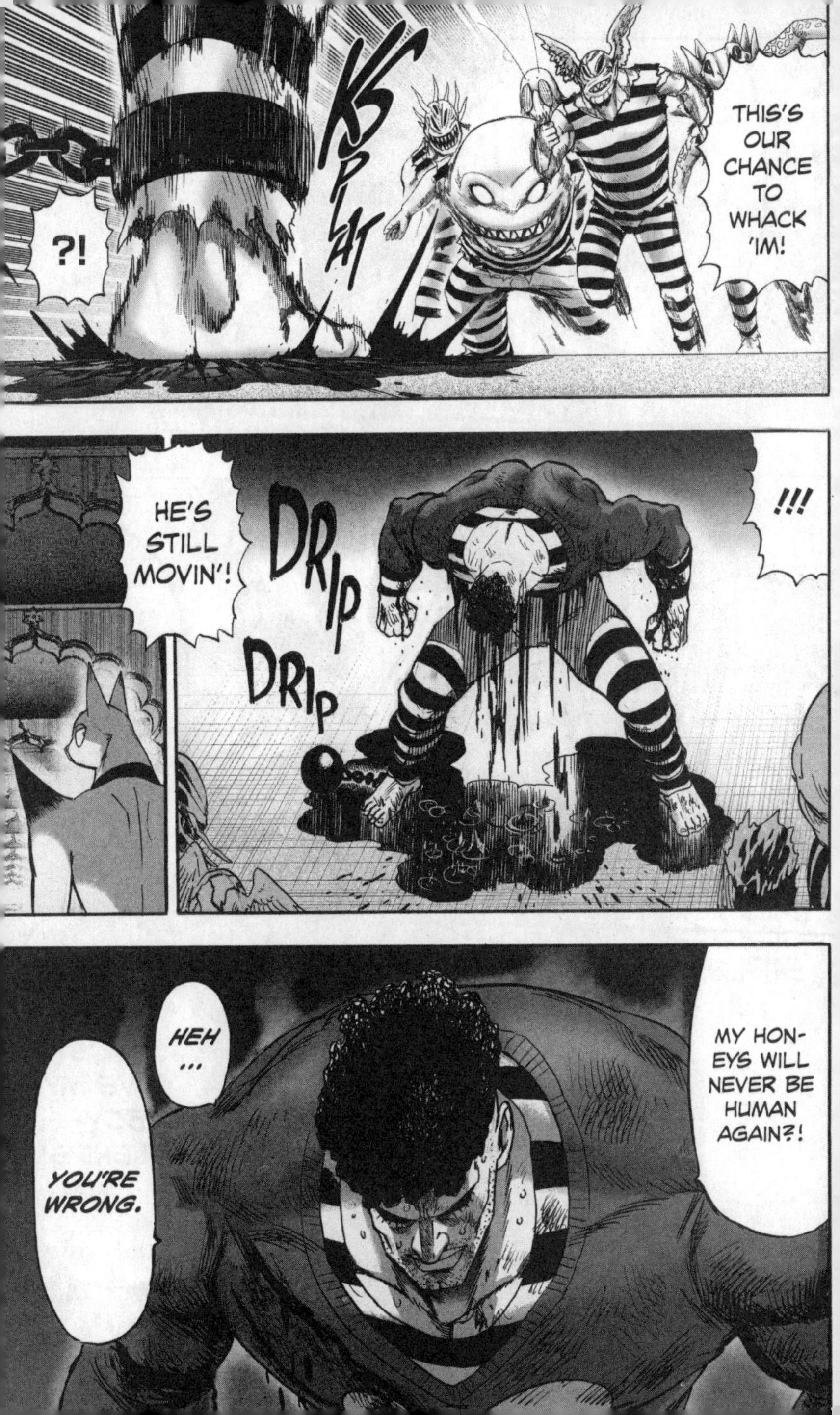
THIS'S OUR CHANCE TO WHACK 'IM!
KSPLAT
?!
!!!
DRIP
DRIP
HE'S STILL MOVIN'!
MY HON-EYS WILL NEVER BE HUMAN AGAIN?!
HEH ...
YOU'RE WRONG.

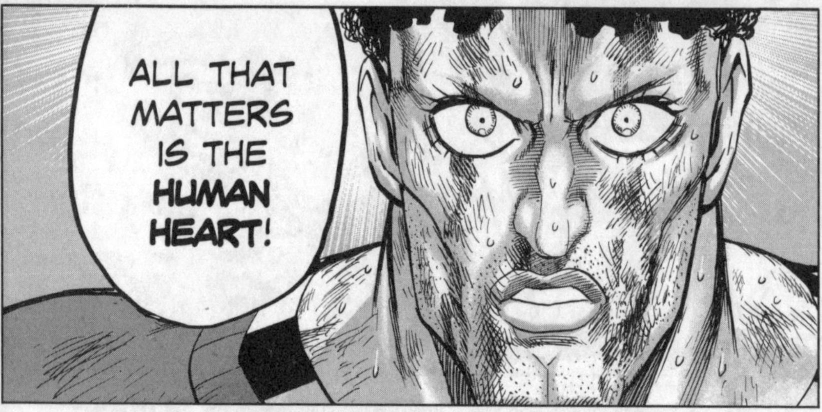
ALL THAT MATTERS IS THE HUMAN HEART!

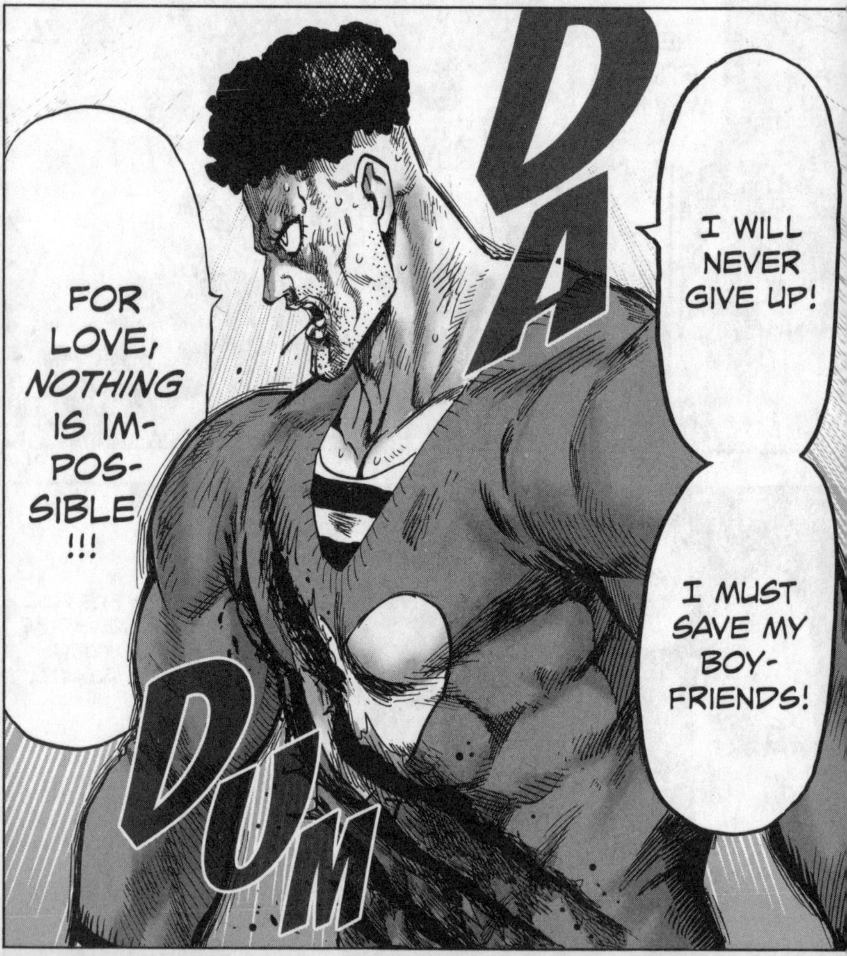
DA
I WILL NEVER GIVE UP!
I MUST SAVE MY BOY-FRIENDS!
FOR LOVE, NOTHING IS IM-POS-SIBLE!!!
DUM

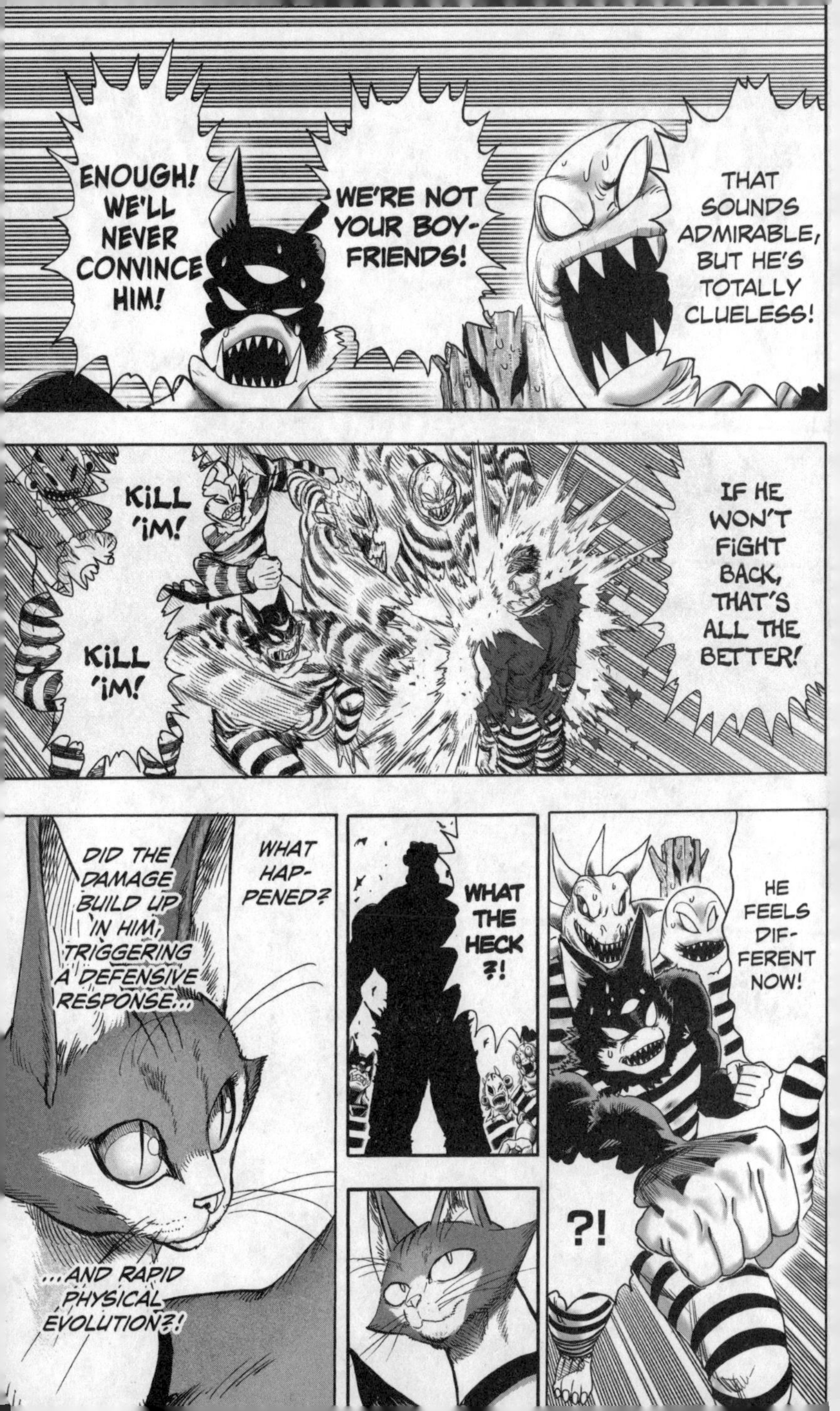
THAT SOUNDS ADMIRABLE, BUT HE'S TOTALLY CLUELESS!
WE'RE NOT YOUR BOY-FRIENDS!
ENOUGH! WE'LL NEVER CONVINCE HIM!
IF HE WON'T FIGHT BACK, THAT'S ALL THE BETTER!
KILL 'IM!
KILL 'IM!
HE FEELS DIF-FERENT NOW!
?!
WHAT THE HECK ?!
WHAT HAP-PENED?
DID THE DAMAGE BUILD UP IN HIM, TRIGGERING A DEFENSIVE RESPONSE...
...AND RAPID PHYSICAL EVOLUTION?!

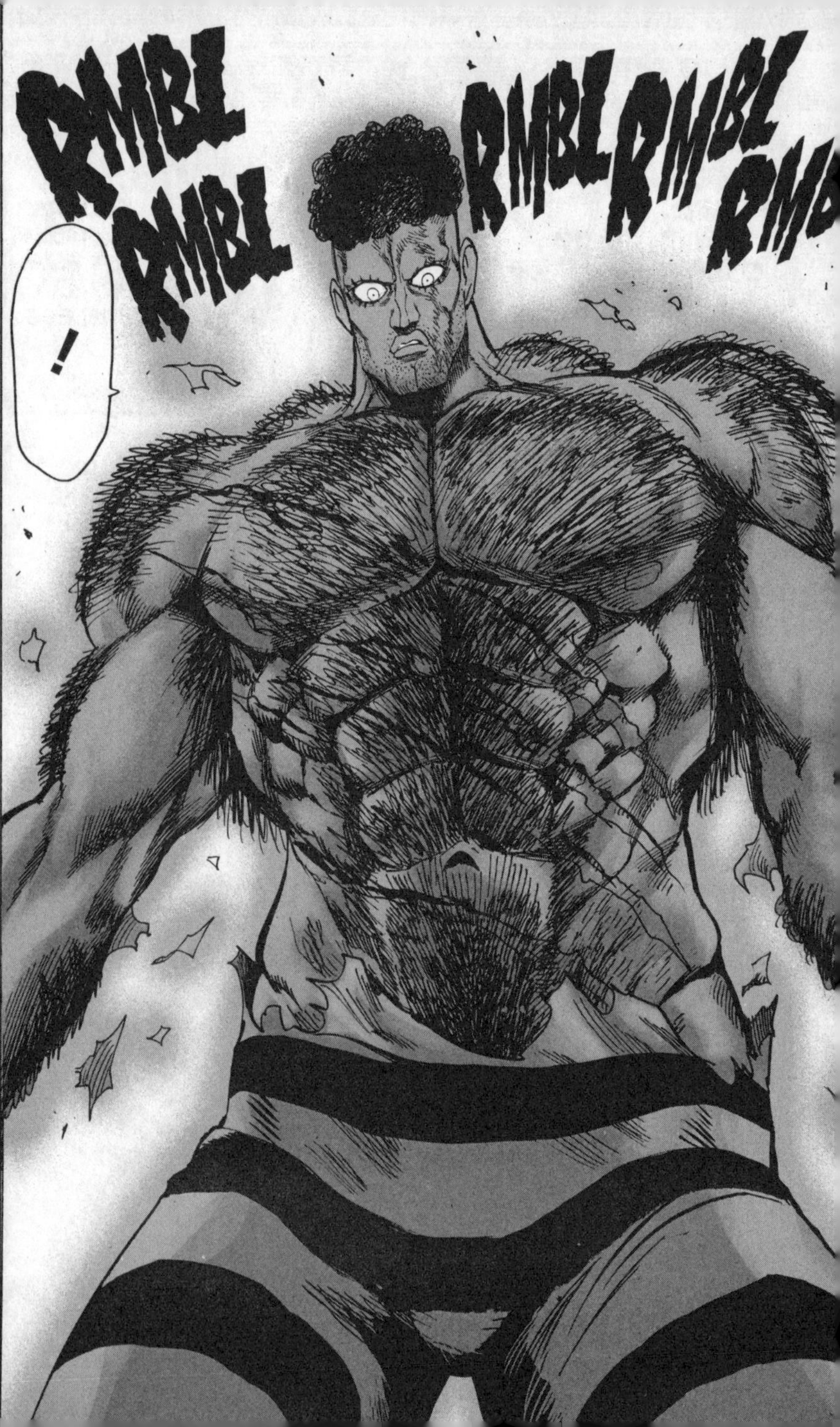
RMBL RMBL RMB
RMBL RMBL
!

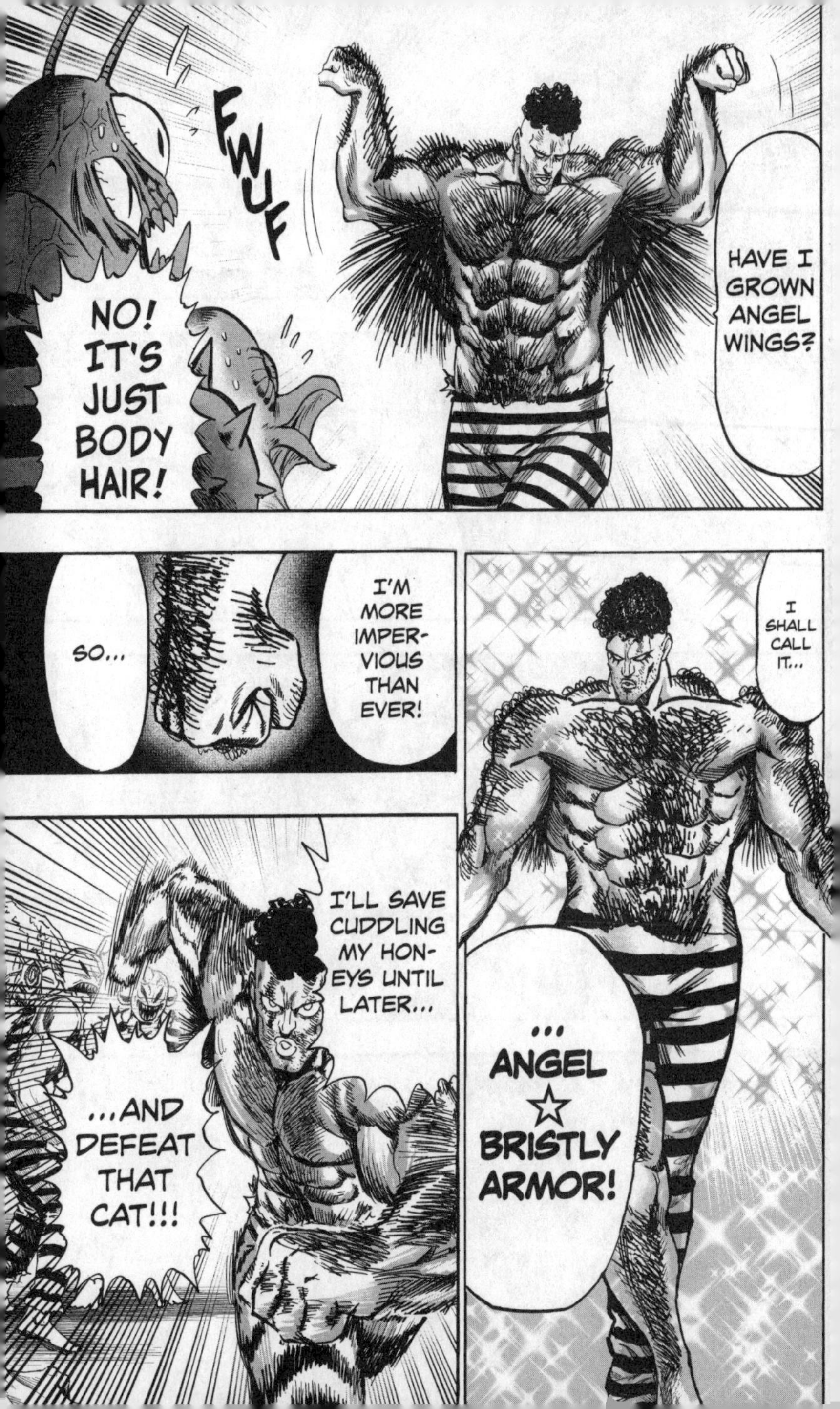
HAVE I GROWN ANGEL WINGS?
FWUF
NO! IT'S JUST BODY HAIR!
I SHALL CALL IT...
...ANGEL☆BRISTLY ARMOR!
I'M MORE IMPERVIOUS THAN EVER!
SO...
I'LL SAVE CUDDLING MY HONEYS UNTIL LATER...
...AND DEFEAT THAT CAT!!!

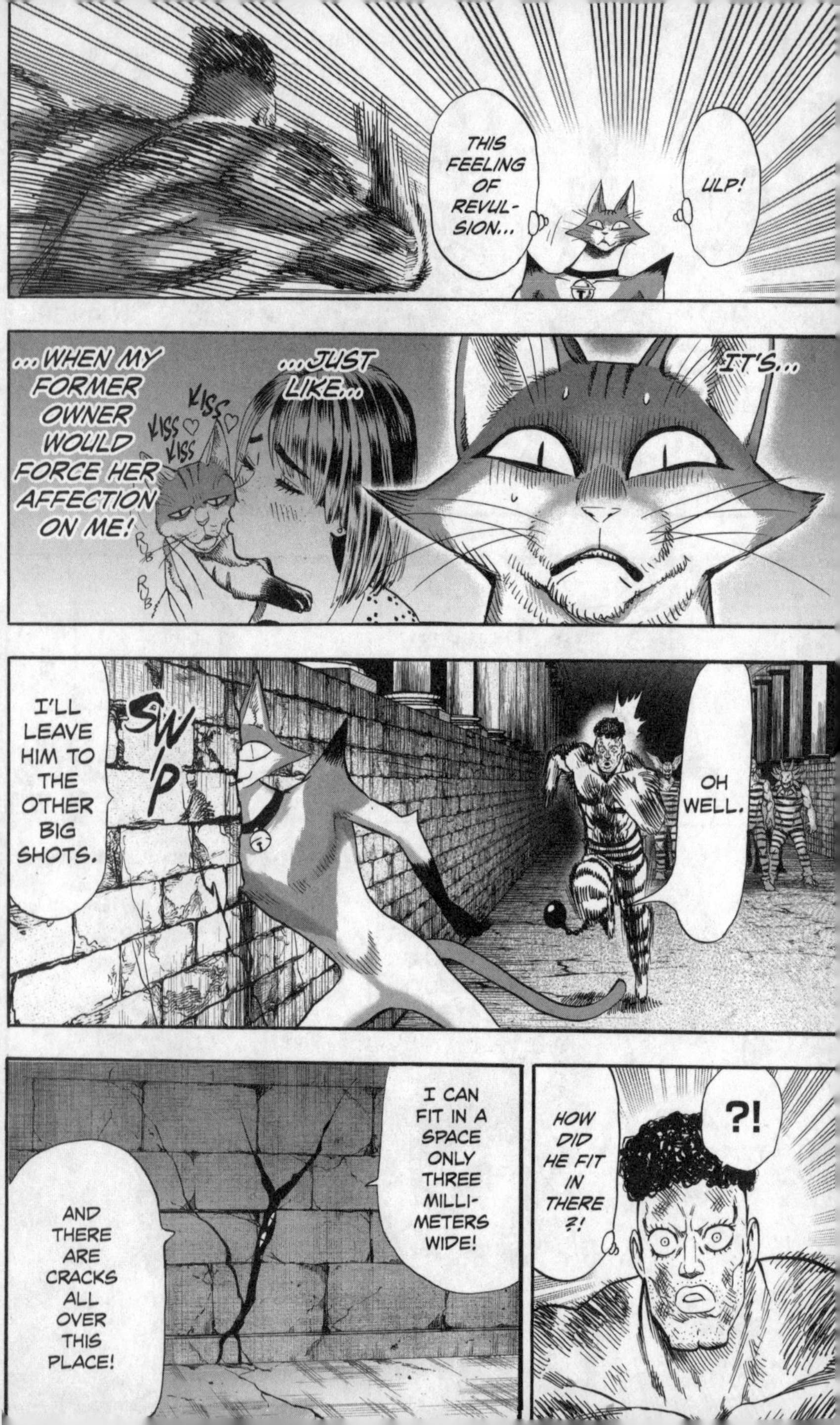
ULP!
THIS FEELING OF REVULSION...
IT'S...
...JUST LIKE...
...WHEN MY FORMER OWNER WOULD FORCE HER AFFECTION ON ME!
KISS KISS KISS
RUB RUB
OH WELL.
SWIP
I'LL LEAVE HIM TO THE OTHER BIG SHOTS.
?!
HOW DID HE FIT IN THERE?!
I CAN FIT IN A SPACE ONLY THREE MILLIMETERS WIDE!
AND THERE ARE CRACKS ALL OVER THIS PLACE!

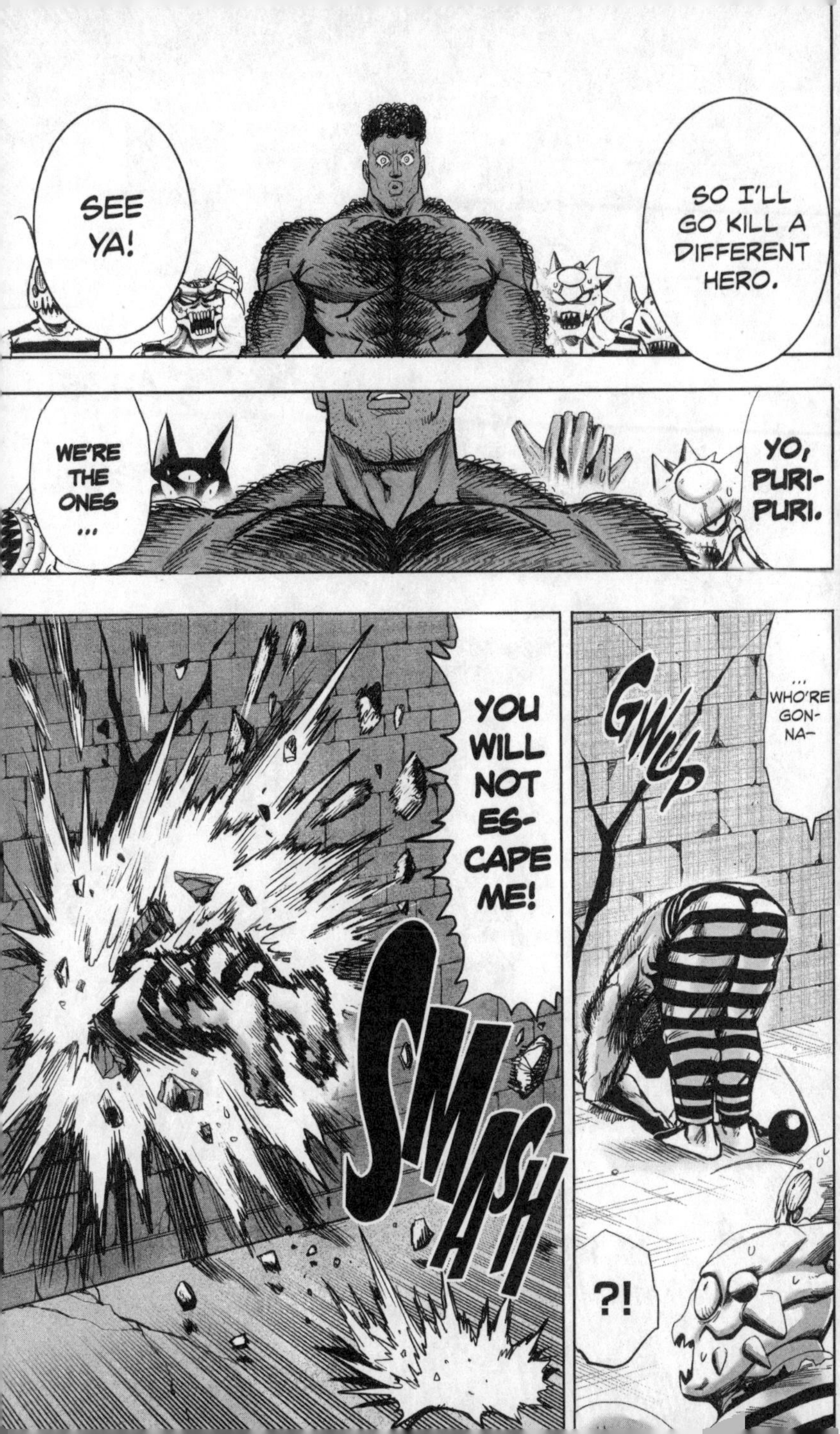
SO I'LL GO KILL A DIFFERENT HERO.
SEE YA!
YO, PURI-PURI.
WE'RE THE ONES...
...WHO'RE GON-NA-
GWUP
?!
YOU WILL NOT ES-CAPE ME!
SMASH

ANGEL ☆ CRAWL!
I'LL SWIM THROUGH THE EARTH TO CHASE THAT CAT MONSTER!!!

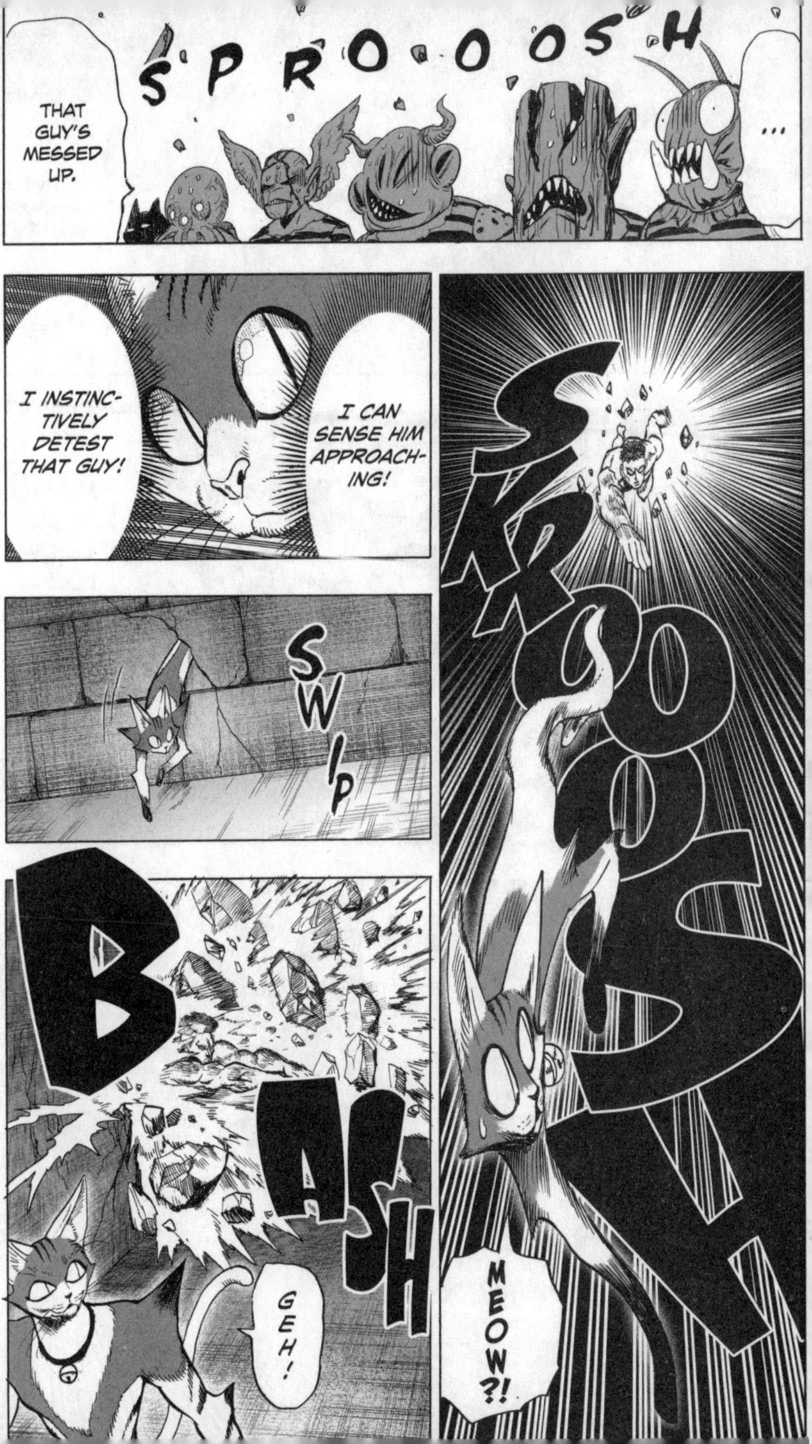
...
SPROOOSH
THAT GUY'S MESSED UP.
SKROOOSH
MEOW?!
I CAN SENSE HIM APPROACHING!
I INSTINCTIVELY DETEST THAT GUY!
SWIP
BASH
GEH!

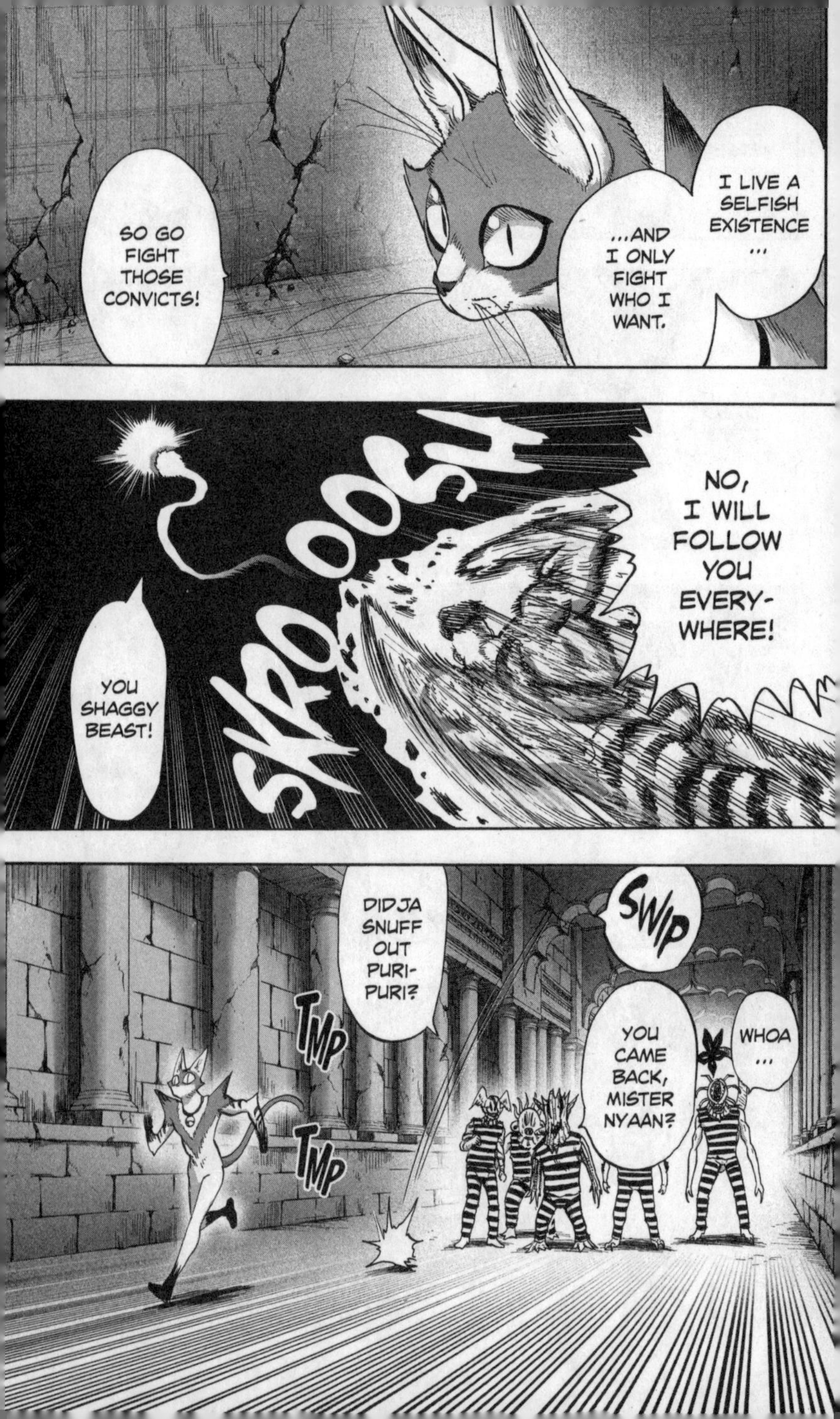
I LIVE A SELFISH EXISTENCE ...
...AND I ONLY FIGHT WHO I WANT.
SO GO FIGHT THOSE CONVICTS!
NO, I WILL FOLLOW YOU EVERY-WHERE!
SKROOOSH
YOU SHAGGY BEAST!
SWIP
WHOA ...
YOU CAME BACK, MISTER NYAAN?
DIDJA SNUFF OUT PURI-PURI?
TMP
TMP

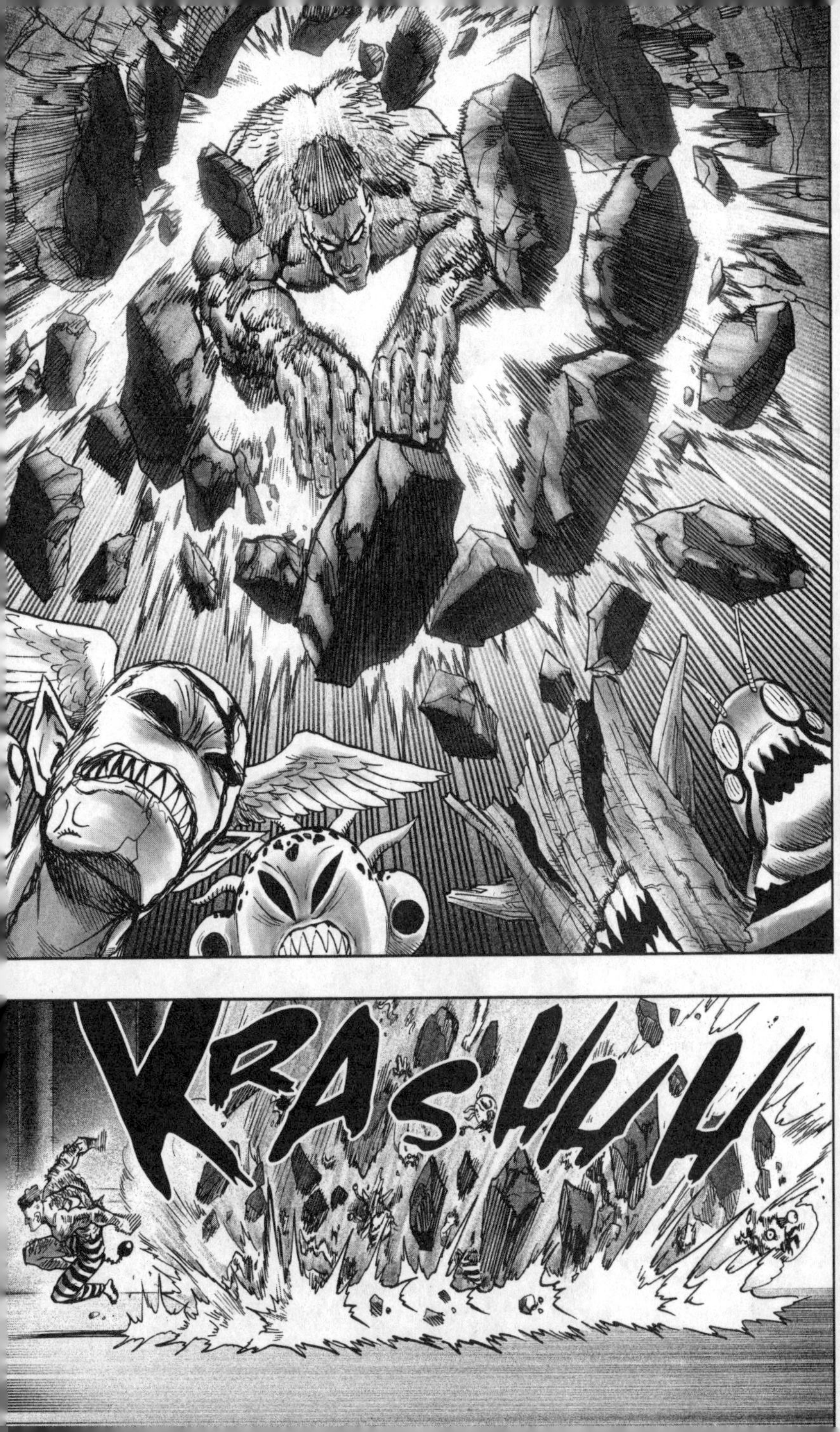
KRASHHH

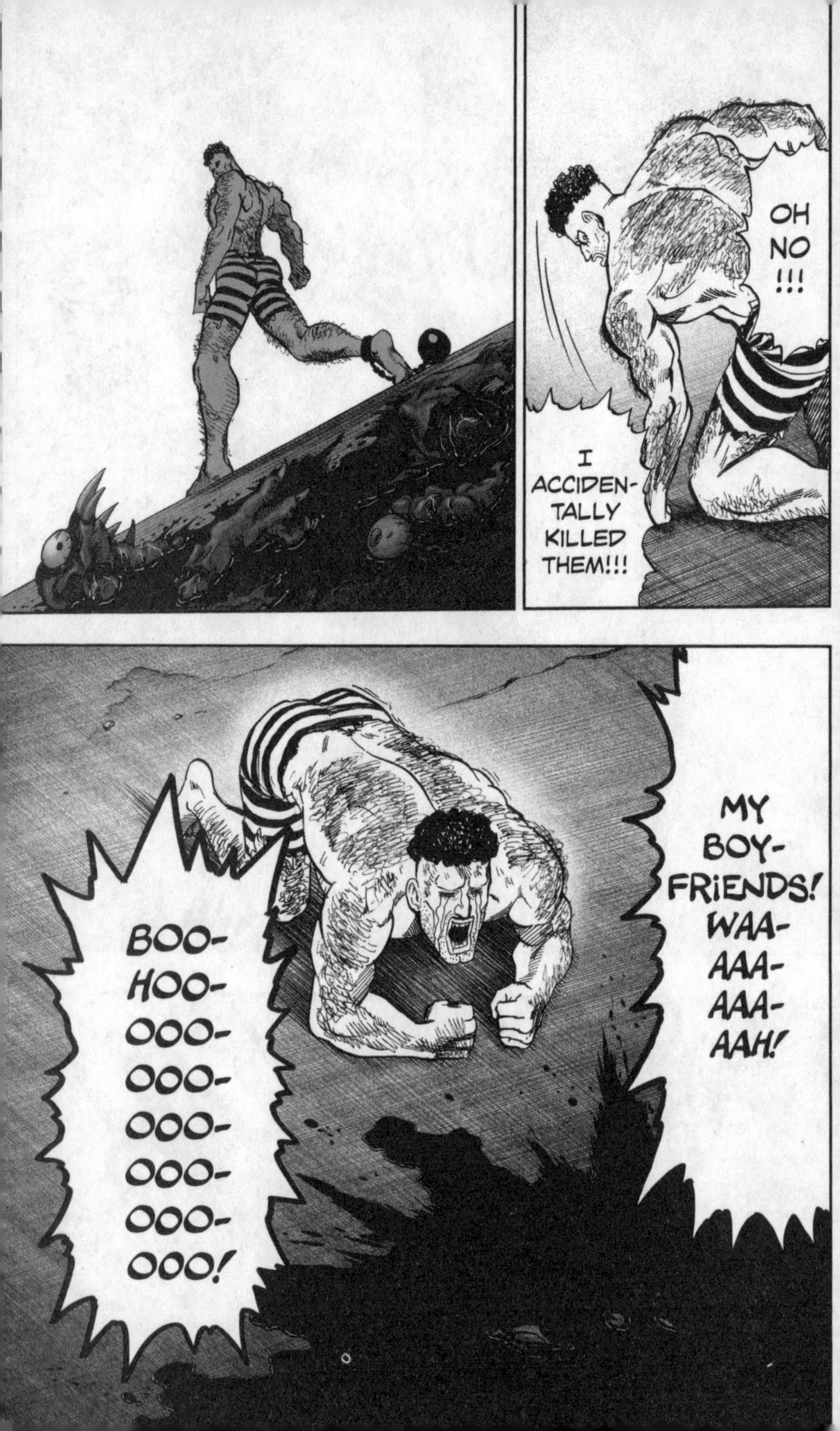
OH NO !!!
I ACCIDEN-TALLY KILLED THEM!!!
MY BOY-FRIENDS! WAA-AAA-AAA-AAH!
BOO-HOO-OOO-OOO-OOO-OOO-OOO-OOO!

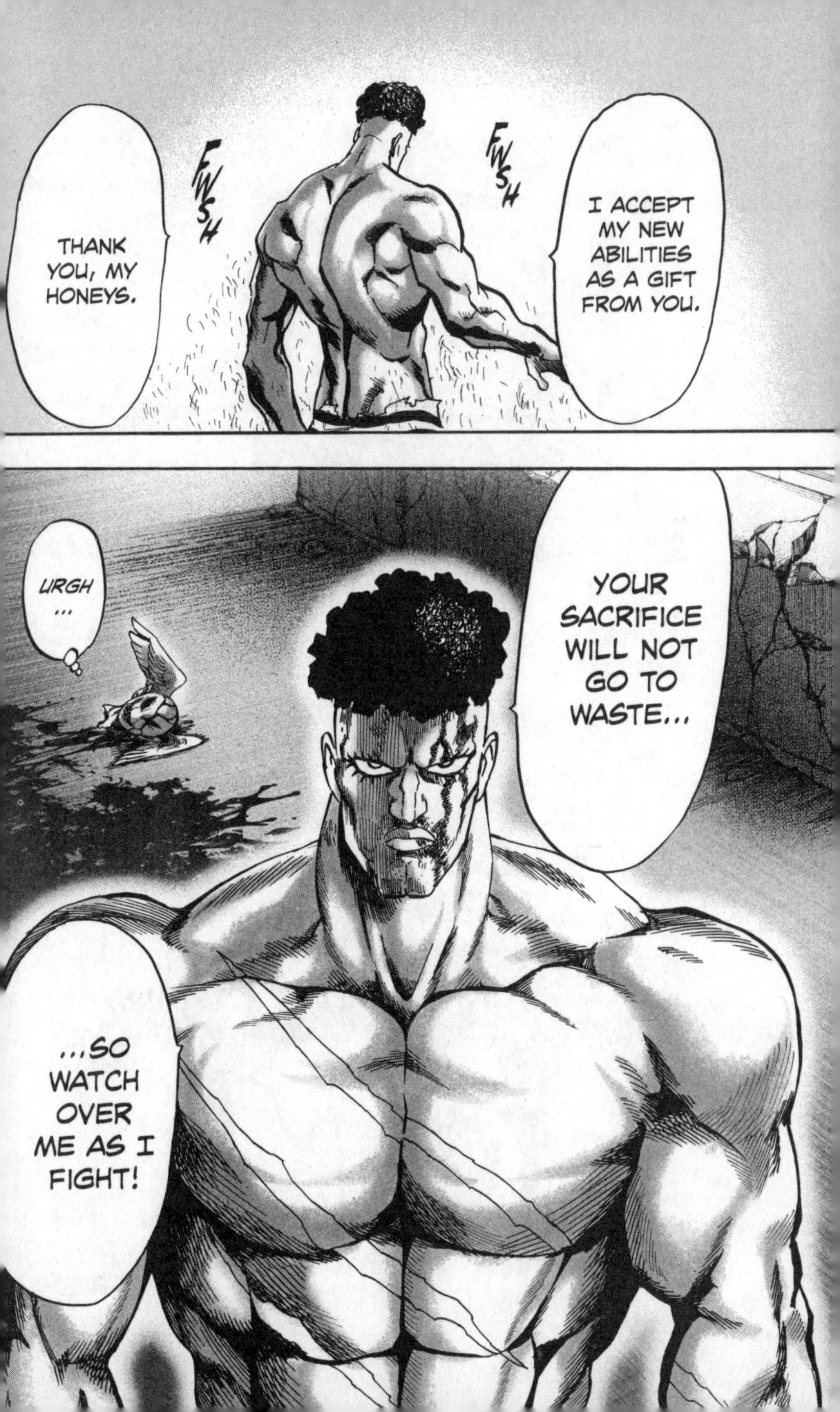
I ACCEPT MY NEW ABILITIES AS A GIFT FROM YOU.
FWSH
FWSH
THANK YOU, MY HONEYS.
YOUR SACRIFICE WILL NOT GO TO WASTE...
URGH ...
...SO WATCH OVER ME AS I FIGHT!

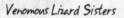

Venomous Lizard Sisters
Raptora (younger)
Raptera (older)

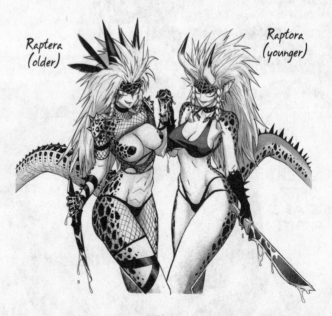

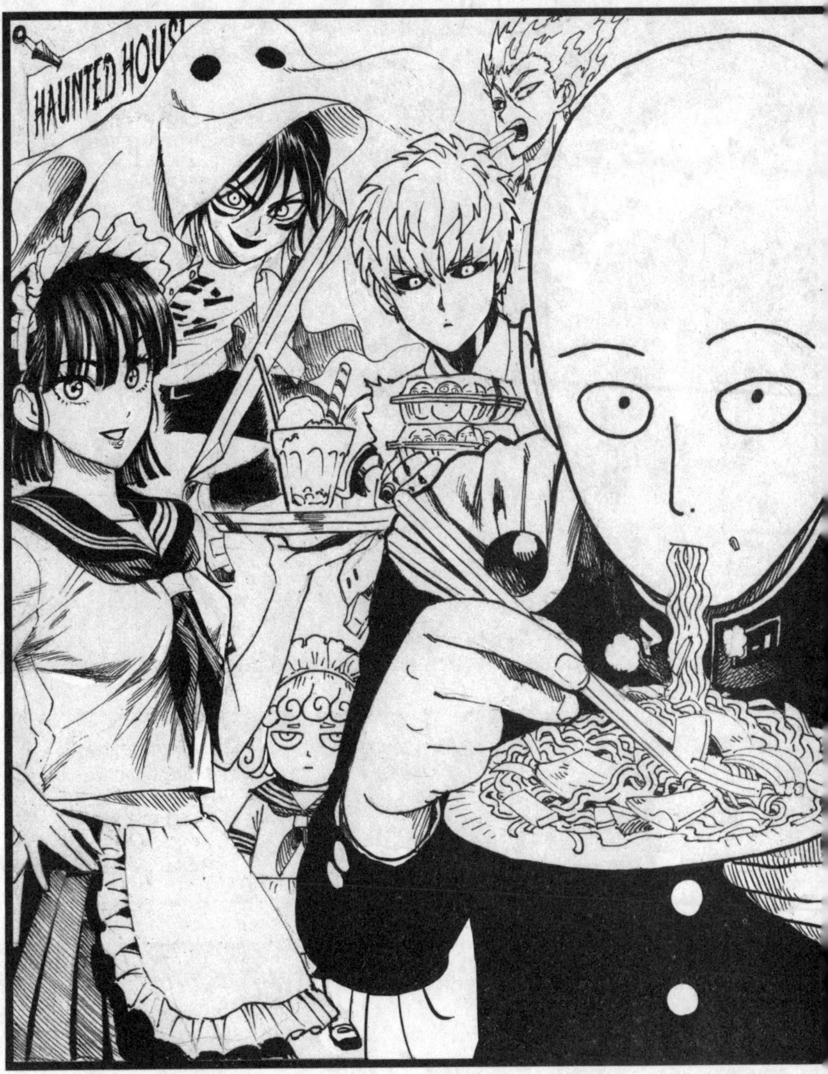
HAUNTED HOUS

PUNCH 111: GLUTTONY

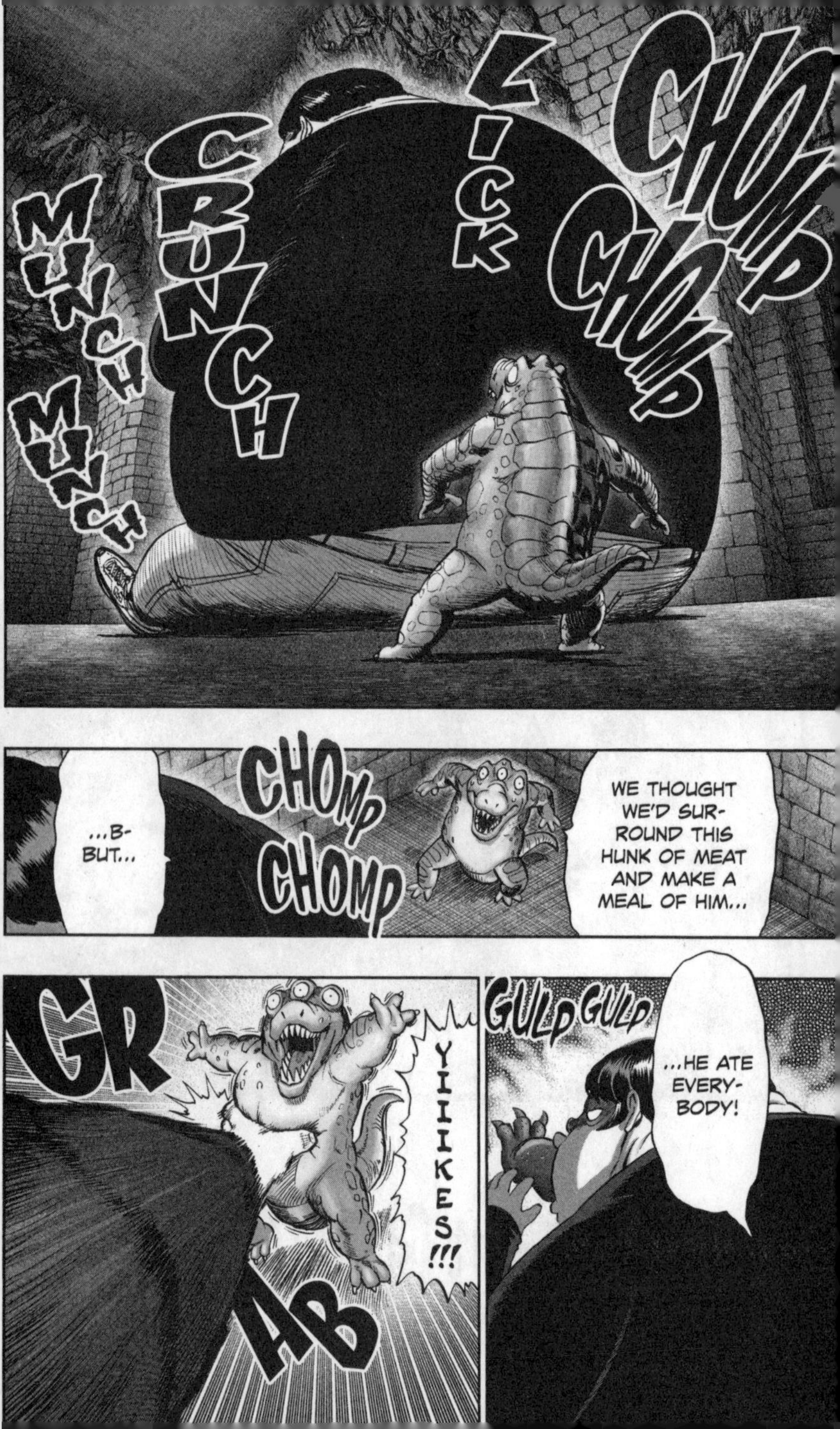
CHOMP
CHOMP
LICK
CRUNCH
MUNCH MUNCH
WE THOUGHT WE'D SUR-ROUND THIS HUNK OF MEAT AND MAKE A MEAL OF HIM...
CHOMP CHOMP
...B-BUT...
GULP GULP
...HE ATE EVERY-BODY!
YIIIKES!!!
GR
AB

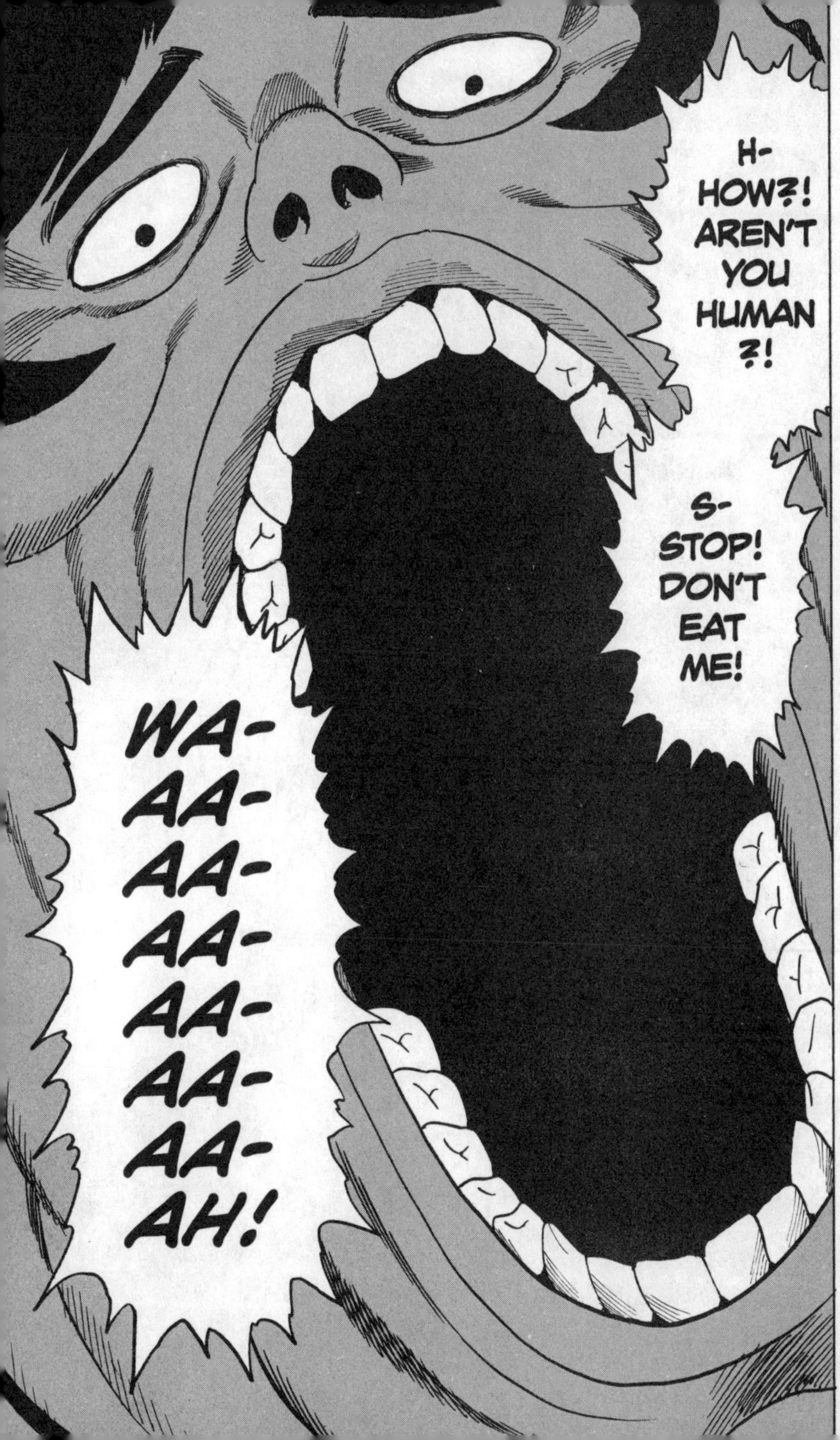
H- HOW?! AREN'T YOU HUMAN ?!
S- STOP! DON'T EAT ME!
WA- AA- AA- AA- AA- AA- AA- AH!

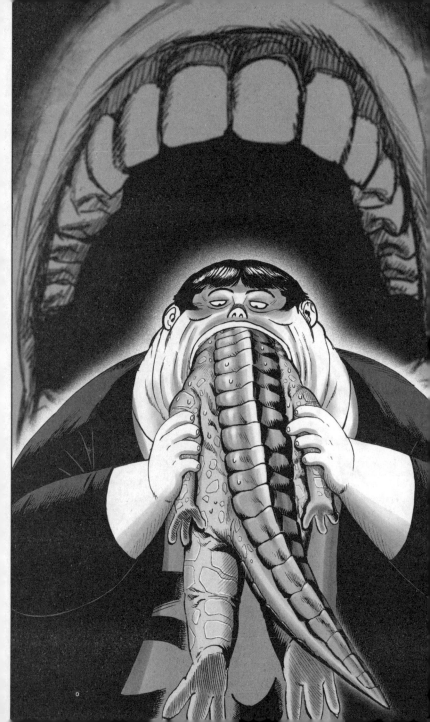

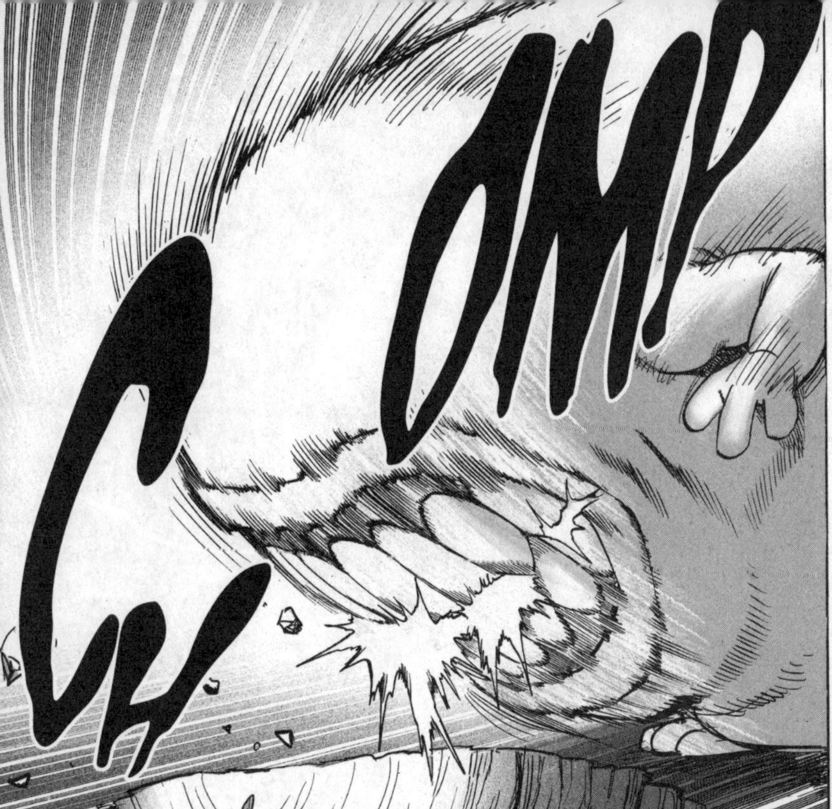
CHOMP
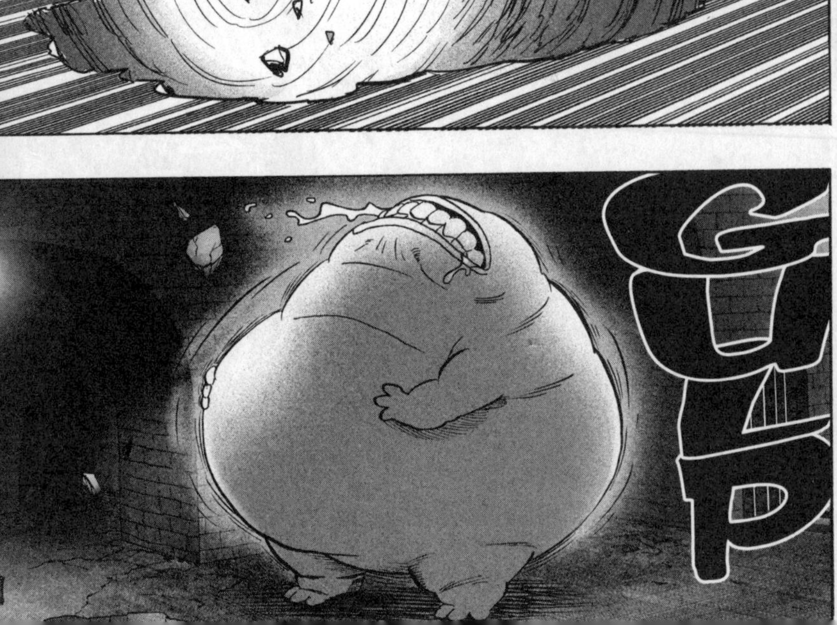
GULP

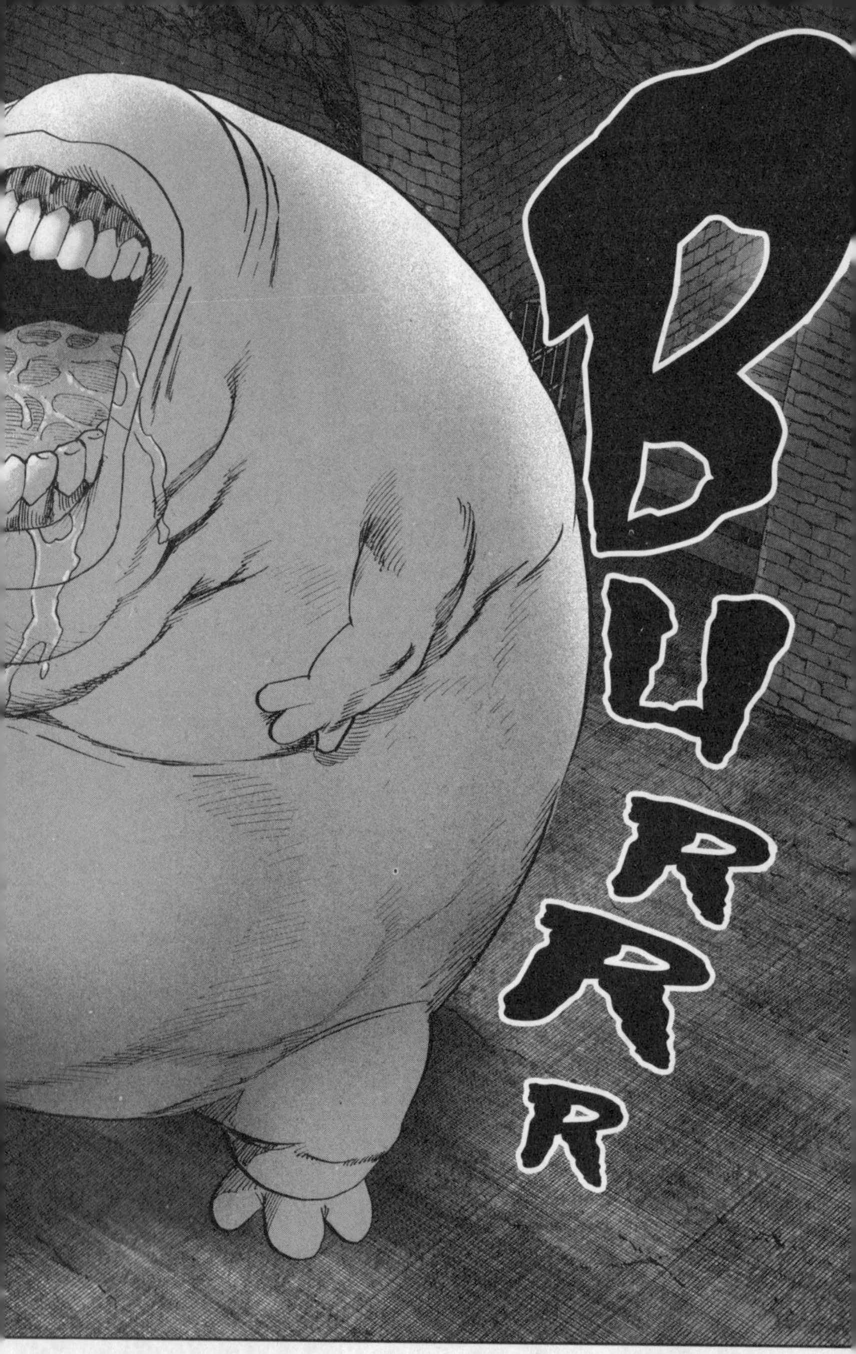
BURRR

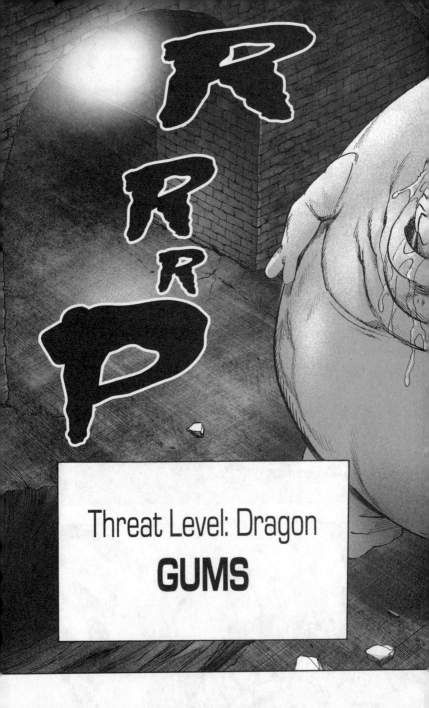

Threat Level: Dragon
GUMS

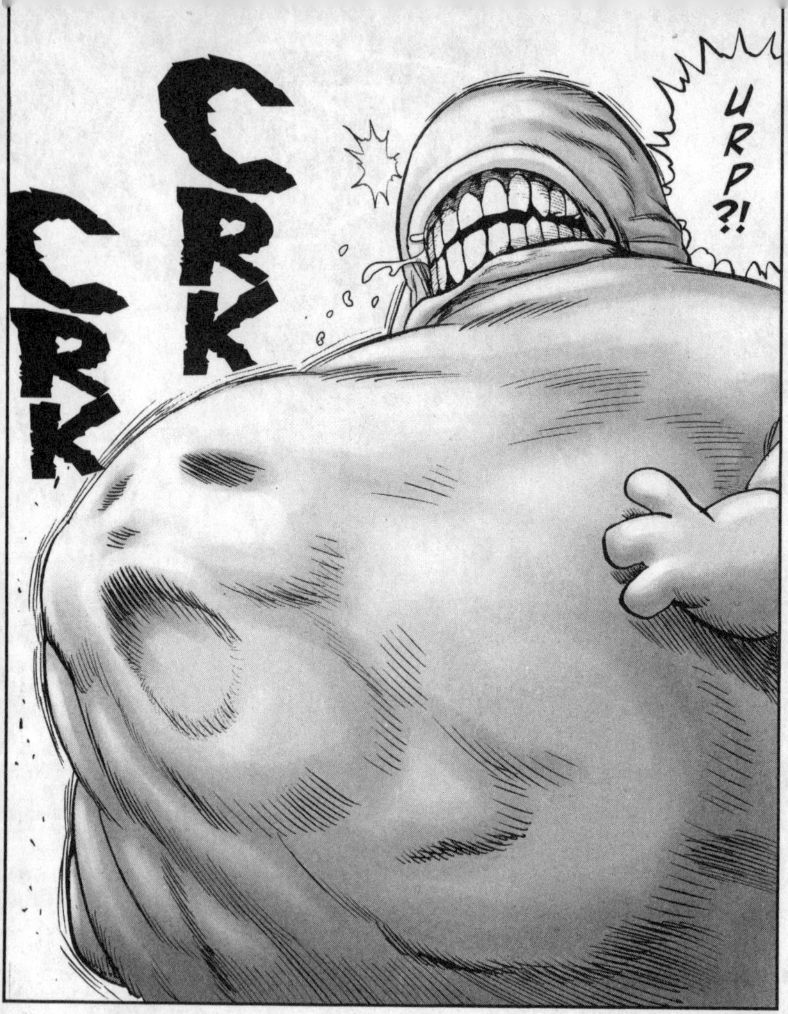
URP?!
CRK
CRK
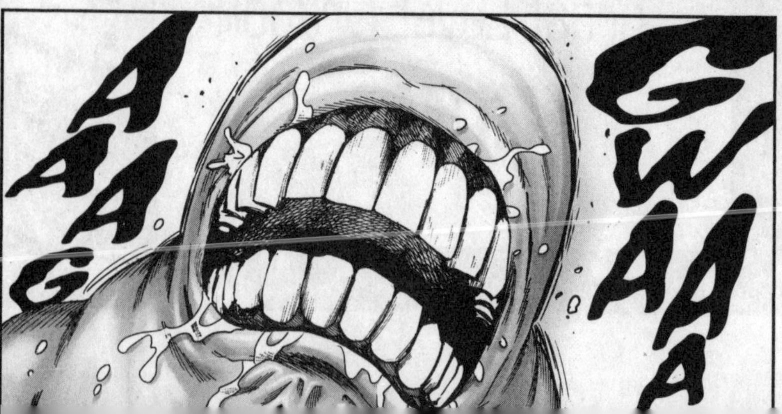
GWAAAA
AAAG

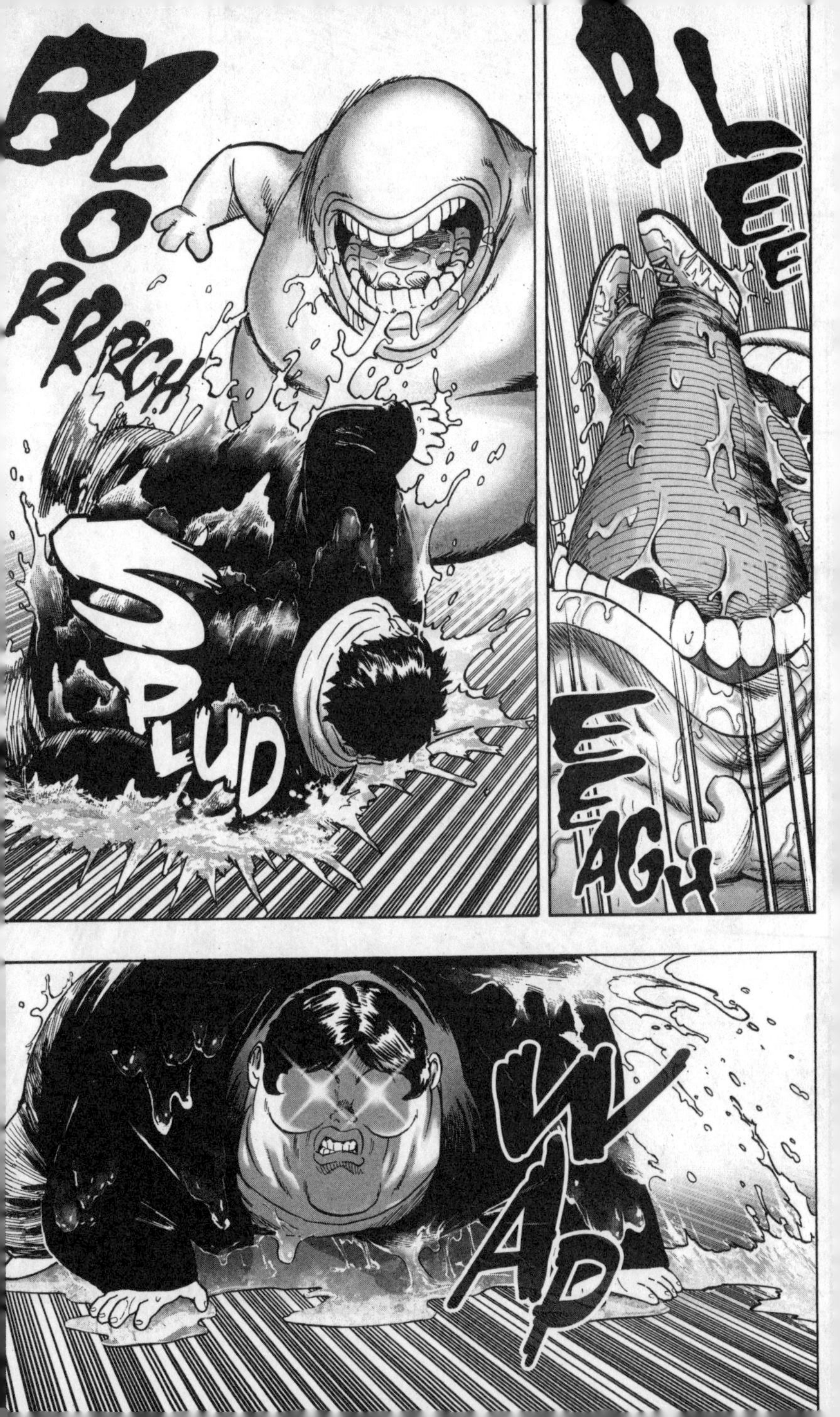
BLEEE
EEAGH
BLORRRRCH
SPLUD
WAD

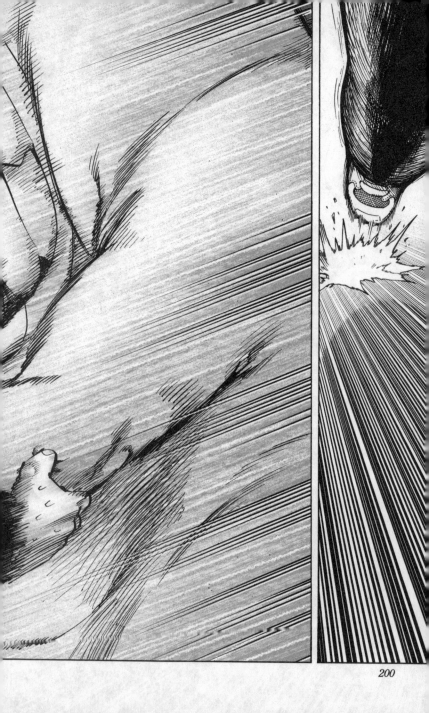

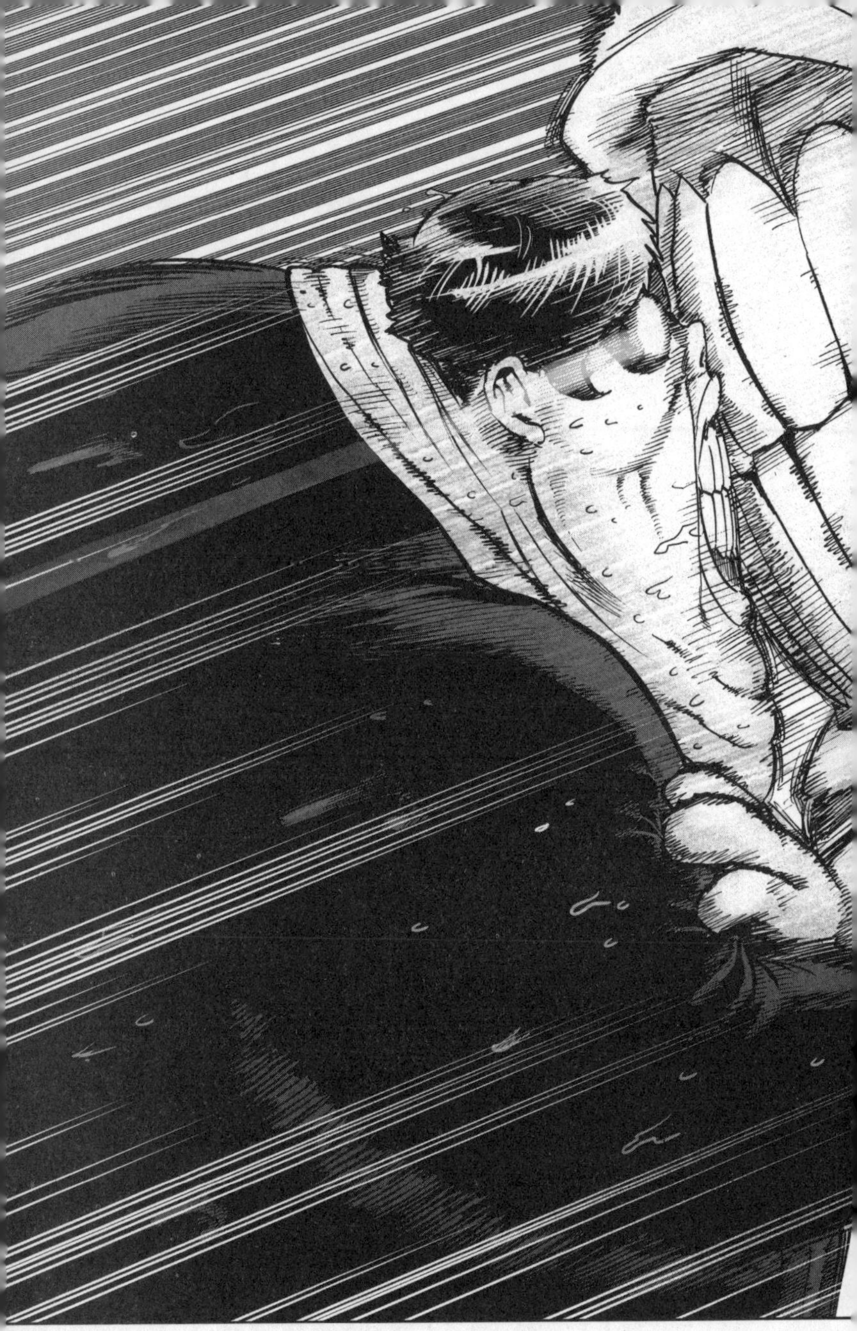

PUNCH 112:
SUPERALLOY BLACKLUSTER

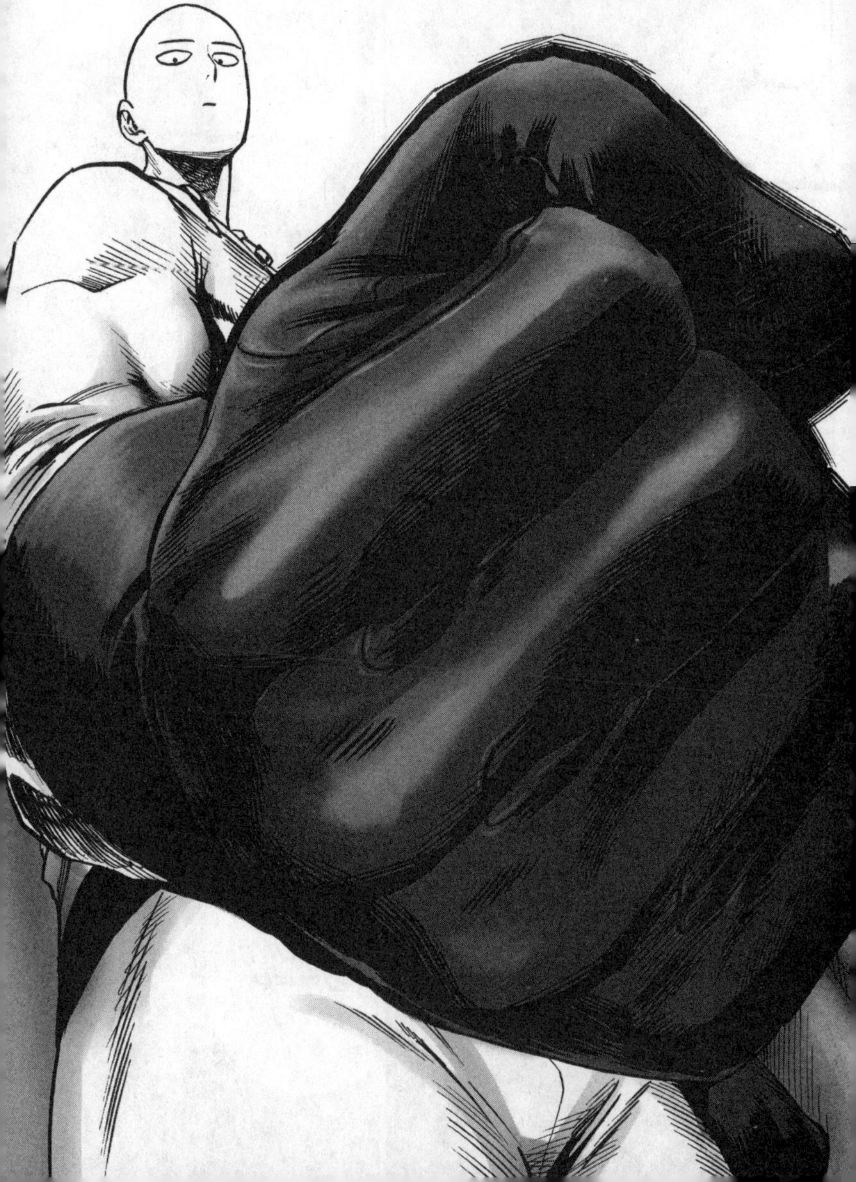

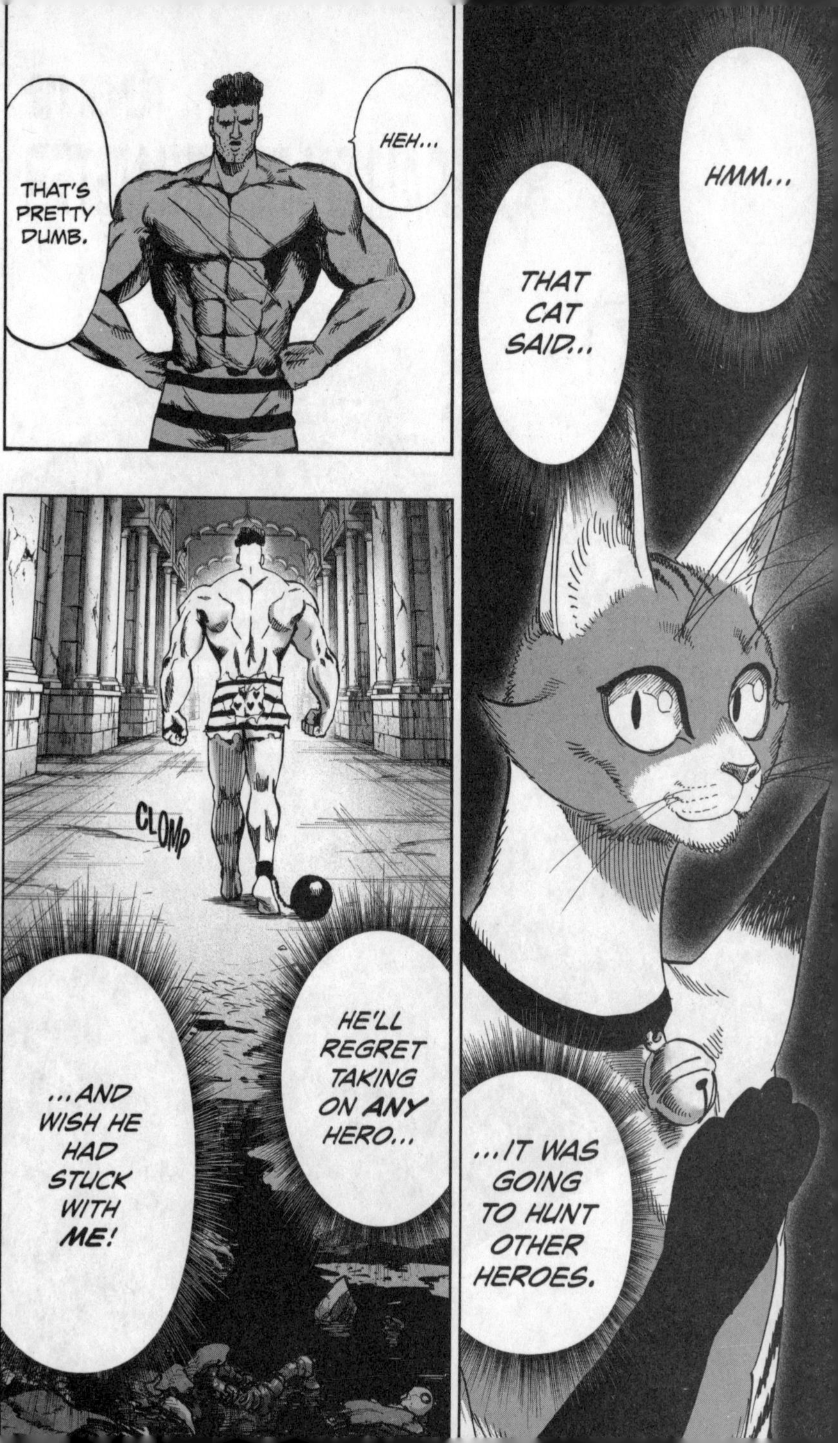
HMM...
THAT CAT SAID...
...IT WAS GOING TO HUNT OTHER HEROES.
HEH...
THAT'S PRETTY DUMB.
CLOMP
HE'LL REGRET TAKING ON ANY HERO...
...AND WISH HE HAD STUCK WITH ME!

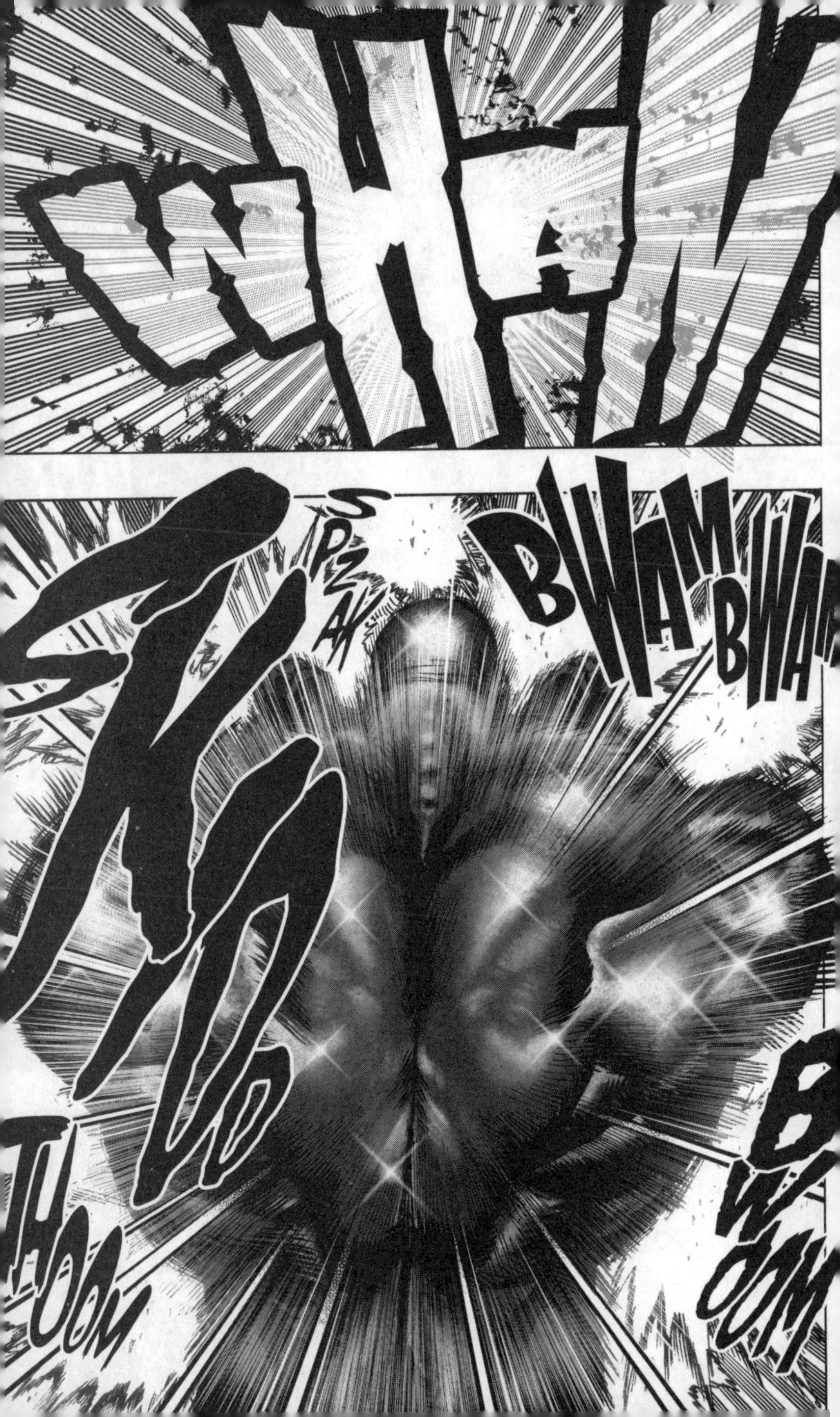
BWOM
BWAM
BWAM
SPZAK
THOOM

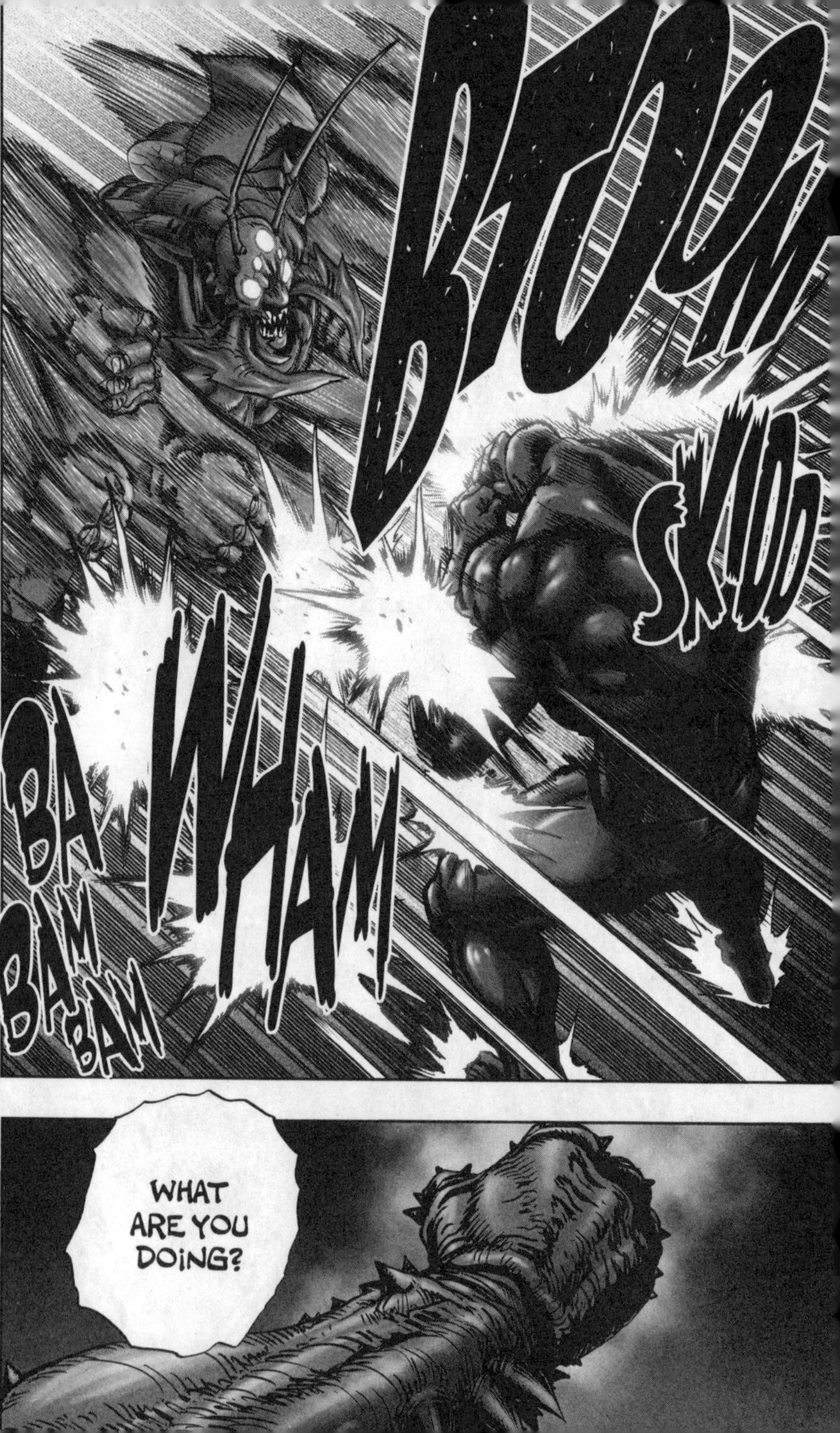
WHAM
BAM BAM BAM
WHAT ARE YOU DOING?

WHY ARE YOU FREEZING UP?
HAVE YOU GIVEN UP?
SUPER-ALLOY BLACKLUSTER...
...WHY DON'T YOU FIGHT BACK?

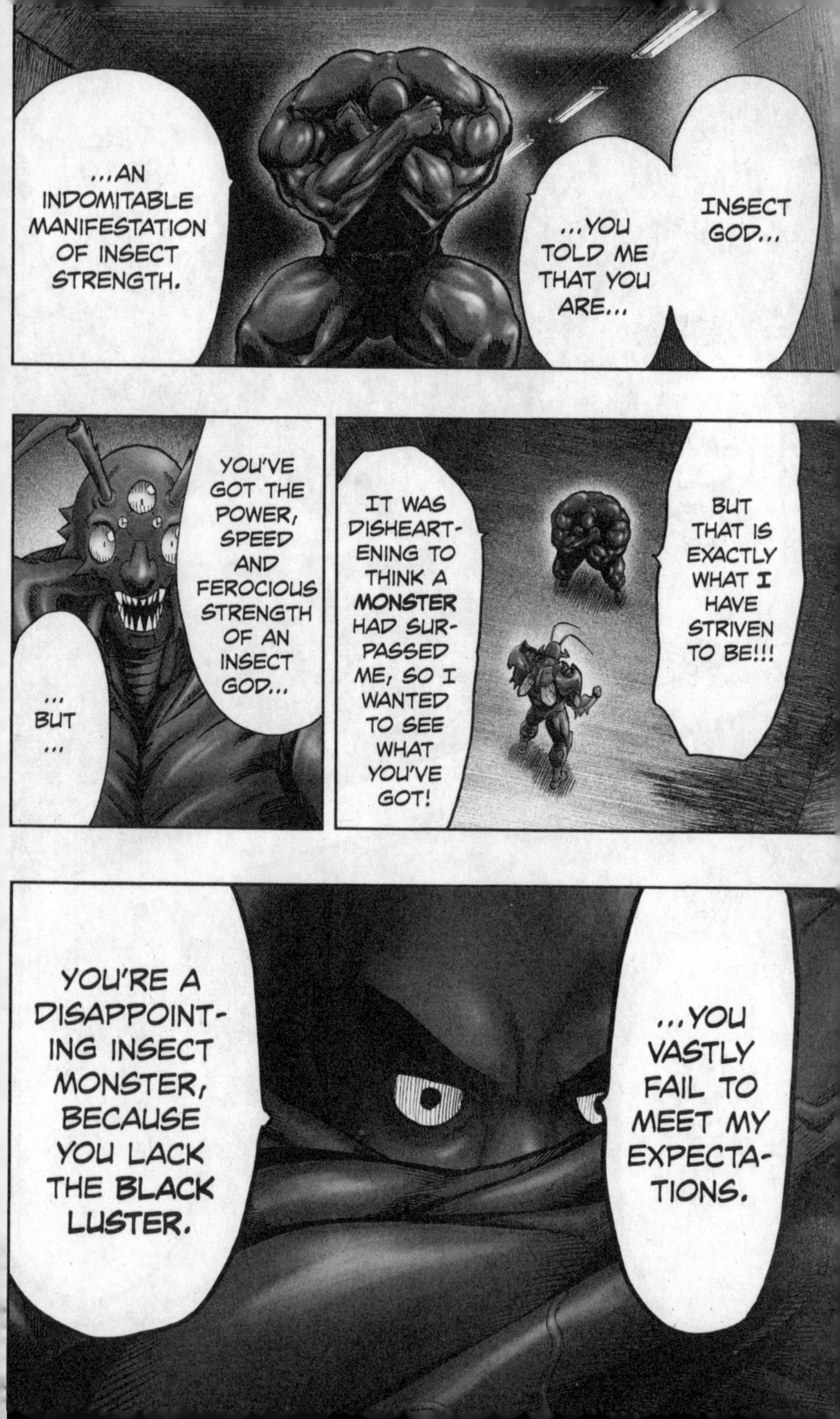
INSECT GOD...
...YOU TOLD ME THAT YOU ARE...
...AN INDOMITABLE MANIFESTATION OF INSECT STRENGTH.
BUT THAT IS EXACTLY WHAT I HAVE STRIVEN TO BE!!!
IT WAS DISHEART-ENING TO THINK A MONSTER HAD SUR-PASSED ME, SO I WANTED TO SEE WHAT YOU'VE GOT!
YOU'VE GOT THE POWER, SPEED AND FEROCIOUS STRENGTH OF AN INSECT GOD...
... BUT ...
...YOU VASTLY FAIL TO MEET MY EXPECTA-TIONS.
YOU'RE A DISAPPOINT-ING INSECT MONSTER, BECAUSE YOU LACK THE BLACK LUSTER.

YOU FOOL! DO NOT THINK THAT WAS A DISPLAY OF MY FULL-
I AM SORELY DISAP-POINTED!
JOLT
MY BODY IS NO MORE THAN EN-LARGED MUSCLE, BUT ITS PERFOR-MANCE OUT-CLASSES *YOURS*, INSECT GOD!
I'M WARNING YOU! THERE ARE THREE HEROES YOU MUST NEVER ANGER!

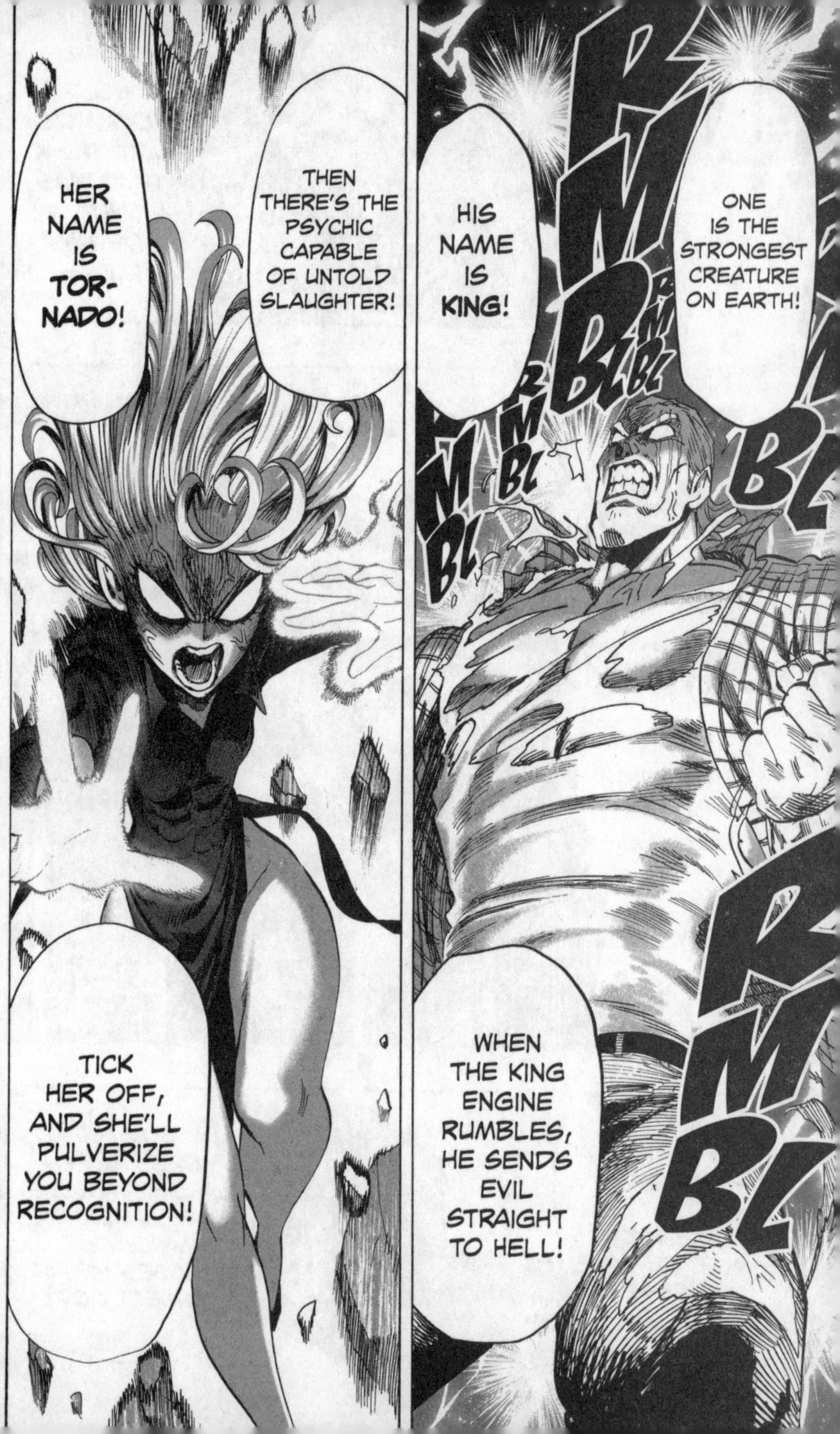
ONE IS THE STRONGEST CREATURE ON EARTH!
HIS NAME IS KING!
RMBL
RMBL
WHEN THE KING ENGINE RUMBLES, HE SENDS EVIL STRAIGHT TO HELL!
THEN THERE'S THE PSYCHIC CAPABLE OF UNTOLD SLAUGHTER!
HER NAME IS TOR-NADO!
TICK HER OFF, AND SHE'LL PULVERIZE YOU BEYOND RECOGNITION!

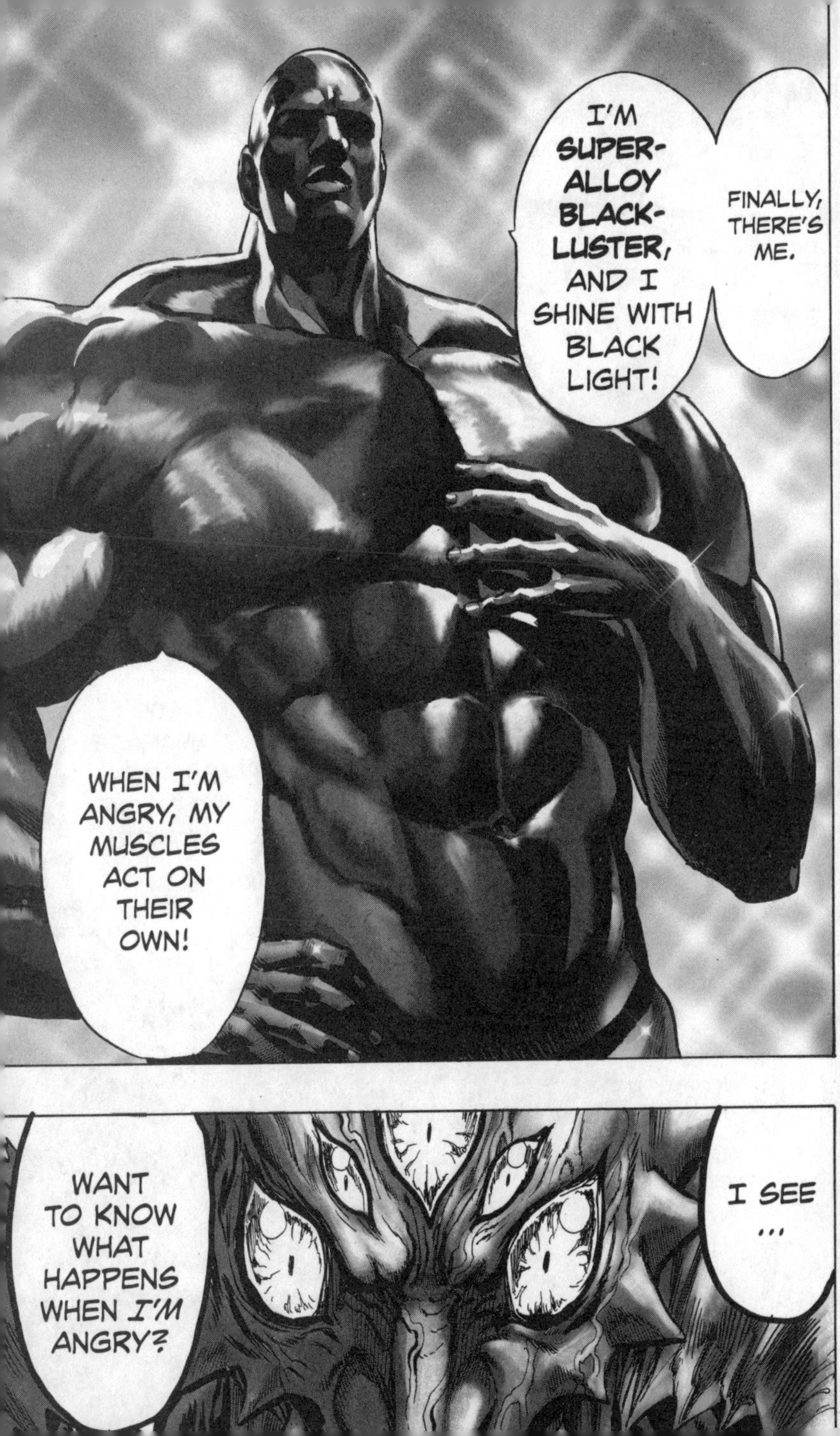
FINALLY, THERE'S ME.
I'M **SUPER-ALLOY BLACK-LUSTER,** AND I SHINE WITH BLACK LIGHT!
WHEN I'M ANGRY, MY MUSCLES ACT ON THEIR OWN!
I SEE ...
WANT TO KNOW WHAT HAPPENS WHEN *I'M* ANGRY?

YOU HEROES HAVE FAILED TO DEFEAT THE HERO HUNTER, AND YET EVEN HIS FISTS WERE POWERLESS AGAINST ME.
MY CARAPACE IS IMPEN-ETRABLE ARMOR!
CRRK
SNAP
POP
I EXIST ON A DIFFERENT PLANE THAN YOU MAMMALS BECAUSE MY INSECT MUSCLES INSTANTA-NEOUSLY IMPEL ME TO FULL POWER!
SNAP POP
KRAK

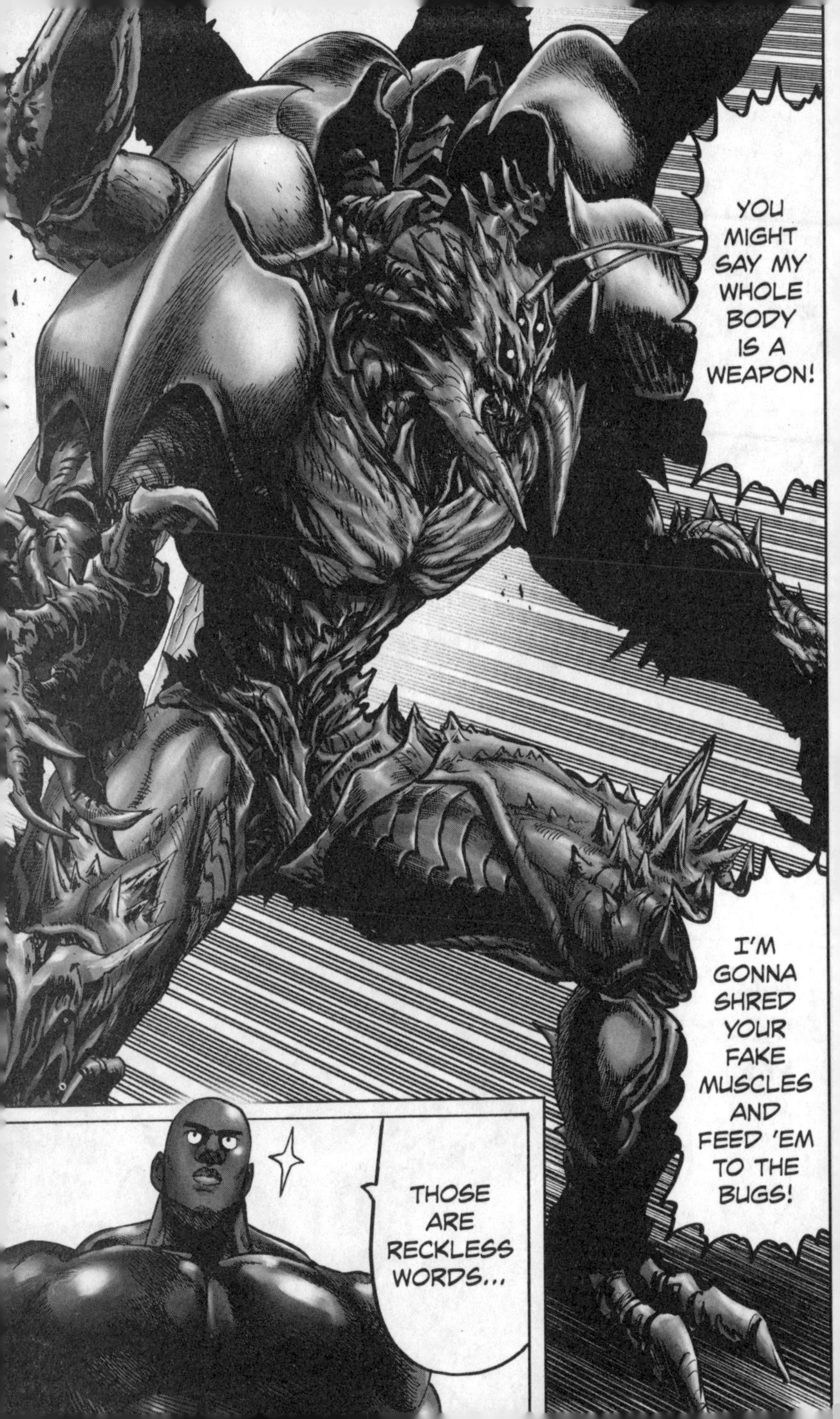
YOU MIGHT SAY MY WHOLE BODY IS A WEAPON!
I'M GONNA SHRED YOUR FAKE MUSCLES AND FEED 'EM TO THE BUGS!
THOSE ARE RECKLESS WORDS...

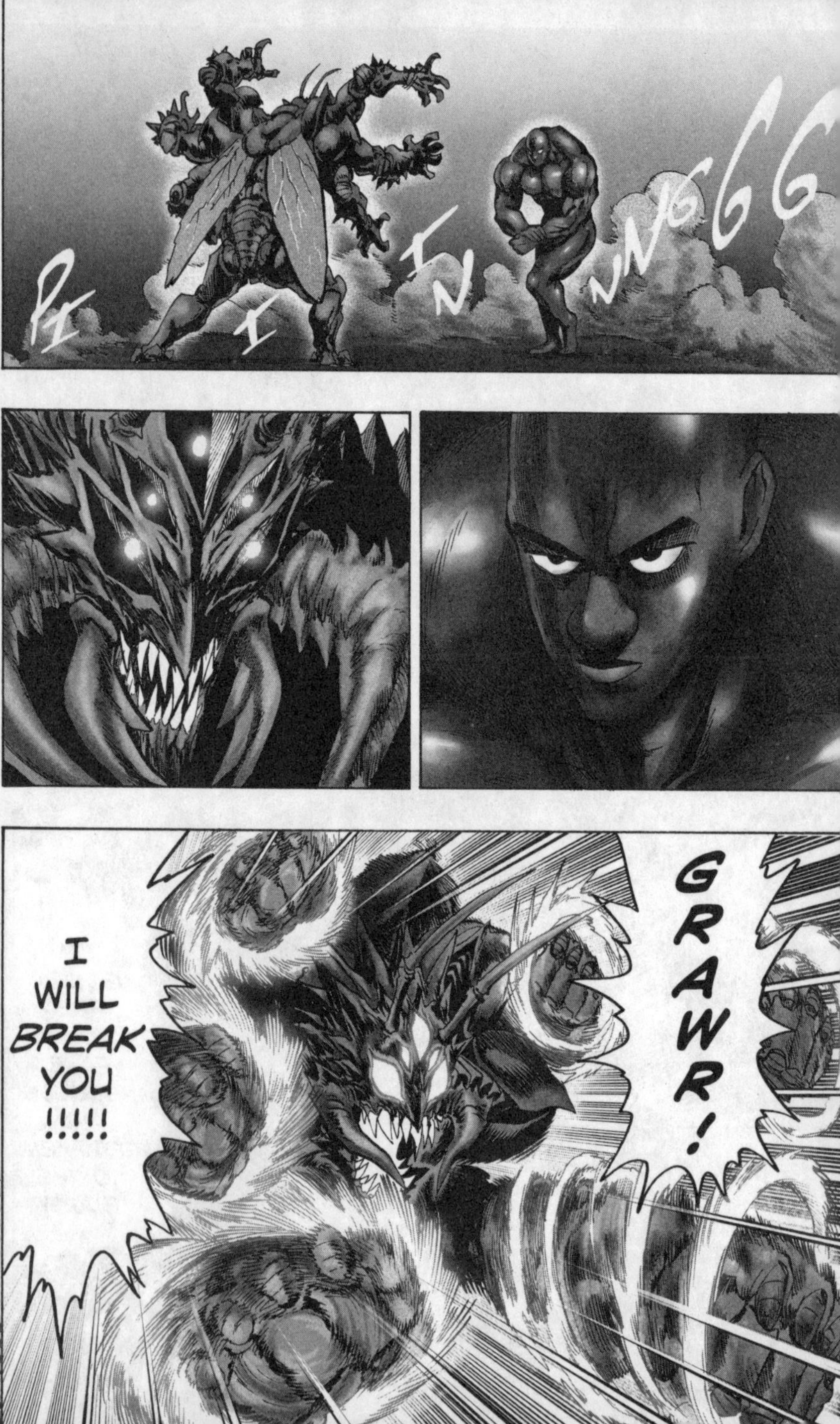
PIIINNNGGG
GRAWR!
I WILL BREAK YOU!!!!!

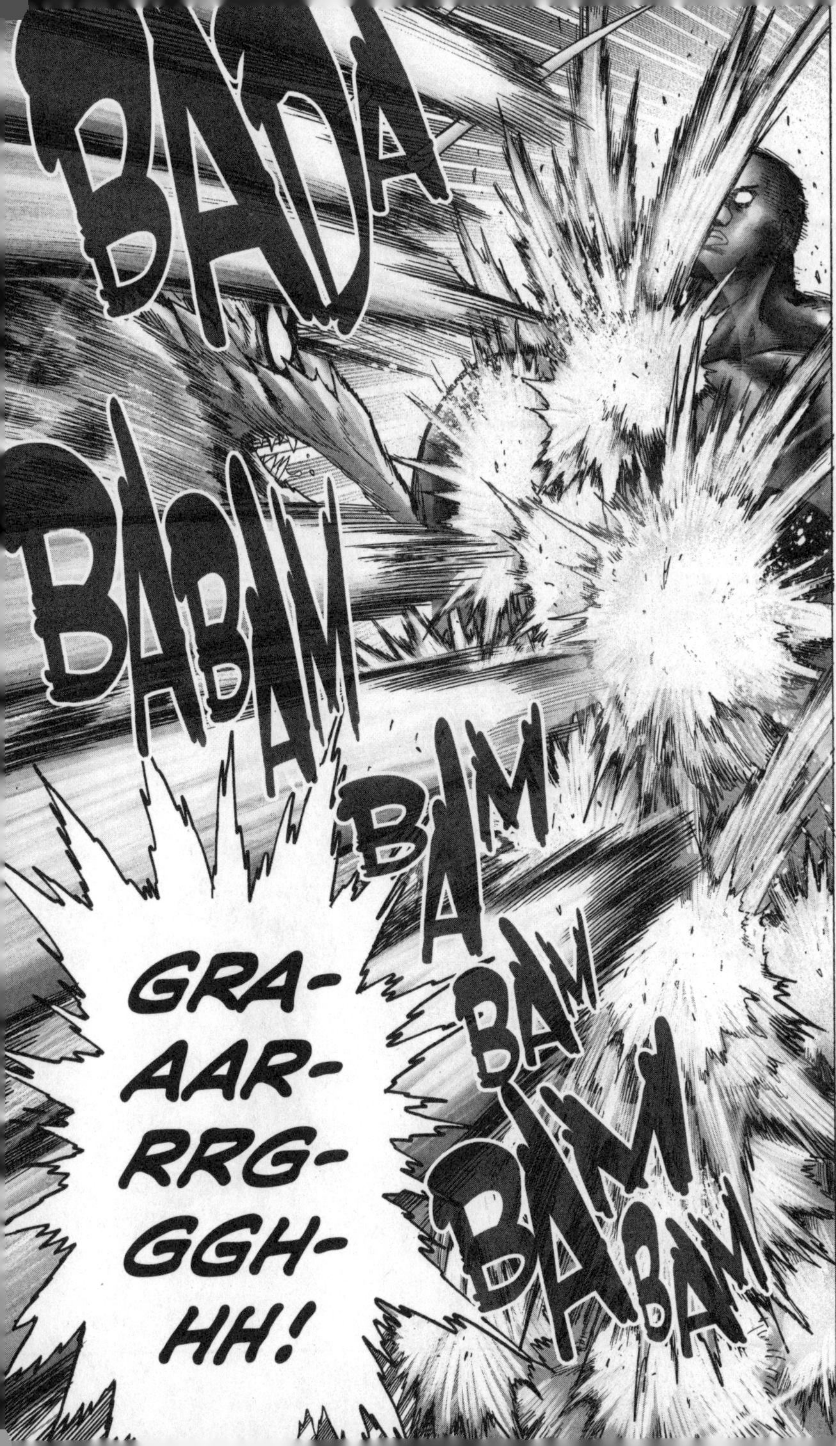
BADA
BABAM
BAM
BAM
BAM
BABAM
GRA-AAR-RRG-GGH-HH!

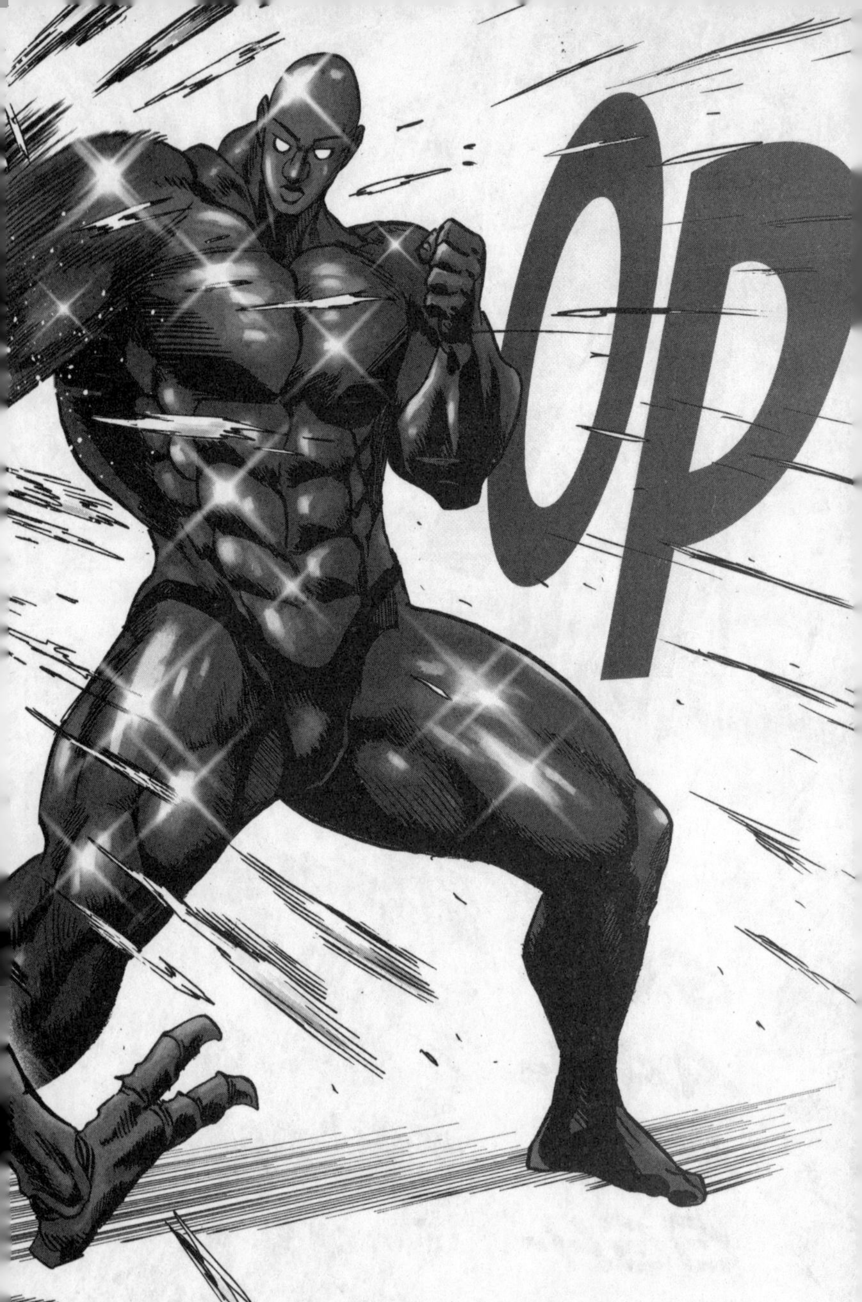
OP

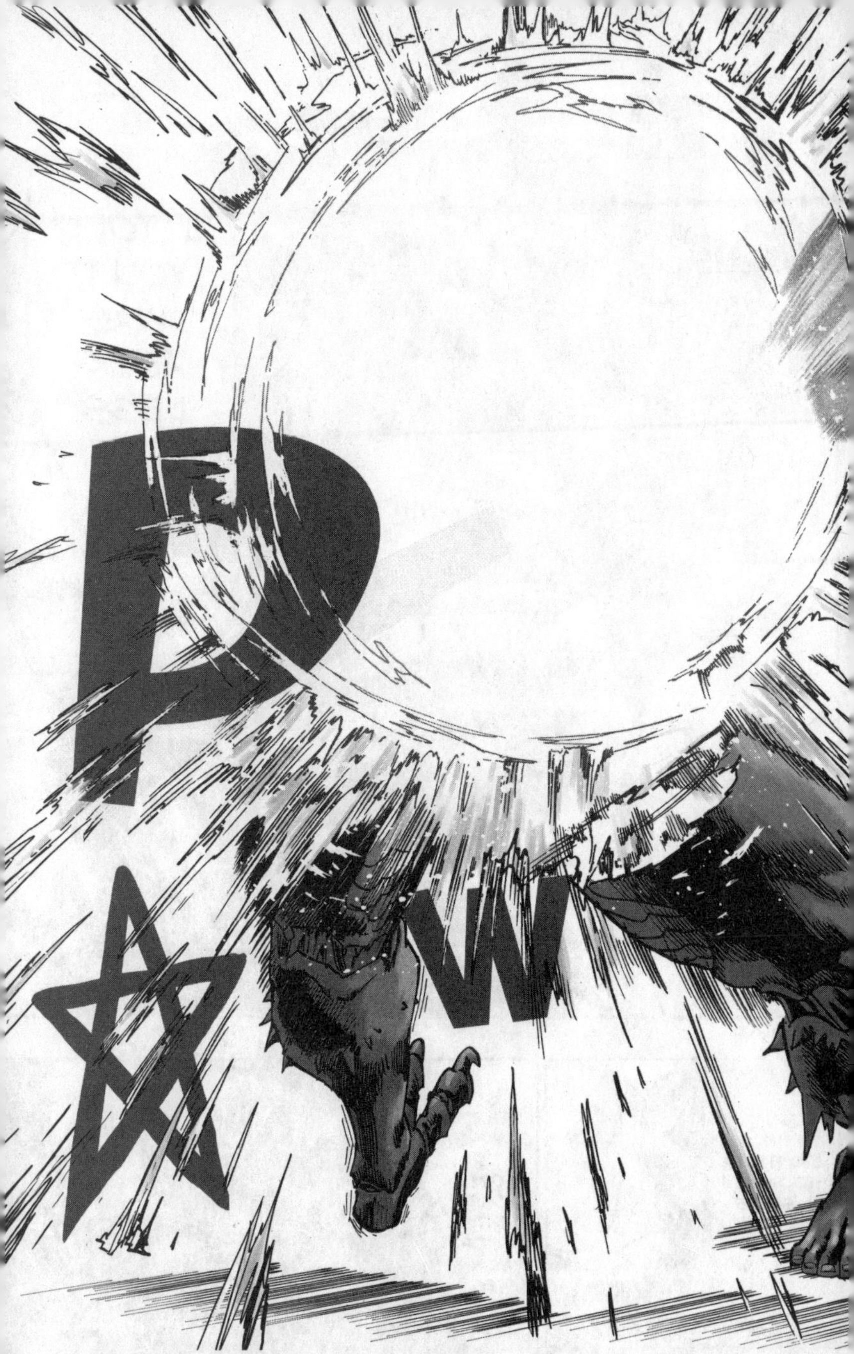
P
W

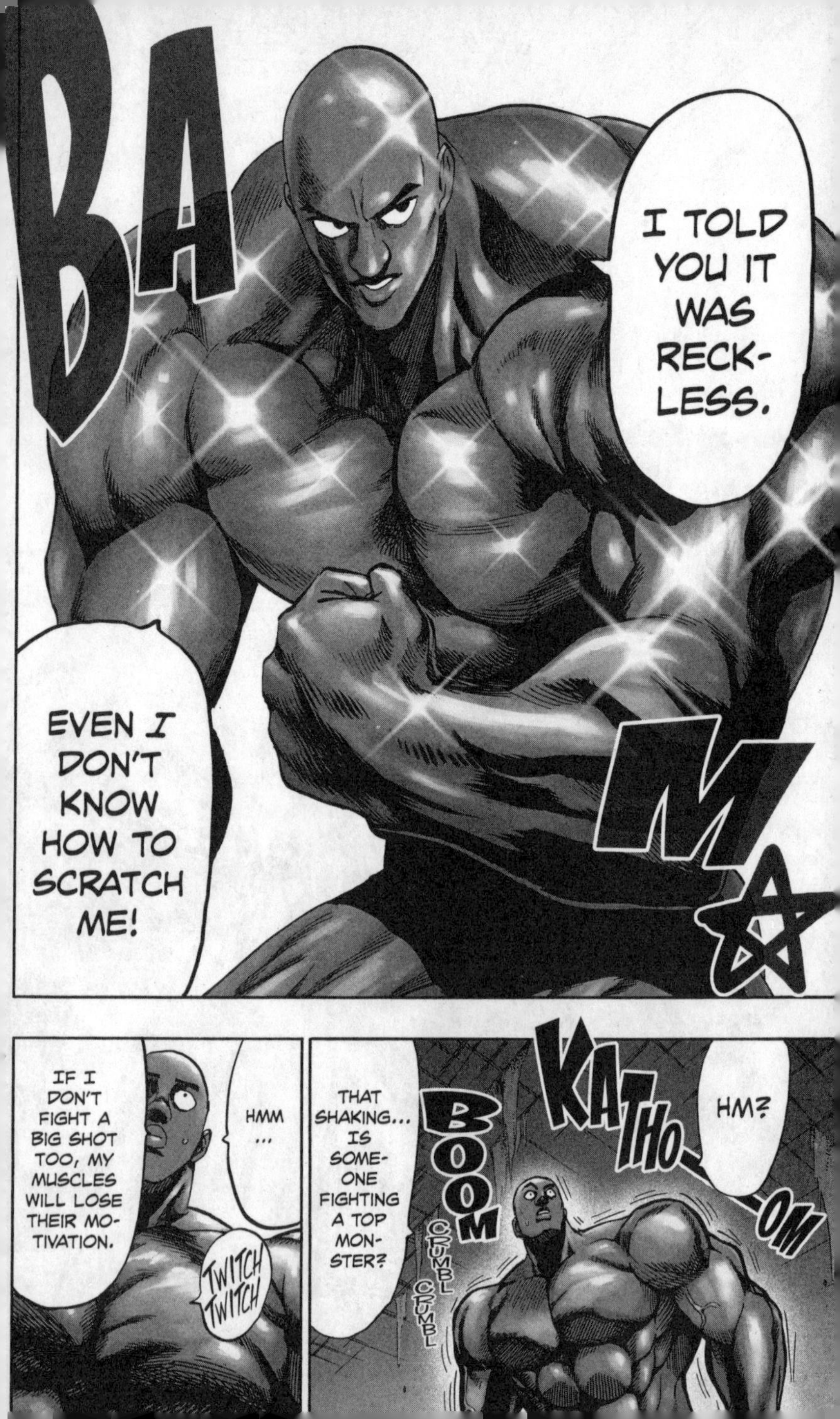
BA
I TOLD YOU IT WAS RECKLESS.
EVEN I DON'T KNOW HOW TO SCRATCH ME!
M
KATHO-OM
HM?
BOOOOM
CRUMBL CRUMBL
THAT SHAKING... IS SOMEONE FIGHTING A TOP MONSTER?
HMM...
IF I DON'T FIGHT A BIG SHOT TOO, MY MUSCLES WILL LOSE THEIR MOTIVATION.
TWITCH TWITCH

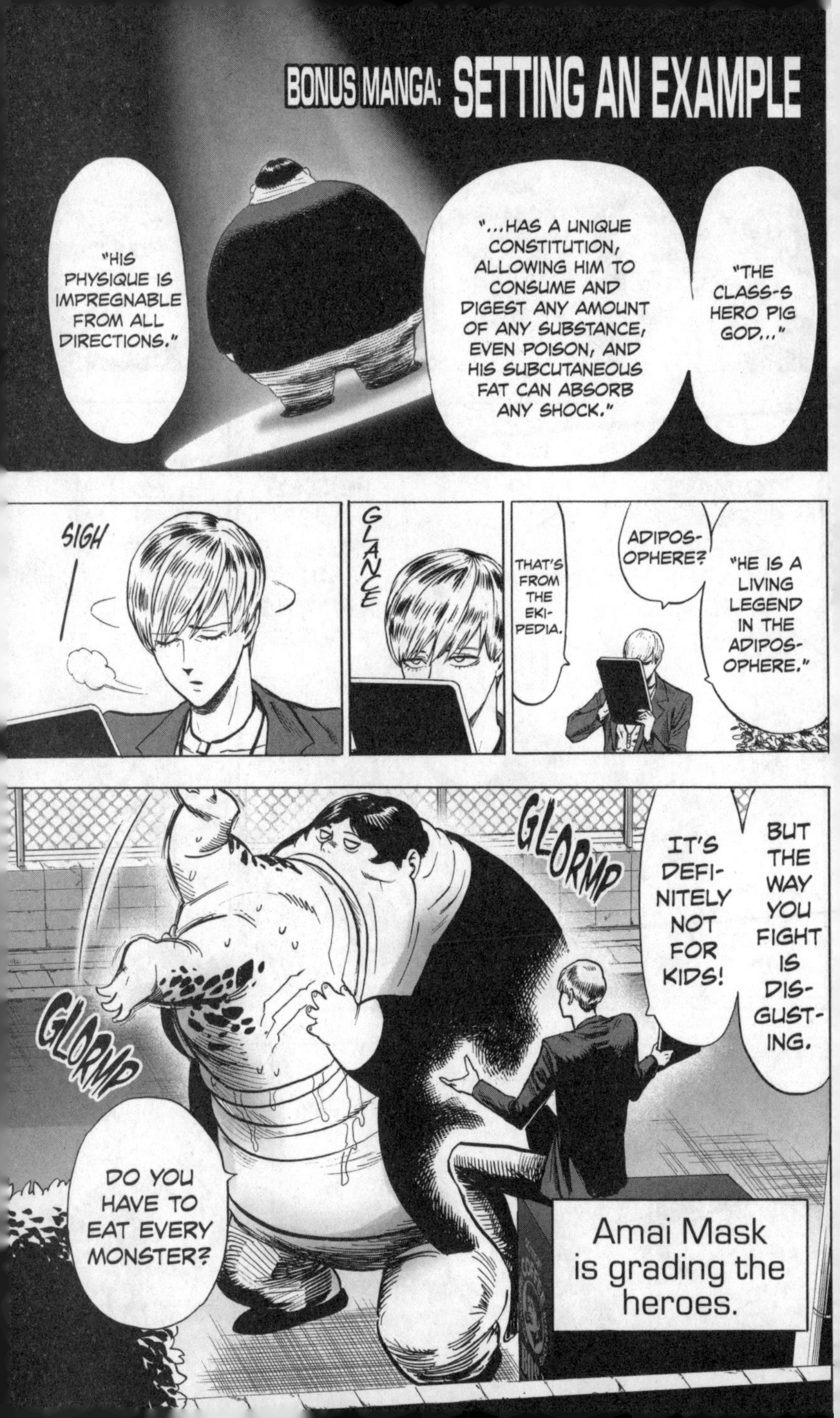
BONUS MANGA: SETTING AN EXAMPLE
"THE CLASS-S HERO PIG GOD..."
"...HAS A UNIQUE CONSTITUTION, ALLOWING HIM TO CONSUME AND DIGEST ANY AMOUNT OF ANY SUBSTANCE, EVEN POISON, AND HIS SUBCUTANEOUS FAT CAN ABSORB ANY SHOCK."
"HIS PHYSIQUE IS IMPREGNABLE FROM ALL DIRECTIONS."
"HE IS A LIVING LEGEND IN THE ADIPOSOPHERE."
ADIPOSOPHERE?
THAT'S FROM THE EKIPEDIA.
GLANCE
SIGH
BUT THE WAY YOU FIGHT IS DISGUSTING.
IT'S DEFINITELY NOT FOR KIDS!
GLORMP
GLORMP
DO YOU HAVE TO EAT EVERY MONSTER?
Amai Mask is grading the heroes.

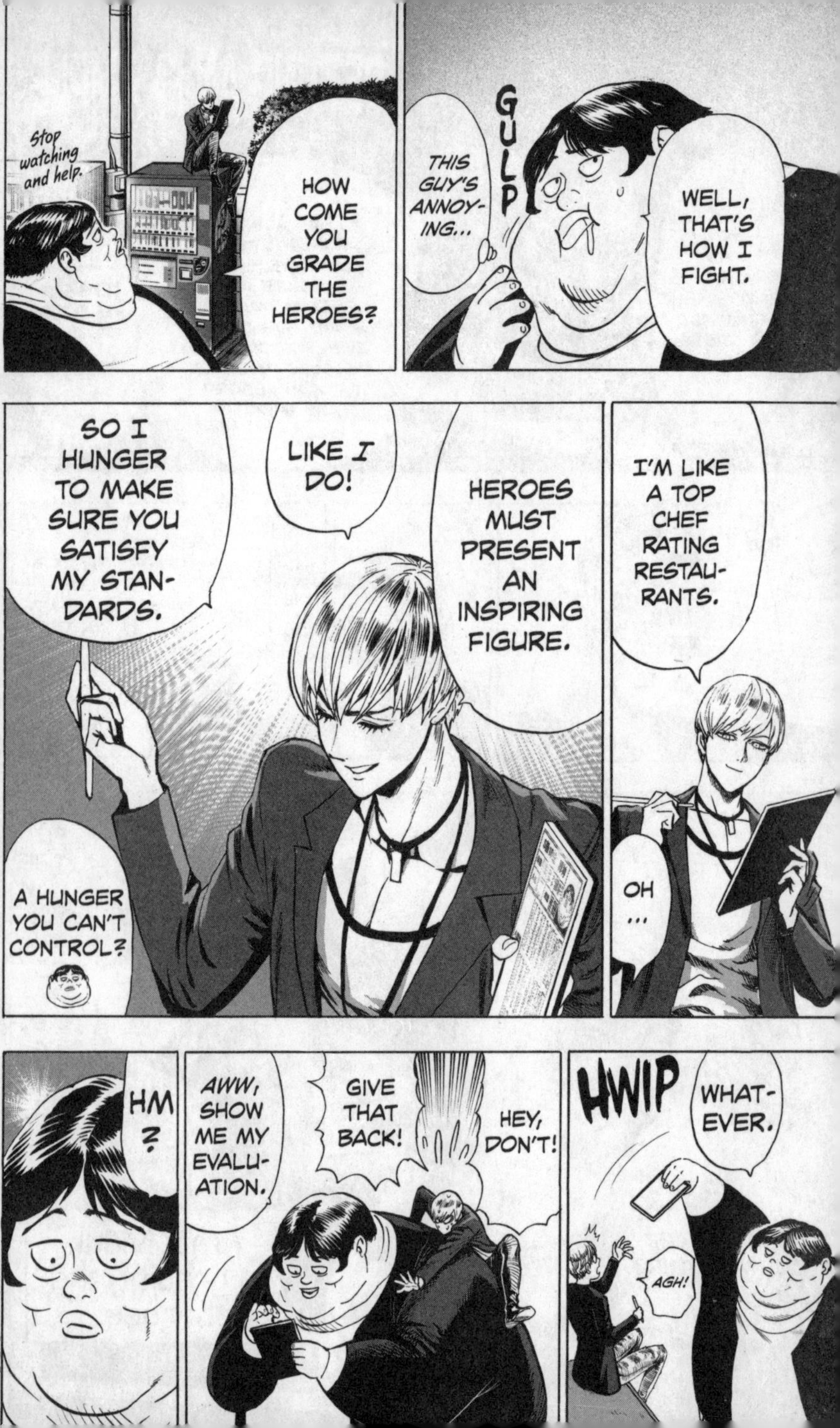
WELL, THAT'S HOW I FIGHT.
GULP
THIS GUY'S ANNOY-ING...
HOW COME YOU GRADE THE HEROES?
Stop watching and help.
I'M LIKE A TOP CHEF RATING RESTAU-RANTS.
OH ...
HEROES MUST PRESENT AN INSPIRING FIGURE.
LIKE I DO!
SO I HUNGER TO MAKE SURE YOU SATISFY MY STAN-DARDS.
A HUNGER YOU CAN'T CONTROL?
WHAT-EVER.
HWIP
AGH!
HEY, DON'T!
GIVE THAT BACK!
AWW, SHOW ME MY EVALU-ATION.
HM ?

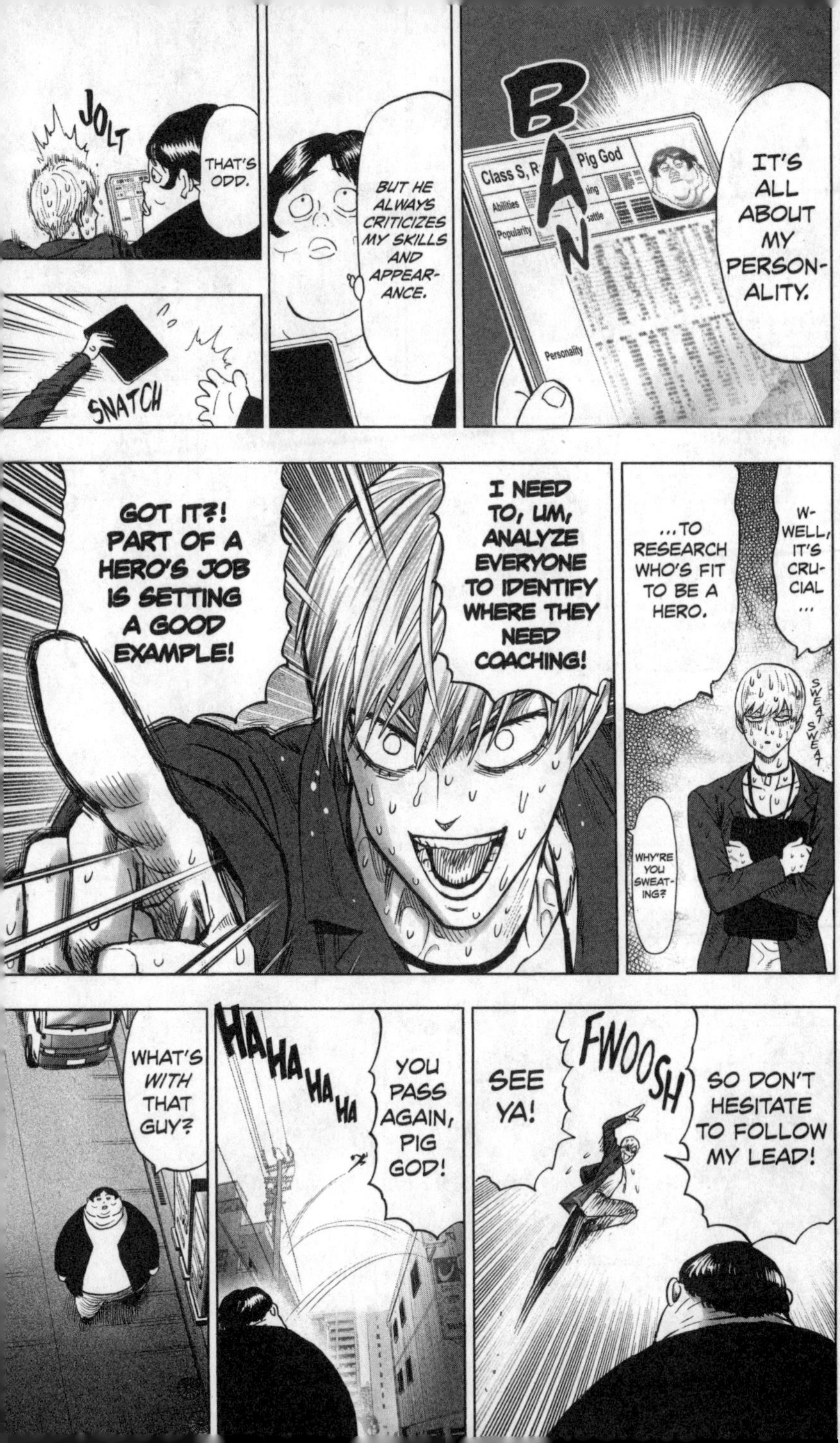
BAN
Pig God
Abilities
Popularity
Personality
IT'S ALL ABOUT MY PERSONALITY.
BUT HE ALWAYS CRITICIZES MY SKILLS AND APPEARANCE.
JOLT
THAT'S ODD.
SNATCH
W-WELL, IT'S CRUCIAL...
...TO RESEARCH WHO'S FIT TO BE A HERO.
SWEAT SWEAT
WHY'RE YOU SWEATING?
I NEED TO, UM, ANALYZE EVERYONE TO IDENTIFY WHERE THEY NEED COACHING!
GOT IT?! PART OF A HERO'S JOB IS SETTING A GOOD EXAMPLE!
SO DON'T HESITATE TO FOLLOW MY LEAD!
FWOOSH
SEE YA!
YOU PASS AGAIN, PIG GOD!
HAHAHAHA
WHAT'S WITH THAT GUY?

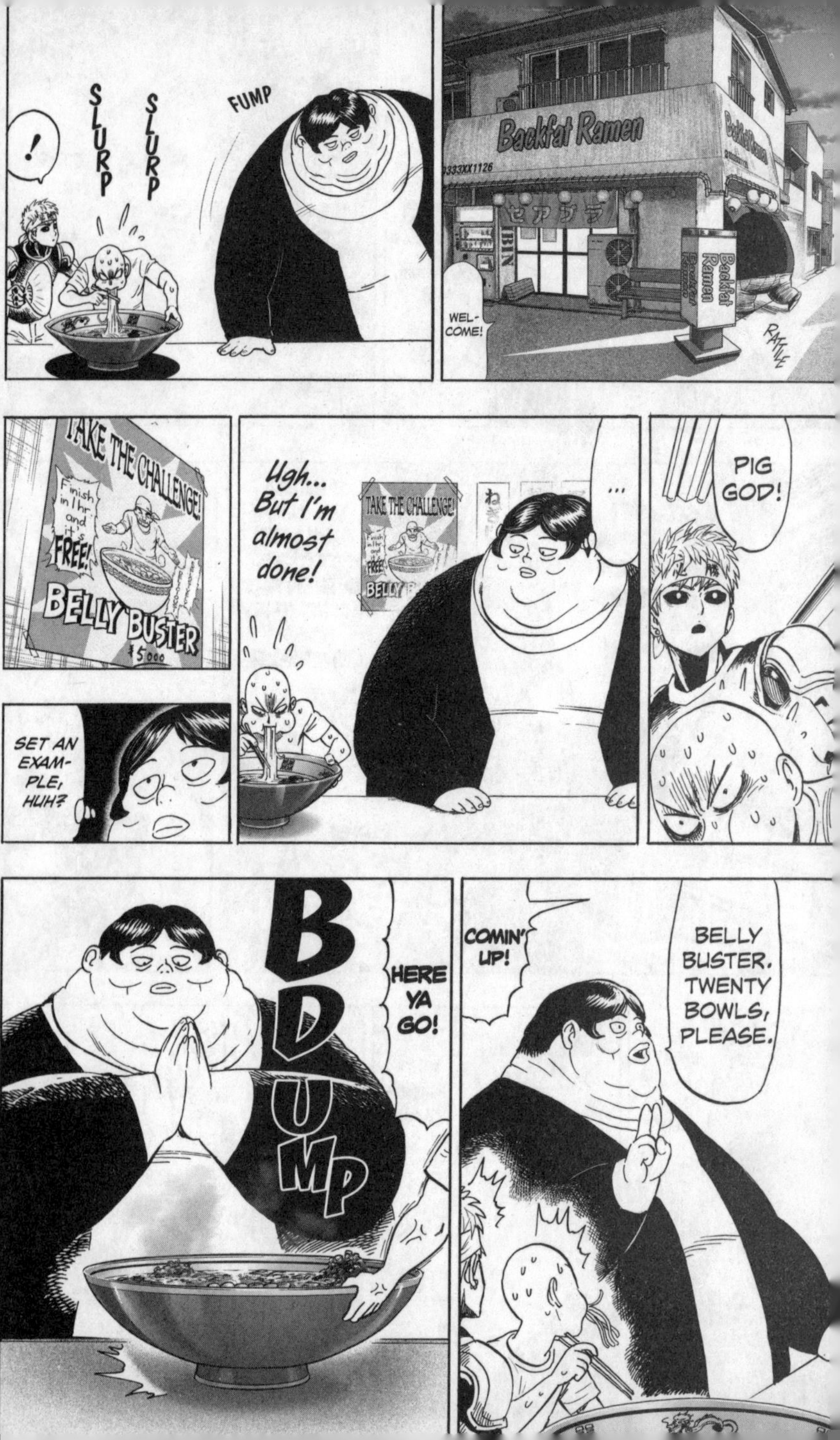
Backfat Ramen
0333XX1126
Backfat Ramen
WEL-COME!
RATTLE
FUMP
SLURP SLURP
!
PIG GOD!
...
Ugh... But I'm almost done!
TAKE THE CHALLENGE!
TAKE THE CHALLENGE!
Finish in 1hr. and it's FREE!
BELLY BUSTER
¥5000
SET AN EXAM-PLE, HUH?
BELLY BUSTER. TWENTY BOWLS, PLEASE.
COMIN' UP!
HERE YA GO!
BDUMP

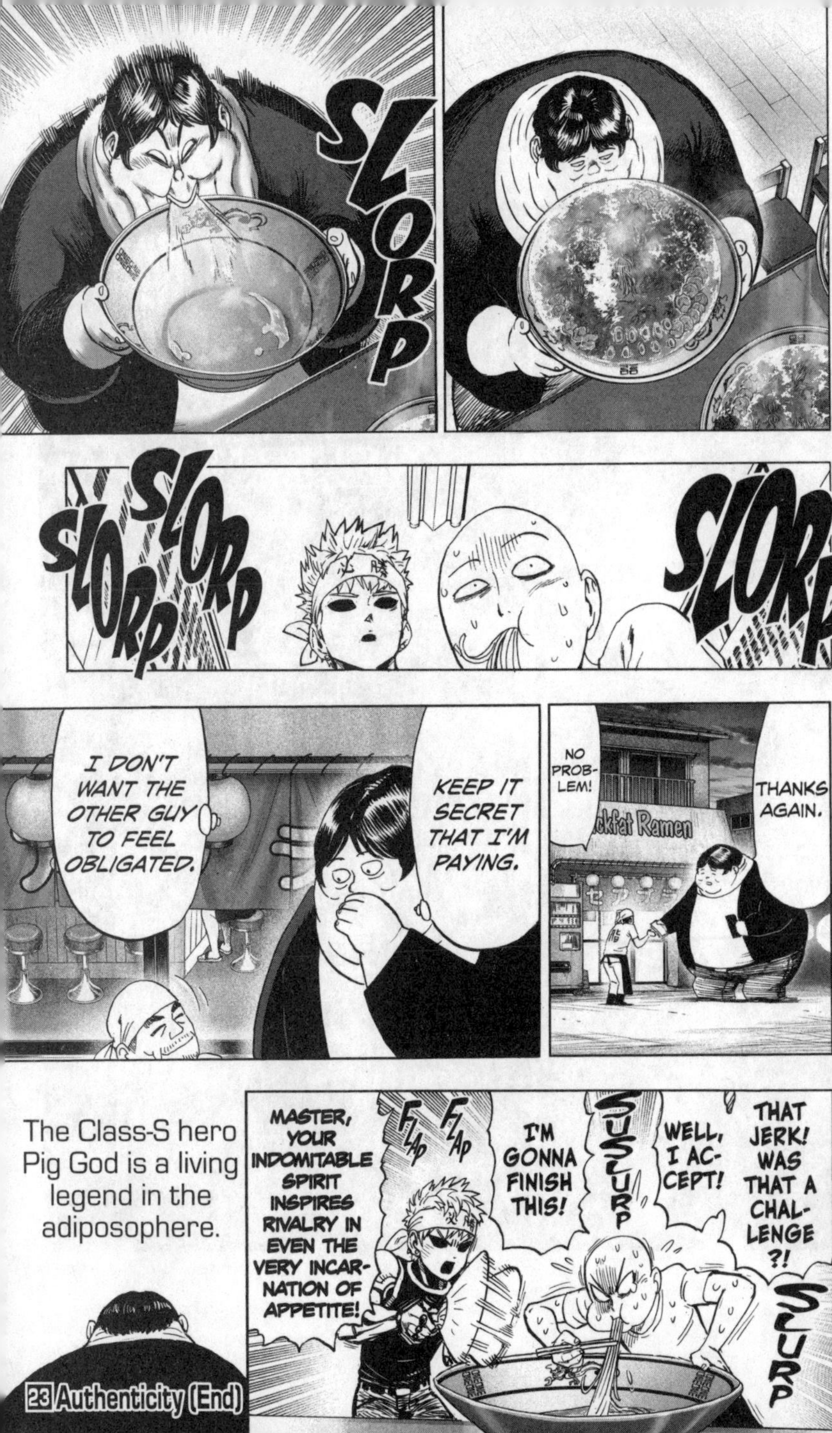
SLORP
SLORP
SLORP
SLORP
THANKS AGAIN.
NO PROB-LEM!
KEEP IT SECRET THAT I'M PAYING.
I DON'T WANT THE OTHER GUY TO FEEL OBLIGATED.
ckfat Ramen
THAT JERK! WAS THAT A CHAL-LENGE?!
SLURP
WELL, I AC-CEPT!
SUSLURP
I'M GONNA FINISH THIS!
FLAP FLAP
MASTER, YOUR INDOMITABLE SPIRIT INSPIRES RIVALRY IN EVEN THE VERY INCAR-NATION OF APPETITE!

The Class-S hero Pig God is a living legend in the adiposophere.

23 Authenticity (End)

ONE-PUNCH MAN

VOLUME 23

SHONEN JUMP MANGA EDITION

STORY BY | ONE

ART BY | YUSUKE MURATA

TRANSLATION | JOHN WERRY

TOUCH-UP ART AND LETTERING | JAMES GAUBATZ

DESIGN | SHAWN CARRICO

SHONEN JUMP SERIES EDITOR | JOHN BAE

GRAPHIC NOVEL EDITOR | JENNIFER LEBLANC

Printed in Canada

Published by VIZ Media, LLC
P.O. Box 77010
San Francisco, CA 94107

VIZ MEDIA
viz.com

SHONEN JUMP

10 9 8 7 6 5 4 3 2 1
First printing, October 2021

ratings.viz.com
RATED T TEEN

PARENTAL ADVISORY
ONE-PUNCH MAN is rated T for Teen and is recommended for ages 13 and up. This volume contains realistic and fantasy violence.